Allende's Chile

edited by
Philip O'Brien

Allende's Chile

PRAEGER SPECIAL STUDIES IN INTERNATIONAL POLITICS AND GOVERNMENT

Praeger Publishers   New York   Washington   London

Library of Congress Cataloging in Publication Data
Main entry under title:

Allende's Chile.

(Praeger special studies in international politics and government)
   Bibliography: p. 295-296.
   1. Chile—Economic policy.   2. Chile—Politics and government—
1970-   3. Unidad Popular.
I. O'Brien, Philip J.
HC192.A69   338.983   75-23987
ISBN 0-275-55750-2

PRAEGER PUBLISHERS
111 Fourth Avenue, New York, N.Y. 10003, U.S.A.

Published in the United States of America in 1976
by Praeger Publishers, Inc.

Printed in the United States of America

This collection of original chapters arose out of a series of
specialist seminars held at the Institute of Latin American Studies,
the University of Glasgow. All too often collections of works lack
coherence and a logical sequence, partly because the editor tries
to represent a wide range of very different viewpoints in the interests
of a "balanced" presentation. This collection makes no pretense at
being balanced in this sense. All the contributors, although highly
critical of many of the policies of Popular Unity, were invited to
submit an article not only because of their detailed knowledge of
the topic, but also because they, by and large, were sympathetic to
the overall objectives of the Popular Unity program. If anything, most
of the chapters argue that Popular Unity was too moderate and too
willing to collaborate with sectors of the Chilean bourgeoisie, and
that it was this lack of firmness which partly explains the success
of the military coup on September 11, 1973.

After the first chapter, which gives an overall analysis of the
Chilean class structure and class politics, the book falls into four
main parts: analyses of the main policies of the Popular Unity government; the response of the working classes; the tactics and strategy
of those opposed to the Popular Unity government; and finally, a
brief account of what is happening in Chile since the coup, and the
main lessons of Chile.

In the first chapter, "Class Structure and Class Struggle in
Chile," Jacqueline F. Roddick sets the background for the subsequent
chapters. She briefly analyzes the essential aspects of Chilean
economy and society, and carefully documents and criticizes the
basis for Popular Unity's fragile strategy of class alliances. Pablo
Lira then shows how this strategy broke down as the Chilean process
moved into different phases. He brings out clearly the different
responses of the various left-wing parties to the different phases,
emphasizing in particular the failure of all left-wing parties to offer
an adequate leadership to the Chilean working class in a growing
revolutionary situation.

The next three chapters, those of Professor Nove, Dr. Kay, and
Mike Gonzalez, analyze in depth three crucial aspects of the Popular
Unity strategy: overall economic policies, agrarian reform, and
ideology and culture. Professor Nove brings out the contradictions
and lack of coherence in the application of economic policies, while
Dr. Kay argues that in their effort to win over "middle sectors" in
the countryside, Popular Unity failed to consolidate a socialist rural
base for itself. In the cultural sphere, as Mike Gonzalez shows, an
increased access to culture and the arts was substituted for the

development of new cultural forms and a new class consciousness.
As a result the opposition's counteroffensive was initially organized
within the ideological system.

Patricia Santa Lucia and Monica Threlfall look at two critical
areas: the response of the organized working class and the response
of the shantytown dwellers, the pobladores, to the Chilean road to
socialism. Both bring out the inability of the existing institutional
structures to respond to their needs, and how when faced with the
political and economic crisis both groups were forced more and more
to take power tentatively into their own hands. This area is undoubtedly one of the key questions of the Popular Unity experience, and anyone
studying the history of Chile between 1970 and 1973 must study the
relationship which the mass movement bore to the existing political
parties and institutions.

The next three chapters, Ian Roxborough's "Reversing the
Revolution: the Chilean Opposition to Allende, " Philip O'Brien's
"Was the United States Responsible for the Chilean Coup?" and
Alain Joxe's "The Chilean Armed Forces and the Making of the Coup, "
look at the right-wing reaction to the unfurling of the Chilean process.
This reaction was not, of course, a passive acceptance of Dr. Allende's
electoral victory. Ian Roxborough convincingly shows how, after an
initial period of confusion, the Chilean opposition slowly came
together around a common strategy to topple Allende. Philip O'Brien
examines in detail the role of the United States in this strategy, and
while accepting that the United States contributed to the overthrow of
Allende, at the same time emphasizes that the U. S. role was a
subordinate one. And in an important chapter, Alain Joxe explains
the historical formation of the Chilean armed forces, and how under
the impact of the Chilean road to socialism the right-wing elements
within and outside the armed forces prepared the way for a successful
coup.

And finally, Philip O'Brien looks at the "social market economy"
as it operates in Chile today, and brings out some of the social and
political aspects overlooked by the economists from the University
of Chicago presently advising the Chilean military. He concludes
with a number of reflections on the main lessons of the Chilean
experience.

In contrast to the majority of the books in English on the Chilean
road to socialism, all of the chapters in this book were written after
the September coup. They therefore have the considerable benefit of
hindsight. But as with the history of the Spanish Civil War, it is
clear that we will have to wait many years before someone has the
information and detachment to write a comprehensive study of Chile
in Allende's period. The information available is still fragmentary:
little detailed information is known about the internal struggles within
Chile's armed forces during Popular Unity's three years in office, and
surprisingly little direct evidence has been published even about the

internal history of working class organizations such as the main Chilean trade union body, the <u>Central Unica de Trabajadores</u> (CUT) during this period. Thus, however objective authors may try to be (and all the contributors in this work have tried to be scrupulously objective about questions of fact), and however much each contributor tries to avoid fitting the complexity of Chilean development into any preconceived pattern, the interpretation that any writer puts upon the Chilean experience should be treated with some caution at this stage. This caveat applies regardless of the political standpoint of any author.

The Chilean road to socialism did not, of course, begin in a historical vacuum. Like any other country Chile does have a unique economy and social structure. All the chapters in this book try to bring out the historical developments leading to the particular problems of the Popular Unity period. But particularly for Europeans, the Chilean road to socialism is of interest not only in its own right, but also for the lessons it offers for similar strategies for achieving socialism. It is this which helps explain why the Chilean attempt at a peaceful transition to socialism and its final collapse into a brutal military dictatorship captured the imagination, passion, and interest of the rest of the world as no other event in Latin America has done for many years. What happened in Chile is important.

Finally, I would like to thank all those who contributed to the preparation of this volume. I would particularly like to thank Mrs. May Townsley and Mrs. Isabel Ovenstone for their secretarial assistance, and my wife, Jackie Roddick, for turning many of the chapters into readable English prose. But above all, I would like to thank all those Chilean socialists who helped me to understand and to appreciate what their struggle was all about.

CONTENTS

LIST OF TABLES AND FIGURES

GLOSSARY

Frequently Mentioned Acronyms of Political Parties and Organizations

UP   Unidad Popular (Popular Unity). The coalition of parties that won the presidential elections of September 1970 with their candidate, Salvador Allende. The coalition consisted of six groups: the Socialist party, the Communist party, the Radical party, the Movement of United Popular Action (MAPU), and the Independent Popular Action party (API), and Social Democratic party.

CODE   Confederacion de la Democracia (Confederation of Democracy). An electoral pact between the PDC, PN, and PIR to oppose the UF.

CORA   Corporacion de Reforma Agraria (Agrarian Reform Corporation). Formed in 1962 under Chile's first agrarian reform law, and became important under the Christian Democrat agrarian reform law.

CORFO   Corporacion de Fomento (State Development Corporation). Created in 1939 during the Popular Front government to finance and promote development projects.

CUT   Central Unico de Trabajadores (Unified Council of Trade Unions). The only trade union federation in Chile, and as such of central importance.

JAP   Junta de Abasteciemientos y Precios (Committee for Prices and Supplies). Originally set up by UP in 1972. Became one of the largest of the mass organizations.

JRR   Juventud Radical Revolucionaria (Radical Revolutionary Youth). Youth section of Radical party in Allende period that frequently diverged from the viewpoints of the Radical party to take up a more revolutionary position.

MAPU   Movimiento de Accion Popular Unitario (Movement of United Popular Action). Formed in 1969 as a left-wing breakaway from the Christian Democrat party. In its first congress in 1970 declared itself a Marxist party. Its first secretary general, Jacques Chonchol, left the party to join the Izquierda Cristiana in 1971. After the March 1973 elections, the party split into two: one side recognized officially as MAPU, adopting a revolutionary position; and the other, which took the name of MAPU Obrero Campesino (MAPU OC) supporting the Communist party positions.

MIC   Movimiento de la Izquierda Cristiana (Movement of the Christian Left). Formed in mid-1971 by a small, breakaway group from the Christian Democrat party. Joined at the same time by some members of MAPU.

MIR   Movimiento de la Izquierda Revolucionaria (Movement of the Revolutionary Left). Formed in 1965 with a guerrilla orientation under the inspiration of the Cuban revolution. Went clandestine in 1969, refused to participate in the 1970 elections. Gave critical support to UP. Was the most important organization to the left of the UP, and although had relatively little support among the organized working class, was important as an ideological alternative to the parliamentary road to socialism. The MIR also organized a number of broad front organizations:

    MCR   Movimiento Campesino Revolucionario (Movement of Revolutionary Peasants).

    FTR   Frente de Trabajadores Revolucionarios (Revolutionary Workers Front).

    FER   Frente de Estudiantes Revolucionarios (Movement of Revolutionary Students).

    MPR   Movimiento de Pobladores Revolucionarios (Movement of Revolutionary Shantytown Dwellers)

ODEPLAN   Oficina de Planificacion Nacional (National Planning Office). Formed by President Frei to oversee Chile's planning efforts.

PC   Partido Comunista (Communist party). Working class party, founded 1922, affiliated to the Third International. Formed part of the Frente Popular (Popular Front) that won the 1938 presidential election under Pedro Aguirre Cerda. In 1949 declared illegal by President Gabriel Gonzales Videla through the Ley de Defensa de la Democracia (Law for the Defense of Democracy), and

forced underground. In 1958 the law was repealed,
and the party returned to legality. Joined with the
Socialist party to form the Frente de Accion Popular
whose candidate, Salvador Allende, was defeated by the
Christian Democrat, Eduardo Frei, in the 1964 presidential elections. In 1969 main force behind formation of
Popular Unity. Obtained 17 percent of the votes in the
municipal elections of 1971, and the largest percentage
of the vote (33 percent) for the 1972 CUT elections.

PDC   Partido Democrata Cristiana (Christian Democrat party).
Founded in 1957 by an amalgam of the Falange party
and the Partido Social Conservador (the Social Conservative Party). Its candidate in the 1958 presidential
elections, Eduardo Frei, came third. In the 1964
election Eduardo Frei stood for the Christian Democrats
again, and this time received the support of the Liberal-
Conservative coalition. In a three-cornered contest
Frei won easily, receiving 56 percent of the vote cast.
The reform program of the Christian Democrats'
"revolution in liberty" ran into increasing difficulties,
and in the 1970 elections the Christian Democrat candidate, Radomiro Tomic, standing on a program very
similar to that of Popular Unity, was beaten into third
place.

PN   Partido Nacional (National party). Formed in 1966 by a
fusion of the two traditional right-wing parties, the
Conservative and the Liberal parties. Party of the
traditional ruling class in Chile. Supported the candidacy of Jorge Alessandri, president of Chile 1958-64,
in the 1970 elections. Alessandri came a very close
second to Allende.

PR   Radical party. Formed in 1862 as a reaction against oligarchic rule. Mainly middle class party. Its candidate,
Pedro Aguirre Cerda, won the 1938 elections as head
of the Popular Front. Its candidate won the elections
again in 1942 and 1946, but the party was crushingly
defeated in the 1952, 1958 and 1964 elections. In
1969 the majority of party decided to enter Popular Unity
leading to a split and the formation of the Democracia
Radical which supported Jorge Alessandri in the 1970
elections. Later in April 1972 a group split off from
the party to form the Izquierda Radical (PIR—the Left
Radical party) which joined forces with the opposition
against Popular Unity.

PS   Partido Socialista (Socialist party). Founded in 1933.
            Marxist party, but never affiliated to any International.
            Supported the Popular Front. Its candidate, Salvador
            Allende stood for the presidential elections in 1952,
            1958, 1964, and finally won the presidency in 1970
            as the Popular Unity candidate. The party has suffered
            numerous divisions in its history. In the 1971 elections
            obtained 22.4 percent of the votes, and came second
            to the Communist party in the CUT elections with 30
            percent of the votes.

PyL   Patria y Libertad (Fatherland and Freedom). Neofascist
            terrorist group. Important force behind the attempted
            coup of June 29, 1973.

                    FREQUENTLY USED SPANISH WORDS

Asentamiento   Agrarian reform settlement first created by the
                        Christian Democrat government.

Campesino   Peasant or farmworker.

Carabineros   Armed police force.

Comando Comunal   Community Council. Grouped together all the
                        various popular organizations in a given area.

Cordones
  Industriales   Industrial assemblies that grouped together
                        workers from different factories in the same
                        geographical area. Called cordones (belts)
                        because they tend to stretch out the length
                        of certain roads in main towns.

Latifundio   Vast rural estate.

Minifundio   Small subsistence farm.

Poblacion   A working class district, made up of both
                        houses and shacks.

Poblador   A person who lives in a poblacion.

1

CLASS STRUCTURE
AND CLASS POLITICS
IN CHILE
Jacqueline F. Roddick

POLITICS AND ECONOMICS

For the past hundred years, Chile's existence has hinged on the revenue from its mines: nitrate mines from 1880-1925, when Chile held a virtual world monopoly of nitrate production, and copper mines from 1935 to the present day. Between 1960 and 1970, mineral exports accounted for 85 percent of all Chile's export revenues, and copper alone accounted for 60 percent.[1] As a Popular Unity slogan coined during the nationalization of the copper companies put it, "Copper is Chile's salary." Throughout most of this century, the source of this salary has been owned by foreign companies. British companies held the largest share in nitrate production: when copper's turn came to play a vital role in the national economy, the three key mines were already American owned.

During the heyday of nitrate production, Chile was a classic example of an enclave economy, as described by Paul Baran or Fernando Cardoso.[2] Most of the state revenues were provided by an export tax on nitrates, with local property owners contributing comparatively little. In return for financial support, the state acted as a policeman for the foreign companies in the mining areas, sending in troops to break up any strike which seemed to be getting out of hand. The Chilean oligarchy made its profits by providing agricultural products and banking services for the mining north, and by taking its share of the proceeds of nitrate revenues channeled through the state in the form of paid employments and public works. Most manufactured goods, particularly luxury goods, were imported from Europe or the United States, successive governments being firmly committed to an economic policy of laissez-faire. Patronage and corruption were the twin characteristics of parliamentary democracy during the nitrate years, with elections being won by the candidate who could buy the most votes, and parties being built on the basis of their ability to control public appointments and dispense patronage.

1

This was the era during which two of the parties in the Popular Unity coalition, which took power in 1970, were formed. The Radical party, one of the minor parties in the coalition, was built during the 1880s on the basis of a "progressive" ideology which challenged the traditional hegemony of the Catholic Church and favored more widespread popular education and public works. Thanks to its rhetoric and its own capacity to dispense patronage, it soon acquired a popular base among empleados or white-collar workers. In 1970, though the Christian Democrats had been able to make their own inroads into this sector on the basis of an ideology of Christian reformism, the great strength of the Radical party was still its support among empleados.

The Communist party was also founded during the nitrate era, but its basis of support was rather different. It was built above all in the mining areas, on the foundations of the nitrate miners' resistance societies or mancomunales, and on a tradition of trade unionism under very difficult conditions. By 1920, when the party affiliated to the Third International as a sympathizing section, it already claimed a national following and dominated the principal Chilean trade union federation of the times, the Foch. By 1970, in spite of its rather varied historical fortunes, it could claim about a hundred thousand party members and was the dominant political force in the working class, although it had a rival in the erratic and often much more left-wing Socialist party, founded in 1933.

Between the nitrate and the copper eras, the Chilean economy changed profoundly, and so did Chilean politics. Thanks to the vivid impression left by the collapse of the international market for nitrates in the 1920s, quickly followed by the Great Depression, the Chilean state abandoned its laissez-faire policies and began to take an active interest in fostering local industry. In 1938, the Frente Popular, a coalition government of Radicals, Communists, and the newly formed Socialist party was elected on an explicit program for the creation of a national industrial base, and copper revenues were turned towards manufacturing investment. Heavy customs duties were levied on imported manufacturing goods. To a greater or lesser degree, succeeding governments followed the same economic policy. By 1970, manufacturing industry accounted for approximately 26 percent of GNP and employed 16 percent of the country's labor force. [3]

Although troops were used to break up a copper strike in 1966, in general, by 1970 the old pattern of violent confrontation between the state and the working class had become a matter of ancient history, sentimentally preserved by the parties of the Left in the form of songs and playlets about the infamous massacre at Santa Maria de Iquique in 1907 where three thousand striking miners died. Strikes and trade unions were legalized, under carefully specified circumstances, by the Labour Code of 1925, which also set up industrial arbitration courts. [4] At the same time, the foundations of a rudimentary welfare

system were laid. In modern Chile, the quaint notion of the old
Chilean ruling class that "the social question is nothing more than
a question for the police" had been laid aside, at least until September 1973, in favor of a more sophisticated and more fruitful policy of
mediation and conciliation, combined with periodic efforts to wean
the working class from its Marxist ideology, spearheaded by the
Christian Democrats. Overt force was used only as a last resort.

Nonetheless, if not a classic enclave economy any longer,
Chile remained heavily dependent on copper revenues, not so much
for the import of manufactured goods as for parts and machinery for
the new industries. Agriculture, a principal source of exports during
the nineteenth century, had declined during the twentieth, and in
spite of Chile's relatively generous natural resources the country
was unable to feed the fast expanding urban population, thus throwing
an added burden on the country's exports, which now also had to pay
for imports of wheat, beef, and milk. Much of the problem with agriculture was due to an antiquated and never challenged system of land
tenure, under which 1.3 percent of landowning families in 1965 owned
63 percent of all agricultural land. [5] The traditional ruling class was
landholding as well as commercial and although in many instances its
great estates were no longer an important source of wealth, they
continued to be important for status reasons—resulting in a highly
inefficient use of the land.

By 1970, the Chilean economy was characterized by persistent
instability, with a high annual rate of inflation (see Table 1.1) and a
large and increasing foreign debt. [6] Rates of inflation of more than
20 percent had become normal from 1950 onwards, thus ensuring that
if Chilean labor relations were no longer violent they were, nonetheless, characterized by permanent tension.

Inflation and the need to support a weak manufacturing industry,
as well as its traditional function of channeling mining revenues into
the urban economy, all tended to reinforce the economic importance of
the state. A Chilean economist sympathetic to Popular Unity calculated in 1970 that the state was directly or indirectly responsible for
some 40 percent of total employment and as much as 75 percent of
total investment. [7] Certainly the high proportion of white-collar
workers, 25 percent of the national labor force, was partly due to
the state's importance as an employer (see Tables 1.5 and 1.6).

The government had long been responsible for fixing an annual
reajuste or wage increase in line with inflation, setting guidelines
for the private sector as well as its own employees. Thus from 1950
onwards, the trade union movement's battle to protect real wages
frequently took on the character of open confrontation with a government bent on imposing a wage freeze. By the 1960s, the centralized
trade union federation, the Central Unica de Trabajadores (CUT), had
begun to formulate a critique of government economic policies and a
theory of the root causes of Chile's economic problems—imperialist

TABLE 1.1

Rising Prices, 1880-1970

Period	Average Annual Rate of Inflation (percent)
1880-90	5
1890-1900	5
1900-10	8
1910-20	6
1920-30	3
1930-40	7
1940-50	18
1950-60	36
1960-70	26

Sources: A. Hirschman, "Inflation in Chile," Journeys Towards Progress; ODEPLAN, Antecedentes sobre el desarrollo chileno 1960-1970, p. 39.

control over key productive sectors such as copper, and a "feudal" agricultural sector; thus it took an important step towards underpinning the Socialist and Communist parties' claims to represent an alternative solution for the country at large.

Such was the economic context in 1970, when a Popular Unity coalition of Communists, Socialists, Radicals, a dissident faction of the Christian Democrats, and other small groups won the presidency, and with it control over the administration.

The Christian Democratic Administration:
1964-70

Allende's election as president followed a decade of increasing radicalization, a decade in which it had become commonplace for Chilean economists to talk of the need for "structural reforms." The Christian Democrats contributed a great deal to this process of political radicalization. In 1964, they had declared themselves firmly in favor of structural reforms and even campaigned on the slogan of a "Revolution in Liberty." Their philosophy at the time was a more or less conscious pseudo-Marxism. It championed the cause of the "marginals," the rural and urban poor and lumpenproletariat and those who inhabited Chile's myriad squatter settlements or poblaciones, as an alternative to the organized working class, claiming, with some justice, that the traditional parties of the Left had ignored these sectors and with even more justice that they were totally excluded from any access to political power, even more so than the organized working class. As an alternative to socialism, it offered "communitarianism," the promise of a society in which capital and labor could live in harmony on the basis of social justice.

In power, the Christian Democratic administration undertook a number of important reforms, particularly in agriculture. Trade unions were legalized in the rural areas for the first time in Chile's history. (In spite of a contemporary Socialist party campaign among the poor peasantry, they had noticeably not been legalized during the 1938-40 Frente Popular, perhaps because the parties of the Left felt insufficiently strong at the time to meddle in the acknowledged stronghold of the oligarchy.) By 1969, there were 105,000 rural workers in unions.[8] Another important gain for agricultural workers was the legal minimum wage, bringing their status into line with empleados, who won a legal minimum in the 1940s, and urban manual workers who won theirs in 1958. The Christian Democratic program for agrarian reform was less successful: intended to replace the under-exploited latifundia with peasant cooperatives run by the farms' previous labor force, by 1970 the reform program had reached only 15 percent of agricultural property.[9] These reforms of agriculture earned the Christian Democrats the undying hostility of the traditional elite, politically represented by the National party, and did much to foster political divisions among the ruling class which prepared the way for Allende's victory.

Less successful were the Christian Democrats' attempts to assert national control over foreign business, possibly because the administration also wanted to encourage foreign private investment and was heavily dependent on loans from the United States. Its Chileanization of the American copper companies, an agreement to buy 51 percent of the companies' shares in local mines, was widely criticized for offering too generous terms of purchase and for leaving the management of the mines, and of new government investments, entirely in American hands.[10] (The extent of national feeling on this issue can be judged from the fact that President Allende's much tougher legislation proposing outright nationalization passed a Congress dominated by opposition parties without a single vote opposed.) Meanwhile, foreign investment and control of local manufacturing industry increased threefold.

However, the Christian Democratic administration's worst failure was its relationship with the trade union movement. Two attempts during the 1964-70 government to set up an independent rival to the Marxist-dominated CUT failed to arouse much enthusiasm even in the party's own ranks.[11] The use of troops to break a copper miners' strike at El Salvador in 1966, resulting in the death of six miners, caused consternation within the party and hardly sweetened

relations with the CUT. The CUT opposed Christian Democratic
legislation reforming the 1925 Labour Code, on the grounds that it
would only weaken the unions; not without justice, since the government's proposals would have allowed for the coexistence of three
rival unions in any one factory and would have made it possible for
the president to order illegal strikers back to work, on pain of bringing
in troops. The administration's attempts to solve inflation through a
novel form of wage freeze in 1967−a forced savings scheme−led to
a brief but successful general strike, and further divisions among the
Christian Democrats.

By 1968, the government's trade union policies were being
criticized formally by a majority of the party's own trade unionists
at its national congress. Alan Angell has summarized the source of
the tension very well:

> . . . Basically it seems that the government, after
> 1965, decided on a policy of conciliating investors,
> both private and foreign. It could not do that and
> continue to grant large wage increases and redistribute
> income−at least not in the short term, whatever its
> long term intentions may have been. But a policy
> relying increasingly on private investment and private
> enterprise was forced to take tough measures against
> the unions. There were also PDC trade unionists,
> however, and their mounting grievances against the
> government help to explain the leftward swing inside
> the party's union movement. [12]

In May 1969, such tensions led a substantial part of the left wing of
the Christian Democrats to leave the party and form the MAPU
(Movimiento de Accion Popular Unitaria)−perhaps a sly reference
to the government's efforts to split the trade union movement. The
same year, this new party formally applied for membership in the
Popular Unity coalition dominated by the two great Marxist parties
(Socialist and Communist) of the working class.

Classes and Class Alliances

Chile's class structure (see Table 1. 2) reflects the economic
weaknesses of an enclave economy, in which so much hinges on the
proceeds of a mining sector which, in terms of the labor force it
employs, is relatively small. Most manual workers are employed
outside the strategic mining and manufacturing sectors, and the
proportion of self-employed in the labor force is unusually high.
Nevertheless, unlike traditional models of the enclave economy,
Chile is not a country of peasants. In 1970, only 21 percent of the

TABLE 1.2

Class Structure, 1970

Group	Number	Percent
Manual workers	1,031,000	38
Empleados[a]	629,000	23
Self-employed	501,000	18
Domestic servants	168,000	6
Unemployed	104,000	4
Employers	81,000	3
Unpaid family labor[b]	43,000	2
Undeclared or unknown	154,000	6
All	2,711,000	100
Active population	2,607,000	

[a]"Empleado" is a legal category to which certain economic privileges were attached in 1970, for instance, a slightly higher minimum wage. (The ruling military junta has since abolished these.) Thus manual workers sometimes campaigned for a higher legal status as empleados, and according to the 1970 Census, 106,000 empleados were actually artisans or blue-collar workers. These have been subtracted from the empleado category and added to the category of manual workers to which, in a strict class analysis, they belong.

[b]Mostly in agriculture.

Source: XIV censo de poblacion . . . muestra de adelanta, 1970, based on a 5 percent sample survey of the whole country (all figures accurate to nearest 1,000).

active population was employed in agriculture and more than half of this labor force were wage laborers (see Table 1.4). If the Chilean proletariat is relatively small, and problems of alliances necessarily dominated left-wing discussions during Popular Unity's years in government, then some of the most important potential allies of the working class were urban, particularly the urban poor (or marginals) and the salaried middle class.

According to the 1970 census, the Chilean working class then accounted for about 40 percent of the active population. In fact, of course, the organized working class was much weaker. Of those the census classified as manual workers, only a quarter were working in manufacturing (see Table 1.3). A third were employed in agriculture and fishing, the largest single category (though the comparison between agriculture and manufacturing is almost certainly overstated,

TABLE 1.3

Salaried Workers in Chile, 1970

Sector	Manual Workers	Empleados
Agriculture	314,000	27,000
Manufacturing	221,000	99,000
Construction	109,000	21,000
Services	76,000	315,000[a]
Mining	50,000	17,000
Commerce	49,000	87,000
Transport	38,000	81,000
Light, gas, etc.	8,000	12,000
Finance	2,000	31,000
Unknown	56,000	45,000
All	924,000	735,000[b]

[a]The majority of these would probably be in the state sector.
[b]Including 106,000 manual workers by occupation.

Source: XIV censo de poblacion . . . muestra de adelanta, 1970, based on a 5 percent sample survey of the whole country (all figures accurate to the nearest 1,000).

since many skilled industrial workers would figure in the census as empleados). Mining, even more important in the history of the Chilean working class, and in times past a solid source of support for the Communist party, accounted for 5 percent of manual workers.

Thus at the time Popular Unity came to power, the majority of working-class Chileans were working in areas of the economy where conditions were very unlike those in the great factories in which Marx had predicted that the proletarian consciousness would be forged. They were employed on farms, recently unionized by the Christian Democrats after years of neglect, where in any case there were great differences of interest between permanent farm workers eligible for the Christian Democratic reform program and migrant laborers who were not. Or (see Table 1.4) they were employed on construction sites, where employment was traditionally unstable and heavily dependent on upswings in the economic cycle, and perhaps 15 percent of workers were unionized (construction workers, employed and unemployed, were a frequent phenomenon in the squatter settlements or poblaciones). Or they were employed in the amorphous commercial and service sector. Or they were employed in small factories and artisanal industries, where there were too few workers

TABLE 1.4

Trade Union Membership, 1967-72

Sector	Labor Force 1970	Union Membership 1967	Union Membership 1972
Agriculture	552,000	23,000	261,000 (45%)
Mining	75,000	58,000	62,000 (82%)
Manufacturing	415,000	163,000	216,000 (52%)
Construction	149,000	16,000	22,000 (15%)
Electricity, gas	21,000	9,000	15,000 (60%)
Commerce	303,000	43,000	61,000 (20%)
Transport, communications	156,000	38,000	59,000 (38%)
Services	668,000	22,000	48,000
Other or unknown	267,000	1,000	n.a.*

*Data not available.

Note: Union membership includes employers' unions, and service sector does not include state employees.

Sources: Labour Force 1970 from the 1970 census; Union Membership 1967 from A. Angell, Politics and the Labour Movement in Chile (London: Oxford University Press, 1972), p. 46.; Union Membership 1972 from Clotario Blest, "La clase obrera organizada en Chile," Punto Final 165, August 1972.

to reach the legal minimum for a plant union under the 1925 Labour Code: in 1960, 46 percent of the labor force in manufacturing was employed in establishments with less than five workers, and perhaps another 7 percent or 8 percent in factories with less than 20 workers, although historically this remarkably high figure seems to have been declining. [13]

The comparative weakness of the industrial proletariat was reflected even within the trade union movement, where by 1970, empleados and farm workers both played an important role. In the June 1972 elections for the CUT executive, 146,000 empleados voted compared to 291,000 manual workers, almost one white-collar worker for every two manual workers.

In 1970, the strength and weakness of the two great Marxist parties (Socialist and Communist) lay in their close identification with the organized trade union movement. Criticism of the two parties for ignoring the needs of unorganized workers and other

TABLE 1.5

Social Composition of the Trade Unions, 1972-73

Group	Number	Percent
Employers' unions	38,000	3
Employers' and workers' unions	4,000	n.a.[a]
Empleados and empleados agricolas	138,000	12
Empleados and manual workers	49,000	4
State sector associations (empleados and manual workers)	351,000	31
Agricultural manual workers	247,000	22
Manual workers	287,000	25
Independent workers[b]	21,000	21
All	1,135,000	

[a]Data not available.
[b]Self-employed.

Sources: Clotario Blest, "La escalada hacia la unidad de la clase trabajadora," Punto Final 177, February 13, 1973, and "Asi esta organizada la clase obrera," Punto Final 192, September 11, 1973.

layers of the poor, and basing themselves on a "labor aristocracy" with a relatively high standard of living, has been a recurring feature of Chilean politics. In some cases the criticism is probably unfair; workers in artisanal or semiartisanal industries, in thousands of small units scattered about the country, are an almost impossible sector to penetrate politically on any permanent basis except in so far as they themselves make contact with other sectors of the working class. It is interesting that many of the founding delegates of the Socialist party seem to have come from this sector.[14] But by 1970, the connection seems to have been lost.

The rural areas and the urban poblaciones are another matter. The Christian Democratic government had made good use of its period in power to set up a substantial popular base in the countryside, particularly among the rural unions, which in many cases were organized by its agents (see Table 1.7). Perhaps as much as a third of this trade union base supported the MAPU when it left the Christian Democratic party in 1969 to join Popular Unity, and the government's own agrarian reform program, which succeeded in expropriating the majority of estates left untouched by the Christian

TABLE 1.6

Party Allegiances in the CUT
(percentages)

Party	1957	1959	1962	1965	1968	1972
Communist	40	45	31	42	46	33.4
Socialist	23	28	28	33	22	28.5
Radical	9	4	6	5	8	3.7
Other left-wing						
MAPU (founded 1969)	—	—	—	—	—	5.7
USP (founded 1967)	—	—	—	—	3	0.9
MIR (founded 1964)	—	—	—	—	1	2.7
Christian Democrats	15	15	18	12	10	25.1

Note: All figures rounded to nearest %; political groups no longer active in 1970-73 have been ignored, so that percentages will not always sum to 100; voting figures for 1972 are for national executive elections.

Source: Alan Angell, "Political Affiliations of Delegates to CUT Congresses," Politics and the Labour Movement in Chile (London: Oxford University Press, 1972), p. 218.

11

TABLE 1.7

Rural Trade Union Confederations, 1969

Confederation	Members	Percent of All Members
"El Triunfo Campesino" (Christian Democrats)	48,000	46
"Libertad," National party*	23,000	22
"Ranquil," Socialists and Communists	31,000	30
All	105,000	

*"Libertad" was organized in 1965 from the union of organizations set up by Catholic activists and others set up by the Church in conjunction with the organization of estate owners, the SNA. Its politics were strongly anticommunist.

Source: D. Lehmann, "Political Incorporation Versus Political Stability: the Case of the Chilean Agrarian Reform," Journal of Development Studies, July 1971.

Democrats, gave the parties of Popular Unity a chance of their own to establish widespread support among farm workers. Nonetheless, Christian Democratic and right-wing influence in the countryside continued to be strong throughout Allende's three years in the presidency.

The Christian Democrats also did a great deal of work in the poblaciones, the only really possible focus for organizing the heterogeneous social layers of the poor. Here it set up neighborhood associations, Centros de Madres and sports associations with a Christian ideology, relying on their ability to contribute to the solution of community problems in order to establish a popular base. Once again, this history of political involvement served the Christian Democrats well during Popular Unity's years in government, particularly among women, where the strength of traditional commitments to church and family was much greater than among men. But there is no way of knowing whether, in a less dramatic political context, such organizations of Promocion Popular would have survived from one political generation to the next; and in some cases, after Allende's victory in the 1970 presidential elections, the organizations themselves turned to the traditional parties of the working class.

These same points of weakness, the "forgotten" layers of the poor, attracted the political attention of the MIR (Movimiento de la Izquierda Revolucionaria) which by 1970 had lost its original belief in the political usefulness of a guerrilla foco, and was looking

for sources of popular support. During Allende's first years of government the MIR took up the interests of <u>pobladores</u> and the general
cause of farm workers on estates which were too small to be expropriated by the existing agrarian reform legislation, and created the
<u>Frente de Pobladores Revolucionarios</u> and the <u>Frente Campesino
Revolucionario</u>. Among the pobladores, in individual cases, it
already had some base, having helped in the struggle to protect
their takeovers of land against police violence in the last years of
President Frei's Christian Democratic administration. In 1972, it
turned its attention to the problems of workers in small and artisanal
industries, in conjunction with an attempt to set up a <u>Frente de
Trabajadores Revolucionarios</u>.

Some of the MIR's successes in organizing squatter settlements
were spectacular: <u>Nueva La Habana</u> in Santiago, for instance, which
rapidly became a showplace. In other areas its gains were political
rather than organizational. It succeeded in pressuring the government
and the parties on the Left of Popular Unity into adopting a more
sympathetic attitude towards demands of farm workers on small farms,
without seemingly acquiring enough local support in the rural areas
to win a secure popular base. Its campaign on behalf of workers
in small industries, combined with a belief that the predominant
Socialist and Communist parties were doing their utmost to exclude
such workers from participation in the CUT or the <u>cordones</u>, seems
to have soured relations with the Socialist party unnecessarily without attracting any real support from this social layer—admittedly very
difficult to organize. The MIR made a poor showing in the April 1972
CUT elections.

In the rural areas, it is relatively easy to judge the opposition's
strength among peasants and farm workers, though perhaps not that
of the MIR. In other marginal layers, any political balance sheet is
necessarily based on impressions. Workers in small industries do
seem to have been drawn into the wave of factory takeovers which
broke out as a result of the 1972 Bosses' Strike, and some at least
participated in the cordones, the spontaneous organizations of self-
defense and self-management which sprang up in industrial areas in
response to the strike. There is no evidence that this social layer
was in any way actively involved in the employers' own mobilizations,
and one concludes that the Left had little difficulty in gaining its
support in the general atmosphere of radicalization which accompanied Allende's three years in power. If anything, the reverse
seems to have been the case: takeovers of factories ran directly
contrary to the government's policy of reconciling the small and
medium-sized bourgeoisie to economic changes, and these workers,
working usually in far worse conditions than those in the big factories
and for less pay, were often difficult for the parties of the Left to
control. But judgements about the political attitudes of this social
layer as a whole are necessarily based on those who played an active
part in political events, and to that extent may be wrong.

As for the squatter settlements (poblaciones) and that amorphous layer of "the people" or the poor who inhabit them, the best guess seems to be that the honors here were well distributed. The Christian Democrats seem to have retained something of a base, at least among women—genuinely marginal to the economy, and always more vulnerable to appeals from the Right. (See Table 1.8.) A careful study of the strategy of the opposition throughout Allende's government would show that the campaign to win and consolidate the support of women was one of its priorities, and the existence of support among working-class women was obvious in opposition demonstrations such as the March for Liberty in March 1972, where they represented the only visible working-class forces (though it was not so evident, strangely enough, in the March of the Empty Pots in December 1971, where the predominant social force seems to have been middle-class housewives). One can show fairly easily that in electoral terms, the opposition's persistent majority over Popular Unity was due to the women's vote. Thus in the 1970 presidential elections, 46 percent of male voters supported Popular Unity but only 26 percent of female voters. By 1973 the gap had narrowed, but it still existed: 906,000 men voted for Popular Unity in the March congressional elections, compared to 683,000 women.

At the same time, the parties of Popular Unity themselves did a great deal of political work in the poblaciones, and there is no reason to doubt that they had a strong popular base of their own.

TABLE 1.8

Women in the Chilean Economy

Group	Number	Percent
Empleados	203,000	34
Domestics	157,000	26
Self-employed	106,000	18
Manual workers	78,000	13
Employers	13,000	2
Unpaid family labor	6,000	1
Unknown	38,000	6
All	602,000*	

*23 percent of the active population.

Source: XIV censo de poblacion . . . muestra de adelanta, 1970, based on a 5 percent sample survey of the whole country (all figures accurate to the nearest 1,000).

The importance of tasks of distribution in the local areas from 1971 onwards gave left-wing militants a useful focus for popular mobilization. The JAPs (Juntas de Abastecimiento y Precios) were formed in 1971 to control prices and liaise with government distribution agencies, and during the 1972 Bosses' Strike, when the lorry owners' strike made supplies more problematic, these committees frequently became mass organizations. They should have and often did provide a focus for involving working-class women in politics in the most natural way possible, through their economic role in organizing consumption.

Such is the political balance sheet of Popular Unity's efforts to win the support of the "marginals" for its political program, in so far as it can be determined. The record is very mixed. There is no doubt that by 1970, the Socialist and Communist parties had allowed the Christian Democrats to steal a march on them in the countryside, and not all of their responsibility in this turn of events can be explained away. There were the missed opportunities of the Frente Popular, and in spite of sporadic efforts of the two parties to organize the peasantry while out of government, a certain historical lack of enthusiasm:

> . . . the main focus of both parties was the urban
> worker, not the peasant, and leaders of marxist rural
> organizations often complained of the indifference of
> the main party. Nor did the rural unions receive any
> assistance from the CUT. [15]

In the poblaciones, by contrast, the parties of Popular Unity had something better to offer than the local organizations originally set up by the Christian Democrats: a chance for the inhabitants to take control over the distribution of local food supplies and other necessities of life on their own behalf. Where left-wing militants within the poblaciones used this opportunity to involve the majority of the inhabitants, local Christian Democrats were more than likely to join in and to support other policies of the government. Where control remained within a small clique of party members and opposition charges of sectarianism were proved at the local level, problems were likely to develop and the opposition of those who did not participate was likely to be confirmed.

Strangely enough, it was the MIR which laid greatest stress during Allende's government on the need to win these layers of the poor, which Christian Democratic ideologues had originally estimated at no less than 50 percent of the population. [16] Throughout Allende's period in office, the president's personal convictions and the political theories of the dominant Communist party led to emphasis being put rather on the need for the government to win support among the middle sectors. The Communist party theorized that it should be possible to win the small and middling bourgeoisie to an alliance with the govern-

TABLE 1.9

Class Composition by Economic Sector
(percentage)

Sector	Employers	Self-Employed	Empleado	Manual Workers	Other*
Commerce	7	42	28	16	7
Manufacturing	4	16	24	53	3
Transport	3	17	52	24	4
Construction	2	7	14	73	4
Services	2	10	43	11	34
Agriculture	3	28	5	57	7
Mining	1	7	23	66	3

*Domestics, unpaid family labor, or unknown.

Source: XIV censo de poblacion . . . muestra de adelanta, 1970, based on a 5 percent sample survey of the whole country (all figures accurate to the nearest 1, 000).

ment against Chilean monopolies and international corporations. One could say this was the essential plank in their strategy; it was coupled with an equal stress on the need not to offend the middle sectors' supposed prejudices in favor of constitutionalism.

It is very difficult to set limits to such an all-embracing concept as the "middle sectors." But as for the small and middling bourgeoisie, in 1970 only 3 percent of the active population were employers; the number of votes which small capital could bring to bear against the government was thus minute, and its only hope of successfully opposing the government's policies lay in mobilizing other social layers. For both government and opposition, the key middle sectors were not small businessmen, but the salaried middle class and perhaps the self-employed. (See Table 1.9.)

Compared to their equivalents in developed countries, Chile's white-collar workers have had a surprisingly left-wing history. Empleados are well unionized, particularly in the state sector (where 96 percent of all employees were members of their appropriate association in 1972).[17] This is undoubtedly a consequence of Chile's long battle with inflation: with salaries eroding at the rate of 25-30 percent a year and often more, middle-class wage earners could not afford to leave their economic interests to employers' benevolence, particularly if their employer was the state, frequently involved in a drive to cut its salaries as part of a counterinflationary program. Furthermore, as Table 1.10 shows, many Chilean white-collar workers are poor. Militant trade unionism is the primary school of the Left, and such economic pressures have occasionally moved the salaried

TABLE 1.10

Estimated Comparative Income of Manual Workers
and Empleados

Income (sueldo vitales)	Percent of All Manual Workers	Percent of All Empleados
Less than 1	54	7
1-2	33	38
2-3	10	28
3-4	1.5	10
4-5	0.5	5.5
5-15	1	11
More than 15	—	0.5

Source: "El reajuste y la luchade clases," Punto Final, no. 183, May 8, 1973.

middle class to play a key role in working class politics, most
noticeably in the formation of the CUT itself. [18] Individually, the
ranks of state-employed white-collar workers have provided two
secretary generals of the Communist party and one of the leading
figures in the foundation of the MIR. (Luis Corvalan, secretary
general of the Communist party during the Allende period, and Ricardo
Fonseca, an earlier secretary general, were both primary school
teachers; Clotario Blest, president of ANEF (the association of government clerks) was first president of the CUT and a founder of the MIR.)
          Nevertheless, historically white-collar workers have been
dominated by Chile's two great center parties, the Radicals and the
Christian Democrats. In 1970, in tune with the political prejudices
of their bases, both parties maintained at least the appearance of
being anticapitalist and in favor of fundamental structural change.
The Radical party had lost its right wing in 1969 (when it left to
form the Democratic Radical party), and thereupon joined the Popular
Unity coalition. Between 1969 and 1972 it was undoubtedly moving
in a confused fashion towards the Left—as the emergence of the
Radical Revolutionary Youth within the party bears witness. Those
who could not accept this leftward trend either abandoned the party
for the Christian Democrats or joined a splinter party, the PIR (Partido
Izquierda Radical, or Left Radical party) which left the parent body
and finally the Popular Unity coalition in 1972.
          In 1970, the Christian Democrats were still suffering from the
conservative policies of President Frei's last years in power. Their
popular support at all levels had dropped substantially: in the 1970
elections, they won only 28 percent of the vote, less than the right-
wing National party. They had lost a sizeable proportion of their
youth wing in 1968, to the group which later formed the MAPU: the
new party, as well as joining Popular Unity, subsequently declared
itself a Leninist organization. Nor was this to be the last split.
In 1971, with Popular Unity in power, a new group left the Christian
Democrats to form the Christian Left—once again, joining Popular
Unity (and subsequently becoming a close ally of the MIR).
          Between 1969 and 1972 there was clearly a profound crisis in
both political organizations which might best be said to represent
the salaried middle class. Political attitudes within this middle
sector were polarizing very quickly, between those in favor of real
structural reforms in Chilean society and willing to join the traditional working-class parties to achieve them, and those who were
not. The almost simultaneous decision of the bulk of the Radicals
and a section of the Christian Democrats to join forces with the
Socialist and Communist parties, even at the cost of the unity of
their own organizations, is hardly a coincidence. Initially, this
process worked very much to the benefit of the Left, which gained
the Radical party, the MAPU, and the Christian Left. The Christian
Democrats were forced into a defensive position, denouncing the

parties of Popular Unity as sectarian and dogmatic and stoutly maintaining their own commitment to revolutionary social change, as
originally promised by the "Revolution in Liberty" of 1964.

By 1972, the Christian Democrats' attitude to the government
had hardened, and their contempt for officialism had changed to a
vigorous denunciation of totalitarianism. This rightward shift enabled
the party to capture support among those sections of the salaried
middle class who felt threatened by substantial social change: for
instance, schoolteachers who felt that a change in the ideological
bias of the school system would threaten their jobs and chances of
promotion, and white-collar workers in private industry whose close
relationship with their employers led them to oppose government
nationalization. By 1972, the submerged conservatives among the
salaried middle class had found a voice and a cause, as the splitting
off of the PIR and its subsequent turn to the opposition testify.

At the same time, the continual pressure within Popular Unity
towards the Left led to further splits within the sections of white-
collar workers who supported reforms, and a hemorrhaging of support
from the Radical party, very noticeable in the 1972 elections for the
national executive of the CUT. Militant members of the Radical party
might feel satisfied working for a transformation of the party into a
revolutionary organization through the Radical Revolutionary Youth,
but more passive supporters were equally likely to register their
wish to break with the party's social democratic traditions through a
vote for the Communists, the Socialists, and even the MIR.

This polarization of white-collar workers emerged very clearly
in the June 1972 elections for the national executive of the CUT, when
the Radicals won only 7 percent of the total vote of empleados compared with 41 percent for the Christian Democrats and 41 percent for
the Communist and Socialist parties. Although a majority of white-
collar workers were in favor of Popular Unity, their support for the
government was no longer channeled through the traditional middle-
class Radical party but through the great traditional parties of the
working class.

Thus in spite of the success of the opposition's campaign
against the government, the salaried middle class divided in the
face of worsening class conflict in the country as a whole. There
is no reason to think that the government lost the salaried middle
class and the opposition gained it: on the evidence of the 1972
CUT elections, it may even be that at the time of the coup a small
majority of this social layer still supported Allende, and it is
certainly not likely that more than a small percentage had changed
their allegiance from the Communist and Socialist parties to the
opposition. At the same time, a good many salaried middle-class
workers clearly felt that their interests were not on the side of
fundamental social change, when it came to the crunch: that in
a social revolution, they would lose a cherished position of privilege.

For some of them, in any case, the privileges were real enough:
more than a quarter of empleados were earning three sueldo vitales
or more in 1973, compared to 3 percent of manual workers.

These were the people who provided the support for strikes
of doctors and other professionals in August 1972, and the occasional
instances of white-collar opposition to government proposals of
nationalization in particular industries. They were also the basis
of the opposition-inspired gremios, "independent" trade unionists
who mobilized against the government as early as 1971, providing
the basis for a mass movement capable of justifying the coup (see
Chapter 4).

The self-employed are such a heterogeneous social layer that
no general statement about them is possible, and even statements
about particular sectors, such as shopkeepers, risk confusing what
are in effect two very different social classes: the lumpenproletariat
of street hawkers and barrow merchants, and the genuine petty
bourgeoisie running a stable family business in a middle-class
district or working-class poblacion. There should perhaps be some
doubt as to whether they are better classified among the middle
sectors or among the marginals. Historically, the average income
of the self-employed was declining, in any case, and they were on
the whole very little better off than workers, and much worse off
than the average empleado. 19 One assumes that small shopkeepers
generally earned about as much as a well-paid manual worker or
lower-middle-class empleado, between 1 and 2 sueldo vitales,
and that the lumpenproletariat belonged to the very poor.

The largest single group within the self-employed, however,
was small agricultural proprietors or minifundistas. Perhaps only
Mao could really do justice to the complications of the real class
composition of this sector—which includes proletarians forced to
hire themselves out as seasonal wage laborers, as well as a bourgeoisie able to hire seasonal wage laborers in their turn. (See Chapter 3).

In 1970, the Chilean Census found that about a quarter of
the self-employed were artisans or manual workers (see Table 1.11).
These can scarcely have belonged to the middle sectors and might
better be labeled part of the subproletariat, along with workers in
artisanal factories or small industries. Certainly the independent
plumber or electrician would be far from qualifying for membership
in the middle class: by the time such a craftsman had sufficient
prosperity to feel himself a cut above other workers on the social
scale, he would almost certainly have employees of his own. At
the other extreme, both professionals and managers and administrators
are clearly bona fide members of the petty bourgeoisie. But the
numbers involved here are small—29,000 in all, 1.1 percent of the
active population. Many professionals were obviously employed,
most probably by the state. Many others must have had employees
of their own.

TABLE 1.11

The Self-Employed, 1970

Occupation	Number	Sector	Number
Farmers	156,000	Agriculture	153,000
Artisans and other		Commerce	128,000
manual workers	124,000	Services	89,000
Shopkeepers, etc.	120,000	Manufacturing	65,000
Truck, bus, and taxi		Transport	27,000
operators	25,000	Construction	12,000
Other services	25,000	Finance	6,000
Professionals	16,000	Mining	5,000
Managers and		Unknown	17,000
administrators	13,000		
Office workers	4,000		
Unknown	13,000		

Source: XIV censo de poblacion . . . muestra de adelanta, 1970, based on a 5 percent sample survey of the whole country (all figures accurate to the nearest 1,000).

Shopkeepers and streetsellers (vendedores y ocupaciones afines) account for nearly a quarter of the self-employed, the next largest group after the minifundistas. Street hawkers had reason to be pleased with the new government in 1970, which gave them freedom to set up their stalls wherever they pleased on the city streets, removing the ban imposed by the Christian Democratic administration. As for the shopkeepers, there are grounds for believing that the majority's reaction to Popular Unity was negative. Local grocers were much affected by the setting up of the JAPs in 1971, with authority to supervise prices and control wholesale supplies being distributed through the government network; and many local shopkeepers seem to have regarded this dose of popular control over their business as inadmissible interference—particularly since such control was almost certain to interfere with their ability to sell scarce supplies on the middle-class black market, at much higher prices. Thus in spite of government propaganda extolling the idea that the interests of the JAPs and the shopkeepers need not be antagonistic, there was bound to be some conflict of interest. As early as December 1971, the National Association of Retailers took a public position of opposition to the government (though once again, the association would include employers as well as the self-employed in its ranks).

However, shopkeepers with a family business in working-class districts or squatter settlements could not afford a policy of long-term opposition to the political interests of their customers, still less if the customers could readily organize an efficient alternative system of distribution through the JAP. Only if the opposition could already count on a substantial popular base within the local poblacion was it worthwhile to take a position of open opposition to government policy. (In this sense, the numbers of small shopkeepers who took an active part in the political struggle against the government, always supposing it were possible to discover them, would provide a fairly accurate guide to the success and failure of the government's mobilization in the poblaciones). This basic economic weakness was also revealed by the Bosses' Strikes of October 1972 and August 1973. Supplies continued to reach working-class consumers with or without the shopkeepers' cooperation, and for many independent small businessmen, the risk of a prolonged loss of business was enough to force them to open. Petty bourgeoisie such as these were unlikely candidates to spearhead the counterrevolution, at least without substantial outside economic aid.

One section of the petty bourgeoisie which is often cited for its vigorous and successful hostility to the government is transport. Independent bus operators converged on Santiago in February 1972 to protest against the government's policy of holding down fares, their mobilization quickly taking on the character of a condemnation of the government as a whole. An even more clearly political tack was taken by the Confederation of Lorry Owners dominated by Leon Vilarin, which in September 1972 organized a national transport strike against the government's supposed threat to nationalize all transport in the remote and sparsely populated province of Aisen. This strike, the signal for strikes of the gremios and other professionals, as well as for employers to close down their factories, was the core of the Bosses' Strike, and for a very clear reason: the transport owners' demands were not limited to transport, but clearly aimed to force the government to retreat on its policies of nationalization or else to create such a state of chaos in the country that the government would fail. The strike was repeated in 1973, playing an important role in the buildup to the coup. [20]

But in spite of the folk image of the copper miner or skilled worker who retires to buy his own truck, the transport industry is not run by the petty bourgeoisie. Only 17 percent of the industry's labor force is self-employed, about the same proportion as in manufacturing, and very much less than in those strongholds of the independent operator, commerce and agriculture. At the time of the Bosses' Strike, the Confederation of Lorry Owners controlled just less than half of Chile's 52,000 lorries, and 35 large firms owned more than a quarter of these, while employing many of the others as subcontractors. Thus, the independent operator or small employer, where

he did exist, was often very far from being independent—not untypical
of the general relationship between the big Chilean monopolies and
the smaller or petty bourgeoisie.

Thus, of the vast numbers of self-employed, only the shopkeepers seem to have emerged as an independent political force during
the three years of Popular Unity, and compared with, say, the doctors,
they were not very strong. This should not be surprising. The
self-employed are a collection of classes rather than a single class—
lumpenproletariat, peasantry, subproletariat of artisans and journeymen,
as well as the classic petty bourgeoisie—and perhaps it is only the
shopkeepers among them who conform readily to the classic model of
the petty bourgeoisie, together with a few of the richer minifundistas.
Even in the case of the shopkeepers, some doubts remain: one would
like to know more about their economic and political relations with
the monopoly-dominated wholesale sector, during the three years. [21]
In many ways, the characteristic weakness of a class structure in an
underdeveloped country posed a challenge to Popular Unity's ability
to wage an ideological and organizational struggle for the loyalty of
the masses, as much as any deep theoretical conundrums over class
alliances. The question of whether an individual journeyman carpen-
ter or street vendor supported the government or not was most likely
to be decided by his relationship with his local Junta de Vecinos,
JAP, comando comunal, or cordon; and in the urban areas, only the
shopkeeper was likely to find such relationships dogged by conflicts
of interest. There is every indication that the opposition understood
this point:

> However the Opposition organizes itself, its methods
> of action must have an immediate root in the bases of
> society: it cannot confine itself to the general propa-
> ganda and traditional use of Assemblies by the old
> political parties. Neighbourhood councils, mothers'
> unions, cooperatives, trade unions and other profes-
> sional bodies require the permanent involvement of
> those representing the best political thinking of the
> citizens: not the reduced contacts characteristic of
> an electoral campaign. The explicit or implicit unity
> of the Opposition should give rise to concrete actions
> at work, in the suburb, in the supermarket, which will
> be capable of counteracting the dictatorship which the
> Marxists are prepared to put into practice at the base.
> It is not enough for the democratic forces to try to
> reach the public through the mass media. They must
> link themselves with the masses. Such a programme
> implies great sacrifice, often a substantial change
> of people's habits and style of life. [22]

    The worst trick which underdevelopment played on the politics
of the Chilean Left was its contribution to one political division
within the proletariat itself, between the copper miners and the
urban industrial sector. Copper accounts for 60 percent of Chile's
foreign exchange: Popular Unity above all, needed the profits from
the copper mines and an increase in copper production and sales in
order to finance not only its plans for greater industrial development
but also the increased consumption of the urban working class itself,
in imported flour, milk, and meat. In Chilean terms copper miners
were well paid in 1970, thanks to a change of policy on the part of
the international companies who had owned the mines during the
Christian Democratic administration. [29] However, like miners everywhere, they had reason to feel that they were underpaid: a short
working life, risks of accident and silicosis, the need to save enough
in ten or fifteen years to set up a small business for the rest of one's
life. In El Teniente, housing and other conditions were deplorable,
the result of many years' neglect. As a result, there were strikes,
confrontations with the government, and political bitterness. In
Chuquicamata in the northern desert, the majority of copper miners
voted for a splinter wing of the Socialist party led by Raul Ampuero,
an old left-winger who owed no loyalties to Popular Unity in the
CUT elections of April 1972. In El Teniente, the country's other
big mine, the miners split; and some of them voted for the Christian
Democrats.

    The result was the El Teniente strike of May-June 1973—a long
and bitter conflict with the government which the opposition used
as evidence of working-class opposition to Allende, and which led
in June to open conflicts in Santiago between El Teniente miners and
their middle-class supporters, and the rest of the urban working class.

    But aside from this tragic episode, the record of the Chilean
working class in overcoming the obstacles posed by the weakness of
its own industrial proletariat is really quite remarkable. An amazing
variety of popular organizations grew up during Allende's three years
in government, all of them bridging in one way or another the gap
between those who were unionized and those who had never had a
chance to join a union organization, those who were already well
acquainted with the political parties of the Left and those who had
traditionally been left by the wayside. Some of these organizations,
such as the Juntas de Vecinos and the JAPs, were originally set in
motion by the government itself. Others, such as the industrial
cordons and comandos comunales, were the spontaneous invention
of workers themselves faced with a political emergency. In the
face of profound economic crisis, these organizations were nevertheless remarkably successful in consolidating a popular movement with
revolutionary aims in the urban areas, in spite of all the odds against
such a development built into the Chilean economy: one can measure
their result numerically in the jump in support for Popular Unity during

the March 1973 congressional elections, in spite of the partial success of the opposition in consolidating its own support among the white-collar middle class. The real failures of the Left in mobilizing popular support lay among women and the peasantry: the one, notoriously difficult to organize along class lines, the other, bitterly divided by the gains and losses of one sector against another inherited from the Christian Democrats' program of agrarian reform.

This upsurge of political militancy and organization in the urban areas gave Allende's period in office a revolutionary impetus which many sectors of Popular Unity would have preferred to avoid, and one can argue that it was largely responsible for the development of bitter political differences within the Chilean Left, as well as for the increasing nervousness shown by the military from October 1972 onwards. Popular militancy combined with the weakness and lack of political agreement within the Popular Unity coalition to produce an explosive mixture. The Communist party and the Radicals would have preferred to establish a tight control over these new organizations of "people's power," if only to preserve their much-beloved alliance with the middle classes and hopes of an alliance with the Christian Democrats. The weight of the Socialist party within the coalition, and the weight of the revolutionary Left within the party, was sufficiently great to prevent any overt attempts at repression however far "people's power" went beyond the government's self-imposed limits. But at the same time, it was not great enough to impose a consistently revolutionary strategy on the government, or to prepare the supporters of "people's power" to meet the coming coup.

However, to understand the radicalization of Chilean politics under Allende, one really has to consider it as a process: a pattern of class alliances which changed periodically in accordance with the actions and reactions of different sectors to the government's policies, and their own developing political ideas. No static survey of different classes and social layers can quite convey the sense of this progression from a campaign to elect a president, to a battle for revolution. Nor is it enough to take the positions and ideology of the various left-wing parties as they were in 1970−to suggest that sectors in the Socialist party were already well to the left of the rest of the coalition, having begun to flirt with the idea of armed revolution following the Cuban Revolution−for the issues and alliances within the Left during this period had a dynamic of their own.

NOTES

1. Cf. Republica de Chile, ODEPLAN, Antecedentes sobre el Desarrollo Chileno, p. 126 (hereafter referred to as Antecedentes).

2. Paul Baran, The Political Economy of Growth (Harmonds-worth: Penguin Books, 1973). Fernando Cardoso, Ideologias de la burguesia en un pais dependiente (Mexico City: Singlo XXI, 1971).

3. Sergio Aranda and Alberto Martinez, "Estructura economica: algunas caracteristicas fundamentales," in Victor Brodersolm, ed., Chile Hoy (Santiago: Siglo XXI, 1970).

4. A brief summary of the Labour Code is given by Alan Angell in Politics and the Labour Movement in Chile (London: Oxford University Press, 1972), p. 57ff.

5. Antecedentes, p. 100.

6. Ibid., p. 436. The state's foreign debts increased from $1,113 million in 1964 to $2,029 in 1970, that is, almost double.

7. Sergio Ramos, Chile: una economia de transicion? (Santiago: Prensa Latinoamericana, 1972).

8. Cf. Angell, op. cit., p. 258.

9. Antecedentes, p. 111.

10. Cf. Keith Griffin, Underdevelopment in Spanish America: an Interpretation (London: Allen and Unwin, 1969).

11. An excellent account of the Christian Democrats' relations with the trade unions and its effect upon the party is given in Angell, op. cit., p. 198ff.

12. Ibid., p. 203.

13. Aranda and Martinez, op. cit.

14. Cf. Fernando Casanueva and Manuel Fernandez Canque, El Partido Socialista y la Lucha de Clases (Santiago: Editorial Quimantu, 1973).

15. Angell, op. cit., p. 255.

16. Ibid., p. 178

17. Cf. Clotario Blest, "La escalada hacia la unidad de la clase trabajadora," Punto Final 177, February 13, 1973.

18. Ibid.

19. Antecedentes, pp. 45, 50, and 53.

20. Cf. P. O'Brien, J. Roddick, and I. Roxborough, Chile: The State and Revolution (London: Macmillan, 1975).

21. Cf. Ramos, op. cit., p. 69. In 1967, 70 large wholesale firms controlled 76 percent of all sales. In the retail sector, very much the reverse was the situation: 100,000 small firms controlling 74 percent of all sales, and small and medium firms together 94 percent of all sales.

22. Armand Mattelart, "La bourgeoisie a l'ecole de Lenine: le gremialismo et la ligne de masse de la bourgeoisie Chilienne," Politique Aujourd'hui, Paris, January 1974, p. 142.

2

THE CRISIS OF HEGEMONY
IN THE CHILEAN LEFT
Pablo Lira

THE VICTORY OF POPULAR UNITY

Popular Unity's victory in Chile in 1970 was not a historical accident. Rather, it was the outcome of a crisis in Chile's dependent capitalist mode of development whose roots lay far in the past. This crisis had come to a head dramatically in 1967, when the Christian Democrat government of Eduardo Frei collapsed in tatters, and with it an attempt to solve the crisis in the spirit of bourgeois reformism. By the 1960s, the increasing social and economic obstacles lying in the way of capitalist development in Chile had forced some sectors of the bourgeoisie, represented by Frei and the Christian Democrats, to implement a series of reforms including an agrarian reform, which brought them directly into conflict with the main sectors of the ruling class represented by the National party.[1] As a result, the ruling class split into different political camps and presented two candidates in the 1970 presidential elections, allowing Allende to win the 1970 election with roughly the same percentage of the total vote that had led to his defeat in 1964 (see Table 2.1). This political division was not an accident or an error of calculation, but an immediate consequence of the contradictions that the crisis of capitalism had created within the ranks of the bourgeoisie; and equally, Allende's victory was a reflection of the unity of the working class, made possible by a political alliance between the Socialist and Communist parties that was originally forged in 1957 and that culminated in 1969 in Popular Unity itself.

However, the very circumstances that brought Allende to the presidency in 1970 also limited the diffusion of revolutionary political

---

This chapter has been translated from the Spanish by Jacqueline F. Roddick.

TABLE 2.1

Election Results, 1964 and 1970

Presidential Election	Total Vote (percent)
1964	
Allende (FRAP[a])	39
Frei (Christian Democrats, Liberals and Conservatives[b])	56
Duran (Radical party)	5
1970	
Allende (Popular Unity)	36
Alessandri (National party[b])	35
Tomic (Christian Democrats)	27

[a]Frente de Accion Popular (Popular Action Front); otherwise the Communist-Socialist alliance.

[b]The Liberals and Conservatives subsequently united to form the National party.

Source: North American Congress on Latin America, New Chile, p. 26.

ideas among the masses. The same legalistic and constitutionalistic beliefs that dominated the majority of those who voted for Radomito Tomic* were widespread among Popular Unity supporters as well. One can see their influence in the strategy that dominated Popular Unity: a strategy based on the belief that the working class could take power through a series of transformations initiated from within the existing state apparatus and its institutions, without having to destroy the old apparatus or create a new one based on its own hegemony as a class—the only way to ensure a genuinely socialist revolution. This "peaceful road to socialism" was essentially the strategy for taking power put forward in Chile by the Communist party (taking power is the principal task of any revolution). It was put forward as part of the Communist party's conception of an anti-imperialist, antioligarchic, agrarian revolution based upon the existing correlation of class forces, as the Communist party perceived

---

*The Christian Democrat candidate for the presidency in 1970; during President Frei's government, the Chilean ambassador to the United States.

them; and this party more than any other saw the key to its strategy
as lying in the presidential elections, which would open the doors
to executive power.

Yet the experience of Popular Unity should not be dismissed
as a piece of reformism that was bound to fail from the very beginning.
This kind of analysis is completely undialectical and just as false
and simplistic as its opposite: the kind that tries to pretend that the
political line that was able to dominate Popular Unity in spite of
differences within the coalition did not fail its historical test in
Chile between 1970 and 1973; that fundamentally it was correct;
that the "peaceful road to socialism" is still a valid strategy and
in Chile there were just a few errors in its application. [2]

What brought the different parties in Popular Unity together,
at the same time as it set out the principles they were bound to
follow, was above all the Basic Program of the Popular Unity Government drawn up in 1969 by all those who participated in the new
alliance: the Socialist party, the Communist party, the MAPU, the
Radical party, and the API (and later, Isquierda Cristiana, the Christian Left). It is on the basis of this program that one should judge
Popular Unity; every argument about the kind of class alliance or
political alliance that it represented should begin here.

The core of the new political alliance that took over the executive in 1970 was an alliance between the Socialist and Communist
parties known originally as the Popular Action Front or FRAP, dating
from 1957. By 1969 other social sectors had joined this coalition
of the two great parties of the working class. Sectors of the peasantry,
represented by MAPU, and sectors of the middle classes gave the
alliance a broader character by bringing into it sections of the small
and medium bourgeoisie: the Radical party, API. The fact that these
last two parties were included reinforced the hegemony of reformism
within the coalition (though one should make a distinction between
"bourgeois reformism, " which attempts to legitimize and secure the
sectoral interests of the working class while denying their class
character, and "workers' reformism," which attempts to realize all
the interests of the working class without letting it be seen that,
in fact, it only takes into account those demands regarded as legitimate by the bourgeoisie).

Nevertheless, the predominance of reformist views within the
coalition did not mean that Popular Unity was in any way solidly
united behind a single political line. Within the same coalition
there were also political sectors that looked towards the establishment
of socialism in Chile within a relatively brief span of time. In 1970
these sectors had no roots in the masses, nor did they have an alternative program or a party of their own. Nonetheless, one can see
the differences emerging in the discussions which accompanied the
drafting of the program, and in the different approaches to the 1970
electoral campaign. Within the framework of the tactical compromise

implied by the program itself, the Left within Popular Unity retained
the right and the duty to mobilize the forces that supported a more
radical and more genuinely socialist interpretation of the program's
provisions: and in this sense, each party within the alliance maintained its own political independence.

It is clear that the program was neither openly reformist, nor
a blueprint for the transition to socialism, in spite of its vagueness
at many points. It proposed that the new government should carry
out a series of reforms attacking imperialism, the monopolies, and
the rural latifundia or large estates, while simultaneously "laying
the foundations for the construction of socialism." It also set out
a series of reforms that could be introduced within the existing legal
framework, with the general aim of introducing rank and file organizations into the state apparatus and even using them to replace existing
state institutions; all this "through the broadest possible mobilization
of the masses," culminating in the creation of a People's Assembly
that was to be the foundation of the "People's state." The ambiguity
in the program's text allowed different sectors within the coalition
to interpret all these provisions in the light of their own political
line: after all, the text was the outcome of an alliance based on
mutual concessions. Later, as it began to be clear that the terms
of the original alliance would have to be changed, this ambiguity
was to create problems, but the real character of the contradictions
with the coalition did not become obvious until mid-1972, when
President Allende himself disowned an attempt to set up a local rank
and file People's Assembly in Concepcion. During 1972, different
conceptions of strategy were suddenly to emerge as the key to debates
within the coalition over day-to-day tactics; but this was not the
case in 1970 or 1971.

Thus when Popular Unity was formed, different conceptions of
strategy were not a sufficient reason a priori, to prevent revolutionary
socialists from participating in the coalition and the government. On
the contrary, failure to participate would have been a major political
error, not only because those outside the government were denied
access to the tools for political intervention which the government
offered, but also because it would have meant isolating oneself from
the masses, who at the time supported Popular Unity. One can see
the weaknesses of a principled stand against Popular Unity in the
results of the April 1972 national elections for the CUT, where the
MIR made a very poor showing (see Table 2.2).

Such real political pressures help to explain why the MIR gave
the government its critical support after Allende was elected, in spite
of its earlier commitment to a strategy of guerrilla war. In fact, the
MIR suspended the armed actions which it had embarked on in 1969,
and even took part in some of the less public activities of Popular
Unity. Yet the MIR was convinced that a military coup was inevitable
from the moment the election results were published; and just as
convinced that, after the coup and after the masses had lost their

TABLE 2.2

CUT Elections, April 1972

Parties	Blue Collar Workers (291,000)	White Collar Workers (146,000)
Communist party	113,000	33,000
Socialist party	95,900	29,000
MAPU	22,000	3,000
Radical party	5,600	11,000
Popular Unity	236,500	76,000
MIR (FTR)[a]	5,800	6,000
Christian Democrats	47,400	61,000
Other groups (mainly USOPO)[b]	1,300	3,000

[a]Frente Trabajadores Revolucionarios
[b]USOPO Union Socialista Popular

Source: Latin American Newsletter, July 1972.

31

illusions in reformism, it would take the lead in the subsequent
struggle for power as the only group with military training, providing
the core of a new revolutionary party around which the rest of the
Chilean Left would regroup. This policy of waiting for the coup lost
the MIR a great deal of support among the masses, and its lack of
understanding of the real political opportunities opened up by the
Popular Unity government condemned it to play a marginal role. The
MIR was never able to provide a real socialist alternative. And
however much the masses may have been dominated by reformism,
that in itself is not a sufficient excuse for the MIR's political weakness throughout these three years. As history has shown, it is
from the most advanced layers of these very masses that the revolutionary party of the proletariat is born: its very birth is a response
to the development of the class struggle as it reaches new levels of
intensity. If there is to be a dialectical interaction between the
nuclei of revolutionaries and the mass struggle, then the nuclei
themselves must be capable of stimulating this dynamic, understanding
it, and providing it with leadership. [3]

    Thus during Allende's term as president, revolutionary organi-
zations faced two fundamental tasks. On the one hand, they had to
battle issue by issue against the hold which reformist and legalist
ideas still held over the masses, offering a concrete alternative to
every problem. On the other hand, they had to try to direct the
masses towards a new political goal: the construction of forms of
"people's power" capable of winning any confrontation between the
classes, and at the same time subordinating the government's activities to the overall aim of creating an alternative to the bourgeois
state. But in contemporary conditions in Chile neither of these
could be achieved if one remained outside Popular Unity and the
government. A different approach would only have been possible or
correct if the government had already demonstrated a total incapacity
and if the left wing within Popular Unity had already definitely lost
the fight for its own political positions within the coalition and
within the government. But in 1970 this was not the case, for the
government had only just taken office.

    Thus at this point in time, rejection of the revolutionary
possibilities opened up by Popular Unity would have been just as
sterile a strategy for the conquest of power as the strategy of limiting
government policies in the interests of an unstinted respect for
legality, as if the rule of law was something that could be guaranteed
by the laws themselves. [4] Both positions denied themselves from the
outset any possibility of forgoing the subjective conditions for turning
the crisis of Chilean capitalism to revolutionary ends. [5]

ALLENDE IN GOVERNMENT

    Allende's installation in government was beset by a number of
problems, and Popular Unity was forced to negotiate with the Chris-

tian Democrats and sign a statute of guarantees that was nothing more than a promise to respect the existing constitution and legal framework. The statute of guarantees did not entail a modification of the government's program in any way, but it did serve to reaffirm the validity of the existing state institutions in the face of any doubts which might be raised as the program was put into practice. The most important clause was the one which reaffirmed "the professional character of the armed forces."[6] Not that this was any concession on the part of hegomonic sectors within Popular Unity: the military had not intervened directly in Chilean politics for forty years, and reformists within the coalition firmly believed that the armed forces were a professional body that had no political interests, respected the constitution, and were thus bound to respect a government that had been freely elected at the polls.

However, within a few months, different views on the factors that would ultimately determine the government's stability could be heard within the government itself. One of Allende's personal advisers, Joan Garces, pointed out in a conference at the Escuela Latinoamericana de Sociologia in 1972,

> Whether or not the Constitution laid down that Popular Unity would control the Presidency from 1970 to 1976 from the night of Allende's installation on September 3, only force could finally determine if the government would last until 1976 and under what conditions it would survive or fall. [Emphasis mine.]

Thus it was more or less clear to everyone that the questions raised as Popular Unity's program was put into effect, could only be solved by the comparative political and military strength that Popular Unity could bring to bear to resolve the fundamental issue of who held power.

During the period between November 1970 and mid-1971, Popular Unity's political strength grew rapidly, both in electoral terms and in terms of its organized support among the masses. One can see this in the results of the municipal elections of 1971 (Table 2.3).

From mid-1971 onwards, however, the government came under increasing pressure from other state institutions: Congress, the judiciary, and the Controleria.* The pressure began with Congress

---

*The Controleria is a peculiar Chilean institution that vets bills passed by Congress for their consistency with previous laws, and where they are inconsistent sends them back to the executive for reformulation. It is supposed to be an arm of the executive.

TABLE 2. 3

Municipal Elections, April 1971

Party	Percent of Total Vote
Popular Unity	50. 9
Christian Democrats	25. 6
National party	18. 1
Democratic Radical party	3. 8
Other	1. 6

laying formal charges of violating the constitution against various
cabinet ministers: Jose Toha, minister of the interior, was only the
first of many to be removed from his post by Congress on such
grounds. [7] This sort of challenge was confined to the level of a
manipulation of political institutions. For its part, the Controleria
began to demonstrate its independence of the executive and call
into question the measures taken by the government to create a
Social Property Area, * and the program's stated intention of nationalizing the monopolies. In the same way, the Supreme Court condemned
the "people's tribunals" proposed by the executive in a bill sent to
Congress for its approval: this initiative was followed by a series
of court actions against government employees and leading figures
in the left-wing political parties, with the clear political aim of
showing that the government was overstepping the bounds laid down
by the law and the constitution.

These tactics culminated in the October strike of 1972 called
by the Unions of the Truck Owners and the Shopkeepers. During the
strike it became obvious that the mass movement was increasingly
an autonomous force in its own right, independent of the government,
though it continued to support the government and defend it as its
own. October 1972 saw the beginning of a long period of political
instability; during this time the bourgeoisie resolved its former
political differences, and emerged as a united political force, while
the government showed itself incapable of confronting the collapse
of the state as an institution and thus of the rule of law itself. For
its part, the mass movement took on new dimensions, sometimes

---

*That is, a nationalized sector of the economy. The government's
economic program envisaged three economic sectors: a nationalized
sector, a private sector, and a sector with mixed or joint state and
private ownership.

overtaking even the left-wing political parties in a fashion never before seen in Chile.

Remembering these basic trends, one can single out a number of phases within this period that were to be particularly important for the definition of the various alternative political options.

The Economic Offensive: November 1970 to June 1971

The first phase corresponds to an economic offensive by the government along the lines set out in the program. Its achievements included a significant redistribution of income, increasing the purchasing power of wages and salaries, a substantial cut in unemployment, increased production as a result of the mobilization of the economy's unused capacity, and, most important, the beginning of the nationalization of the monopolies and banks through mobilization of the workers and the use of the executive's hitherto-forgotten legal powers.* The government set in motion the nationalization of the North American copper companies, and a massive application of the existing Agrarian Reform Laws to all rural properties of more than 200 irrigated acres. [8]

Policies towards national and international capital such as these principally benefited the working class and the urban and rural sub- and semiproletariat, about 40 percent of Chile's working population in the first case and 30 percent in the second. The enthusiasm that the government's offensive aroused among these classes explains why the vote for Popular Unity shot up from 36 percent in the 1970 presidential elections to just over 50 percent in the municipal elections of April 1971. As for the petty bourgeoisie, the salaried middle sectors and small- and medium-sized capitalists who account for virtually all the remaining 30 percent of the labor force, [9] these sectors still on the whole resented the prospect that Popular Unity might survive, although they had lost nothing by the government's policies and had even made substantial gains. [10] The vast majority of these people continued to vote for the Christian Democrats and even for the National party. On the other hand, they did not actively oppose the government; their attitude was rather one of waiting for a clear definition of the government's attitude towards their interests, above all towards the private sector of the economy. Thus for the moment they were neutral.

---

*The Allende government made liberal use of a decree passed by a military government in 1932 (the "Socialist republic") allowing the administration to take over industries if their owners were threatening to halt or reduce production.

For their part, the big bourgeoisie and its imperialist allies had suffered a severe blow. [11] They were taken aback by the government's unexpected resources, and unable to lay their hands on a strategy for counteraction, finding themselves trapped by an institutional order that was now being used against them and without having made the necessary preparations or having the forces behind them to bring that institutional order down through a coup d'etat. (Though, of course, there were already plots to overthrow Allende. The ITT papers show that the intention to provoke a coup d'etat was there, before Allende had even taken office, as does the wide-ranging collection of documentary evidence collected by the military tribunal that spent two years investigating the assassination of General Schneider, commander in chief of the armed forces, in October 1970.)

During this phase, then, the correlation of forces politically and socially was exceptionally favorable to the working class and its allies, while the military were neutralized by the high command's formal loyalty to the government (see Chapter 6). Thus the dynamic of the situation created by Popular Unity was rapidly leading towards a prerevolutionary situation. Following the municipal elections, some sectors within Popular Unity suggested that the government should hold a plebiscite, asking for support for a widening of the powers of the executive which would allow it to introduce the institutional reforms promised in the program without running the risks of a boycott by the opposition majority in Congress.* The same sectors were also in favor of securing the government's control over the economy through the introduction of workers' control, [12] as laid down in the Normas de Participacion (Guidelines on Workers' Participation) agreed on by the CUT and the government—on the grounds that this would allow workers and the government together to plan the activities of the Social Property Area and exercise an effective control over the private sectors. Simultaneously, they argued, the government should define its policy towards small- and medium-sized firms more clearly. Certainly this kind of policy was put forward within the coalition and within the government; one can see here the first manifestation of the coming struggle between two different conceptions of strategy, though the differences still appeared to be about questions of tactics and straddled party boundaries rather than emerging as a struggle between parties. However, for the moment the differences were resolved in favor of the reformist line on both politics and economics. The process of nationalization and expropriation continued, but with the clear intention that it should be confined to certain sectors of industry; the participation of workers in the administration of the Social Property Area was postponed.

———

*In 1970 the opposition had 32 seats in the Senate and 93 seats in the Chamber of Deputies compared to the government's 17 seats in the Senate and 60 seats in the Chamber of Deputies.

The Ambiguous Phase: July 1971 to May 1972

The next phase in the dynamic process set in motion by Popular
Unity corresponds to the eleven months between July 1971 and May
1972. Its most notable characteristic was Popular Unity's manifest
inability to cope with the problems which its own initiatives were
creating, and the ambiguity of its response to the opposition's
counteroffensive as a result. The real root of this inability to cope
was that the consequences of the policies being carried out were
not forseen in the government's conception of strategy and tactics;
and this in turn was due to the contradiction between the peaceful
road to socialism and the real economic and political possibilities
open to the government. The growing unity of the opposition also
made the government's life more difficult: during this period the
Christian Democrats were moving towards a much closer alliance
with the National party, with the result that the government was
under much greater pressure from the branches of the state apparatus
that it did not control (Congress, the judiciary) while simultaneously
the U. S. economic blockade of Chile was intensifying as the copper
companies attempted to gain control over Chile's exported copper
through European courts.

The government was aware that the limitations of the economic
policies applied during the first phase would become obvious very
quickly. But its economic strategy had not been based on purely
technical considerations, nor was it designed to provide a solution
to the chronic ills of the Chilean economy (inflation, balance-of-
payments deficits, and so on). The primary aim of the policy was
to dismantle capitalist relations of production and inaugurate a new
economy based on social ownership of the means of production, the
planned use of economic resources, and state participation and
control in the management of the economy. For this very reason,
far from solving the crisis of capitalism, it made the "normal"
functioning of a capitalist economy impossible—thus provoking a
political reaction from the class sectors most directly affected. The
problem was that elsewhere, within the political apparatus and in
its relations to the masses, the government's policies were not
guided by the same conception of strategy and were hardly designed
to prepare for the kind of political breakdown that was coming or
to confront it when it came. Rather, they were designed to stabilize
the situation within the state apparatus and channel the class
struggle along electoral lines.

Toward the end of 1971 there were shortages of some products
for which demand greatly exceeded supply, and lines and a black
market began to appear, as well as the kind of speculation that
tended to create an artificial and uncontrolled increase in demand.
These all increased inflationary pressures on the economy while
simultaneously leading to an even worse scarcity of popular consumer

goods. The government and the reformist sector within Popular Unity sought to solve such problems by calling on workers to increase production, seeing the shortages as a technical and economic problem rather than a political one. The left wing of Popular Unity and the government also recognized that the problem was partly economic, suggesting voluntary labor and overtime as a partial solution. At the same time, however, they argued that a political response was needed and that Production Control Committees should be set up to keep an eye on production in the private sector, as well as Price and Supply Committees (Juntas de Abastecimiento y Precios or JAPS) to keep an eye on the retail trade. [13] These organizations would be the instruments that allowed the masses to control production and distribution, ensuring that supplies were available for working class consumption and reducing the bourgeoisie's superfluous consumption along with its hoarded stocks of consumer goods. But at the same time, the Left itself did not as yet understand the full implications of this incipient policy, not yet having reached a full understanding of its own political identity and its differences with the hegemonic sectors of Popular Unity.

Here as elsewhere, the government's inability to cope and its ambiguity created a climate that threw the petty bourgeoisie and other middle sectors into militant counterrevolutionary activity, abandoning the relative neutrality they had maintained during the first phase. In turn, the government's hesitation and this revival of strong right-wing sentiment among the middle classes allowed the bourgeoisie to make further strides towards political reunification and provided it with the material for its own mass movement. An example of this was the December 1971 "March of the Empty Pots" led by National party women in protest against the government's economic policies. Similarly, the bourgeoisie was able to make gains in the February 1972 by-elections in Linares and Colchagua, where the opposition presented a single candidate. For its part, Congress openly took on the executive with a Constitutional Reform Bill designed to set limits to the legal loopholes that had allowed Popular Unity to create the Social Property Area (see Chapter 4). Thus the opposition learned very quickly how to combine legal methods of struggle with extralegal methods, a lesson that passed Popular Unity by.

For their part, the masses countered the government's vacillations with mobilizations of their own, slipping beyond the government's control as they did so. This new development created a situation the reformists could not accept. The conflict was to break out into the open for the first time in July 1972 as a result of a mass rally in Concepcion—the so-called People's Assembly—called by left-wing parties inside and outside Popular Unity, with the exception of the Communist party, with the aim of bringing rank and file workers' organizations together to coordinate their activities within the general perspective of popular power. [14]

Thus at the beginning of 1972, the government found itself in a situation that was completely the reverse of its position only a year before: encircled within the state apparatus, confronted by a mass mobilization in favor of the bourgeoisie, confined to using loopholes in the law that were also under attack. It was now clear that the much-vaunted flexibility of the Chilean political system would stretch just as far as the point at which the ruling class saw its own interests being affected and a threat to replace it emerging. At that point, the ruling class would react with the full weight of its economic and political power.

Throughout the Popular Unity period, the intensification of the class struggle in all departments of Chilean life led sectors of classes and political parties to shift their political position in line with the general correlation of class forces. Thus in June 1971 the most progressive wing of the Christian Democrats left the party to join Popular Unity as the Izquierda Cristiana. In the same way, in April 1972 a fraction of the Radical party led by Alberto Baltra, the PIR (the Left Radical party), left Popular Unity to join the opposition, alleging that Popular Unity had gone beyond the limits of the constitution and the rule of law.

"Advanced Democracy" or the Conquest of Power?: May 1972 to August 1972

A third phase lasting from May until August 1972 can be identified, as the political line of the reformists began to harden and the line of the left wing inside and outside Popular Unity became more self-conscious, more precise and more clearly based on a global conception of politics.

The strategy of the reformists took as its starting point the need, above all, for the revolution to gain forces within the state apparatus, necessarily in a gradualist fashion. They envisaged two distinct, successive stages: first, the construction of an "advanced democracy" designed to hammer the principal enemies of revolution and win the support of a democratic majority through the ballot box; and secondly, the "transition to socialism" through reforms in the character of the state and its institutions (Congress, the judiciary, the executive, and so on), carried out in such a way as to avoid a confrontation between classes and thus also any armed trial of strength.

The second strategy supported by sectors inside and outside Popular Unity was that of the revolutionary Left (the most convenient way of describing those in the Socialist party, the MAPU, the Izquierda Cristiana, the Juventud Radical Revolucionario [JRR], and the MIR who disagreed with the political methods that the Communist party was following in implementing Popular Unity's program). The revolutionary Left did not underestimate the vital role that the government could play in the revolutionary process, nor the objective possibilities of turning the bourgeoisie's own institutional order against it. Nevertheless, they understood that these tactics must be subordinated to the strategic goal of building "people's power,"* the power of the masses themselves, as a force independent of the state apparatus and capable at a later point of coping with the breakdown of the existing state. They believed that the revolutionary process would be uninterrupted, and that the Chilean revolution would be a socialist revolution, which, while completing democratic tasks for the benefit of the majority, would also have to carry out the socialist task of paving the way for the working class at rank-and-file level to develop its own power and its own mechanisms of control—the power that would eventually provide both the aims and the material foundations for a new "people's state."[15]

Where the economy was concerned, the reformists sought to use the mechanisms of the capitalist market, balancing supply and demand by adjustments of prices and wages in the belief that this sort of measure would bring problems of scarcity to an end. Such a policy was bound to favor those with higher incomes and a consequently greater ability to manipulate the market, as against the poorer layers of the population, who saw their powers of consumption beginning to decline. The pattern of class alliances that this kind of policy implied, however, could only really bear fruit if it was complemented by a political alliance with the same middle sectors: that is, with the wing of the Christian Democrats that currently seemed to be in control of the party. There was no other way of guaranteeing the middle sectors that the private, capitalist sector of the economy would survive, and that the character of the existing state would remain unchanged. The policy as a whole was designed to avoid a revolutionary crisis, by ensuring a stable period of "democracy" and supposedly preparing the way for a second "people's government" in 1976.

The Left insisted that part of the surplus controlled by the bourgeoisie must be appropriated, by extending the Social Property Area, raising taxes, and carefully manipulating prices which affected this class. It also argued that the bourgeoisie could not be allowed to compensate for its loss of profits by sidestepping the prices fixed by the government or engaging in speculative activities, and that the way to prevent such abuses was to bring all productive activities under workers' control. Something must be done about the imperialist blockade, they pointed out; payments on the external debt would

---

*"People's power" was the collective term used for the JAPS, Production Control Committees, Industrial Cordons, Communal Commands, and all other self-governing rank-and-file organizations.

have to be suspended and Chile would have to negotiate bilaterally with other countries in order to ensure a continuing flow of imports. (See Chapter 5.)

Within the camp of the bourgeoisie, two different strategies were being put forward with contradictory implications. One was the openly reactionary line of the imperialists and the monopoly bourgeoisie, who saw no alternative to the violent overthrow of the government and whose slogan was "civil resistance": this was the position of the National party, the Radical Democrats and Patria y Libertad ("fatherland and freedom"), an ultraright paramilitary and terrorist organization. The other was the line of the small- and medium-sized bourgeoisie who were still engaged in defending their livelihood, who wanted to prevent the collapse of the state and simultaneously halt the advance of socialism. During this phase, it was the second conception of strategy that still held sway, being supported by the majority of the Christian Democrats and the PIR. The immediate aim of this strategy was to hamper the activities of the masses while forcing the government to bargain and make concessions that would effectively prevent the implementation of the program, thus leading it to lose the support of the masses. In this fashion, the opposition would be able to create the preconditions for defeating Popular Unity at the polls, or at least forcing it into a subordinate political role, without itself being driven to break down the existing institutional order through a coup d'etat.

It was in this context, under pressure from the right-wing offensive in Congress and the courts and faced with growing economic difficulties, that the government called the parties of Popular Unity together at Lo Curro near Santiago, to draw up a balance sheet of the country's economic and political situation and decide on future strategy. Simultaneously, in June 1972, parallel discussions were being held with the Christian Democrats.

The Lo Curro conclave saw a formal victory for the reformists and their policies within Popular Unity. The result was that in August, the government authorized a series of price increases which raised the rate of inflation to the spectacular level of 20 percent a month in August and September. In spite of the promise that wages would be raised in October, in fact these increases meant a cut in the buying power of wages and salaries. However, the actual outcome of the policy was not what had been expected. The dynamic of the masses' own political activity, combined with the inability of the government to solve trade union demands by calling up the state's repressive apparatus, allowed the trade union movement to resist these attempts to cut the real level of wages with some success. The government only succeeded in creating a situation in which inflation ran wild, reaching 162 percent a year by the end of the year. The scarcity of supplies, the lines, and the black market in goods and dollars all grew worse, for they were rooted not in an

economic distortion of the market but in a political disturbance of the
system as a whole.

As far as political initiatives were concerned, the government's
hands were tied. Negotiations with the Christian Democrats had
ended in failure, not because the government was unwilling to reach
an agreement but because the Christian Democrats were preoccupied
by their own tactical need to preserve an alliance with the National
party, an alliance which was already serving them well in congressional elections. In fact, in Chile in 1972, as in other historical
experiences, political weakness in the face of the middle classes'
political representatives was not only no help in cementing a class
alliance, but actually drove the middle sectors towards those classes
or class fractions that showed greater political strength. The defensive attitude of the reformists within Popular Unity and the government
was a sign of weakness; and as such, it reinforced the argument put
forward within the Christian Democrats by the faction of ex-President
Frei that a harder line towards the government was necessary. Thus
the way was paved for a subordination of the Christian Democrats
to a strategy of overthrowing the government by force.

The government's willingness in principle to move towards
active repression of the mass movement when it slipped out of the
control of its traditional organizations was shown concretely in
police attacks against demonstrators and shantytown dwellers in
Concepcion in May 1972, and Lo Hermida in August 1972.* Even
so, there was no stopping the movement, which increasingly became
an autonomous force acting independently of the government. The
clearest expression of this independence prior to the October strike
was the People's Assembly held on July 26 in Concepcion, which
brought together all the different organizations of the rank and file
of the working class to coordinate political and economic responsibilities within the general perspective of "people's power" (see
Chapter 7).

October 1972: the Bosses' Strike

The fourth phase of the process was the great political crisis
of October 1972, which hardened the emerging prerevolutionary
situation while culminating in a new lurch towards reformism on
the part of the government. The Truck Owners' and the Shopkeepers'
Unions, and the professional colleges of university graduates such

---

*In Concepcion, the occasion was a left-wing counterdemonstra-
tion against an opposition march; in Lo Hermida, police searched the
shantytown and provoked a confrontation with the inhabitants in the
course of which two were killed.

as engineers, doctors, lawyers and architects, set in motion a new opposition offensive somewhat misleadingly called the "transport strike." National party and Christian Democrat supporters followed their initiative, and the strikes found strong financial backing from organizations such as the CIA. (For an analysis of the evidence on CIA involvement, see Chapter 5.) The objective of the strikes was to make the existing shortages acute by preventing the flow of food and fuel to consumers and paralyzing production and trade. This economic offensive, together with the activities of terrorist groups, was intended to create a climate of chaos and lead to the kinds of clashes that would provoke workers into a violent reaction, thus inviting the intervention of the armed forces and the overthrow of the government.

The bourgeoisie failed in its objectives for two principal reasons. First, the masses showed an amazing sense of discipline and initiative, as well as a capacity for organization that kept the economy going and prevented any truly chaotic situation from developing while restraining the terrorist outrages of the opposition paramilitary groups. Second was the attitude adopted by the armed forces, who cooperated with workers in organizing the transportation and distribution of fuel, thus demonstrating their formal loyalty to the executive.

Within the armed forces, in fact, a discussion had already begun around the concept of "national security." For some military men, apparently the majority, "national security" required an active military participation in the economic and social development of the country. Thus the concept could be interpreted in a progressive fashion, as it was interpreted by the commander in chief of the armed forces, General Prats, as a clear call for loyalty to the constitution and the rule of law that entailed a rejection of any move to break these limits. It could also be interpreted in a more conservative fashion: "participation" meaning nothing more than the defense of the state and the modernization of its apparatus, a modernization whose limits Popular Unity had already gone beyond. In October, the armed forces as a whole were undecided between the two camps, and which way they would swing in the future depended very much on the comparative strength demonstrated by each of them. There was a possibility that the armed forces would divide, though only at the point when they were forced to do so by the class struggle: a struggle that was also taking shape within their own ranks, slipping out of the control of the officers who on the whole belonged to the middle and upper classes. Meanwhile, the most reactionary politicians had been trying to mobilize support for a plot against the government among some sectors of the officer corps; but the plot, led by General Canales, failed, and he was later forced to retire.

For its part, the Left had done no political work worth mentioning within the armed forces, nor even defined what the character of their political work should be. Given the weakness of the Left, it was the strength and discipline of the masses which provided the decisive factor in swinging the armed forces against the strike and behind the government. As General Prats put it in an interview with the magazine Ercilla in July 1973, "So long as the rule of law continues, there will be no divisions within the armed forces. . . if President Allende had not retained the ability to control the workers, and if the workers themselves had not demonstrated an exemplary discipline, what would have happened? The armed forces would have divided and a violent confrontation would have taken place."

The October strike showed that, just as working class attempts to use the general strike as a key weapon in a revolutionary situation have failed historically time after time, the general strike was equally unreliable as the key weapon in a counterrevolutionary offensive by the bourgeoisie. In both cases, the decisive factor was access to military power. The opposition learned its lesson, and thereafter worked consistently within the armed forces to win their support for the overthrow of the constitutional government. Popular Unity, for its part, failed to learn the same lesson. Instead of developing a military strategy of its own, within the armed forces and among the masses, it took the armed forces to be nothing more portentious than one political sector among others: a sector with which one could cement political alliances, by making concessions and using a little flattery to "win them over"—the same tactics that had shown such poor results with the middle sectors.

Thus the October strike ended in a compromise. As a result of the strength and discipline shown by the masses, the armed forces supported the government and joined the cabinet, taking over three ministries. But the military were well aware of the government's weakness in the face of the October political crisis, just as they were well aware that the advance of the masses and their demonstrable capacities represented a danger. So the cabinet was a "cabinet of social peace" that aimed to preserve "national unity" and prevent a polarization of Chilean politics with the risk that the armed forces would split. At the same time, it was a guarantee that congressional elections would be held in March 1973. Once again, the government had shown its lack of confidence in the masses and had reaffirmed its faith in the state apparatus, a policy that flowed directly from the hegemony of the reformists within Popular Unity.

The Congressional Elections: November 1972 to March 1973

Between November, when the strike ended and the civilian-military cabinet was formed, and the elections in March, Chilean politics entered a new phase characterized by worsening economic difficulties (the presence of the armed forces within the cabinet with the power to make political decisions), and the development of the class struggle within the general framework of a struggle over votes.

As far as initiatives for further changes were concerned, the presence of the armed forces within the executive tied the government's hands. Henceforth, in fact, the opposition was able to use military cabinet members such as Admiral Huerta* to exert pressure within the cabinet in its own right, holding back the activity of the masses and putting obstacles in the way of any measures advocated by the Left.

The clearest instance of this kind of pressure was an episode which followed a speech by the MAPU minister of the Treasury, Fernando Flores, on March 8, 1973. The speech set out as official government policy the kinds of measures that had been rejected at Lo Curro some months back and that were advocated by the Left within the coalition: principally, that real power should be given to the JAPs or People's Supply Committees. Threats from the three military cabinet ministers to resign if this policy were carried out forced the government to change its mind, and far from the JAPs being given more power, control over distribution was handed over to the armed forces in the person of General Bachelet. †

The civilian-military cabinet also entailed a progressive dismantling of the organizations of popular power that had sprung up in October, these being incompatible with a strengthening of the state apparatus and a reassertion of its power. In practice, organs of workers' power such as the industrial cordons continued to exist or at least preserve the same name, but they were no longer really the seeds of dual power, at least until the final phase leading up to the overthrow of President Allende in September 1973. Instead, they became a new instrument in the masses' political struggle, the means of giving expression to the left wing's political line.

The political unification of the bourgeoisie proceeded by leaps and bounds, taking advantage of the electoral campaign. Yet tactical differences persisted within its ranks, particularly over the proper attitude to the armed forces and the possibilities of winning an electoral victory which would allow Congress to impeach the president. The most reactionary sectors embarked on a camapign of slanders against the three military cabinet ministers, hoping to kill two birds with one stone: the withdrawal of the armed forces from the government on the grounds that it was an unconstitutional and illegal government, and the removal of generals in the high command who were loyal to the constitution to make way for officers who were

---

*Later minister of Foreign Affairs in the military junta until August 1974.

†Later imprisoned by the military junta and found dead in suspicious circumstances in a Santiago prison.

in favor of overthrowing the government. The "democratic" sectors
of the bourgeoisie were in favor of strengthening the role of the
armed forces within the government, seeing this as the best way
of progressively stripping the political process of its revolutionary
content and paving the way for a new compromise that would mean
the final surrender of the government. Which way the bourgeoisie
as a whole would go, however, depended on the outcome of the March
elections.

Although all Popular Unity's energies were concentrated on the
March elections, real problems existed that forced the masses to
take initiatives and make use of the new tools available in the
organizations they had invented. Thus they continued to keep the
JAPs and the Production Control Committees alive as a means of
controlling production and distribution.

Meanwhile, within the parties and organizations of the Left,
the polarization of militants between two different conceptions of
strategy continued. The two sectors confronted one another clearly
during the electoral campaign, with slogans such as, on the one
hand, "We must face and reject the provocations of ultra Right and
ultra Left" and on the other "We must advance without compromise. "
The two lines were now a matter of public debate, overflowing the
limits of the coalition, and to the revolutionary Left it was clear
that the hegemony of the reformists within Popular Unity would have
to be challenged and that the government's limitations must be overcome, through a call for the realization of the socialist demands in
Popular Unity's program. Within Popular Unity this polarization led
some parties to divide and created an internal struggle between
different tendencies in others. But it is clear that no party was able
to escape this experience of a polarization and radicalization among
its militants; for these were the internal signs of the dynamics of
a revolutionary process and the radicalized views of the masses.

The Watershed: March 1973 to June 1973

The announcement of the election results marked the beginning
of a sixth phase in the revolutionary process. The 44 percent that
the Left had obtained was a substantial increase over the 36 percent
who voted for Allende in 1970, though it was less than the 50 percent
who voted for Popular Unity in the municipal elections of 1971.
Given the country's dire economic difficulties, it was a sign of
renewed electoral support among the masses for the government and
the process of change that Popular Unity had set in motion. It meant
that, in spite of their own hardships, scepticism, and even discontent with some of the government's policies, the masses were
prepared to support the government and to defend it whatever the
consequences. From March onwards the reformists saw new hope

for their plans of constructing a stage of "advanced democracy" that would avoid the breakdown of the existing state, interpreting the election as they did, as a vote of confidence in the legal road and the government. What they failed to understand was that the bourgeoisie had exhausted its legal alternatives, and that as a result there were only two immediate options: fascist reaction or socialist revolution.

The "democratic" sector of the bourgeoisie now understood that it would be impossible to achieve any stability by negotiating with the government, for the government was no longer in control of the revolutionary process, and however much it might be prepared to surrender, the masses (who had found their own forms of organization) would not accept any deals. The way was now open for the most reactionary sector of the bourgeoisie finally to consolidate its hegemony over the other factions and unite the bourgeoisie as a class behind its strategy of organizing civil and military resistance in order to overthrow the government.

The government, for its part, persisted in looking for an alliance with the Christian Democrats, using the slogan "No to Civil War"; hoping that a pact with the Christian Democrats and the high command of the armed forces would allow it to assemble a power bloc representing the national majority. These efforts were accompanied by a marginalization of the revolutionary Left within the government, the result of which was simply an increasing alienation of the masses from the state apparatus that Popular Unity controlled.

The military left the cabinet, arguing that the objectives that had originally led to their participation in the November civilian-military cabinet had been achieved. In point of fact, they continued to take an important part in government decisions, particularly through their control over distribution and other sectors where they were active. Thus the government grew more and more isolated, an increasingly weak political force with little or no initiative. But in spite of its isolation, everyone understood his own need and duty to defend it in every way possible, because its presence was a necessary part of the revolutionary process through which the country was living.

The reformists devoted all their energies to evading and avoiding the political and military confrontation that now was clearly inevitable. Meanwhile, the bourgeoisie was engaged in preparing the most favorable conditions for a confrontation. Politically, its representatives insisted on the unconstitutional character of the Social Property Area and on the government's failure to respect the decisions of the courts (since it had not obeyed judicial orders to return some firms under government control) as well as its failure to respect the Controleria, which was challenging the Executive's interpretation of the legal process. At the military level, work was going on within the armed forces, along with the armed activities of

the terrorist groups who were perpetually provoking clashes in the
rural areas and in the streets.

The effects soon became visible. High ranking officers of the
armed forces began to condemn government policies in public as
unconstitutional, for instance the government's program of educational
reform.* At the same time, right-wing politicians began to refer
constantly to the economic grievances of the rank and file of the
armed forces, laying the blame for shortages, the black market, and
so on, at the government's door.

The executive's reply to this offensive by the Right was purely
defensive. It tried to win over the high ranking officers in the armed
forces with flattery and concessions, while replying to all the charges
from other sections of the state apparatus through Congress, and
postponing reforms that provoked a reaction within the armed forces.
There was strong criticism of those sectors of the revolutionary Left
who tried to win over officers, NCOs, and soldiers loyal to the
constitution by taking up their economic grievances and their demands
for democratic rights. (For example the MIR, who distributed pamphlets in military barracks in Concepcion, and the MAPU who called
publicly on NCOs and soldiers to disobey their officers.) This
situation reached a climax on June 29, 1973 (the Tancazo), when
a group of military men supported and led by the terrorist organization
Patria y Libertad (Fatherland and Freedom) made an abortive attempt
at a coup. (Led by the Second Tank Regiment commanded by Colonel
Souper, this mutiny was defeated within three hours by loyal government troops commanded by General Prato.) As a result, the officers
were arrested and the leaders of the terrorist organization sought
asylum.

Defensive Policies and Defeat

The last phase covers the period between the Tancazo and
the military coup of September 11. It was a period characterized
by a high level of internal decomposition within the armed forces,
by the isolation of constitutionalist officers, by the repression of
soldiers and left-wing workers, and by the government's inability
to find a way out.

The abortive coup of June 29 made it quite clear to the masses
that a violent confrontation between classes, so often predicted,

---

*The Escuela Nacional Unificada, the National Unified School
was designed to merge the three existing varieties of academic,
technical and commercial schools into a single "comprehensive"
system.

was a real threat and would take place within a very short time. The organizations of the masses took up the struggle once again, occupying their workplaces and creating organs of "people's power" that were now attempting to play a paramilitary role. None of this was enough, not because the masses lacked the ability to face an eventual confrontation but because the left-wing parties within Popular Unity lacked the capacity to give this movement leadership and tell it what to do next, while the reformists were insisting that civil war must be avoided. Thus the Left had no military strategy of the kind that the masses were demanding.

Left-wing NCOs and soldiers began to make their own political position known, hoping for the backing of the Left and the government. The politicization, loss of discipline, and decomposition within the armed forces were extraordinary. At this moment in time, the government could have turned such decomposition to the advantage of the Left, and it was vital that it should do so. It could have united the rank and file of the workers' movement around a military policy that would also have won soldiers over to the support of the government and the revolutionary process. A revolutionary policy would not have attempted to avoid civil war, but to lay the basis for organizing resistance to any attempted confrontation, and make a left-wing military victory feasible. The revolutionary Left, inside and outside Popular Unity, understood this point, without being able to put understanding into practice, as events proved.

The section of the armed forces that favored a coup embarked on a campaign of fierce repression against the masses, invoking the Arms Control Law passed by Congress in October 1972 as a justification for attacking all the organizations of "people's power," Industrial Cordons, Communal Commands, and so on. Peasants and trade union leaders were arrested and then tortured to force them to confess where they had hidden their supposed caches of arms. At the beginning of August, a group of sailors was charged with mutiny, arrested, and tried for high treason, and leading figures in Popular Unity were publicly accused of being behind their "plot." Those generals within the high command who remained loyal to the constitution were forced to resign through a series of public provocations that culminated in the removal of General Prats from command of the armed forces and his replacement by General Pinochet, today president of Chile.

All this was carried out through a large scale mobilization of the armed forces. Meanwhile the government continued to insist on the need to negotiate with the Christian Democrats, while simultaneously it was losing its remaining support among the high command. A new strike of truck owners, shopkeepers, and professionals was called; but now they were no longer demanding economic concessions, but the overthrow of President Allende himself.

Thus, in spite of the fact that it had the votes of almost 50 percent of the population, the government avoided civil war without being able to avoid a coup d'etat; and this coup was organized with the active support of the state institutions and the bourgeois legal order that Allende respected so much. After the coup, both the institutions and the legal order were destroyed by the very classes that had built them, for they no longer served the interests of capital.

NOTES

1. See J. Roddick, Chapter 1.

2. See A. I. Sobolev, "Revolucion y Contrarevolucion: la Experienca Chilena y el problema de la Lucha de Clases." The original article first appeared in Russian in the Soviet journal Rabotchi Klas i Sovromenny mir (Moscow, March-April, 1974).

3. See Rosa Luxembourg, "The Mass Strike" in Dick Howard, ed., Selected Political Writings of Rosa Luxembourg, (New York: Monthly Review Press, 1971).

4. See Joan Garces, El Estado y los Problemas Tacticos en el Gobierno de Allende (Mexico: Siglo XXI, 1974) pp. 117-18.

5. For an analysis of the crisis in Chilean capitalism see S. Aranda y A. Martinez "Estructura Economica: Algunas Carac-teristicas Fundamentales," in Victor Brodersohn, ed., Chile Hoy (Mexico: Siglo XXI, 1970).

6. Garces, op. cit.

7. See Joan Garces, Revolucion, Congreso y Constitucion: el caso Toha, (Santiago: Quimantu, 1972).

8. See Jacques Chonchol "La politica agricola en una economia de transicion al socialismo El caso chileno" in G. Martner, ed., El Pensamiento Economico del Gobierno de Allende (Santiago: Editorial Universitaria, 1971).

9. For 1970 Census figures see J. Roddick, op. cit.

10. See Patricio Biedma, "El comportamiento politico de la pequena burguesia," Marxismo y Revolucion, no. 1 (Santiago, 1973): 87.

11. See R. M. Marini, "El desarrollo industrial dependiente y la crisis del sistema de dominacion," Marxismo y Revolucion, no. 1 (Santiago, 1973): 22.

12. See Luis Vargas "La formacion del Area Social: del programa de la UP a la lucha de clases" Marxismo y Revolucion, no. 1 (Santiago, 1973): 35.

13. See Patricio Biedma, "El comportamiento de la pequena burguesia," op. cit.

14. See "Asamblea del Pueblo" in Chile Hoy, no. 8, August 1972.

15. For a clear statement of "people's power" and the "people's state," see "Proposicion de programa del Partido MAPU al segundo Congreso," Documentos del MAPU (Santiago, 1972).

3

THE POLITICAL ECONOMY
OF THE ALLENDE REGIME
Alec Nove

I taught in the planning institute of the Universidad Catolica de Chile in September-November 1972, and revisited the country in March 1973. I tried to the best of my ability to understand what was happening, what the policy of the government was, and the causes of the economic troubles that were besetting it. What follows is an attempt to analyze the economic policies that, beyond doubt, contributed to the disaster that befell the Allende regime. It may be of interest to note that, when I expressed many of the same ideas in Santiago in November 1972, I was criticized by most of those who heard me for a harsh and unsympathetic approach. I denied then, and I deny now, any harshness or lack of sympathy. The facts point to a great deal of unclarity, contradiction, confusion, due partly to divided counsels, partly to political constraints, and partly to a fundamental dichotomy in the economico-political strategy of the administration. Of course defeat was due also to the actions of the government's enemies, but grave errors gave these enemies far too many opportunities to exploit. To pretend that the government merely fell victim of a conspiracy between the CIA and the extreme Right is of no help to anyone, least of all the Chilean Left—which is not to deny the obvious facts of conspiracy and sabotage. In any conflict in which one is defeated, it is self-evident that the enemy's actions made a major contribution to the outcome (and deserve more careful study than they will get in this paper). However, in any inquest on a lost battle attention is usually and rightly devoted to analyzing one's own errors, and to discovering why one was not successful and the enemy was. The conspiracy-based explanation leads logically to far-reaching conclusions about the impossibility of a peaceful road to socialism. In one such version the onward march towards a just society was violently interrupted because it was in fact succeeding, whereas (in my view) by early 1973, indeed, by the second half of 1972, catastrophe faced the economy, with the gravest political consequences plainly discernible. It may indeed be true that there is no "peaceful road" in Latin America (or Italy, or

51

anywhere), but the case for this proposition should not rest on myths about Chile.

One first must take cognizance of the class structure of Chile. It is a country with a very large class of small shopkeepers, owners of workshops, artisans, owner-drivers of trucks, small peasantry, and other members of what must be called the petty bourgeoisie. There was, of course, a group of big businessmen, many of them linked with foreign corporations, and an upper stratum of senior civil servants, officers, and professional people; the officers were (by Latin American standards) rather poorly paid, but took great pride in their disciplined nationalism, as could be seen each Independence day in their spectacularly precise goose-stepping. The tactic appropriate to a left-wing president was, it seemed, to attract or at least neutralize the petty bourgeoisie, while gaining peasant support by pressing ahead with land reform, which had been begun slowly under the previous president, Eduardo Frei. Allende, understandably, sought to reassure the petty bourgeoisie and to promise to take action only against the foreign corporations and the few Chilean big monopolists. It was surely essential for the security of the regime not to antagonize the "small men."

I appreciate that constraints and limitations are not unchange-able, and that observers can and do differ in interpreting the limits of the possible. But it is sufficient here to stress that economic policies were conceived and carried out within a social and political structure that set limits to what Allende and most of his colleagues considered it possible to do.

THE ECONOMIC LEGACY OF THE
FREI ADMINISTRATION

Chile, when I first visited it in 1965, was facing economic difficulties. First, there was the chronic inflation, which had gone on for many decades. The price index behaved as follows in the years of Frei's presidency:

TABLE 3.1

Price Rises
(percent)

	Retail Prices	Wholesale Prices
1967	18.1	19.3
1968	26.6	30.5
1969	30.7	36.5
1970	32.5	36.1

Source: Antecedentes sobre el desarollo Chileno, ODEPLAN 1971, p. 39.

Food supplies were adequate only because of substantial imports, and this for a country that, a generation earlier, had been a significant exporter of grain and meat. Agriculture had for too long been in the doldrums, and this was attributed by most Chilean economists at least in part to the inefficiency or inactivity of the landed proprietors, whose liking for horse riding in ponchos—and holding land as a hedge against inflation—exceeded their interest in productive activity. Frei's Christian Democrat administration did indeed adopt land reform laws, and we shall see that Allende's speeded-up land reforms were based on these very same laws.

Industrial output rose only slowly, or stagnated. Chile is not a populous country, and the industries that operated under cover of a high tariff wall were unable to benefit from economies of scale. A foolish policy of indiscriminate encouragement to foreign capital led to setting up more than twenty small car assembly plants, all far below optimum size. Unemployment grew, and there was much underutilization of industrial capacity. The following 1971 ODEPLAN figures give one some idea of the trend:

	1967	1968	1969	1970
Industrial output (percent increase)	2.8	2.4	3.7	0.8
Unemployment percent (incomplete figures)	4.7	4.9	5.0	6.0

Thus in the last three Frei years inflation rates rose, industrial output showed little upward trend, and unemployment increased.

The balance of payments was a constant source of concern. With nitrates no longer significant, and an increasing food import bill to meet, Chile's exports consisted largely of copper, which accounted for around 80 percent of the total. The country was thus very vulnerable to price changes of this one commodity. "Import-saving" industrialization led to increasing imports of machinery and components, and the bulk of Chile's oil also had to be imported. In addition, Chile had to carry a large burden of debt, both governmental and commercial. Frei succeeded in coping with the balance of payments, building up reserves in the process:

TABLE 3.2

Balance of Payments
(U. S. dollars)

	Net Balance	Reserves
1967	-25.0	-91.5
1968	+127.0	37.7
1969	+222.8	220.0
1970	+108.2	343.2

Source: Antecedentes, op. cit., pp. 435-36.

However, this increase in reserves was achieved by damping down
activity, and this contributed to unemployment of human and material
resources.

The copper mines were, in the main, U. S. -run, by the Anaconda and Kennecott companies. Frei decided to "Chileanize" them,
acquiring a 51 percent controlling shareholding. However, the terms
of the agreement proved highly favorable to the copper companies,
who made and remitted unusually high profits in the years following
this "Chileanization."

ALLENDE'S ECONOMIC PROGRAM

Allende's victory was unexpected, and there is some evidence
that he was caught unprepared, with no defined plan of action. His
program promised to contain inflation, to redistribute income in favor
of the poor, to carry out a rapid land reform, and to nationalize the
copper companies, other foreign-owned corporations, and big monopolies. Thereby it was hoped to weaken the economic-political
basis of the right-wing parties, to strengthen the electoral popularity
of the regime and to move onwards towards socialism. These onward
moves were by no means clear. Nor were the ways in which the
various elements of the immediate program were to be carried out.
There was, we may be sure, much improvisation.

Two factors must be stressed. The first was that the election
of Allende touched off great expectations among the working-class
supporters of Popular Unity (UP). Life would become better, wages
would go up, they would soak the rich. The strength of these expectations, as well as the government's own commitment to income
redistribution, made it politically essential to grant large wage
increases, while simultaneously combating inflation. The other
factor was disunity, or rather divisions, on the Left. The trade
unions were united under CUT (Confederacion Unica de Trabajadores),
but within them the parties competed, with the Christian Democrats
vying with the Communists, who controlled CUT, in promising or
demanding immediate benefits. Politically, too, there were those
who urged massive concessions to the workers, to win their enthusias-
tic support as a first and essential step towards mobilizing them for
the march towards socialism. Some of Allende's supporters thought
of the possibility of a plebiscite to amend the constitution to give
the government greater powers, and large benefits for the masses
could mean votes. Some of the parties in the UP coalition, especially
the socialists under their secretary Altamirano and two of the smaller
parties (MAPU and the Left-Christians) were for a vigorous socialist
offensive and for extensive redistributive measures in favor of the
poor. Allende himself seems to have been nearer the Communists
in urging caution. It was, above all, the Communists who sought to

reassure the middle classes, insisting that legality should be respected and attention paid to economic possibilities. They were outflanked from the left not only by the MIRistas, who were urging seizures of property and challenging the very concept of legality, but by the other members of the coalition. (I recall the mocking tones of Chilean postgraduates whom I met at an international seminar in the summer of 1971: the Communists were a bourgeois party, they insisted).

The government knew that it could nationalize copper with the overwhelming support of the people and of Congress. It promptly did so, virtually denying compensation by claiming that excess profits and unpaid taxes in the past should be deducted from the compensation entitlements of Kennecott and Anaconda. Whether it was wise to do this is a matter of opinion, for the government risked more trouble with the United States as well as with the firms in question; the latter were important as suppliers of equipment to the mines, the former could (and did) take steps to cut Chile off from credits which, possibly, might have helped to mitigate the balance-of-payments problem. It is worth inquiring whether the failure to compensate caused, on balance, more loss than gain. Chilean delegates could have dragged out compensation negotiations for years, while accepting the principle, thus weakening the argument of its enemies, who (as the ITT files show) were hard at work persuading American official agencies to take hostile action. (It is, of course, also arguable that the United States would in any case have done its worst, whatever the compensation paid for copper.) Could it be that the fine "declaratory" value of the no-compensation principle was a luxury that Chile could not afford? Whether one accepts this view or not, there is no doubt at all that the action was popular. Even the right-wing deputies in Congress voted for it.

The nationalization of other enterprises was more difficult. A list of 90 firms was drawn up and submitted to Congress, which turned it down. There was thus no direct legal road, and so the government was forced to resort to a number of expedients. These included participation on a 51 percent basis in the case of foreign-owned enterprises, a procedure that covered, among other things, some enterprises owned by ITT (such as the Sheraton hotel). Participation could be achieved by direct negotiation with the enterprises concerned, in the knowledge that their foreign ownership would give the government political strength in dealing with them. If the enterprises refused—as I was told Philips refused—they were sometimes allowed to carry on, because of the loss that would follow from their withdrawal. Chilean-owned big firms would be, and were, tackled on the basis of existing legislation or by indirect forms of executive ingenuity, including:

1. The government acquired control by purchasing controlling shares. For example, this was how banks were acquired, and some

industrial firms also. The process was in some cases facilitated by related actions: demands for large wage increases, price control, and denial of import licenses could, separately or in combination, cause sufficient losses to "persuade" the directors to sell.

2. Use was made of legislation adopted under the short-lived rule of a left-wing president, Davila, in 1932 and never repealed. This provided for control over (not nationalization of) enterprises that were not being operated in a vaguely defined public interest. The government put in an interventor, who replaced the board of directors. By this means, state control was much expanded. Again, the incomes of owners could be reduced by a combination of price control and wage increases.

3. Finally there was action from below, often encouraged by one or more of the UP parties but sometimes spontaneous (or MIR-inspired), in which workers occupied factories and/or demanded that the government take over control from the owners.

By these and similar means the so-called area social (Social Property Area), that is, the state-controlled sector, was substantially expanded by stages. But these methods caused not only bitterness but also confusion and uncertainty. Bitterness because they were seen as a way of evading legislative opposition to nationalization. Confusion because there was uncertainty about who might be national-ized or "intervented" next. It would have been better and clearer if Congress had passed the law nationalizing the 90 named enterprises and the government had combined this with a clear guarantee that other firms were free of the danger of takeover. Of course, it was not Allende's fault that Congress refused to pass the law. But the fact remains that, as things were, business nervousness increased, paralyzing private investment and causing many conflicts with particu-lar firms, who used the press and the commercial radio to lambaste the real or alleged efforts of the government to nationalize them. I recall the daily "commercials" on behalf of the large Chilean-owned paper company, Papeles y Cartones, whose losses, due to price control, were suspected of being a deliberate prelude to a state takeover; the commercial ended with the words, shouted in chorus: "La Papelera: NO!" At the other end of the scale, the nervousness of owner-drivers about alleged plans to nationalize road transport contributed to the mobilization of these key petty bourgeois against the government in 1972, with deplorable results. Of course these fears were played upon by right-wing elements.

The government did make friendly declarations towards small business, and the banks that it controlled were generous with credit. Allende announced: "Although monopolies will be abolished, because that is in the greater interests of the country, for this same reason we guarantee that middle and small-scale businesses may rely on the close collaboration of the state to ensure the sound development of their activities."[1] Maximum interest rates were reduced from

44 percent to 31 percent. [2] But one factor—probably not the most important—in alienating the medium- and small-scale business community was the method by which state control was expanded.

It is noteworthy that, of the 90 enterprises originally scheduled for nationalization (or for mixed state-private ownership), 20 were foreign-controlled, that is, over 50 percent of their capital was held by foreign companies. Of these, only 6 were to be nationalized outright, the others would be mixed, that is, Chilean state organs would operate them in joint ownership with the foreign interests. Progress was in fact not very rapid, as the situation in December 1972 shows (see Table 3. 3).

TABLE 3. 3

Nationalization of Industrial Enterprises
(December 1972)

	Number of Enterprises	Percent	Percent Share of Production
Social and mixed area	103	12. 7	13. 4
Requisitioned and "intervened" enterprises	99	6. 9	8. 5
Total	202	19. 6	21. 9

Source: La Economía Chilena en 1972, Universidad de Chile, 1973, pp. 134-35; with acknowledgment to Cristobal Kay for help in finding these and some other statistics.

Although it was intended to expand the Social Property Area in 1973, the large majority of industrial production (around 70 percent) would still have remained in the private sector even if Allende had survived to the end of that year and carried out his program. This underlines the vital importance to the health of the economy of enabling private industry to function effectively.

Land reform proceeded rapidly, but, while the government could take credit for carrying out its promises, once again there were unfortunate consequences, attributable partly to the actions of the ultraleft, and partly (perhaps mainly) to the legal provisions upon which the reform process was based. There was also a persistent dispute among the government's supporters concerning the maximum size of holding that was to be exempted from redistribution. The reform proceeded on the basis of 80 hectares (much more than

this when the land was of inferior quality), but many left-wing critics
demanded limits of 40 hectares or even less.

There were two disruptive features of the reform as it was
carried out (and in my view the second of them was the most serious).
First, the owners were, under the Frei land reform law, allowed to
remove their assets, and this meant loss of equipment and, in some
cases, also of livestock. Second, the fate of the redistributed land
was uncertain. The peasants did not, as a rule, acquire it as personal
property; it was run on a semicooperative basis under the name of
asentamiento. This was an ill-defined and provisional arrangement,
pending a final settlement that could be either private ownership or
collective or cooperative farming. There were differences of opinion
about what was to be done, and what the peasants wanted, and great
unclarity over how the asentamientos were to be run, how the peasants were to work within them, how the produce was to be disposed
of, and the resultant income distributed. Since many peasants also
had private holdings, all this greatly confused the system of incentives: how much cooperative work should the peasants undertake,
and what remuneration should they receive? Since a black market
soon grew up, these issues became linked with the problem of selling
through legal channels at legal prices.

The government set up institutions for land reform, but these
never had clearly defined powers or an agreed strategy. Credits
were lavished upon agriculture, but these were seldom repaid. In
these circumstances, it is hardly surprising that output and marketing
did not come up to expectation. [3]

One example of lack of control of the reform process was the
speed-up of migration from rural to urban areas. According to statements made to me in Santiago, this was because many casually
employed landless laborers employed on estates were denied any
land, as the estates' land was divided among existing regular laborers
(or rather that one had to be such to be a member of the asentamiento.
These laborers often also cultivated small landholdings of their own).
This was a consequence of local influence on the process of reform.
Since smallholders could not afford to employ laborers, many casual
laborers on the old estates had no alternative but to join the slum
dwellers whose shacks disfigured the outskirts of Santiago and
Valparaiso.

Finally, the MIR encouraged illegal land seizure, presenting
the government with a dilemma. To use force against the peasants
would be to outrage much of the Left. Not to use force would greatly
upset the constitutionalists among the military (upon whom, in the
last resort, the government had to rely) and also contradict the
government's claim to keep within legal norms, a claim that it relied
upon to secure acceptance of its measures by its more moderate
opponents. Obviously, the intransigents would be against all its
actions, but the moderate center of public opinion was not to be too

greatly antagonized, and certainly not on an issue—land reform—on which the government could legitimately claim that it was carrying out Christian Democrat policy based upon Frei's own legislation, which Frei himself had not speedily enforced, in the event, the government compromised, offending both the extreme Left and the center by repressing some illegal seizures and tolerating others. Allende's speech on the subject made on December 21, 1970 in Santiago is an example of the discomfort of the authorities faced with this problem. [4]

THE UNSOUND POLICIES OF 1971

Large increases in wages followed the election of Allende. In a country with a long tradition of inflation, regular wage rises were a feature of life. Allende's first year was not out of the ordinary. The exact extent of the rise in money and real wages depends considerably on the months chosen for the comparison, hence the evidence of a number of different estimates. The figures in Tables 3.4 and 3.5 seem reasonably reliable.

It seems clear that, in the first year, money wages did not rise faster than in the last year of Frei's presidency. The difference, as can be seen, was entirely due to the behavior of the price index, and this, in turn, was due to tighter price control. Probably, in holding down prices, the government hoped that money wages would not rise so fast. If so, its hopes were disappointed. It should be added that the magnitude of the increase was due in part to autonomous trade union actions, and to the willingness of many employers to

TABLE 3.4

Percentage Increases in Real Wages, 1970-71

	Wages and Salaries	Retail Prices	Real Wages[a]
January-January	43.2	28.1	11.8
April-April	53.0	20.2	27.0
July-July	54.9	19.1	30.1
October-October	51.9	16.5	34.1

[a]Derived from first two columns.

Source: La Economia Chilena en 1972, op. cit., p. 265.

TABLE 3.5

Percentage Increases in Real Wages, 1968-71

	Wages and Salaries (Index, un- known base)	Percent Increase over Pre- vious Figure	Price Increase	Real Wages Percent Increase
October 1968	1187.0	–	–	–
October 1969	1605.4	35.2	27.2	6.2
October 1970	2450.7	52.7	35.6	12.6
July 1971	3529.3	44.0	12.2	28.3

Source: ODEPLAN, Informe annual, 1971, pp. 27-28 (calculated from figures there given).

concede large claims to "buy off" possible demands for nationalization or "intervention." So the rises were not solely the consequence
of deliberate government policy. However, the large increase was
a fact.

Powers to control prices had existed long before Allende, but
his government sought to exercise them with greater toughness to
prevent the money wage rise from evaporating through inflation.
The effect was remarkable: in the period from October 1970 to
October 1971, inflation was brought down to a mere $16\frac{1}{2}$ percent,
as measured by the retail price index against an average of 29 percent in Frei's last three years. This meant a rise in "real wages"
of 34 percent. It seems to me that in this single figure one sees
most clearly expressed the basic unsoundness of the government's
political-economic strategy. It was a fatal and large step on the
road to disaster.

It did not look that way at first. The large increase in purchasing
power, under conditions of underemployment of human and material
resources, had favorable effects on industrial production, which rose
by 12 percent in 1971. But common economic sense showed that
this was unrepeatable: once the slack was taken up, there could be
no more increase without investments, and investments (as we shall
see) were reduced, not only in the private but also in the nationalized
productive sector (housing construction and public works did increase).

In any case part of the inflated demand of 1971 was met out of
higher domestic industrial production. But the bulk of the extra
demand was for food, and agricultural output was quite insufficient
to meet it. So, at the controlled prices, food had to be imported in
ever-growing quantities, as Table 3.6 clearly demonstrates.

TABLE 3. 6

Balance of payments, 1970-72
(U. S. dollars, millions)

	1970	1971	1972
Exports	1129	1076	853
Imports	1020	1123	1287
Balance of services	-39	-45	-10
Net commercial balance	71	-122	-444
Net foreign remittances	-129	-90	-120
Net current account	-57	-212	-564
Capital movements	149	-100	-17
Net balance of payments	91	-311	-581
Renegotiation of external debt	–	–	200
Imports of foodstuffs	178. 2[a]	314. 2[a]	444[b]
Imports of machinery	–	178[a]	137[b]

[a]From pp. 47, 145.
[b]Estimate

Source: Comentarios sobre la situacion economica, Universidad de Chile, 2nd semester, 1972, (1973), p. 138.

The table is quite clear: imports of food rose very steeply, imports of capital goods fell (reflecting falling investments), total imports rose, and capital movements made matters worse. Reserves fell precipitately, indeed virtually disappeared by the end of the year, as we shall see.

An important factor was an unfortunate and unpredictable fall in copper prices from their 1969 peak of $66 per ton to only $48-49 in 1971 and 1972. This found reflection in the fall in export revenues shown in the above table. Exports of other items also fell. There is absolutely no evidence that the fall in prices was planned by anyone, any more than was the sharp rise that occurred during 1973. It could not have come at a worse time from Allende's point of view. It made a bad situation worse, though it would have been bad even if copper had remained at $66.

The same requires to be said of the reduction of credits and aid. The United States did not help, it hindered (except, significantly, that military aid continued). Needless to say, if Allende had had aid from the United States on the scale of (say) U. S. subsidies to Taiwan or South Vietnam, he might well have been able to ride out the balance-of-payments consequences of his policy.

But one can hardly envisage a road to socialism, including confisca-
tion of U. S. assets, based on U. S. aid. It has also been argued
that, while new lines of credit were indeed fewer, renegotiation of
past debts and drawings on credits previously negotiated continued
to help the Chilean balance of payments. [5]

Why have I used the word "disaster" about the policy of 1971?
Because of the exhaustion of currency reserves, which fell from $377.6
million in September 1970 to $32.3 million in December 1971, [6] the
impossible increase in "real wages," the price controls, the inevitable
material shortages, the exaggerated expectations of the workers, the
fall in investments, made a major crisis quite inevitable in 1972.
When I argued this on an earlier occasion, a Chilean responded
indignantly: "We were not concerned with economic efficiency, we
were concerned with power." This meant that the aim of policy as
he saw it was primarily of a short-term political nature: to secure a
jumping-off ground to get mass support, either to amend the constitution or to achieve "workers' power" by mobilizing and "ideologizing"
the masses. It is pointed out that in the municipal elections of
April 1971, when the costs of the policies were not yet apparent, the
UP did win more votes, indeed very close to 50 percent. Then, so
the political argument ran, was the time to attack.

The chance, if it existed, was missed. But did it exist? Was
such a strategy politically feasible? Much depends on the answer,
but this basically economic survey is not the place to attempt to find
it. We can agree, surely, that unless some drastic political change
could have been engineered during 1971, political disaster as well
as economic chaos were likely during 1972, and that economic inefficiency would threaten the hold on power. Even if a change in the
power balance could have occurred, economic troubles would still
have followed the utterly unsustainable and totally unsound increase
in real wages. All that could be argued is that the government might
have been in a stronger position to repress the resultant discontent.

The government chose not only to control prices but also to
peg the official exchange rates. A growing gap developed between
these and the black market rate, diverting transactions and currency
away from official channels. (There were a number of rates, depending
on the nature of the transaction.)

The statistics in Table 3.7 show Gross National Product (GNP)
figures for 1970-72. The increase in industrial output in 1971 looked
gratifying, but could not be maintained. The agricultural figure is
likely to be inaccurate. The 1970 and 1971 figures are official
(ODEPLAN); the 1972 estimates are those of the University of Chile's
economic department.

GNP thus rose by 9.56 percent in 1971, but only by 0.8 percent
in 1972.

Investments fell, according to the same source, from 17.4
percent of GNP in the decade 1960-70 to 13.3 percent in 1971 and

TABLE 3. 7

Gross National Product by Sector
(millions of 1965 escudos)

	1970	1971	1972
Agriculture and fishing	2015	2130	2032
Mining and quarries	2259	2324	2240
Manufacturing	5366	6037	6128
Construction	1071	1173	1100
Public utilities	347	398	414
Transport and communication	996	1049	1065
Wholesale and retail trade	4617	4977	5032
Other services	4901	5308	5578
Total	21357	23396	23590

Source: Comentarios, op. cit., p. 176.

12. 4 percent in 1972. They fell absolutely both in 1971 and 1972.
Stocks of materials also declined.

Finally, the quantity of money in the possession of the private
sector increased by 120 percent in 1971, and by 140 percent in 1972. [7]

THE ACCELERATING CRISIS OF 1972

With no currency reserves to fall back on, the Allende administration found itself unable to meet demand at controlled prices. Wages
continued to rise. Goods began to disappear. Black markets grew.
As costs soared and output stopped rising owing to shortages of
capacity, private business found itself in a squeeze. It was not
inflation as such that was the sole cause of the trouble, at least
until it accelerated in the second half of 1972. Latin American
countries learned long ago to live with inflation. The trouble was
the combination of cost inflation, price control, and import restric-
tion, plus unpredictability and uncertainty.

Since these circumstances greatly contributed to the alienation
of the middle and petty bourgeoisie, it is necessary to dwell on them
in a little more detail. To do so it is useful to imagine oneself to
be a Chilean small-business man: say a petty manufacturer, a shopkeeper, an owner of two or three trucks, and to consider his difficulties
and his frustrations. If he required spare parts, materials, or commodi-
ties from abroad, these were subject to strict import licensing, owing
to the desperate shortage of foreign exchange. A license may be

unavailable. Or it may be available at one of a large number of
widely varying exchange rates, according to the category of essen-
tiality judged by the Central Bank to apply to the proposed transaction.
By 1972 the would-be importer might or might not be called upon to
make a deposit in escudos worth 10,000 percent of the value of the
imports for three months. (Provision for a 10,000 percent deposit
existed also under Frei, but applied to only a few goods. It was
extended.) Insofar as imports were involved, therefore, a high degree
of uncertainty and frustration prevailed, both as regards the cost and
the availability of the necessary permit.

Wages and material costs were subject to steep and sudden
change. When, during 1972, the government began to allow large
price rises, these were conceded reluctantly and after a long delay.
Some foodstuffs, manufactures, or services, might be held at 10
escudos for six months, so that production began to be carried on
at a loss, and then suddenly the price was raised to 26 escudos,
resulting in a profit for a few months until costs once again surpassed
the authorized selling price. Wages were readjusted to keep pace
with the rising prices, and price rises and wage increases speeded
up and reinforced each other, as futile attempts were made to hold
on to the excessive gains allowed in 1971. (The government was,
of course, aware that these gains were in fact unsustainable, and,
as we shall see, tried to make a downward correction in the real
wage level during the second half of 1972.) As price control was
inevitably highly complex, and adjustments tended to be resisted
until pressures built up, anomalies were extremely common. In
September 1972 most bus rides in Santiago were 1.50 escudos, a
daily newspaper was 4 escudos, the maximum price for cinema seats
was 10 escudos, the toll for the Valparaiso road was 12 escudos,
excellent wine was 25 escudos a bottle (but one had to bring a bottle),
a portion of pizza cost 60 escudos, a tin of Paraguayan corned beef
cost 120 escudos, and imported consumer durables cost thousands,
but petrol (almost all of it imported) was phenomenally cheap. There
was neither rhyme, nor reason, nor predictability. While cheap
necessities may have been a form of redistribution of income, cheap
petrol benefited the middle classes. Failure to keep prices of public
utilities and of other nationalized industries ahead of costs necessi-
tated large subsidies, which led to further money creation and
stimulated inflation.

Many items at fixed prices became unobtainable. Others,
which were not controlled, were available at high prices, so that,
for instance, I could get cream but not milk. By September 1972,
despite the price rise in August (see below) meat was exceedingly
scarce, and it was almost impossible to find sugar, flour, butter,
margarine, rice, potatoes (though these latter did appear in October).
It soon became very difficult to buy detergents, cigarettes, razor
blades, toilet paper, and toothpaste.

The government increasingly sought to supply the working-class areas with goods at official prices, using organizations set up for the purpose, the JAP (Juntas de Abastacimiento Popular–Popular Supply Committees), but this caused friction with traders and led to accusations of political favoritism. Undoubtedly the UP supporters in the industrial "bidonvilles" around Santiago did reasonably well. In middle-class areas protests mounted, with housewives banging saucepan-lids every evening.

So the petty bourgeoisie had a difficult time as consumers and suffered great frustration in their professional capacities. Consequently, their hostility to the government mounted. Was this inevitable, given the desire to move towards socialism? Some have argued so. Others did not and do not agree. In a paper circulated in the summer of 1972, Jose Vera wrote the following. After listing the critical problems of the period (balance-of-payments deficit, supply shortages, deficiencies in economic administration, inflationary pressures due in part to excessive wage demands, and insufficient investments), he went on: "The above-mentioned difficulties are the logical result of the peculiar form of the advance to socialism chosen by the government. In principle, the costs such methods imply are justified by the aim being pursued: to establish a just and dynamic socialist society. But it is clear that if the government cannot find speedy effective solutions which will permit a continued advance towards socialism, the aim will not be accomplished and the cost will no longer be justified. Furthermore the government would then face a period of grave political difficulties." The author then makes some suggestions, some of them socially very progressive, calling for reinforced government controls over the economy, and also for "the creation of real and stable incentives for the private sector, which today faces a situation of great uncertainty and despair."[8]

It is, of course, clear that Allende had no wish to antagonize the small man. It happened because of the economic crisis of 1972. The question is only: how far did the policies adopted earlier lead to this crisis and so to these consequences?

How far were these consequences foreseen? To some extent they were, or so I was assured in interviews before and since the coup. The initial economic strategy of 1971 was undertaken on political assumptions that proved unreal or inconsistent with the political strategy actually followed by the Allende administration. One view expressed to me is that calling the policies followed a "strategy" would be misleading. There was ninguna politica coherente, there were several inconsistent strategies, reflecting the splits within the UP and the fact that key ministries were controlled by different parties (and also splits within parties, especially the Socialists).

In this connection, it may be interesting to quote the pro-UP (Marxist) publication of the Facultad de Economia Politica of the Universidad de Chile, La Economia Chilena en 1972. Noting the

huge increase in real wages of 1971, the authors commented as follows:
"This line of economic policy aimed at demonstrating clearly the class
nature of the revolutionary forces which controlled the executive power,
with the ultimate objective of uniting with revolutionary forces sectors
alien to them"[9] (that is, nonrevolutionary and nonproletarian elements).
After deploring the insufficiency of the organizational measures of mass
activity, the authors noted that "To isolate the 'powerful enemy, '
i. e. the big bourgeoisie and the imperialist interests, requires the
support or at least neutralization of elements of vacillating classes
. . . . i. e. the petty bourgeoisie and also the middle bourgeoisie.
But in an economy predominantly dependent-capitalist, which is subject to the law of value, commodity producers (whether capitalist or
not) must respond to prices, and derive their profit margins from the
difference between prices and costs. . . . Consequently a policy
designed to win or neutralize these middle-class strata. . . must be
accompanied by a price-level linked with a certain level of profits,
particularly if there exist upward pressures in levels in workers'
wages."[10] This is described as a "contradiction within an alliance
of classes." We shall see that, by the middle of 1972, this view
affected price policy. However, the authors do not show awareness
that, by then, the damage had been done, and that the earlier policy
ran directly counter to their own class analysis. Perhaps the way
out they envisaged was a very large increase in the Social Property
Area, which they imagined as withdrawn from the operation of the
market and the 'law of value', plus a total change in the political
balance, based upon mass activity. They do not make this clear.

It is also necessary to mention the government's policies in
the fields of foreign exchange, industrial planning, and agricultural
procurements.

As inflation speeded up during 1972, the gap between the
official and the black market exchange rates grew so wide that illegal
transactions became normal. Thus in September 1972 the official
"tourist" rate of 45 escudos to the U. S. dollar contrasted with a
black market rate of over 300. When, in March, the official rate
was belatedly moved to 90, the unofficial one approached 600. The
few tourists were compelled to exchange a minimum at the official
rate on arrival, but obviously the illegal market flourished. I was
told by an American visitor how she went into a (nationalized!) bank
to change a travellers' cheque, and the bank clerk told her she was
crazy to change it officially, offering to give her a much better rate
if she would step outside.

As for planning, it was almost nonexistent. The state sector's
enterprises operated autonomously, and were as confused by the
price pattern as was private enterprise. It had been understood that
they were to make a profit. Indeed, this had been one of the hopes
placed upon nationalization: that the state would be able to use
industrial profits to finance its welfare and investment measures,

independently of Congress's grip on the pursestrings. However, escalating wages and other costs, and price control, soon turned profits into losses in many cases. Far from contributing to the state budget, the nationalized sector became a charge on the budget. While market and price indicators lost their significance, the Allende administration was never able to make up its mind about what central planning powers there should be, or who should exercise them. Two "competitors" emerged: CORFO, an industrial promotion organ originally set up in 1939, and ODEPLAN, the nearest equivalent to Gosplan. One reason for government indecisiveness was unclarity over the desirable degree of centralization. The parties were not of one mind on this. Allende himself spoke to workers and told them: We are not your masters, you are your own masters. Such sentiments would have ill accorded with the issuance of binding orders from Santiago. It would not be correct to assert that the government sought planning powers that were denied it by Congress: the government probably did not know what powers it should seek. This would not have mattered too much if the state and private sectors had been effectively governed by the market, since this would have provided some sort of basis for operation. But the market was becoming hopelessly distorted.

Inflation speeded up for several mutually reinforcing reasons. Incomes had greatly increased in 1971, and continued to rise in 1972. Supplies could not be adequate at existing prices. So long as Pedro Vuskovic was responsible for economic policies, prices of necessities were kept low, despite the lines and empty shops. Then Vuskovic was replaced by Matus, who apparently decided that prices must rise to more realistic levels. The reasoning was that cited on page 66 above, in the citation from the Facultad de Economica Politica. The results are shown in Table 3.8.

TABLE 3.8

Rise in Consumer Prices, August 1972
(in escudos)

	July 31	August 31
Fillet steak	55.00	160.00
Stewing steak	29.00	70.00
Lamb chops	33.00	52.00
Chicken	18.50	33.00
Cooking oil	9.60	14.40
Tea	17.60	37.60
Coffee	17.50	31.70
Milk	1.70	3.50
Granulated sugar	6.00	12.00
Rice	2.90	7.10

Source: El Mercurio, September 23, 1972.

This was to be part of an anti-inflationary strategy. Once set
at more realistic levels, prices were to be frozen. However, this
policy turn was half-hearted, doubtless because of its intense unpopu-
larity, especially among UP supporters. Prices were still, as a rule,
below the levels at which supplies balanced demand. Nor was it
politically possible to reduce the level of real wages far from the
unrealistic levels of 1971, especially as there was an election due
in the following March.

Wages had to be raised to keep pace with rising prices. Thus
in October 1972, the announced reajuste was 100 percent, that is, a
doubling of wages, and the consequences would naturally be a further
major twist to the inflationary spiral.

However, to the government's credit it did face the necessity
of some decline in real wages, and this is reflected in the following
figures:

TABLE 3. 9

Percentage Increases in Real Wages 1971-72

	Wages and Salaries	Prices	Real Wages
January-January	52. 5	24. 8	+20. 2
April-April	40. 3	38. 1	+1. 6
July-July	44. 9	45. 9	- 0. 7
October-October	121. 2	142. 9	-15

Source: Facultad de Economia Politica, La Economia Chilena
in 1972 (Santiago: Universidad de Chile, 1973), p. 265.

The 100 percent increase was not to apply to everyone and it
was calculated to incorporate increases already made during the year,
except that the lowest paid were favorably treated. This policy caused
irritation among the copper miners, who had been relatively well paid,
and in 1973 this led to a damaging strike. Meanwhile, other forces
were rapidly pushing up the supply of money. The nationalized
industries required subsidies. The purchase of some private enterprises by the state was also financed by money creation. Indeed
the executive power to print money was a way round congressional
financial control. Tax collection was not effective, and any new
tough redistributive fiscal legislation would not pass Congress. Such
desirable social measures as free milk for children, for instance, were
in the last analysis, paid for by the printing press.

Agricultural procurements suffered from the inflation and from
the growing black market. Thus in late September 1972 the official

price of potatoes was 4 escudos per kilo, the free or black price was 14 escudos. Peasants and middlemen naturally diverted potatoes (and many other products) to the black market. The one more or less sure source of supply under the government's control came from imports, as and when they could be afforded. Agricultural production was also discouraged by uncertainty over the prices and availability of goods, which might obtain when the crop ripened. Because of the black market, and also the confusion between private and cooperative activities on the asentamientos, statistics of sowings and production became less and less reliable. Output was probably higher than was reported.

By September 1972 the situation was plainly deteriorating. The events of the following month would make a bad situation worse.

THE GENERAL STRIKE OF BOURGEOISIE

The opposition parties were split over the tactic to adopt. Congressional elections in March 1973 would theoretically give them the opportunity to impeach Allende, provided they obtained more than a two-thirds majority. This seemed unlikely. The more extreme members of the Right (Patria y Libertad, and much of the National party) seemed increasingly to have thought of persuading the military to intervene. But the military at this date were only likely to intervene to save the country either from a left-wing coup or from chaos. In the absence of a real danger of a left-wing coup, and given the grave economic situation that already existed, the best bet for the Right seemed to be to worsen this situation by economic sabotage. This policy was facilitated by the bitter grievance felt by much of the petty as well as by the grande bourgeoisie. If the country could be made ungovernable, the army would have to step in. If chaos spread, then perhaps the disenchanted voters would abandon the UP by the time of the March elections.

The pretext chosen was a minor misunderstanding: In the distant southern province of Aisen, the provincial CORFO proposed a nationalized goods transport service, in an area poorly provided with transport. In intent it was certainly not more revolutionary than the activities of British Road Services in the Highlands of Scotland. However, the truck owners, mostly very small men, saw here the thin end of the wedge. Nationalization, backed by the state's control over imports of trucks, buses, spare parts, was alleged to be threatening. Denials were of no avail. The truckers stopped work, in a country overwhelmingly dependent on road transport. Since so many of the truckers were owner-drivers, trade union action was no remedy. (A damaging strike by small truck owners in the United States in January-February 1974 reminds us that such troubles can also occur here.)

The government detained some of the ringleaders. This led to politically concerted action by other groups and associations (gremios). In mid-October, doctors, dentists, accountants, engineers, bank officials, pharmacists, shopkeepers, petty manufacturers, and some university staffs stopped work. Allende declared a state of emergency (October 12) and tried a mixture of threats and negotiations, which ended in deadlock. The gremios presented joint demands, enshrined in a so-called "Pliego de Chile," which included political conditions that amounted to surrender.

The CUT ordered its members to go on working. Volunteers loaded and unloaded railway wagons. Some trucks were requisitioned. The government improvised a distribution system for essential supplies, giving priority to working-class areas. However, disorganization of production was inevitable and considerable. Serious damage was being done, with the gremios repeating their determination to stay out, and Allende having no way of compelling them to return to normal activities within the bounds set by the constitution and legality.

Indeed, even within these bounds he was compelled to invoke the aid of the military. The state of emergency brought generals and admirals into the role of maintaining order. General Hector Bravo, for example, was appointed to command in Santiago and issued emergency regulations. Armed soldiers toured the streets and guarded the petrol stations, where long lines of motorists waited their turn. At this stage the military did their duty without fear or favor, but this did not include the use of violence against the strikers (as distinct from groups of demonstrators). Nor were they ordered to use such violence. The effect of their new role on the senior officers could have been significant for the future. A U.S. correspondent in Santiago told me that as he was interviewing General Bravo, "his phone was ringing, there was a line of petitioners outside his office. He was exercising power. And, you know, I thought he was beginning to enjoy it!"

A way out of the impasse was found, when the commanders of the army, navy, and air force joined a reconstructed government. General Prats, commander in chief, became Minister of the Interior, which not only made him responsible for public order but also ex officio vice-president (this minister acts if the president is incapacitated, or abroad). Some of the less popular ministers were dropped at the same time. General Prats successfully negotiated an end to the general strike of the bourgeoisie in early November 1972. These events are not our primary concern in this chapter. What matters in the present context are their economic consequences.

First, of course, industrial output diminished. The effect of this on inflation was muted at first by the strike of retail traders: the diminished output of consumer goods piled up in warehouses. Consequently, although a wage reajuste of 100 percent occurred during this strike, the additional money chased more unsold goods in the short run. Second, while the crisis gave rise to some improvisations by the government in the field of planning, allocation, and transportation, based in some degree on requisitioning, a precondition of the peace negotiated by Prats was a return to the status quo, that is, private capital assets had to be returned to their owners insofar as they had been acquired during the crisis. (The strikers had demanded more, including a reduction in the Social Property Area acquired or controlled in previous years.) A virtual guarantee had to be given that further nationalization would be halted. Third, this left the Allende administration with no further politicoeconomic perspective, except a vaguely-defined consolidation of gains already made. Although Prats was a constitutionalist and acted at all times as a loyal servant of the president, in fact it was clear to all that the military members of the cabinet had a virtual right of veto: measures to which they took exception were unlikely to be adopted. There was little room for maneuver left.

The government was politically relieved, if economically further embarrassed, by the series of court actions by the Kennecott Copper Corporation, which sought to prevent payments being made by the purchasers of Chilean copper in Western Europe by claiming property rights to the (nationalized) mines. While these actions lasted, payments were delayed, but the public in Chile supported Allende on this issue, and in fact even the Right in Congress voted with the government over the Kennecott case.

The crisis showed a notable split in the Christian Democrat party, with contrasting speeches by the intransigent ex-President Frei and the more conciliatory and left-wing ex-candidate Tomic. Tomic clearly supported the compromise that left Allende in office with the military in the government (indeed he told me so). It seemed at the time that Frei wished Allende's regime to fall, and it was therefore not surprising in September 1973 that Frei expressed support for the coup.

In November-December 1972 Allende visited New York and also Moscow. In Moscow he was given high honors. The Chilean Communist leader Corvalan was there too. No doubt they asked for immediate large-scale economic assistance. They got promises of delivery of Soviet equipment on credit, and some immediate help, but too little. "We overestimated greatly the amount of aid we might get from Socialist countries, " said an official exiled after the coup. The USSR had its own balance of payments problem, and was pursuing detente with the United States.

THE ELECTION AND THE DEADLOCK

The civil-military government held on to power until the March elections, with inflation resumed at a rapid rate; there was a mixture as before of price controls, giving way at irregular intervals in the face of ever-rising costs; shortage of many foodstuffs and consumers' goods was a constant source of worry. January and February are summer holiday months, and everyone waited for March.

The elections were hailed by the Left as a victory, because the UP vote was higher than at the presidential elections, and certainly higher than the Left had anticipated—over 43 percent of the total. Partly this must be explained by the fact that the Christian Democrats in March 1973 were aligned with the Right, so that some left-wing supporters who had voted for Tomic in the presidential elections switched to the UP in the Congressional elections. In fact, bearing in mind the economic chaos and social dangers of the situation, the result of the elections represented a fatal deadlock. The actual votes were:

	(thousands)
Christian Democrats	1005
National party	750
Socialists	700
Communists	570
Other UP (MAPU, IC, etc.)	330
Other Right	220
Total UP	1600
Total opposition	1975

Allende had three more years to go. Could the country survive that long, with continuing deadlock between executive and legislature, and with economic disintegration threatening? The government could take no decisive action against the will of Congress and without the support of the military within its own ranks. At best it would hope to hold on to the social gains it had registered and survive until 1976. However, its chances were reduced when Prats and the other generals left the government after the elections. Their presence had been a source of irritation to the more left-wing members of the UP coalition: thus it was an open secret that the secretary of the Socialist party, Altamirano, opposed their participation. In retrospect, their resignation was a grave setback to the hopes of Allende's survival. In fact it was the UP who desired them to resign, but the generals may well have been uneasy in a UP government, and under increasing pressure from their own fellow-officers to withdraw, now that they had guaranteed the holding of free elections (they would in all probability have been free and honest anyhow, but the Right had expressed deep suspicion on this point).

The accelerating inflation and growing sense of disintegration was faced in April to June 1973 by an all-civilian government, amid vigorous and often unscrupulous opposition from the Right and from the majority of the Christian Democrats. The one external factor that turned favorable was an increase in the price of copper. But this proved to be too late to save the government, the more so because of the continuing high prices of items that needed to be imported, for instance wheat. It might be argued that, without oppositionist sabotage, the government could have tightened economic controls and begun a program of economic recovery. Allende did speak of the need for sacrifice and for increased productive investments. But the government's grip on power, the means available to enforce its decisions, had become dangerously weak.

What could Allende now do? He had not the power to impose any drastic economic policies, he faced a hostile Congress, a mainly hostile free press and radio; and the armed forces and carabineros, who had hitherto protected the constitution, were watching from the sidelines, with increasing evidence of the emergence of a faction willing to consider the overthrow of the president. The ultraleft was calling for tough measures ("la mana dura," to cite a popular left-wing song of the period). Enforced how? There were militant (not military) working-class organizations, but to arm them would mean instantly provoking the military into decisive and overwhelming counteraction. The sad story of the last six months of Allende's rule was of a gradual slide into disaster, without any real means of averting it or of taking any new policy initiatives in the economic field. A precondition for action (other than a civil war that the army would win) was a coalition with the Christian Democrats, if a joint program could be devised under some umbrella of a "government of national salvation" with Allende still as president. Discussions along these lines were begun, very late because of opposition among many of the UP leaders. There was no time even to see whether something could have been achieved by this route, which was known to be favored by the Communist party.

Two further setbacks weakened the government and disrupted the economy. One was the strike of many copper miners. This, the first major conflict with a group of workers, arose from their desire to maintain their position, won under the American companies, of being much better paid than other Chilean workers. The particular reason for their strike was that they demanded that the 100 percent wage reajuste due in April 1973 should be added to a 40 percent interim rise already granted them a few months earlier. The government refused, since other workers due a 100 percent rise had not received this interim increase. A damaging loss of copper production and exports ensued in an obstinate dispute that lasted two months.

The second and ultimately fatal attack came once again from the gremios, again led by the road transport organization, under the right-winger Leon Vilarin. Again paralysis threatened. Again the government mobilized its supporters and declared a state of emergency. Again they brought the military into the government. But history refused to repeat itself. The occasional acts of sabotage that occurred in October 1972 became more frequent; electric pylons were blown up, one of Allende's own personal assistants murdered. Inflation speeded up even further, to an annual rate of 400 percent (the index for June 1973 was already 207 [January 1973 = 100]). Amid growing chaos, it became clear that, whatever the personal views of General Prats and a few other loyal senior officers, the bulk of the armed forces would not play any longer the role assigned to them. Allende must have pinned hopes upon a split in the military, who seemed more likely to split if he observed legality scrupulously. This was not altogether baseless. Prats went into exile, and some other senior and junior officers were dealt with severely by the conspirators, after the coup. But in practice the conspiracy developed unhindered, while no steps were taken to organize "unofficial" resistance for fear of upsetting the military. In fact, such feeble efforts as were made to form groups loyal to the UP, notably in the navy, were apparently undertaken by individuals without Allende's authorization (Altamirano was said to have played a leading part), and this helped the conspirators to present to vacillating officers a picture of a left-wing conspiracy to "subvert" the navy. The last opportunity presented to the government was perhaps the premature rebellion of a tank regiment on June 29 (the Tancazo); this would have required drastic action, including mass dismissals of potentially disloyal officers, but this opportunity, if it existed, was not taken, and two months afterwards Prats was forced to resign by his fellow-officers. Even in distant Glasgow I could see that this was the end. Meanwhile, with no means of enforcing any policy, the government could only watch the continuing collapse of the economy. Aware of the increasing likelihood of a coup, the striking bourgeoisie refused any compromise, did not negotiate, and waited for the political dividends that would flow from economic disasters. Allende had now neither policy nor power to impose a policy. He could only stagger on, improvising solutions to crises as they arose, until in the end the more ruthless elements in the armed forces destroyed him, the UP parties, and the constitution, on that tragic day of September 11, 1973.

The problem for the political economist is to draw any possible morals. That errors were made is self-evident, but which of the errors were the fatal ones, which could have been avoided? Between the expectations and pressures of its own supporters and the objective difficulties, exacerbated by domestic opposition and foreign obstruction, how much room for maneuver was there for Allende? What could he do without a majority and without control over the legislature? Was there a more moderate policy that could have won the support of at least the left wing of the Christian Democrats in Congress? Or was such a policy, or a coalition that included Tomic, rendered impossible by the political attitudes of the UP supporters and of the leadership of most of its constituent parties? In any case, could it have been right so greatly as to raise real wages and expectations, reduce investments, greatly increase imports of food, and use up all currency reserves and material stocks?

Among the errors that can be diagnosed was one that could be called economic naivete, of a kind common in far left-wing circles in Britain and elsewhere. There is little realization that real incomes depend decisively on productivity. Wage restraint is equated with impermissible "reformism" or with betraying the working class. By some UP leaders inflation was blamed airily on capitalism and curable by altering los estructuras (the structures), enlarging the Social Property Area, freeing Chile from subordination to foreign capital, and carrying out land reform. High output accompanied by price control would then halt inflation. (The above remarks on inflation are paraphrased from the Programa basica del gobierno de la Unidad Popular, cited from an editorial in Panorama economico devoted to el desborde inflacionario.)[11] A critic called this a vision facilista, and cited in illustration a speech by Millas made at the end of 1970, shortly after the Allende government took office: "Until 3 November inflation galloped on in Chile. From this day the problem begins to slow down. No more antipatriotic devaluations of the escudo rate against the dollar! We will cancel various increases in price, for instance for electricity. Necessities will be subsidized. During the course of 1971 the new economic measures will take effect, with the result that rising prices will become a thing of the past, remembered as a burden carried in the days when governments served large-scale Capital."[12]

The fact that a large expansion of the money supply would stimulate a speed-up in inflation was either forgotten or regarded as unimportant. So was the pressure of rising wages upon costs. By contrast, there was a gross overestimation of the antiinflationary effects of price control, and an underestimation of the effect of such control in stimulating imports. A large budget deficit financed by money-creation, plus higher wages, plus strict price control, equals shortages and lines. This simple lesson may yet have to be learned in other countries. Falling profits, as costs rose, cut down the possibility of investing out of profits in the public and private sectors alike. The price adjustments that then had to be made in the middle of 1972 were so drastic that they caused the economy to stagger towards hyperinflation.

The editorial of Panorama Economico makes a further important point: that while the organized working class did gain large increases in money wages, the price rises of 1972 hit a large and poor segment of the population that was deemed self-employed, or was in small workshops or petty services where no trade unions or wage regulations operated, or finally was poor peasants. "The potential political consequences of this phenomenon are not difficult to imagine and could constitute another element of tension in the already acute process of political radicalization."[13] How many of these, perhaps

lumpen-bourgeoisie as well as lumpen-proletariat, turned to the
radical Right?

For an economist who writes and works in Great Britain, a further
question poses itself. Certain errors not dissimilar to Allende's
were committed under the Conservative government presided over by
Edward Heath. Allende was a Marxist, Heath is a conservative.
Britain too ran headlong into a crisis. Some of its elements do have
certain parallels with Chile. Heath reduced taxes for political reasons;
Allende was unable to increase them for political reasons. Both had
a large and growing budget deficit, which contributed to inflation.
Both faced a labor movement that demanded, and got, large wage
increases. Both froze prices charged by nationalized industries,
and had to subsidize their growing losses. A huge balance-of-payments
deficit developed. This was made worse by a sharp worsening (in both
countries) of the terms of trade. It was complicated, at a critical
moment, by industrial action on the part of miners (copper and coal
miners respectively). Given the balance-of-payments situation of
1973-75, suppose Britain were faced with the prospect of paying her
way without incurring further foreign indebtedness? Few would doubt
that the resulting chaos would have had (perhaps still might have)
profound effects on the British political system. It is only by vast
borrowings that Heath, and after him Wilson, has (so far) avoided
disaster. Allende had no such choice; massive credits were denied
him.

These parallels are not drawn in order to forecast the fate of
the British government (Wilson is hardly likely to be overthrown by
the chiefs of staff), but because it serves as a useful reminder of
the limitations of political power in a democracy. It is easy to say:
why did Allende not impose a sound economic policy? A future
historian might say the same thing about Heath or Wilson: why did
he tolerate so high a rate of inflation (of course never as high as
Chile's, but too high by European standards), why did he not balance
the budget, and so on. We who live in Britain know that, along with
genuine errors of policy and judgment, Heath and Wilson were hemmed
in by political and social constraints, by forces they could only
partially control or could not control at all. To remember this is a
first step towards understanding some of the causes of the economic
failings of the Allende administration. They had the best intentions,
they (or most of them) wished to conciliate the small businessmen,
to reduce inflation, to redistribute income in favor of the very poor,
and to nationalize key sectors in order to use their revenues for the
public good. It is surely too simple, in the light of the evidence, to
say that they were overthrown because of what they tried to do. Many
of their policies led to results quite other than they had intended, and
strengthened the hand of those who wished to eliminate the UP and
all that it stood for. The present chapter is written much more in
sorrow than anger. It does not pretend to answer all the questions

that it poses, directly or by implication. There is much more research to be done. The UP leaders who are abroad—for instance Teitelboim and Altamirano—could cast light on some puzzling policy decisions in which they participated. We must gather evidence from other actors in the drama.

Meanwhile, we should (in my view) refrain from tempting generalizations about the inevitable failure of a parliamentary road, particularly if one bears in mind the fact of an antisocialist parliamentary majority. One cannot legislate one's way towards socialism if the antisocialists control the legislature.

Finally, a word on the junta's economic policies. Having eliminated political parties and suppressed trade unions, an attempt was made to raise prices to "realistic" levels: they rose by 87. 6 percent in the single month of October 1973. This caused much hardship, as did the rise in unemployment that accompanied the attempts to impose deflation. However, it proved necessary to allow some increases in money wages, which had fallen way below subsistence levels in many cases. Therefore, while in November and December the price rises were small (5. 7 percent and 4. 7 percent respectively), the upward trend was resumed thereafter, the total rise in the first three months of 1974 being 63 percent, and inflation has roared on since. The junta has been disappointed at the lack of foreign aid, and hit by falling copper prices. Its policies have no doubt been bitterly unpopular, but the military have had the power to enforce them by organized terror.

Perhaps the generals are hoping to follow the Brazilian model, where there has been an industrial boom based upon large-scale import of capital, a military regime, low wages, and high profits. However, the Brazilian model may be quite inapplicable to Chile, with its much smaller population and relatively restricted internal market. The junta may well face political as well as economic crises, unless it receives aid from abroad. (The rise in copper prices in their first year was reversed, and there have been large rises in prices of oil and grain.) The outlook is still stormy.

NOTES

1. Speech of November 5, 1970 in Salvador Allende, Chile's Road to Socialism, (Harmondsworth: Penguin Books, 1973), p. 65.
2. Ibid. , p. 84.
3. An excellent account of the whole problem was written by S. Barraclough and A. Affonso, "Diagnostico de la reforma agraria chilena, " in Cuadernos de la Realidad Nacional (Santiago: April 1973).
4. Salvador Allende, Chile's Road to Socialism, op. cit.
5. Comentarios sobre la situacion economica, (Santiago: Universidad de Chile, 2nd semester 1972, 1973), p. 229.

6. Ibid., p. 249.

7. _Comentarios_, op. cit., p. 7.

8. _Documentos del Consejo de Rectores_, (Santiago: Universidades Chilenas, July-August 1972), pp. 43, 45.

9. Facultad de Economia Politica, _La Economia Chilena en 1972_, (Santiago: Universidad de Chile, 1973), p. 40.

10. Ibid., pp. 63-64.

11. _Panorama Economico_ (Santiago, October 1972).

12. El Siglo, December 13, 1970, cited from _Panorama Economico_ (Santiago, October 1972).

13. _Panorama Economico_ (Santiago: October 1972), p. 8.

AGRARIAN REFORM AND THE
TRANSITION TO SOCIALISM
Cristobal Kay

The purpose of this chapter is to examine Popular Unity's agrarian policy in the light of the failure of the revolutionary forces to capture power and initiate a transition to socialism in Chile. We argue that Popular Unity's agrarian policy reflects the limitations and contradictions in its overall strategy for gaining power. For although President Allende's land reform was extensive, drastic, and rapidly executed, it nevertheless limited the peasantry's contribution to a revolutionary struggle for power.

In the first part we briefly examine the agrarian legacy left by the previous Christian Democrat government and outline the agrarian program of Allende's government. We proceed in the second part of the chapter with an analysis of peasant mobilization and organization, focusing on land seizures and peasant councils. In the third part, we devote our attention to the organization and functioning of the expropriated latifundia that constituted the reformed sector and examine to what extent it formed a vanguard of the revolutionary struggle in the countryside. Finally, in the fourth and last part, we attempt an assessment of Popular Unity's agrarian policy from the viewpoint of the accumulation of revolutionary forces in the rural sector.

FREI'S AND ALLENDE'S AGRARIAN REFORM

Frei's Agrarian Reform: Aims and Legacy

In 1967 the Christian Democrat government introduced a land reform and union legislation law meant to modernize and consolidate the capitalist mode of production and to obtain a solid base of political support for the Christian Democrat party from the peasantry. (We are using the term peasantry in the more general Latin American sense of campesinado meaning small landed proprietors, tenants, and wage laborers). The aims of the land reform were to increase agricultural production and productivity, to create 100,000 new peasant proprietors, to incorporate the peasantry into the economic, social, and political decision-making processes of the country, and to raise rural living standards. Frei's agrarian policy represented a reform strategy resting on four pillars—the expropriation of the large and badly worked estates, incentives for efficient producers, government sponsored organization of the peasants, and an increase in rural wages and job security. [1]

Although the land reform law of 1967 permitted the expropriation of all large estates, less than a third of Chile's latifundios were expropriated between 1965 and 1970 and only 21,000 of the promised 100,000 peasant families received land. [2] Moreover, the law did not provide for the expropriation of livestock and machinery and the Christian Democrats let the landowner choose a large reserve equal to 80 hectares of good irrigated land. The new organizational structure that emerged from the expropriated latifundio was the asentamiento, a loose form of rural cooperative of peasant households, in which the land and capital belongs to CORA—the State land reform agency—and the major administrative decisions are taken by CORA. The asentamiento was conceived as a transitional organization in which after a trial period of three to five years the peasants, called asentados, would be free to determine if they wanted to continue as a cooperative enterprise, if they preferred to divide the land into individual family plots, or if they wanted to organize a farm in mixed property arrangements. The asentamiento was a system that maintained and even increased economic and social inequality among rural laborers. At the end of the Christian Democrat administration only 6 percent of the rural workers (excluding the minifundistas—small peasant proprietors) gained control over roughly 20 percent of total irrigated land, averaging about 10 irrigated hectares per asentado. [3] An asentado thus possessed on average ten times more land than a minifundista. The asentamiento also maintained the differences between the various types of laborer of the ex-latifundio. The inquilinos (tenants) kept their rights of use over a plot of irrigated land and of about three-quarters to one and a half hectares (regulia de tierra), as well as their pasture rights for a few animals (talajes). The voluntarios (resident wage workers) remained with no, or only minor, access to production fringe benefits. Furthermore, the inquilinos, now asentados, enjoyed full rights in the administrative council of the asentamiento, while the voluntarios, now socios, had only the right to speak, not to vote. A third category of laborers, the afuerinos (literally outsiders), who as seasonal wage laborers used to supply up to half the workforce during harvesting time, were left out completely from the asentamiento. In some cases the asentados continued to employ these afuerinos for a traditional wage, thus transforming themselves into nuevos patrones (new landlords). [4]

Thus the Christian Democrats had the clear intention of forming a privileged group of peasants, the asentados, who with the subdivision of the asentamientos would eventually become a rural petty bourgeoisie, spreading the peasant mode of production in the countryside, acting as a buffer for the social tensions resulting from the conflicts between the rural bourgeoisie and the agrarian proletariat, and opposing a more radical land reform. [5]

The Christian Democrat's effort to organize the peasantry was more successful. Before Frei, legislation virtually prohibited peasant organization, so it was not surprising that only 2,000 rural workers belonged to unions (largely vineyard workers). In the last year of the Frei administration (1970), rural unions had over 140,000 members and a further 100,000 peasants had become incorporated into cooperative or precooperative committees. [6] Only a small percentage of the unionized peasants, however, were among the poorest and most oppressed sector, the afuerinos, while the multiplication of peasant organizations created or deepened already existing divisions among the peasantry, instead of promoting peasant unity. [7] For example, peasants working on the same farm could belong to rival unions.

By the end of the Frei administration, agricultural production had increased significantly and real wages had doubled, but at the cost of growing unemployment. Cheap government credits, facilities for importing agricultural machinery to the medium and large landowners, and a favorable agricultural price policy, coupled with the threat of expropriation, encouraged latifundistas (big landowners) to subdivide their farms and become efficient commercial farmers. [8] On balance, the Christian Democrat agrarian reform improved the situation of the rural capitalists and the asentados, but did little for the poorer strata—the afuerinos, the minifundistas and Indian communities—who remained largely unorganized, unassisted, unemployed and, most importantly, with no or insufficient land. As Winn and Kay conclude: "The Christian Democrats, therefore, left a mixed rural legacy to Allende in 1970. They had legitimised the idea of agrarian reform and initiated the redistribution of land and the organization of the peasantry, but limited the scope of these changes. The land reform law was deficient, but it could provide the legal basis for the elimination of the latifundio if applied by a government determined to enforce its provisions. The asentamiento had serious flaws, but it was a precedent for the transformation of private estates into peasant and state cooperatives. The Christian Democrats left an inefficient and overlapping agrarian bureaucracy, but also agencies and officials with some experience in the implementation of an agrarian reform." [9]

Allende's Agrarian Reform Program

The main instrument for carrying out Popular Unity's agrarian
reform program was the existing Christian Democrat land reform legislation. The main problem was overcoming its negative aspects. This
inherited legal framework was to be given a different political purpose
and setting under Popular Unity—that of initiating and advancing a
transition to socialism. [10] Popular Unity's class analysis of the
countryside led it to consider that the main enemy for a future socialist
transformation were the latifundistas. Thus one of the main aims of
the agrarian reform policy was to expropriate all latifundia, defined
as every farm exceeding 80 HRB (hectare as de riego basico) in size,
regardless of their efficiency. (The total amount of land of each farm
was reduced to a homogeneous unit, the HRB [standard irrigated hec-
tare], which is a unit of best quality land). It was thought possible
to win over or neutralize the 'medium producers' (defined as owners
of farms between 20 to 80 HRB) who were therefore to be supported
economically. [11]

Little was said in Popular Unity's program about the organization of the reformed sector. It was hinted that in order to speed up
the expropriation process and facilitate planning, expropriation should
proceed by regions and that the new reformed unit should be a regional
cooperative incorporating various adjacent farms and unemployed
peasants. Another aim of Popular Unity's agrarian policy was to
reverse the traditional outflow of economic resources from the rural
to the urban sector to augment rural investment and raise peasant
living standards. Popular Unity did not envisage the agrarian reform
in isolation. Its program stipulated that its objective of raising
peasant living standards and developing an economically strong
reformed sector would be achieved by nationalizing the banking system to control the allocation of credits and by expropriating the
monopolistic wholesalers to prevent them from capturing the rural
surplus. [12] Popular Unity realized that in order to fulfill these aims
it needed the firm support of the peasantry. For this purpose it
envisaged the creation of consejos campesinos (peasant councils)
that would foster peasant unity by bringing together representatives
from different peasant organizations.

Thus part of Popular Unity's agrarian reform aims was directed
at fully exploiting the Christian Democrat land reform legislation by
expropriating all latifundia and extending unionization. Other aims
pointed toward a new direction, such as the creation of peasant
councils and regional cooperatives, and the nationalization of the
banking and wholesale distribution system. Although Popular Unity
intended to initiate a transition to socialism, its agrarian program
could not strictly be called socialist as its measures were compatible
with state or peasant capitalism, as other sweeping agrarian reforms

had revealed in Latin America in the cases of Mexico, Bolivia, and Peru. [13] Moreover, with the election of Allende to the presidency, Popular Unity could use part of the government's administrative and economic resources to weaken the economic base of the bourgeoisie via expropriations, and strengthen the social power of the urban proletariat and the peasantry via political mobilizations. If Popular Unity wanted to initiate a transition to socialism it was essential for it to capture state power and neutralize the armed forces. Socialist relations of production cannot be introduced in the countryside until the proletariat exercise hegemonic control of the state apparatus. Generalizing, agriculture can only be called socialist if the following two conditions are fulfilled. First, when most or all of the means of production (land, water, and capital) are social or state property. Second, the proletariat as a class (worker and peasant alliance) control the allocation of the economic surplus they have generated. This control is exercised through the proletariat playing a major role in the planning of production and distribution, which replaces the market system.

PEASANT CONFLICTS AND POWER: THE NEW CHARACTER OF THE RURAL CLASS STRUGGLE

Unionization and Strikes

One of the main legacies of the Christian Democrat agrarian reform was the organization of the peasantry in unions. The Christian Democrat hoped through unionization to gain a solid base of political support among the peasantry, creating an alliance between the peasantry and the urban bourgeoisie. To make this alliance feasible union action was confined to the traditional role performed by unions in capitalist society, that is, to represent the corporative interests of its members through collective bargaining. Union demands were confined to wage claims, better working conditions, enforcement of social security and minimum wage payments, defense from landlords' encroachment upon production fringe benefits, and so on. [14] When negotiations failed, the unions resorted to strike action; the seizure of estates was rarely contemplated as this was illegal and would have been violently repressed by the government or the landlords themselves. Thus unions under the Christian Democrat government confined their role to these purely trade unionist (corporative) demands and rarely constituted a mobilizing factor in the expropriation process. [15]
The Christian Democrat's political expectations were realized to some extent as about two-thirds of unionized rural workers belonged to unions controlled by, or sympathetic to, the Christian Democrat party. The remainder were supporters of a left-wing rural union

federation, jointly controlled by the Socialist and Communist parties. Popular Unity continued with the unionization effort and by 1973 had more than doubled union membership as compared with 1970, which meant that about two-thirds of the peasantry were now affiliated to trade unions. It is estimated that almost the whole of the rural proletariat (permanent wage workers, voluntarios, and inquilinos) was unionized, that the subproletariat (seasonal and casual wage laborers, afuerinos, and unemployed) had still not joined unions in any significant numbers and that over one third of the minifundistas belonged to unions. In the end the Popular Unity succeeded in gaining the support of roughly two-thirds of the unionized peasantry due to their recruiting efforts but also because they won over some previously controlled Christian Democrat unions. [16]

With the advent into government of the Popular Unity coalition, strikes continued to escalate as shown by the following figures: in 1967, 693 strikes, in 1968, 648 strikes, in 1969, 1,127 strikes, in 1970, 1,580 strikes and in 1971, 1,758 strikes. [17] Although the aims of these strikes still revolved around the solution of labor and economic problems, they increasingly became an expression of peasant solidarity. Solidarity strikes, which accounted for a third of the strikes in 1970 and 1971, were those in which unionized peasants supported the grievances and strike action of another farm in which they were not directly involved.

Land Seizures: The "Tomas"

Popular Unity's promises to radicalize the land reform, and its unwillingness to use the repressive apparatus against peasants or workers facilitated a series of land and factory seizures—the tomas. Decades of pent-up peasant frustrations and resentment against the landlords' exploitation expressed itself in a forceful manner with the tomas de tierra. Land seizures were not common under the Christian Democrat government as peasants were forcefully evicted. Christian Democrat policy was predio tomado no sera expropiado (any farm taken will not be expropriated). Although Popular Unity did not support tomas, it responded not by forceful eviction but by accelerating expropriations. [18]

Tomas under Popular Unity increased dramatically in numbers as evidenced by the following data: in 1967, 9 seizures; in 1968, 26 seizures; in 1969, 148 seizures; in 1970, 456 seizures; and in 1971, 1,278 seizures. A qualitative change in peasant action was involved, too. [19] First, there occurred tomas of a collective nature, in which various estates undertook joint action. These collective seizures revealed a greater organization, coordination, and solidarity among the peasants compared with previous peasant action. Second, tomas were no longer organized to such an extent by an external agent

as happened under the Frei government. Peasants seized farms by
themselves without always awaiting outside organization. Peasants
revealed a greater political independence and ability to act on their
own. Third, tomas had as their main objective the expropriation of
the farm and were only secondarily concerned with economic and
labor issues, although these continued to be important. Another
feature of interest about tomas is that they involved a greater social
spectrum of participants than had strikes. In half of the tomas such
social groups participated as unemployed laborers, smallholders
and seasonal wage workers, who also wanted to belong to the reformed
sector. [20] We must not forget that the number of rural unemployed
had greatly increased as a result of the modernization drive of the
Christian Democrat land reform, aggravating conflicts in the countryside. Peasants also became impatient with the agrarian bureaucracy.
When they did not receive prompt attention to their demands for expropriation they sometimes proceeded to occupy the local CORA offices.

Land seizures started on a massive scale in the Mapuche
indian regions of the south, where Mapuche peasants had traditionally
claimed land from the latifundia as theirs and had a history of corridas
de cercos (land invasion). They soon spread to other regions, especially the southern provinces of Valdivia, Osorno, and Llanquihue
that had barely been touched by expropriations during the Frei administration. It can generally be observed that tomas were initially
predominant in those regions in which expropriations had previously
made few inroads, [21] and that new peasant groups of a more proletarian
character (except for the Mapuche peasants), who had previously been
excluded from the expropriation process, were active participants. [22]

The tomas, which were the most radical expression of class
conflict in the Chilean countryside, were not confined to the latifundio.
Half of the land seizures occurred on farms smaller than 80 HRB, [23]
the legal limit below which initially the Popular Unity government did
not want to expropriate, not to upset the alliance that they were trying
to establish (or keep) between the proletariat and the middle sectors.
In any case only under special circumstances could the government
legally expropriate farms smaller than 80 HRB. This fact reveals that
the class conflict was as intense on the modernized farms of the new
rural bourgeoisie in the 40 to 80 HRB bracket, as on the latifundio. [24]
It was only after almost all latifundia had been expropriated, (that is,
towards the end of 1972), that Popular Unity began selective expropriation of farms between 40 to 80 HRB, but these were few and
confined to cases in which the rural workers were determined to
achieve the expropriation of the farm.

It was only in the final stage of the expropriation process, when
the large-scale peasant mobilizations were ebbing, that two parties
of the Popular Unity coalition began to endorse and direct some farm
seizures. In the southern province of Nuble, a socialist-led peasant
federation organized the peasant mobilization for tomas. In the

Melipilla area (Santiago province), MAPU–a party belonging to the
Popular Unity coalition–directed and mobilized tomas through the
peasant federation "Campesinos al Poder, " which they controlled. [25]
The novelty of the peasant demands in the Melipilla case was that
they went beyond the expropriation of the various seized farms and
included political demands. For example, in their fighting platform
they demanded that government action should be taken against those
landlords who they knew were preparing to overthrow the government.
The mobilization was also directed against the bourgeois judiciary
system and particularly against the local court, where the judge had
ordered the police to evict and imprison 41 peasants who had seized
the farm "Millahuin. " They also demanded that all remaining farms
above 80 HRB should be expropriated without delay, that landlords
should not be granted a reserve, and that expropriation should include
all the livestock and farm machinery. This peasant mobilization that
engulfed a whole region of Santiago province viewed the class struggle
not only in terms of expropriation but in the wider terms of a political
struggle against the courts and the bourgeoisie that were attempting
to overthrow the government. However, MAPU and the Socialist party
support for the tomas came at the end of the expropriation process
when the peasant struggle was subsiding and problems of agricultural
production and organization of the reformed sector gained importance.
For these and other political reasons, the experiences of Nuble and
Melipilla remained isolated events and did not inaugurate a new phase
in the peasant struggle as the "revolutionary" tendency within Popular
Unity had hoped.

Peasant Power via Peasant Councils?

        A few months after taking office, Popular Unity issued a decree
creating peasant councils. These were conceived by the government
not as an expression of an independent peasant power but as an
organization that would be a channel of communication between the
government and the various peasant organizations on such issues as
expropriations, credits, prices, marketing, taxation, and so on.
The role of the councils was confined to giving advice and receiving
information and instructions from the government. Peasant councils
would be formed at local, regional, and national levels, grouping
together into one organization representatives of the various peasant
organizations, such as the asentados through their Federacion de
Asentamientos, the minifundistas through their Comite de Minifundistas,
and the inquilinos, voluntarios, and other wage laborers through their
rural unions. [26] Thus peasant groups were represented that did not
share exactly the same interests. There were those of a petty
bourgeois character like the asentados, sharecroppers, lease- and
smallholders, who were interested in expanding the peasant economy;

there were those of more proletarian character, voluntarios, afuerinos, obreros agricolas, and the rural unemployed who were more interested in obtaining secure employment, good work conditions, and a fair wage. The small-holders or minifundistas are a mixed category. Some minifundistas are also seasonal and casual wage laborers and thus have proletarian characteristics. Others belong to communities of an indian or nonindian type. Mapuche communities were involved in occupations of latifundios reclaiming land that had once belonged to them. Thus this type of smallholder can and partially did, play a revolutionary role. In quantitative terms, by 1970 the rural proletariat (obreros agricolas, voluntarios, and in part the inquilinos) constituted less than 25 percent of the rural labor force, the subproletariat (afuerinos, casual wage laborers, and rural unemployed) 25 percent, the minifundistas over 40 percent, and the asentados less than 5 percent. Therefore, even without taking into account the proletarian character of some minifundistas, about half of rural workers were of a proletarian nature.

The original government conception of peasant councils excluded all those peasants who did not belong to an organization, and these were half the peasants at the beginning of the Popular Unity government. Furthermore, the majority of organized peasants were controlled by Christian Democrat organizations so that peasant councils came to be dominated by them and were an opposing force to the government's agrarian policy. This explains why some peasant groups demanded a different formulation of the peasant councils. In Cautin, a predominantly rural Mapuche province, peasants supported by the Socialist party and the MCR–the Revolutionary Peasant Movement– an organization associated with the MIR, demanded the creation of peasant councils por la base (by the grass roots), thus giving representation to the organized as well as to the unorganized peasantry. The councils formed under the original decree were referred to as consejos creados por decreto (councils created by decree) and those that were modified by peasant pressure to incorporate the nonorganized peasantry were called consejos ampliados por la base (councils enlarged by the base). The government approved this latter type of council after peasants of Cautin had mobilized in support.[27] Later, in some localities, councils in which no organized peasantry participated were formed; these were named consejos creados por la base. In the latter two types of councils some or all the representatives were elected directly in various local peasant assemblies, specifically called for that matter, in which all the peasants had the right to participate. These additional or alternative ways of constituting councils were not only more democratic but also more favorable to Popular Unity, as many of the yet unorganized peasantry tended to be supporters of the government. However, Christian Democrat organizations withdrew from those councils in which they had lost control through base mobilization, arguing that they were no longer democratic. Other councils came to represent peasants of one particular party of Popular Unity as other parties adopted sectarian attitudes, and councils became party organizations instead of representing the various peasant groups.

By early 1972 in almost all the 200-plus rural comunas (districts) of the country peasant councils had been formed, but a third did not function at all and many functioned irregularly. Two-thirds of these councils were established by the original decree and the remainder were ampliados or exclusively por la base; thus the original idea of the government predominated. This was unfortunate as those councils formed por la base functioned more regularly and actively, thus appearing to represent more closely the peasants' interests. The social composition of the leadership was mixed in 42 percent of the councils, 27 percent were of a proletarian nature, 16 percent were small farmers, and 15 percent were asentados. When this leadership composition is compared with the rural class structure, the proletarian and minifundista elements are greatly underrepresented and the asentados are overrepresented. [28]

Although by the end of 1972 three-fifths of the peasant councils were either ampliados or por la base, they were not particularly successful for several reasons. First, councils should have been established after all peasants had been mobilized in each region. The organized as well as the unorganized peasants should have been incorporated right from the start through direct elections in assemblies. This could have made a difference in the functioning of the councils, as some case studies point to the fact that those councils in which proletarian elements and nonorganized peasantry participated were more actively engaged in the expropriation process, had been trying to incorporate more workers on the expropriated farms, and were in favor of more advanced forms of cooperative farm organization. [29] Second, councils did not receive full political backing from the government and all the Popular Unity parties. This was the crucial factor in determining the lack of success of the councils, as peasants were still predominantly dependent on outside political support. Political support was limited to the Socialist and MAPU parties who most actively campaigned for the creation of peasant councils. Sectarian attitudes of Popular Unity parties emerged as each of them tried to retain control over their particular peasant organization, thus further weakening the unity of action of the councils. [30] Third, following from the previous factor, councils were unsuccessful because the government failed to assign them concrete tasks and to give them the necessary political power and economic resources to carry these out. Councils should have been more than advisory bodies and transmission belts for governmental policies, if they were to be a true expression of peasant power. [31]

As peasant councils never functioned well, unions continued to be the most important organization of the peasantry. Unions often gave advice and in some cases supported land seizures, and in many cases unions were the most active organization sustaining the councils, particularly those controlled by the Socialist party. [32] Perhaps only an agrarian reform process that eliminates the differences between peasants of a petty bourgeois and a proletarian character by trans- forming them all into collective farm workers can succeed in working towards a unified and effective peasant organization, [33] thereby increasing the revolutionary power of the peasantry. However, this would have required a new and radically different land reform legisla- tion.

THE REFORMED SECTOR: A SOCIALIST RELATIONS OF PRODUCTION?

The Various Types of Reformed Units

The Popular Unity government was well aware of the limitations and inequalities of the asentamiento but it took some time before an alternative organization was agreed upon. This was the CERA (Centro de Reforma Agraria), which would bring together various neighboring farms to rationalize the use of infrastructure and capital equipment and to incorporate landless seasonal laborers who had traditionally worked on these farms. (In some areas even minifundistas were to be integrated in the CERA.) The CERA was also to be characterized by its greater internal equality as all members would have equal rights on the administrative council and equal but restricted rights to produc- tion fringe benefits, as the emphasis of the CERA was to develop the collective economy. Economic differences arising from different productive capacities would be reduced by socializing the surplus produced by each CERA through the contribution of a percentage of profits to a regional development fund. [34] However, the CERA was not well received by much of the peasantry. In theory the CERA was both economically rational and politically correct, but it clashed with the social reality and the degree of political consciousness of the peasantry of the latifundia. The permanent workers of the expropriated latifundio, particularly the inquilinos, having become accustomed to the idea of their privileged position on the asentamiento were unwilling to accept the outside seasonal laborers with equal rights on the farm, as this would reduce production fringe benefits and the share in profits for each member.

The government, therefore, reached a compromise solution with the comite campesino that became the most widespread reformed unit. The comite was similar to the asentamiento but eliminated the differ- ences between members who all had equal rights in the running of the farm and in the distribution of production fringe benefits. It still left out the seasonal laborers and the minifundistas who could be incorporated as full members only if the majority of the permanent laborers so wished.   Often the economically most successful reformed units were the CEPROs (Centros de Produccion) and the 'intervened' farms. The CEPROs were state farms that were established on those expropriated latifundia with an agro-industrial character (for example, a timber complex) or had to tackle complex technical processes (for example, stock breeding).   The CEPROs were financed by the state and run by its technical experts.   Agricultural laborers were paid a fixed daily wage. [35]

Those farms that experienced a major labor conflict, or had been seized by the peasants without the government being able to expropriate them, were immediately intervened by the state, which appointed an interventor who ran the farm in the name of the owner until the conflict was solved or the farm legally expropriated.   Interventions were convenient because the government could take over the management of the farm much more quickly than under the lengthy process of expropriation and because the owner could not remove his capital equipment.   These farms became almost a new type of reformed unit, as they often remained intervened for long periods and were slowly expropriated. [36]

The Conflict Between the Collective and Peasant Economy

With the asentamiento the Christian Democrat government sought to replace the landlord by the state agrarian bureaucracy. CORA (the land reform agency) owned the land and capital equipment and paid an anticipo to the members of the asentamiento for the days worked on the collective land.   The anticipo was a monthly advance payment on future profits but as most asentamientos suffered losses during the first years, it became a wage payment.   The running of the asentamiento was jointly managed by government functionaries and the peasant administrative council.   Although Popular Unity replaced the asentamiento by the CERA and the comite campesino, these were managed on a similar basis.   The state owned the land and capital equipment and paid an anticipo, that is, a wage.   The state also provided most of the inputs, fertilizers, seeds, tractors, spare parts, and so on.

Popular Unity hoped that peasant control over the reformed sector would lead to the development of cooperative relationships of a socialistic nature and that the administrative controls could be lessened.   In order to encourage this, campaigns of concientizacion and capacitacion, directed at raising the political consciousness and technical ability of the peasantry, were carried out.   However, the opposite occurred.   The land cultivated for the private benefit of the peasant household (the peasant economy) encroached upon the land cultivated for the common benefit of all members of the producers' cooperative (the collective), channeling collective resources for private appropriation by the peasant household enterprise. [37] The traditional conflict over the resources of the hacienda system between the landlord—not state collective in the sense that the land was still legally the property of CORA—and the peasant economy came to the fore once more. How did such a process, which contradicted the ideological goal of socialism of Popular Unity, occur? Before we attempt to answer this question we must point out, however, that this deterioration of the collective economy in relation to the peasants' did not occur on the CEPROs where the state control over administration and collective resources was almost absolute. We also have to bear in mind that CEPROs were highly capitalized enterprises that paid high wages to the members but therefore restricted production fringe benefits. Although the government could have established more CEPROs, there were limitations because capital intensive latifundios were not common and because governmental technical experts to run these state farms were scarce. [38]

The peasant economy appropriated collective resources in the reformed units by the following mechanisms. One way was by expanding production fringe benefits; the amount of land cultivated privately and the number of pasture rights for livestock on the common pastures increased. This expansion occurred not only because more land and more pasture rights were appropriated by each member but also because the number of workers on the reformed units increased. It was Popular Unity policy to work on the principle of equality, and therefore workers who previously had had no, or restricted, production fringe benefits (like the voluntarios and the new members) now received a similar amount as inquilinos, thus reducing the collective lands and pastures. This equality principle was not completely effective as those peasant families with a greater number of adult males (most of the voluntarios were sons or relatives living and belonging to an inquilino peasant household) benefited more than others. [39] The increase in consumption fringe benefits (such as harvested allowances, milk allowances, wood for fuel, and so on) reduced the collective's production for the market. As peasant plots expanded both in numbers and size more labor time was needed for working on the peasant economy, particularly during harvest time, and the collective economy suffered as peasants worked fewer days per year and fewer hours per day on the collective. Collective land was left uncultivated or neglected, reducing output per hectare. Reformed peasants were reluctant to hire seasonal wage laborers to amend this situation as they feared their incorporation as full members. Finally, the productive capacity of the collective was reduced when, in some cases, resources belonging to the collective such as machinery, seeds, fertilizers were allocated to and utilized by the peasant household, without payment to the collective. [40]

Why Did the Collective Economy Deteriorate?

We shall single out the following factors as the most important ones in explaining the expansion of the peasant economy to the detriment of the collective in the reformed sector. First, lack of economic incentives for working on the collectives. Second, lack of capital resources for fully exploiting the collective. Third, lack of sufficient administrative and technical advice and controls by the state bureaucracy, and fourth, the development of the black market.

The lack of economic incentives for working on the collective largely derived from the character of the anticipo, by which each member received an equal monthly wage, regardless of the number of days worked on the collective. The anticipo did not differentiate between the various skills and efforts required by particular tasks.[41] Furthermore, as the reformed units made no profits during the first years, the incentive of profit distribution according to days worked on the collective by each member did not hold. Reformed units accumulated debts that were never fully repaid as the government was unwilling or unable to enforce a stricter repayment policy in order not to lose the peasants' political support. Thus, reformed peasants began to view the anticipo as a political right and not as an incentive to work on the collective, as it has been originally designed.

The lack of machinery, equipment, and tools, together with insufficient seeds and fertilizers meant that land was left uncultivated or was not as intensively exploited as it might have been. Much land was left as natural pasture, thus continuing with the extensive pattern of land exploitation that had been a negative and predominant characteristic of the private latifundio. This lack of capital was often imposed by the limitations of the land reform legislation in which expropriated landlords kept possession of their machinery and livestock. The government tried to offset this decapitalization of the expropriated farms by purchasing the landlords' machinery and livestock whenever possible. Often landlords preferred to sell these for higher prices in the market, or kept them to work the reserve. Although the government imported large numbers of tractors and other agricultural equipment for the reformed units, the massive scale of the expropriations within a period of only two years meant that a partial decapitalization of the collectives was inevitable.[42]

A third factor that prejudiced production on the collective lands was the insufficient provision of technical advice, training, and supervision by the agrarian bureaucracy. This particularly affected the raising of livestock and the maintenance of machinery and equipment. Livestock death rates increased and quality fell. Machinery broke down more frequently and lay idle for long periods before it was repaired. This situation was helped by the fact that reformed peasants did not repay the debts incurred by the purchase of machinery and livestock, or purchased them at a highly subsidized rate. Therefore, they did not become cost-conscious and easily mis-used expensive resources. [43]

An additional factor that conspired against the development of the collective economy and provided additional incentives for enlarging the peasant economy was the emergence and growth of the black market in foodstuffs from mid-1972. [44] The peasant was free to sell the produce of his household enterprise independently, while some of the products of the collective like wheat were sold to the state marketing agencies at official prices that were many times below black market prices. This differential price system certainly acted as powerful incentive for expanding production on the private peasant economy.

In spite of all the above-mentioned factors that encouraged the expansion of the peasant economy, peasants of the reformed sector did not generally want to split up the cooperative into private plots, as by doing so they would have to pay accumulated debts, pay for the land, no longer receive the anticipo, and perhaps most important-ly of all they would no longer receive state subsidized credits, machinery, and inputs. [45]

The negative economic effects resulting from the deterioration in collective cultivation were only felt with catastrophic consequences in the last year of the Popular Unity government. According to data from the World Bank, [46] agricultural and livestock production grew at an annual average rate of 2.7 percent during the first two years of the Popular Unity government. In 1973, however, production fell by an estimated 18 percent compared with 1972. (This figure over-estimates the drop in production, as the official statistics failed to register part of the output which was increasingly sold in the black market.) It is likely that production fell mainly in the reformed sector for the reasons mentioned above. However, production may also have fallen in the private commercial farm sector due to the compulsory purchase of wheat and sugar beet (at comparatively low prices) by the state. The area cultivated with wheat and sugar beet—wheat accounting for over half of the total cultivated crop area—fell by about 25 percent for both crops between 1972 and 1973. Yields also diminished during the same period by over 15 and 20 percent respectively. [47] The truck owners' strike that took place during the spring planting season of 1972 disrupted the distribution of crucial seeds, fertilizers, and fuel to the rural areas, and thus was another contributory factor to the fall in production. The reduction in agri-cultural production together with the redistribution of income had the effect of greatly increasing food imports between 1970 and 1973 from about 110 million U.S. dollars to about 400 million U.S. dollars, thereby plunging the country into one of its worst foreign exchange crises.

From this description of the reformed sector, it follows that the hacienda system, defined as a conflicting relationship between

a landlord—or in this case state or collective—enterprise and the
peasant enterprise, had not yet disappeared in Chile. [48] However,
this conflict was being resolved to the peasants' favor insofar as he
gained joint or individual control over the whole of the reformed sector.   Before the land reform process started the peasant economy
within the latifundia was in its last stage of proletarianization, as
the inquilino and sharecropper had lost much of their peasant character, and demesne production (instead of peasant production) with
wage labor (instead of tenant labor) had already become dominant. [49]
Under the land reform of the Christian Democrat and Popular Unity
governments this proletarianization process was reversed and a
strengthened and enlarged peasant economy emerged at the expense
of the collective economy in the reformed sector.   In the next section
we shall examine the implications of this reformed hacienda system
for the Popular Unity revolutionary process.

Reformed Peasants: Socialist Vanguard?

We must bear in mind that the socialist character of the reformed
sector primarily depends on the socialist nature of the whole revolutionary process.   Thus it is impossible to have a socialist reformed
sector within a capitalist economy. However, it is possible to have
a socialist society, albeit with distortions, in which the rural sector
is not yet socialized, as for example Poland, where the peasant
economy is the predominant agrarian unit. Nevertheless, it is necessary to advance as far as possible towards a socialistic type of
economic and social relationship in the reformed sector, as otherwise
this can later become a political obstacle, or fail to perform the role
of a revolutionary vanguard as expected in the countryside. This is
particularly true in a nation like Chile, where the socialist forces had
not yet captured power. Let us therefore examine the political implications of the existence of a hacienda system type of reformed sector
from the perspective of a revolutionary process commited to initiate
a transition to socialism.
The spread of a peasant economy within the reformed sector
multiplied the petty mode of production in the countryside. This
petty mode of production carried with it the future development of a
petty bourgeois consciousness that would create political obstacles
for a further socializing of the means of production in the rural sector.
Widespread opposition to Popular Unity government policies already
existed in those asentamientos formed during the Christian Democrat
period. These asentamientos, grouped in the Federacion de Asentamientos controlled by the Christian Democrat party, had led campaigns
against the CERAs saying that the CERA was a state farm in which
peasants would have no rights whatsoever, less so over a piece of
land. This federation even attempted to join forces with landlords'

organizations like SNA (Sociedad Nacional de Agricultura), CAS (Confederacion de Agricultores del Sur) and CONSEMACH (Confederacion de Empleadores Agricolas)[50] in solidarity with the strike of the truck owners, a group who were instrumental in the coup d'etat. Although eventually only a few asentamientos actually went on strike and then only for a day, they had joined the opposition's ideological campaign against the government and there was no guarantee that in the future other reformed units might not swing over to the opposition.

An interesting case study of what can happen on a reformed unit if a petty bourgeois tendency is not controlled is the ex-hacienda Culipran in Melipilla. Culipran was one of the first of the few estates to be forcefully seized by the peasants during the Frei administration. Some peasants were Christian Democrat supporters; others were Socialist party supporters and when they planned the takeover they had contact with Socialist leaders. The farm was expropriated and worked as a cooperative for three years. It was then parceled out following demands from the peasants and in line with Christian Democrat goals of creating peasant proprietors. Problems of property and agricultural prices increasingly shaped peasants' attitudes. Although the union continued to be led by some Socialist party members, Culipran peasants only thought of enriching themselves by working on their little farms and by using their contacts with the agrarian bureaucracy to secure subsidized credits and supplies. They were no longer involved in expressing solidarity with those peasants in the Melipilla region who were still struggling to achieve the expropriation of the latifundia, as for example in the Millahuin case already cited. The book by Petras and Zemelman on the Culipran reaches this warning conclusion: "The end result of the land invasion in our case study illustrates this process of bourgeoisification: the once insurgent peasants turned entrepreneurs exploiting labor and accumulating property and capital at the expense of their former companeros.[51] Other case studies of estate seizures during Popular Unity government reveal that it is during the most intense phase of peasant mobilization—between the organization of the toma and when the farm is finally expropriated—that peasants are most amenable to government and union pressures to incorporate as many peasants as possible with full rights by forming a CERA instead of less collectivistic reformed units.[52] From this it follows that Popular Unity should have fully supported and directed tomas, as this would have created greater acceptance of the CERA among the peasants. Soon after expropriation a phase of demobilization seemed to emerge as production and organizational problems created strains and divisions in peasant solidarity.

This petty bourgeois behavior by peasants of the reformed sector was furthered by the continuing existence of the capitalist rural bourgeoisie[53] and by the emergence of the black market. Under the land reform process the big medium-sized rural bourgeoisie (defined tentatively as farmers between 40 and 80 HRB) had doubled in number.

Furthermore, they supplied 40 percent of the marketed agricultural surplus.[54] A fact that is often overlooked is that Frei's union legislation also permitted the creation of an employers' union, CONSEMACH.[55] CONSEMACH soon outnumbered the members of the traditional landlords' organization (the SNA) and was actively engaged in opposing Popular Unity agrarian policy and in confronting the radicalism of the insurgent peasants. This new rural bourgeoisie that partially emerged from those latifundistas who had subdivided their estates to avoid expropriation, or who had retained a reserve, soon established a variety of links with some farms of the reformed sector. Their control of capital enabled them to rent out machinery and capital equipment to the reformed farms and some even provided technical and repair services. Nor was this a one way process. Some reformed units rented out pasture rights and land to the rural bourgeoisie who had livestock but insufficient land.[56] The rural bourgeoisie together with the commercial middlemen with whom they were in contact often purchased the agricultural produce of the reformed peasantry and then channeled it into the black market, reaping large profits.

This bourgeois tendency of the reformed peasantry and the fact that they constituted a privileged sector made necessary a socialist land reform that would go beyond the Christian Democrat legislation. By 1973 the reformed sector incorporated 20 percent of the total rural labor force, controlled over half of the irrigated land of the country (over 40 percent in terms of HRB) and produced over a third of the agricultural output. More than a third of the labor force still obtained a subsistence income from the minifundia, the remainder being wage laborers and unemployed.[57] The Chilean road to socialism unfortunately never reached a second land reform and the coup d'etat reminds us how central the question of power is if a process of transition to socialism is to be initiated.

CONCLUSIONS

Allende's agrarian reform must now be seen from the viewpoint of the failure of Popular Unity to capture power in the revolutionary struggle. In this final part of the chapter we shall not focus on the remarkable achievements of Popular Unity in the agrarian sector, such as the great rise in the peasant standard of living, the upsurge of peasant power and participation in society, the expropriation of all latifundia, and a dramatic growth in the peasants' class consciousness, but concentrate on the limitations of its agrarian policy in relation to the political struggle in the countryside. We maintain, and hope to have shown in the paper, that Popular Unity could have increased the revolutionary mobilization of the peasantry and also weakened the counterrevolutionary power of the rural bourgeoisie more than it did. However, we are not saying that if a greater revolutionary stronghold could have been fostered in the countryside, this by itself would have been sufficient to swing the balance of forces towards the revolutionary side in the capture of power in the whole of society. Nevertheless, it may have meant that the present class struggle could have been carried out on a more favorable basis for the revolutionary forces.

We have mentioned in the second part of this paper how a new phase of peasant mobilization and consciousness erupted as soon as Popular Unity was elected. The large number of farm seizures shows the revolutionary fervor of the peasantry. The multiplication of solidarity strikes is also evidence of radicalization. Although the government did not support or encourage land seizures, it was due to the peasant movement, which was pressing further ahead than the government was willing to concede at that stage, that the government was forced to speed up the expropriation process giving the death kiss to the traditional latifundia. A similar situation happened with regard to the constitution of peasant councils: The peasant base demanded a less bureaucratic formation by pressurizing for the incorporation of the nonorganized peasantry. The government acceded to this demand because it helped lessen the influence of Christian Democrat dominated peasant councils, but it did not give in to those demands for greater economic, and, above all, political power. The government was afraid that such peasant councils might gain a revolutionary independence from the government and radicalize too much and too quickly the rural struggle. It should also be pointed out that half of the tomas occurred on farms smaller than 80 HRB, the limit below which the government intended not to expropriate. Again peasant pressure brought about a partial change in Popular Unity's agrarian policy on this point. By mid-1972 it started expropriating farms between 40 to 80 HRB, but only those that were badly managed or that had particularly bad labor relations.

If we analyze the class composition of the peasantry who were in the forefront of the revolutionary class struggle, we observe that it tended to be the more proletarian elements (as opposed to petty bourgeois) of the peasantry, such as the voluntarios, the rural wage laborers, and the afuerinos. However, Popular Unity did not succeed in incorporating these proletarian sectors as much as it could have done into the unions, councils, and the reformed sector, as data indicates that rural wage laborers and afuerinos were particularly underrepresented in these institutions, thus arresting a further radicalization of the process. There certainly were some objective constraints that could not be removed and pushed the reformed sector towards acquiring a petty bourgeois character. However, some of these petty bourgeois tendencies (which we described in the third part of this chapter) need not have arisen if Popular Unity had implemented different policies.

Only macroeconomic policies of a socialistic type coupled with the constant mobilization and organization of the peasantry, particularly of its proletarian elements, towards socialist goals could have reversed the trend towards petty bourgeois behavior by the reformed peasantry and further weakened the rural bourgeoisie. [58] Such policies would have replaced the private marketing system by a state system for most important agricultural products, and would have limited the black market, withdrawing one of the main factors that accounted for the expansion of the peasant economy to the detriment of the collective economy in the reformed sector, and would have prevented the rural bourgeoisie from capturing part of the reformed sector's surplus. A taxation system could have been introduced to capture the differential rent arising from different productive capacities. The additional tax income derived could have been used to finance investments in depressed rural areas. As for microeconomic policies, an incentive for working on the collective land could have been introduced and was beginning to be introduced on an experimental basis in some reformed units by early 1973. This incentive scheme related wages to the individual and/or group work effort and to output. [59]

With regard to peasant mobilization, the Popular Unity parties should have changed their attitude towards tomas, that is, they should have organized and conducted the seizure of estates. In doing so they could have incorporated to a much greater extent the proletarian groups into the expropriation process, thus strengthening the forces favoring collectives. Such a mobilization policy could have led to a socialized reformed sector, as land for viable peasant units would not have been sufficient and the peasants would have had to rely exclusively on the collective enterprise, a fact that would have been favored by the proletarian elements. Although such a reformed sector without a petty bourgeois peasant character might not have become a socialist vanguard, at least it would not have grown into a rural capitalist sector, providing future fertile ground for the antisocialist forces.

Thus we would finally conclude that through the political mobilization of the proletarian groups within the peasantry, Popular Unity could have achieved the following situation that would have greatly strengthened the revolutionary forces. First, it would have further weakened the rural bourgeoisie by expropriating not only the latifundistas, but also the new rural bourgeoisie, which, as we have described, had doubled in size and increased in power because of the type of land reform that had been carried out, particularly during the Christian Democrat period. Second, a more collective type of reformed sector would have emerged and the potential threat of the reformed sector moving into the opposition camp of the bourgeoisie would have been eliminated. Finally, peasant councils could have become an effective revolutionary organization of the peasantry in the struggle against the new rural bourgeoisie and for a more collective reformed sector.

Although we do not fully analyze the objective limitations that Popular Unity would have faced in implementing the above-mentioned

policies, they should be borne in mind.   One of the consequences
would certainly have been to intensify the class conflict.   We would
also agree that the class struggle in the rural sector had to be subordinated to the general class struggle in the country, particularly in
Chile where the urban proletariat was in the forefront of the revolutionary struggle. [60]   (Less than a quarter of the active population
is engaged in the rural sector that produces only one-tenth of Chile's
gross national product.)   Therefore, any agrarian policy pursued by
Popular Unity had to be subordinated to the problem of the revolutionary
strategy and tactics to gain power and the necessary class alliances.
We have not tackled these essential problems here but it is our con-
tention that a more radical agrarian policy could have been implemented.
That this was not the case was largely the result of different strategies
and tactics to capture state power within the Popular Unity coalition
itself.   This lead to different analyses of the correlation of forces in
the countryside, that is, with whom it was possible to form a tactical
alliance and who was the class enemy.   It also meant disagreements
over the relative importance to be attached to the different peasant
organizations—unions, councils—and their composition and function,
disagreements over forms of peasant participation and mobilization,
disagreements over the organization of the reformed sector and over
the nature of the new agrarian reform law. [61]   These and other differences amongst Popular Unity (or in other words the absence of a
unified revolutionary party) were the factors that led to the victory
of the counterrevolutionary forces. [62]

Some of the increasing difficulties of Popular Unity's electoral
road to socialism and its contradictions could have been predicted.
Popular Unity could only obtain an overall electoral majority (with
which it would have gained control over congress but not yet hegemonic control of the state) by winning the support of a large section
of the middle classes.   To facilitate this, the economy needed to
grow at such a rate as to enable middle class incomes to expand or
at least prevent their deterioration.   The deterioration of the economy
during the last year of the Popular Unity administration (increasing
shortages and spiraling inflation) did not enable Popular Unity to
buy off the middle class with financial benefits.   Economic policy
makers could have predicted that production on the reformed sector
was likely to fall in the short run, until a certain level of capitaliza-
tion and reorganization was achieved.   Instead the Popular Unity
economic policy makers greatly underestimated the upheaval in
production that a drastic agrarian reform attempted within the limitations of the existing Christian Democrat land reform legislation
meant. [63]   This gave the middle classes economic as well as political
reasons for opposing the Popular Unity government, thereby blocking
the democratic road to socialism.

Another factor that Popular Unity did not consider in its policy
was the survival of the economic base of the rural capitalists.   The

expropriated agrarian bourgeoisie transfered its capital towards the distribution of agricultural supplies and provision of services, the marketing of agricultural products, and the creation of agroindustries. With the emergence of the black market, large profits could be obtained through speculative activities. Thus the expropriation of the land of part of the agrarian bourgeoisie did not totally curtail their economic power, as this was displaced to new speculative ventures in the rural sector. This agrarian bourgeoisie was active politically in sustaining the trucker's strikes (besides, of course, the CIA) which not only crippled the distribution of inputs to the reformed sector but led to the overthrow of Allende's government. This shows that the rural capitalists could still use their economic power to undermine the economic policies of the Popular Unity government and launch subversive activities.

A further difficulty that Popular Unity encountered was, as we have already analyzed, that the social relations of production were not automatically transformed with the expropriation of the latifundia in the reformed sector. Under conditions of speculative capitalism, and without having hegemonic control over the state, it became virtually impossible to develop the nationalized sector on socialist principles. On the contrary, in the reformed sector new capitalist relations of production became entrenched as analyzed in section three. The policies of Popular Unity often had the opposite effect of what was intended.

In order to solve the above-mentioned contradictions it was crucial for Popular Unity to take the initiative with regard to the question of power. However, it failed to do so even when faced with the open subversion of the bourgeoisie and sectors of the armed forces. In actual fact the Popular Unity government opposed the tomas, as we analyzed in the second section, instead of supporting and guiding this spectacular upsurge in the political mobilization of farm workers in the expropriation of the estates and around wider political goals, such as the fight against the speculative and subversive rural capitalists and ultimately for the seizure of power. Political demobilization set in after the initial phase of expropriations was over by mid-1972.

The shortcomings of the Popular Unity agrarian policy led to a series of contradictions which contributed to its overthrow. The vast seizure of estates by the peasants forced Popular Unity to accelerate expropriations under legally unfavorable circumstances. As a result agricultural production diminished substantially, contributing overwhelmingly to the general economic crisis. It thereby alienated the middle-class vote it had set out to win in order to make the democratic road to socialism viable. Popular Unity also failed to capitalize on the vast political mobilization of the peasantry insofar as the question of power was concerned. Furthermore, the rural bourgeoisie established links with the reformed sector that, together with the development of speculative capitalism, encouraged the spread of peasant capitalism in this sector, undermining its socialist purpose. Instead of seizing power to resolve some of these contradictions, the Popular Unity government reaffirmed its faith in the Chilean democracy (including the armed forces), when the opposition parties together with sections of the armed forces were organizing not only the overthrow of Allende's government but democracy itself. [64] However there is no guarantee that a unified revolutionary party would have been successful in capturing power, although the chances would have been more favorable. The purpose of this chapter, as already mentioned, is not to condemn Popular Unity but to draw some lessons from this frustrated revolutionary process. Our intention has been limited to highlighting some of the contradictions of the Popular Unity agrarian policy and above all to illustrate that the objective conditions prevailing in the Chilean rural sector contained greater revolutionary potential than Popular Unity brought to the fore.

NOTES

1. Eduardo Frei, "Proyecto de Ley de la Reforma Agraria propuesto por S. E. el Presidente de la Republica al H. Congreso Nacional," El Mercurio (Santiago: El Mercurio, November 22, 1965).

2. Corporacion de la Reforma Agraria, "Expropriaciones desde 1965 al 31- XI- 1970," Boletin Estadistico, mimeographed (Santiago, 1970).

3. ICIRA, Instituto de Capacitacion e Investigacion en Reforma Agraria, Diagnostico de la Reforma Agraria Chilena, Noviembre 1970 - Junio 1972, Report by ICIRA to the Minister of Agriculture, (Santiago, 1972).

4. Jorge Echenique, "Las Expropiaciones y la Organizacion de Asentamientos en el Periodo 1965-70" in David Alaluf et al., Reforma Agraria Chilena: Seis Ensayos de Interpretacion, ICIRA, (Santiago, 1970).

5. Solon Barraclough, "Reforma Agraria: Historia y Perspectivas," Cuadernos de la Realidad Nacional 7 (Santiago, March 1971): 57; and see also Silvia Hernandez, "El Desarrollo Capitalista del Campo Chileno," Sociedad y Desarrollo 3 CESO (Santiago, July-September 1972): 35-38.

6. FEES, Fondo de Extension y Educacion Sindical, "Afiliacion Sindical por Federaciones y Provincias," mimeographed, (Santiago, 1973).

7. Almino Affonso et al., Movimiento Campesino Chileno, 2 vols. (Santiago: ICIRA, 1970), p. 161.

8. Wayne Ringlien, "Economic Effects of Chilean National Expropriation Policy on the Private Commercial Farm Sector, 1964-69" (Ph.D. diss., University of Maryland, 1971), pp. 13-47, 110-43.

9. P. Winn and C. Kay, "Agrarian Reform and Rural Revolution in Allende's Chile," Journal of Latin American Studies 6, pt. 1 (May 1974): 138.

10. "The Popular Unity Programme" in Salvador Allende, Chile's Road to Socialism (Harmondsworth, England: Penguin, 1974); and particularly "The Twenty Basic Points of the Popular Unity Government's Agrarian Reform" in Ann Zammit, ed., The Chilean Road to Socialism (Brighton, England: Institute of Development Studies at Sussex University, 1973): 281-84.

11. Jacques Chonchol, "La Politica Agricola en una Economia de Transicion al Socialismo. El Caso Chileno," in Gonzalo Martner, ed., El Pensamiento Economico del Gobierno de Allende (Santiago: Editorial Universitaria, 1971), pp. 217-44. Rene Billaz and Eugenio Maffei, "La Reforma Agraria Chilena y el Camino al Socialismo: Algunas Consideraciones," Cuadernos de la Realidad Nacional 11 (Santiago, January 1972).

12. For a good exposition of Popular Unity's agrarian objectives, see Chonchol, op. cit.

13. For a good discussion on the capitalist nature of land reforms in Latin America, see Michel Gutelman, "Reforma Agraria y Desarrollo del Capitalismo" and Ruy Mauro Marini, "La Reforma Agraria en America Latina," both articles in Transicion al Socialismo y Experiencia Chilena, CESO-CEREN, PLA, (Santiago, 1972).

14. For the best analysis of the peasant movement in Chile under the Frei government see Affonso et al., op. cit.

15. Juan Carlos Marin, "Las Tomas, 1970-72," Marxismo y Revolucion 1 (Santiago, July-September 1973): 49-78.

16. FEES, op. cit.; S. Barraclough and A. Affonso, "Diagnostico de la Reforma Agraria Chilena," Cuadernos de la Realidad Nacional 16 (Santiago, April 1973): 112-15.

17. Emilio Klein, "Antecedentes para el Estudio de Conflictos Colectivos en el Campo 1967-1971," mimeographed, ICIRA (Santiago, 1972), p. 6.

18. Jacques Chonchol, "The Agrarian Policy of the Popular Unity Government," in Zammit, ed., op. cit., p. 108.

19. Klein, op. cit., for the data and evidence of the qualitative change of tomas.

20. Marin, op. cit., pp. 63-65.

21. Klein, op. cit., p. 11.

22. Marin, op. cit., pp. 69-77.

23. Zammit, ed., op. cit., pp. 129-30.

24. Solon Barraclough, "The Structure and Problems of the Chilean Agrarian Sector," in Zammit, op. cit., pp. 115-22.

25. Jose Bengoa, "Movilizacion Campesina: Analisis y Perspectivas," Sociedad y Desarrollo 3 CESO, (Santiago, July-September 1972), pp. 57-76.

26.   Cristobal Kay, "La Participacion Campesina en el Gobierno de la Unidad Popular, " Revista Mexicana de Sociologia 36, no. 2, (1974); and Republica de Chile, "Decreto 481 que Crea Consejos Campesinos, " mimeographed, CORA (Santiago, 1971).

27.   David Lehmann, "Agrarian Reform in Chile: 1965-1972, An Essay in Contradictions, " in D. Lehmann, ed. Agrarian Reform and Agrarian Reformism (London: Faber and Faber, 1974), pp. 96-106.

28.   Sergio Gomez and Emilio Klein, "Informe Sobre el Estado Actual de los Consejos Comunales Campesinos, " mimeographed, ICIRA (Santiago, April 1972).

29.   Eugenio Maffei and Emilio Marchetti, "Estructura Agraria y Consejos Comunales Campesinos: Situacion Actual, Analisis y Estrategia, " Cuadernos de la Realidad Nacional 14 (Santiago, October 1972): 126-51.

30.   Sergio Gomez, "El Rol del Sector Agricola y la Estructura de Clases en Chile, " Sociedad y Desarrollo 3, CESO (Santiato, July-September 1972): 80-89.

31.   Wilson Cantoni, "Poder Campesino, " mimeographed, FEES (Santiago, 1971); and W. Cantoni, "Poder Popular en el Agro Chileno, " Cuadernos de la Realidad Nacional 11 (Santiago, January 1972), pp. 80-103.

32.   Maffei and Marchetti, op. cit., pp. 138, 146.

33.   On the problems facing consejos campesinos see Chonchol, "La Reforma Agraria y la Experiencia Chilena, " in CESO-CEREN, eds., Transicion al Socialismo y Experiencia Chilena (Santiago: Prensa Latinoamericana, 1972), see pp. 158-59.

34.   On the CERA, see "Organizacion Transitoria de la Nueva Area de la Reforma Agraria: Los Centros de Reforma Agraria" mimeographed, CORA (Santiago, 1971).

35.   Eugenio Maffei, "Los Centros de Produccion y la Buro-cracia del Agro: Problemas y Analisis" mimeographed, ICIRA (Santiago, February 1973).

36.   E. Maffei and E. Marchetti, "Pre-informe sobre Interven-ciones en el Sector Agrario" (Santiago: ICIRA, June 1972). "Interven-ciones y Conflictos en el Sector Rural" (Santiago: ICIRA 1972).

37.   ICIRA, Diagnostico. . ., op. cit.; and Michel Langand, "El Sector Reformado: ? Area Social de la Agricultura?", Revista Agraria 2 (Santiago, January 1973), Supplement of Chile Hoy weekly magazine, CEA (Centro de Estudios Agrarios), pp. 3-4.

38.   Maffei, "Los Centros, " op. cit., pp. 31-35.

39.   Lehmann, "Agrarian Reform in Chile, " op. cit., pp. 90-97.

40.   Omar Brevis, coordinator of project "Proyecto Analisis de las Unidades Reformadas en la IV Zona de Reforma Agraria (Estudio de Casos), " mimeographed, ICIRA (Santiago, 1972). See also Michel Langand and Alberto Pena, "Relaciones de Produccion en un Sector de Comuna, " mimeographed, ICIRA (Santiago, June 1973).

41. Lehmann, "La Agricultura Chilena y el Periodo de Transicion, " Sociedad y Desarrollo 3, CESO (Santiago, July-September 1972), pp. 133-34.

42. Langand and Pena, op. cit. and Salvador Allende, Tercer Mensaje del Presidente Allende ante el Congress Pleno (Santiago: Presidencia de la Republica, 1973), p. 282.

43. ICIRA, Diagnostico, op. cit., chapter 3.

44. On the discussion of pricing and rationing see Lehmann, "La Agricultura, " op. cit., pp. 103-09, 122-27.

45. Lehmann, "Agrarian Reform in Chile, " op. cit.

46. World Bank, Special Report on the Chilean Economic Outlook, 1974, Statistical Appendix, Table 7.1.

47. World Bank, op. cit., Statistical Appendix, Table 7.2.

48. For a conceptualization of hacienda system see chapter 1 of C. Kay, Comparative Development of the European Manorial System and the Latin American Hacienda System: A Theory of Agrarian Change for Chile (Ph.D. diss., University of Sussex, 1971). For a more concise characterization of the hacienda or manorial system see C. Kay, "Comparative Development of the European Manorial System and the Latin American Hacienda System, " Journal of Peasant Studies 2, no. 1 (October, 1974).

49. For an historical periodization of the Chilean hacienda system see C. Kay, "The Development of the Chilean Hacienda System 1850's-1973" in Landlord and Peasant in Latin America and the Caribbean, eds. K. Duncan et al. (London: Cambridge University Press, [forthcoming]).

50. For a study of landlords organizations during the Frei administration see Sergio Gomez, Los Empresarios Agricolas ICIRA (Santiago, 1972).

51. James Petras and Hugo Zemelman, Peasants in Revolt: A Chilean Case Study, 1965-1971 (Austin: University of Texas Press, 1972), p. xii.

52. Field interviews carried out by Cristobal Kay and Peter Winn in the El Monte and Melipilla area during the period of the Millahuin conflict in 1972. Also private communication by Ian Roxborough who undertook extensive field research in that area during the Millahuin conflict period. See also I. Roxborough, "The Political Mobilization of Farm Workers during the Chilean Agrarian Reform" (Ph.D. diss., University of Wisconsin, in progress).

53. On the emergence of the new rural bourgeoisie and its political implications see Gonzalo Arroyo, "Despues del Latifundio: Que?", Mensaje 113 (Santiago, October, 1972): 591-99.

54. Solon Barraclough and Almino Affonso, "Diagnostico de la Reforma Agraria Chilena, " Cuadernos de la Realidad Nacional 16, CEREN (Santiago, April 1973): 77-82.

55. Gomez, Los Empresarios, op. cit., pp. 33-52.

56. Langand and Pena, "Relaciones, " op. cit., pp. 39-40, and O. Brevis "Proyecto, " op. cit.

57. Barraclough and Affonso, "Diagnostico de la Reforma, " op. cit., pp. 77-81.

58. For suggestions on what Popular Unity's new agrarian economic policy could have been, see Jaime Crispi and Vicente Garces, "Consideraciones acerca de una Nueva Politica Economica Agraria para la Fase Actual del Proceso Revolucionario Chileno, " Cuadernos de la Realidad Nacional 17 (Santiago, June 1973); and for advice to the Minister of Agriculture see ICIRA, "Diagnostico, " op. cit., chapters 7 and 8.

59. Oficina de Planificacion Agricola (ODEPA), "Sistema de Gestion Predial para el Area Reformada, " mimeographed, (Santiago, 1973); ODEPA, "Algunas Experiencias de Aplicacion de los Criterios Basicos del Sistema de Gestion Predial, " mimeographed (Santiago, 1973).

60. For an analysis of the dependent role of the peasantry in the transformation of society see Barrington Moore, Social Origins of Dictatorship and Democracy: Lord and Peasant in the Making of the Modern World (Harmondsworth, England: Penguin, 1967); Eric Wolf, Peasant Wars of the Twentieth Century (London: Faber and Faber, 1971); V. I. Lenin, The Development of Capitalism in Russia (Moscow: Progress Publishers, 1964); and Karl Marx, Eighteenth Brumaire of Louis Bonaparte (Moscow: Progress Publishers, 1967). For the Chilean case see E. Klein, "Tipos de Dependencia y Obreros Agricolas en Chile, " Boletin de Estudios Latino-americanos y del Caribe, no. 16, (June 1974): 16-27.

61. Ian Roxborough, "Agrarian Policy in the Popular Unity Government, " Institute of Latin American Studies Occasional Paper, no. 14 (Glasgow: University of Glasgow, 1974).

62. For an analysis of Popular Unity's strategy to power, see Sweezy's article "Chile: The Question of Power" in P. M. Sweezy and H. Magdoff, eds., Revolution and Counter-Revolution in Chile (New York: Monthly Review Press, 1974), pp. 11-21.

63. The failure to foresee the drop in agricultural output and to grasp the wider political and economic consequences of the agrarian crisis by high level Popular Unity government economic policy makers can be ascertained in various articles written by them in, for example, Zammit, ed., op. cit.

64. Cristobal Kay, "Chile: The Making of a Coup d'Etat, " Science and Society 39, no. 1, (Spring 1975).

**IDEOLOGY AND CULTURE
UNDER POPULAR UNITY**
Mike Gonzalez

When Allende came to the presidency in 1970, he faced a cultural system dominated by a small sector of the bourgeoisie. The men who owned industry, or who administered it on behalf of foreign capital, also owned or administered the mass media—the press, television, radio, the commercial theater, the schools of art, etc. [1] In Article 40, the program of Popular Unity (UP) acknowledged that the class struggle would be fought out in the field of culture just as it was on the heights of the economy. The expropriation by the state of the system of production was no more urgent than the need to return to the exploited masses their dominion over their everyday life; after all, the self-consciousness of the working classes must begin by asserting in practice the totality of social relations. The role of bourgeois ideology, on the other hand, is to fragment that totality into a series of disconnected and self-sufficient universes; it is no coincidence that the same U. S. capital that exploited the natural resources of Chile, as well as the rest of Latin America, has also made the means of ideological and cultural control an important area of investment throughout the continent. [2]

The appearance of the three years of UP is one of intense and sustained activity in every field of culture. The theater left the proscenium arch and went into the fields and the factories; the easels were abandoned for the walls of the shantytowns where the anonymous brigadas painted the slogans and images of the political process. The new magazines of the Left debated the transition to socialism, and workers and peasants appeared for the first time on television screens. That is one side of the picture. Yet the bourgeoisie remained firmly in control of the most important means of mass communication—dominating the instruments of hegemony. [3] And that domination was never systematically challenged by Popular Unity—despite Article 40 of its program. It was only the action of workers, without government support, that extended popular control over the mass media

(the takeover of Channel 9, for example). Throughout the three years
El Mercurio, the voice of the Right, sustained its daily defamation of
UP and provided an important focus of regroupment and cohesion for
the bourgeoisie. The Right certainly recognized the significance of
ideology in the class struggle, and organized accordingly; the Left,
on the other hand, never recognized the extent to which advances
at the level of production (the experience of occupation, of popular
power) could be neutralized, or at best confused, at the level of
ideology, and in the course of everyday life. [4] It is this contradiction
that must provide the starting point for the analysis of culture under
Popular Unity.

CULTURE AND THE UP PROGRAM

   The UP program envisaged the capture of one part of the state
apparatus–the executive. With massive popular support the transition
to socialism could then begin from within the state machine. In
practice, the first phase of the implementation of the program involved
drawing large sectors of the dispossessed masses into the economy.
But from the outset, the most important question within the UP coalition was who should be the principal protagonist of this transition
towards socialism. Was it to be the Allende government, the state,
or was it to be the working class with its allies in the countryside
and the shantytowns? In practice, UP's response was ambiguous.
At this stage, the protagonist was to be a coalition of antiimperialist,
antimonopolist forces (see Chapter 7); the struggle would center upon
winning the uncommitted sectors–the capas medias–whose frustration
and impotence under previous regimes provided a fertile field for the
politics of UP.
   The consequences of this perception at the economic level are
considered elsewhere in this volume. The central ideological question,
however, was this: which social forces would be dominant, ideologically, within the coalition–whose interests and whose historical
project would determine the pace and character of the transition?
For if Popular Unity was the representative of the working classes,
and if its program was a preparation for the seizure of power by those
classes, then its task was to actively encourage and initiate the
creation of the appropriate conditions. As far as the middle sectors
were concerned, they would be drawn towards socialism on the basis
of clear alternatives–a bourgeois society, albeit a reformed one, on
the one hand and a socialist society on the other. In the period of
transition, the self-activity of the exploited classes required, too,
the determined development of a class consciousness–an understanding
of the nature of the enemy, the growth of the seeds of a new culture,
preparing for the creation of the new social relations of production:

> . . . we should in no way see our educational objectives
> to be the creation, under laboratory conditions, of the
> harmonious communard during this extremely disharmonious
> transitional phase of society. Such an objective would
> be pitiful and puerile utopianism. We want to create
> fighters who will be the guardians and successors of
> the historical revolutionary traditions that we have not
> yet completely fulfilled. [5]

The first step, however, would necessarily be a challenge to bourgeois domination over the means of ideological production—the expropriation of the instruments of ideology—and a sustained program of reeducation, developing socialist consciousness in an epoch of class struggle— the expropriation of the content of ideology. In the event, neither was actually carried out. The lack of any organized expression of the struggle of the working class at the level of ideology left the field open to the bourgeoisie to develop and extend its definitions of everyday life, its dominion over the organization of consciousness. Thus its temporary loss of control over the means of coercion and repression—the state—left it nonetheless, at this crucial point of crisis, in control of "civil society." And from there it organized and initiated its assault upon UP and the reassertion of bourgeois control over the other institutions of the state.

Given its electoral orientation, the leadership of UP clearly saw its initial acts as ways of winning support. Its first economic measures set out to raise living standards by extending consumption; the benefits of socialism were experienced in the first place, then, at the level of consumption in strictly quantitative terms. In the same way, UP's cultural program envisaged a democratization of culture, extending the availability of ideological messages to new and broader sectors of Chilean society. The irony was that this very process of democratization, because it was not accompanied by any qualitative assault upon the content of those messages, enabled the Right to extend the scope of its counterattack. In the end, democrati- zation was a criterion at the level of consumption, but not at the level of politics. The conviction that a rising standard of living, coupled with state control over the key areas of the economy, would slow automatically into a transition to socialism, therefore found its most glaring contradiction at the level of ideology and culture. For while the pattern of distribution of ideological messages may have changed, the pattern of production did not. In an era of sharpening class struggle, then, culture and consciousness—the organization of everyday life—were deemed to lie outside the class struggle. The clearest evidence of this is the Statute of Guarantees, signed by Allende in exchange for right-wing support in Congress before he reached the presidency; for what that document guaranteed was pre- cisely continuing bourgeois control over education, the mass media, the armed forces, etc.

UP cultural policy (to the extent that it was ever formulated as conscious policy) rested squarely on the criteria of distribution, of the market. Where it did intervene (by publishing new magazines, for example) it accepted the concept of diffuse and distinct publics, each with a separate universe, which determined bourgeois policy towards mass communication. In quite specific terms, this was a direct abrogation of the concept of a totality which had to underpin any socialist policy on ideology and culture. It was this which enabled the Right to take advantage of UP cultural policy; the criteria elaborated by UP in no way contradicted the decision to popularize cultural activity, and thus effectively to extend ideological control, which had been taken by the government of Eduardo Frei. For its plan, too, had been to extend consumption and incorporate in this way whole new layers of the population. [6] What was involved was a populist perspective, drawing increasing numbers of people into the area of bourgeois ideology by denying its class character and stressing its universality. The bourgeois offensive at the ideological level began, as soon as Allende had taken power, by asserting the validity of those universal truths against the partiality of Popular Unity's rhetoric. The bourgeoisie, with El Mercurio at its head, became the champion of democracy and the guardian of the classless concepts of bourgeois democracy. The ambiguity of UP's own position, its appeals to the people, the masses, the nation, both obfuscated the development of a class consciousness among the working class and its allies, and provided the bourgeoisie with the ideological instruments which had been, historically, the patrimony of the bourgeoisie, and which were thus easily and rapidly appropriated, or rather reappropriated by it. [7] In the field of ideology the struggle was waged in terms of a war over the use of identical concepts—people, nation, masses—concepts which clearly expressed the hegemony of the middle sectors within Popular Unity and the postponement of the development of socialist consciousness until some later stage, presumably when UP's electoral majority was assured. Government and opposition, then, both sought to conceal or deny their class character and assert their proprietorship over the democratic language of the petty bourgeoisie. The battle thus became a matter of logistics rather than politics; furthermore, the struggle was located in the market, and not in production where class contradictions were experienced as a qualitative distinction (worker v. capitalist). In the arenas of consumption all distinctions are quantitative; some are more and some are less—but this is presented as an individual, not a collective question. By locating the ideological struggle there, Popular Unity ensured that it would always be at a disadvantage, for control over the means of ideological production remained in the hands of the bourgeoisie.

The attempt to reform the capitalist system through its own instruments had immediate and ultimately tragic consequences in the field of culture. While the monopolies and the key areas of foreign

domination in the economy were expropriated, the monopoly over the
cultural system remained sacrosanct. Thus Edwards, Yarur, and the
other members of the monopoly groups, were able to continue and
extend the class war, the assault by the bourgeoisie upon Popular
Unity, from the redoubt of the mass media, the press, and the ideological system as a whole. Popular Unity itself did not, could not,
challenge the ideological hegemony of the bourgeoisie. Where such
a challenge was mounted, it was precisely at those moments when
the working class itself drew the ideological struggle out of the
market and into the organizations of the class at the level of production—when the working class forged its own ideological instruments
in the cordones and comandos comunales.

Middle Sectors, Popular Culture, and
Socialist Consciousness

It is a well-known dictum that the ruling ideas in each historical
epoch are those of the materially dominant class. [8] Where that domination is challenged, or where there is a crisis in the domination of a
class divided against itself, these ideas also enter into crisis. The
germs of working-class consciousness both reflect and contribute
to that crisis. The essential element of such a "crisis of hegemony"
(the term is A. Gramsci's) is the incapacity of the state to govern on
behalf of the whole bourgeoisie; factions of the dominant class
appropriate different elements of the dominant ideology, just as they
defend their partial interests from points of retrenchment in different
parts of the economy. Between 1964 and 1970, but particularly after
1968, for example, the reactionary project of the landed oligarchy
appeared to come into direct conflict with the reformism of Frei and
the PDC. The failure to implement the reform of Chilean capitalism,
however, brought bourgeois ideology as a whole into question, and
UP seized the resulting crisis by the horns.

The electoral strategy that dominated the UP coalition, however,
determined the way in which the coalition perceived its own social
base. In quantitative terms the uncommitted middle sectors were the
determining factor; had the question been posed in qualitative terms,
as a struggle between alternative class perspectives, then the working class would have been seen to occupy the center of the historical
stage, and to have the initiative in the bourgeoisie's moment of
crisis. But it was not. The democratic language of UP reflected the
ideological domination within the coalition of those sectors whose
interests would be better served by the achievement of national independence than by the overthrow of bourgeois society. [9] The language
of antiimperialism was not antibourgeois as such. It was aimed
clearly at the petty bourgeoisie, whose fundamental class experience
is that of a dispossessed sector within the bourgeois bloc, and whose

project is the extension of power within that bloc. Since they were
the key to electoral victory, Popular Unity limited its ideological
demands to the appeal for democracy, representing directly a petty
bourgeoisie caught within the state machine and the managerial and
professional classes and fraught with frustration and a sense of
impotence which the Frei regime had merely exacerbated by compro-
mising with the oligarchy after promising a democratization of the
political system. Thus the central rhetoric of UP concerned participation, democratic control, democratic freedom, and so on.[10] We
shall see how useful an instrument for the bourgeoisie were these
freedoms, and how significant a victory was the Statute of Guarantees
which Allende signed prior to assuming power.

What was the alternative? By concentrating its attention on
the economy alone, UP implicitly accepted a definition of man as
homo oeconomicus and restricted its intervention in the struggle to
the economic field. This fundamental misunderstanding of the nature
of political economy[11] left social man to be defined by the hegemonic
ideology—the bourgeois. For what was at issue was the transition,
from practice (mere behavior) to praxis (conscious purposive action),
of the working class. This fundamental confusion made the leaders,
the actors, in the field of ideology not the working class but the
radicalized petty bourgeois intelligentsia, acting apparently on behalf
of the exploited classes, but in fact in terms of their own interests
which temporarily coincided with those of the working class in a
common struggle to conquer and consolidate the democratic freedoms;
the difference, of course, was that for the petty bourgeoisie, those
freedoms were the end, for the working class movement no more than
an instrument in the transition to socialism and the struggle for
power.[12] UP argued, quite correctly, that even these freedoms had
never existed in Chile; it was precisely on that basis that the tactical
alliance that was UP could be built around a minimum program of
demands that were common to the reformists and the revolutionary
sectors. The distinction came at the level of strategy—and as the
prerevolutionary crisis developed under UP, the bifurcation of the
via chilena and the revolutionary process came during the October
crisis of 1972.

The first half of the UP period has to be seen in terms of subsequent developments; it was a period during which both Right and
Left prepared for the confrontation to come. While UP had conquered
the executive, the bourgeoisie took refuge in the other institutions
of the state apparatus where its ideological predominance had been
assured by the Statute of Guarantees. In Congress, the judiciary,
the army, and the ideological apparatus of the state, the bourgeoisie
began the regroupment of its forces. The fact that UP took no account
of the class struggle except at the level of production enabled that
regroupment to be carried through with impunity. The result was that
the hegemonic ideological expression within UP was economism—a

theory which sees socialism as the result of a redistribution of income
such that capitalism will not be overthrown so much as undermined. [13]
For the working class, the ideological development was towards consumer and trade union consciousness; that is why the government
continually emphasized that the leading organizations in the process
were the trade unions. At one stage, this was undoubtedly correct;
the ambiguity became manifest, however, in October 1972, when UP
completely failed to take its lead from the embryonic organizational
expressions of class consciousness—cordones and comandos
comunales—but instead coincided with the bourgeoisie on the primacy
of the traditional organizations of the class whose political expression
was the state itself.

If the objective was the transition to socialism, then the issue
during the prerevolutionary period was to use the time to establish
and build the consciousness of the class, to prepare the working
class to assume its dynamic historical role in the overthrow of
capitalist society. Each tactical victory had to be assessed and
used in that light. The elections of 1970 opened up a possibility of
winning large sections of the working class to revolutionary socialism.
But socialism and class consciousness are not merely the result of
improved material conditions:

> No, we must help the masses through their vanguard
> elements to examine their way of life, to think about it
> critically, to understand the need for change and to
> firmly want to change it. . . . The fact of the matter
> is that between the vague sense of community and the
> determination to consciously reconstruct the mode of
> life is an enormously long historical road. [14]

The struggle must be systematically carried out at every level, not
only in the factories but also in everyday life where capitalist relations
of production are maintained and reaffirmed. A revolutionary perspective demands that the idea of the fragmentation of the bourgeois world
(the division of each area of social activity into a separate universe
with its own historical logic, and the atomization of social classes
into a mass of individuals innately distinct and with nothing more
than accidental common interests) be opposed by a socialist perspective where the various areas of social activity are seen to be governed
by the same structural imperative within the system—the maintenance
of the social relations of capitalism.

UP was not, of course, in a position to develop its hegemony
from the weak fortress of the executive. The essential point was to
what extent it was consciously engaged in a struggle for hegemony.
Clearly the struggle was already under way at the end of 1970; UP's
task then was to arm the working class for that struggle in every
field, to drive a wedge into bourgeois dominance and take full advan-

tage of its tactical superiority at that point. What did this mean in practice? In a bourgeois culture, the characteristic role of the working class is a passive, consumer role. It receives ideological messages produced by the ideological apparatus of the state, which are in their turn the property of a bourgeoisie whose role, in Latin America, is to transmit the cultural values and definitions of the metropolitan bourgeoisie–the hegemonic class. [15] The pattern of ownership and control of the mass media in Latin America is sufficient evidence of the source of the message. But crucial to a socialist program for culture is a clear view of the significance of the relationship between producer and consumer that characterizes cultural activity under capitalism–and a program for changing it. It is important not only for the working class to know, but also to act upon that knowledge. The failure to understand that distinction is at the roots of UP's failure to develop the self-consciousness of the working class.

The official policy of UP was based on the acceptance of bourgeois freedoms–freedom of expression, freedom of the press, etc. This left the initiative firmly in the hands of the bourgeoisie, not only because these freedoms were the historic expression of the bourgeoisie's own struggle for hegemony, but because those freedoms have to be set in a context of power. Freedom of the press in a situation where the bourgeoisie holds monopoly control over the press and the mass media is a concession, and a crucial one, to the bourgeoisie. UP recognized this, but its solution was to compete (unequally) with the bourgeoisie on its own ground. It sought to build a presence within the pluralist universe of bourgeois ideology–worked within the fragmentation of everyday life that corresponds to the vision of the bourgeoisie. But it failed to attack the relationship between producer and consumer in the field of culture. The magazines of the Left were simply the obverse of the right-wing journals; but their method of capturing audiences still derived from the market entertainment value, specialist appeal, and so on. On strange ground, it was bound to lose.

The central question, however, is whether consciousness and ideology are seen as elements of a total political activity of the class, or rather as a special and distinct area of activity with its own rules and development. The answer to that question will determine whether the historical actor in the field of culture is the class itself–for example, where a developing consciousness is the elaboration of the self-activity of the class for itself–or a specialist–the intellectual, who elaborates ideas on behalf of the class. [16] The latter corresponds to a division of labor that is characteristic of bourgeois market relations. In a transition to socialism, it is class consciousness that must be built and expressed in the assumption by the working class of its leading historical role. In this light, no socialist program for culture can operate in terms of formal democracy alone; the only freedoms that matter are those that are conquered in

the struggle for power. The ideology of UP, however, restricted the
activity of the working class to the economic field; elsewhere, specialists would represent the class. In the field of culture, this meant
that the leading role was given to the petty bourgeois intelligentsia,
whose objective was the conquest of the individual freedom to create. [17]
In the end, these sectors would see their task as making bourgeois
culture more widely available, rather than developing proletarian
culture. [18] This is not to say that all previous cultural expressions
should be rejected; the working class must know and understand its
own history, and recognize the dialectical continuity of culture, as
Lenin emphasized. [19] At the same time, the elements of previous
culture must be selected by the working class on the basis of their
significance for the workers. And this reveals a central contradiction;
in a period of transition, the argument for individual freedom, for the
development of individual consciousness, is opposed to the need to
develop the collective consciousness of the class. [20]

What follows is a survey of the repercussions of UP policy in
the central areas of ideological struggle. It is a gloomy picture,
albeit slightly alleviated by developments that occurred as a result
of the direct intervention of the organizations of the working class
itself. In culture, as in every other field, two strategies emerged—
the reformist and the revolutionary. Thus the struggle to develop
class consciousness did not go by default. The compromises of
Popular Unity led ultimately to the predominance of reformism, whose
inherent ambiguities ensured the defeat of the working class at the
level of culture and of ideology. At the rank and file level, however,
the embryonic expressions of working-class organization, of the
self-consciousness of the working class, gave rise to new and specific ideological forms. The policies of UP, however, ensured that
the conditions under which these new forms emerged were highly
disadvantageous; the failure of the leadership of the working-class
movement to take its lead from the class it claimed to represent
restored the historical initiative to the bourgeoisie every time it came
into question. Thus the fragmented expressions of class consciousness never found coherence, cohesion, or a unified direction; what
Gramsci calls the "collective intellectual," the revolutionary party,
never emerged, and the challenge for the institutions of state power
was postponed. The result was the military coup.

MANIFESTATIONS OF AN IDEOLOGICAL CLASS WAR

The Press

When UP came to power, the press was firmly in monopoly
hands. The right-wing domination of the press was further supported
by the Alessandri group monopoly over the production of paper and

newsprint; furthermore, the Edwards family, owners of El Mercurio, La Segunda, and Las Ultimas Noticias, also owned the Lord Cochrane agency representative and administrator of the UPI and Hearst interests in Chile. [21]

In June 1971 the opposition, having added two dailies to its previous four, reached some 340,000 readers. The left's press, comprising five national newspapers and two provincial papers whose columns were open to the Left, had a circulation of 250,000. By October 1972, Vaccaro estimated the opposition readership at 540,000, the Left's at 312,000. In the provinces the situation was still worse, since the Right controlled 41 out of a total of 61 provincial newspapers, with only 11 in the hands of the Left. [22]

The Right also maintained control over the weekly and magazine field. The seven right-wing weeklies covered a readership of 250,000. The opposition also retained the distribution rights for American comics of which some 750,000 were sold each month. Here too, new comics were added to the list and the existing ones published more frequently. Add to this a virtual monopoly of imported material and specialist magazines.

The Left was slow to respond to this unequal situation. There is a long tradition of good working-class journalism in Chile, [23] yet on the eve of UP government, Senator Teitelboim of the Communist party acknowledged that the Left was ill-prepared in the field of the press. [24] The tradition of a popular press had been swallowed up by mass culture, which provided bourgeois values and bourgeois messages for a passive working-class audience, or at least a nonparticipating public. Clearly the immediate task for the Left after the UP victory was to destroy that relationship by generating a popular workers' press that would be an instrument of mobilization and rising self-consciousness. Yet by mid-1971, there was still no journal of the Left. [25] Chile Hoy, the excellent news magazine published by Empresa Editorial Quimantu, did not begin publication until mid-1972. The political parties continued to produce their newspapers and periodicals; but there was no new workers' paper able to organize and give coherence to the developing consciousness of the working class as a whole in a period of rapid transition. [26] More importantly, the relationship between the class and the Left's press was never attacked; the lessons that could be learned from the workers' correspondents of the Russian Revolution who would play a new, educative, and mobilizing role within the working class, [27] were never taken seriously. There were corresponsales obreros during the first months of UP; but they were rather token workers, new recruits to an old profession—the lack of a cultural policy ensured that they were not the advanced guard of a new level of worker participation in the political process. Only when the working class intervened directly, when the class struggle erupted in the factories and the organs of dual power—cordones, comandos—were built, did such a newspaper appear. That was Tarea

Urgente; it too disappeared as the initiatives of the working class were recuperated by the leadership of the existing working-class organizations.

Quimantu did project a number of magazines. The problem, as A. Mattelart indicates, [28] was that the publication criteria remained within the bourgeois conception of publics. Women, children, mechanics, skiers were separate audiences, divided not by their relation to the system of production, nor yet by areas of common activity, but rather in terms of a casual, and temporary, identity in consumption. The UP press, then, set out from the beginning to win audiences in market terms; it never challenged the pattern of reception nor the bourgeois view of the newspaper/magazine reader as a passive receiver of news, opinions, and values. Here, too, democratization implied an extension of the readership, rising circulation, but not a frontal assault on the definition of what news is or the way in which it is received. [29]

This confused populism facilitated matters for the Right, which was much quicker to respond to the changing situation. On the press front it rapidly developed a clear and coherent policy, the leading edge of which was El Mercurio. UP did not see its job as extending politics into the realm of everyday life, and the bourgeoisie was able to use that separation to its own advantage. The intervention of politics into any area of social life was bitterly attacked—there was to be no questioning of personal or family relations, the position of women, the education of children, etc. Incredibly, UP accepted and honored these criteria. Thus the Right was able to heal its broken ranks through the defense of bourgeois freedoms and those universal values which underpin the fragmentation of daily life under capitalism; its appeal to the middle sectors was carried forward, in the early stages, on the basis of a general humanist platform. The first battleground was everyday life—for both UP and the Right agreed that this was an area where politics had no place. Thus UP was able to permit the production by Quimantu of a pop idols magazine—the clearest expression of bourgeois manipulation of the market.

At this stage, then, the strategy of the Right at the ideological level, and specifically as far as the press was concerned, was clear: (1) to reassert the pluralist view of a world composed of an infinity of publics each with different needs, each served by a different press, cutting across class lines and defined by patterns of consumption. This was abetted by the right-wing organizations, who ordered their members not to give advertising to the Left's press, thus retaining control of the market in right-wing hands; (2) to ensure the proliferation of magazines and newspapers, with the aim of reemphasizing the characteristic atomization of bourgeois culture; (3) to present the Right as the defender of universal human values, and the bourgeois world order as the only guarantee of those values. Ultimately the objective was to present the question of growth and change in Chile

as a technical problem, falsely rendered ideological by UP and its
allies. The campaign on freedom of the press must be seen in this
light.

By mid-1972 the bourgeoisie had regrouped its forces and
developed its central political strategy. It then changed its line,
choosing as the tribune from which to launch the new line the congress
of the Interamerican Press Association (SIP) in July 1972 in Santiago.
This was appropriate since the SIP (dominated by U. S. press monopolies) had been charged with orchestrating the campaign against UP
outside Chile. At this point, then, the bourgeoisie moved on to an
offensive line, mounting a sustained and direct assault upon UP, and
seeking to reestablish its hegemony through what Mattelart and Waksman call the "mass line"[30] – mobilizing large sectors of the population
behind it through the provocation of successive confrontations aided
by the judicious use of scaremongering and panic news stories.

Because their effective monopoly was never seriously challenged,
it is the activity of the Right that has claimed most of our attention.
There were, of course, a Left press and a number of initiatives (like
the political comic Firme) to reach new audiences. But the truth of
the matter is that UP was never on the offensive in the ideological
field; it failed to establish a new and different criterion for the press,
limiting itself to criticism of and competition with the Right. The
monopoly of paper was a key – yet not until October 1972 was that
monopoly expropriated directly by the working class. The import of
material from the United States declined by 40 percent, yet it was
this material that dominated the market and retained a majority readership. In Chile itself, the agents of U. S. interests ensured that news
continued to be defined by those agencies who define the news for
two-thirds of the world's population.

Quimantu

In February 1971, the state intervened and took over the biggest
publishing enterprise in Chile, Zig-Zag. Seven months later, the
Empresa Editorial Quimantu began operations. By the end of 1972,
it had sold 5 million volumes. Its brief was broad and exciting; it
saw itself as much more than a publishing house – rather as an institution and an expression of developing consciousness. It made books
available at very low prices on a wide range of themes – extending a
socialist library for the working class. It went outside the traditional
circuits of distribution, and by the end of 1972 had established book-
stalls in factories and working-class areas. At the same time those
who administered Quimantu increasingly saw their role as one of
servicing political developments with educative material. Its Cuadernos de Educacion Popular, and the "Nosotros los chilenos" series
were of uneven but generally high quality. Its potential was undoubted-

ly enormous, for it had continuous access to the working class and
its allies; with a more positive policy on UP's part, Quimantu could
have driven a burgeoning wedge into the bourgeois cultural monopoly.
Instead, it was subject to constraints that severely limited that
function—political as much as commercial.

Quimantu was a state publishing house; its primary function,
therefore, was to disseminate and popularize government policy. The
problem, here as elsewhere, was that this was a one-way process
set within a context of reception which had not changed. This was
further emphasized by the consequences of UP's pluralism at the
level of culture. Paradoxically, 60 percent of Quimantu's printing
time was given to strictly commercial work. But it not only accepted
the work of its predecessor; it accepted, furthermore, a market conception of the audience, the public, which led Quimantu to publish
magazines for specific publics just as its predecessor had done. It
is important to distinguish between a magazine which addresses
itself, say, to women by discussing women's problems, advertising
goods for women and so on (Paula, Vanidades) and a magazine which
particularizes for women the general problems, questions, and perspectives of the revolutionary process. In the latter case it is a
question of how the historical role of women places particular obstacles
in the way of their participation. Ramona, Quimantu's magazine for
women, fell neatly between two stools; it said different things to
women, but implicitly accepted the specialness of their universe.
The general editorial criterion of Quimantu was undoubtedly a market
one;[31] it addressed itself to increasing sales rather than to raising
levels of consciousness. Had it faced the latter question, it would
have assessed its activities not only in terms of what it was saying,
but also taking into account the way in which those messages would
be received and used.

The market was still flooded with pulp, imported books mainly
from the United States, and so on. Quimantu was forced to compete
with them, to justify itself in their terms. Its initiatives and program
were never subject to anything but the most general political determination—the needs of particular groups as regards political education
and so on. In the end Quimantu, though it claimed to speak for the
working-class movement, was controlled not by the working-class
movement but by the market. [32]

The Mass Media

Television clearly has a central role to play in the maintenance
of ideological dependency. The changes in the structure of dependency that occurred during the late 1950s and 1960s had important
implications for the mass media. Latin America ceased to be merely
a producer of raw materials and became a market for manufactures.

The immediate result was an extension of the consumer market; in this process the mass media were of key importance. [33] The task was the creation of a mass culture in Latin America. What was involved was the popularization of bourgeois values, those values which sell goods and unite all consumers—individualism, technological determinism, social mobility, etc. In concrete terms this involved the direct export of ideological material from the metropolis—the United States—and the creation of an adequate apparatus through which to diffuse that material. The extension of the television and radio audience, therefore, automatically meant the extension of imperialist influence throughout society. For the mass media represent a possibility of a sustained and instantaneous definition of the world on a day-to-day basis; this definition is broadcast from an issuing center where there is a coherent vision and corresponding broadcasting policies. The same messages, however, are received by an atomized public, inured in the incoherence and fragmentation of social life. The centrality of the ideological element finds its clearest proof in the massive intervention of metropolitan monopoly capital into the field of the mass media. [34] For television and radio provide a crucial vehicle for the dissemination of ideology shaping the world view of mass audiences. In Chile, under Popular Unity, that process provided a constant counterbalance, negation at times, to what was happening in industry.

In the field of the mass media the characteristic ideological pluralism of UP proved catastrophic. There were three national TV channels in Chile—Channels 13, 9, and 7. Channels 7 and 13 were basically popular channels, entertainment media, while Channel 9, emanating from the University of Chile, was more culturally specialized. In 1970, audiences divided as follows: Channel 13—50 percent; Channel 9—10 percent; Channel 7—40 percent. [35] The program policies of all three were supervised through a state agency, as a result of a much earlier decree. From 1971 onwards, the Right sustained a continuous campaign, one aspect of the struggle for freedom of the press, to release television from state control; this was the source of several bitter struggles between UP and the Right. Where UP regarded this area of confrontation as rather marginal, the Right recognized how important it was to maintain its control of the media. It immediately took over Channel 13 and placed at its head the neo-Fascist cleric Hasbun. Channel 9, administered by a right-wing-led University of Chile, was the object of constant and bitter struggles. Boeninger, the right-wing rector of the university, had already attempted to starve it of funds in 1970—and Channel 9 had been maintained for six months by workers in occupation. In early 1973 it was again occupied after a dispute over the administration of the channel, and remained so until the coup. The Right had attempted to take over Channel 9 in order to ensure a monopoly of right-wing TV coverage of the March elections; the response of the workers of the channel

was to expropriate it; there was an immediate response from the working class which gave massive and constant support. At one point
workers from local factories surrounded the studios when a Patria y
Libertad group attempted to eject the occupying workers. Channel 9,
then, could be maintained because it was located in an industrial area
whose inhabitants were prepared to defend every advance through
their own organizations. The government, however, took no attitude
on the question, beyond the threat to use limited legal instruments.

Channel 13, on the other hand, operated throughout in flagrant
violation of the constitution. By early 1973, and particularly after
the March elections, it became the voice of those who were preparing
the military coup. Its increasingly hysterical attacks on government,
its overt links with the terrorists of the Right, brought only confused
complaints from the UP leadership. The irony is that Channel 13's
audience grew during 1971 and 1972 while Channel 9's fell, for the
simple reason that Channel 13 had exclusive rights to the American
TV programs that had always claimed the highest audience ratings—
"Bonanza," "Combat," etc. Channel 9, pursuing government policy,
responded by booking "Patrulla Juvenil" and the epic soap opera
"Simplemente Maria" in order to conserve its audience. Instead of
using whatever instruments were at its disposal to enforce constraints
upon the use of the media by the Right (and the Channel 9 affair showed
that it would have had massive popular support had it done so)[36] it
preferred to enter into competition with an opposition which had
control over, and spoke through, both the form and the content of
the media—and this in itself was a radical new departure. On the
other hand, the extensive use of access television in the industrialized
countries has shown clearly that unless it is an instrument subordinated
to the organizations of a conscious working class, access is no more
than a method of assimilation. The TV workers become personalities,
become performers, and the relationship between viewer and medium
survives unchanged. Government policy towards the mass media,
then, envisaged participation for workers as the aim, but never
workers' control. Thus it made no statement on the question of
Channel 9, and it left Channel 13 to mobilize freely for the military
coup.

In radio, the picture was similar. UP controlled 33 percent of
total transmission power but in quantitative terms the proliferation of
radio stations in Chile gave the Right enormous weight. There were
155 radio stations in all, 115 of them controlled by the opposition,
which also controlled the three most powerful networks, allowing
them to link up with provincial radio. Furthermore, they retained
exclusive control over the shortwave networks which enabled them
to virtually monopolize all external broadcasting. Radio Agricultura,
the voice of the landed oligarchy, was an important mobilizing point
for the Right. Its attacks on UP were unstinted, and it cynically
attempted to generate waves of mass hysteria and panic; yet UP acted

against it only once, closing it down for 48 hours for broadcasting seditious libel. [37]

The mass media and the press, then, were used by the Right in two ways. First, as transmitters of right-wing propaganda: this was made simple by the Right's control over the media and the lack of any consistent policy of restraint at government level. Second, and less directly, the lack of a politics of everyday life on the part of the Left meant that social man, man in his social life, was defined and redefined in terms of a continuous bourgeois culture. The vision of man that was being developed and encouraged in the economic arena found no corresponding new vision at the level of ideology. There the American dream, the pluralist view found no serious challenge. [38]

The Film Industry

The Chilean cinema before 1970 was very like the rest of Latin America; cinema was a cheap form of popular entertainment (entry prices were held down by state decree) and were dominated by the images of Hollywood or their Mexican versions. Cinema lies at the core of the leisure industry, maintaining the separation between men and women at work and men and women in their everyday life. The transference of the American dream to Latin America was a paradoxical phenomenon; the illusions of consumption—the solid gold Cadillacs—flash before audiences deprived of the possibility of consumption; the mythology of the white conquest of the world—John Wayne yet again victorious over Indians/Japs/assorted Commies, James Bond proving the superiority of the Western mind—plays to the colonized victims of these triumphs.

From the 1930s onwards, Hollywood colonized and destroyed a nascent Latin American film industry, [39] and either directly or through its Mexican satellite, began to produce that endless parade of singing cowboys, sexy priests, and moralizing vedettes characteristic of the popular cinema in Latin America today. The new Latin American cinema of the 1960s (Sanjines, etc.) which did introduce important elements of social criticism, was either banned altogether or shown only to restricted (and well-off) audiences in cinema clubs and salons. The colonization of the popular film industry was almost complete. Before 1970, 70 percent of the films shown in Chile came directly from the United States. After that the United States placed an embargo on the export of films to Chile as part of its economic blockade. Presumably the anticipated response was a massive reaction to this deprivation of the familiar tinsel images of Hollywood.

UP's response was to create Chile Films, and to support the so-called independent distributors whose stock came mainly from Western Europe, Eastern Europe, and Cuba. From 1971 onwards Chileans were able to see socialist films, the new Latin American

cinema, and so on. Yet the independent distributors were, and
remained, commercial operations, their criteria exclusively related
to the market. Chile Films, for its part, was seen by government as
a producer of films, but without a budget or a clear policy statement
which would have enabled it to use the cinema as an instrument in
the political process. During the three years of UP the function of
Chile Films expanded from production into distribution and, by early
1973, into direct finance. Yet it was incumbent upon filmmakers
throughout this period to find their own finance, mainly from bank
loans–the criteria for which, of course, were hardly likely to be
political. UP never recognized the significance of film as a political
or educative instrument. [40]

There were filmmakers in Chile who saw their work as directly
and explicitly linked to the struggle for socialism; it is ironic in many
ways that these were precisely the people who worked most enthusias-
tically within Chile Films, where the MIR had a significant political
presence. Young directors like Patricio Guzman and Raul Ruiz were
taking their hand-held cameras into the factories and the poblaciones;
yet it was always a shoestring affair, and UP's attitude towards these
elements was always cool and ambiguous in the extreme. Guzman's
"El primer año, " for example, was conceived by its director as an
instrument of education–the point was not to make good films but
useful ones. Yet early in 1973 Guzman could still complain bitterly
of the lack of any national policy towards the film industry, and
argue for the urgent need to create a Chilean Institute of Film which
would give a clear line on the role of film in the ideological process. [41]
His call was taken up by many workers in the industry and a first
General Assembly of Filmworkers was arranged for September 1973.
It never took place. In the meantime, the cinema screens reflected
the pluralism typical of all fields of cultural activity; the lack of any
policy guidelines made no distinction between James Bond and Sanjines.

Music, Theater, Art

In the aftermath of the military coup, it is the music of Chile
that has most poignantly carried the lessons of Chile throughout the
world. Victor Jara Quilapayun, Inti-Illimani, and others, all of them
direct actors in the political process, have maintained an image for
the world of what Chile was. Certainly it was true that the folk music
boom of the early sixties had developed towards a committed music–
la nueva cancion–which had used those identifiably Latin American
sounds to carry an assertion of Latin America's own cultural heritage.
In Chile the Parra family, particularly Violeta, had taken a central
part in that change. When UP came to power, its program was trans-
mitted through song. Yet it remained a didactic form, a music for
the people. It has to be said, however, that popular music, the music

most working men and women listened to most of the time, was not
this type of music. It was the sentimental ballads of Mexico, the
popular dances, that claimed their attention. The difference could
only be clearly seen when a new music began to emerge from the day-
to-day experience of the working class, particularly in the inspired
work of Tito Fernandez, El Temucano, among others. [42]

As far as the theatre was concerned, the "turn to the people" had
anticipated UP by two years. In 1968, the university reform movement had had very specific repercussions in the schools of drama.
It was the generation of 1968 that, in the aftermath of the UP victory,
rejected the theaters and the salons and took its activity into the
factories, the field, the working-class areas. The commercial theater
continued, though it introduced new elements of social theater into
its repertoire directly. But its audience remained the same, extremely
select one it had always been. The real developments in theater and
in ballet were taking place outside; several factories (Sumar for
example) had its own theater groups whose presentations were directly linked to the experience of its members. Increasingly theater
became a participatory activity and a political one, dramatizing political questions and providing new ways in which workers could raise
and discuss them among themselves.

Art, too, left the easels, as anonymous teams painted the walls
of the working-class districts and taught those who lived there how to
use those walls for their own purposes. Since the coup, it is those
walls that have carried on the propaganda war.

A Socialist Education, A Socialist Culture

Central to any program for socialism is the question of education;
it is the core of the ideological system. For it is as children that
workers first absorb, and effortlessly, the ideas that explain away
or divert attention from their alienated condition under capitalism.
It is at school where women imbibe the justification of their future
role and in the classroom that the patterns of family life are reinforced
and legitimated. And it is through the textbooks and the disciplines
of school life that children assimilate the illusions and the myths
that make them receptive to the reinforcing messages of the ideological apparatus. In Latin America, the system of education is directly
and intimately linked with the institution of religion—with the Catholic
church. Ironically, although these are the central columns of civil
society, they were in Chile the most remote from the class struggle.
Bourgeois dominion over the system of education was never challenged
at the level of content. In early 1973, when Popular Unity introduced
its plan for a unified, national education system the response was
immediate and virulent. The armed forces issued a statement con-
demning the plan and warning of the dire consequences that would

follow on any attempt to implement it. [43] The plan was quietly dropped, and never even reached the stage of parliamentary debate. The paradox is that it was not a fundamental challenge to bourgeois education, but rather a rationalization of the chaotic education system, and an attempt to introduce a vocational element.

As far as the church was concerned, the Chilean church had undergone the same upheavals as in the rest of Latin America. Some Catholics had rejected the church as such and taken an open and clear commitment to socialism; [44] groups of Catholic workers became increasingly radicalized as the process developed. But as an institution the church demonstrated once again its fast allegiance to the constitutional order, and its enmity towards socialism.

The subject of education deserves a separate study; here it will have to suffice to say, simply, that any serious challenge to the dominion of bourgeois ideas must begin there. The fact that UP had no policy towards education in many ways meant that it would necessarily lose the ideological struggle. The problem was that it never recognized the centrality of that struggle. Thus, in its anxiety to hold on to the middle sectors, it lost them by not posing any kind of clear challenge to the bourgeois organization of social life. Because it never posed the central question of the family, and of personal relations, it lost hundreds of young people to the pernicious ideas of Silo, an odd semimystical movement which attracted many young people through its radical rhetoric about sexual and personal liberation and so on. Because it never recognized that "in order to change the conditions of life we must learn to see them through the eyes of women,"[45] thousands of women were lost to the revolutionary cause and trapped within the family, the traditional roles that the ideological system imposed upon them.

A socialist culture in a period of transition cannot of course be generated by governmental dictate; this can only be the result of the creative initiative of the working class which redefines history in the past and creates the history of the future through its own collective consciousness in practice. The criticism of UP should not be posed at that level. What is involved is a recognition of the distinction between a reformist and a revolutionary perspective on the question of socialist education, ideology and class consciousness. The fundamental difference, of course, is that the former has no perspective on the question. Where socialism is seen to stem automatically from material advance then there is no concept of class struggle necessary. The result is that the neutrality of the state and its ideological system and the universality of bourgeois ideas are not contested. To the extent that this perception is dominant within the movement, the development of socialist ideas, or class consciousness, is inhibited and diverted. This was the case in Chile. The very separation of economic, ideological, social, and political activity into discrete areas with distinct specialists created conditions that were directly adverse to the development of class consciousness. And the strategy of the Right took as its starting point the maintenance of that fragmentation.

Yet the UP period in Chile was a period of bitter class struggle—testimony to the creativity of the working-class organizations. The lack of an overall policy did not prevent the working class from building the links between the struggle in various areas of social and economic life—the cordones and the comandos were the concrete evidence of that. The ideological struggle can only be waged where class consciousness can have practical expression; in a period of transition that expression is in the combat organizations of the working class. In a period of transition it is they who must retain the initiative, they who must exercise the ideological hegemony. Where that is not the case, as in Chile, those initiatives will not cease—but they will not be given the coherence and the collective force that will enable the exploited classes to carry through the assault on the bourgeois state and all its institutions.

NOTES

1. Cf. A. Mattelart, "La industria cultural no es una industria ligera," Casa de las Americas, no. 77, (March/April 1973): 27-60.

2. Much has been written on this subject in recent years, but see particularly Mattelart, op. cit.; Mattelart, et al., La ideologia en una sociedad dependiente (Buenos Aires: Signos, 1970); and H. Mujica, El imperio de la noticia (Caracas: Universidad Central de Venezuela, 1971).

3. See A. Gramsci, Prison Notebooks (London: Lawrence and Wishart, 1974), for a characterization of hegemony. Cf. also New Edinburgh Review, no. 27, (1974).

4. See H. Valdes in Cuadernos de la Realidad Nacional (hereafter cited as CEREN), no. 8, (June 1971); and L. Razeto in Revista de la Universidad Tecnica del Estado, no. 6, (1971).

5. L. Trotsky, Problems of Everyday Life (New York: Monad Press, 1973), pp. 108-09.

6. A. Mattelart and M. Mattelart, "Ruptura y continuidad en la Comunicacion," in CEREN, no. 12, (April 1972): 100-43.

7. Chile Hoy, no. 21, (November 3-9, 1972): 23-25.

8. K. Marx, The German Ideology, (London: Lawrence and Wishart, 1965).

9. Cf. A. Gramsci, Literatura y vida nacional (Buenos Aires: Editorial Lautaro, 1952), pp. 21-22.

10. Cf. Chile Hoy, no. 8, (August 4-10, 1972): 13-19. The pages of Chile Hoy closely reflect the debate around this question in the quoted and succeeding issues.

11. Cf. Peter Madsen, "The Critique of Political Economy and the Sociology of Literature" (Working paper, Copenhagen, 1973).

12. Rosa Luxemburg, Rosa Luxemburg Speaks (New York: Pathfinder Press, 1970), pp. 63-69.

13. Ibid, p. 75.

14. Trotsky, op. cit., p. 59.

15. See Ludovico Silva, La plusvalia ideologica (Caracas: Universidad Central de Venezuela, 1969).

16. Cf. A. Gramsci, The Modern Prince (London: Lawrence and Wishart, 1967).

17. Ibid.

18. Cf. A. Mattelart, "Hacia una cultura de la movilizacion cotidiana?", in CEREN, no. 10, (December 1971): 49-97.

19. V. I. Lenin, speech of November 3, 1920, in La cultura y la revolucion cultural (Moscow: Editorial Progresso, 1966), pp. 142-56.

20. Cf. J. Collazos, J. Cortazar, and M. Vargas Llosa, Literatura en la revolucion y revolucion en la literatura (Mexico City: Siglo XXI, 1970).

21. Cf. A. Mattelart and D. Waksman, "Mas alla de la SIP," in Chile Hoy, no. 19, (October 20-26, 1972); and no. 20, (October 27-November 2, 1972).

22. See A. Mattelart et al., Comunicacion masiva y revolucion socialista (Santiago: Ed. Prensa Latinoamericana, 1971), particularly pp. 13-205.

23. Cf. P. Biedma, "Prensa burguesa, prensa popular y prensa revolucionaria," in Mattelart et al., op. cit.

24. El Siglo, February 9, 1970.

25. See C. Ossa, "Conciencia, ideologia y cultura en el actual proceso chileno," in CEREN, no. 12, (April 1972): 85-99.

26. T. Cliff, "Lenin's Pravda," International Socialism, January 1975.

27. Cf. Trotsky, op. cit., pp. 120-28.

28. CEREN, no. 12, (April 1972): 107.

29. See C. Ossa, op. cit.

30. Cf. Mattelart and Waksman, op. cit.

31. CEREN, no. 12, (April 1972): 108.

32. Ibid.

33. Cf. L. Silva, Teoria y practica de la ideologia (Caracas: Universidad Central de Venezuela, 1972).

34. CEREN, no. 12, (April 1972).

35. CEREN, no. 12, (April 1972): 100-04.

36. See Chile Hoy, no. 34, (February 2-8, 1973).

37. V. Vaccaro, "Desigual enfrentamiento en la radio," Chile Hoy, no. 18, (October 13-19, 1972): 16-17.

38. A. Dorfman, Como leer el Pato Donald (Santiago: Editorial Universitaria, 1972).

39. See for example J. Ayala Blanco, La aventura del cine mexicano (Mexico City: Ediciones ERA, 1969).

40. As Trotsky did for example in op. cit., pp. 35: "The cinema is the great competitor not only of the tavern but also of the church. Here is an instrument which we must secure at all costs!"

41. Cf. interview with Patricio Guzman, Chile Hoy, no. 35, (February 9-15, 1973): 24-25.

42. Cf. interview with El Temucano, Chile Hoy, no. 61, (August 10-16, 1973).

43. Cf. A. Silva and R. Vera, "Sobre el problema del poder en la educacion," CEREN, no. 17, (July 1973): 3-46 and Chile Hoy, no. 46, (April 23-May 3, 1973).

44. Cf. interview with Guido Lebret, Chile Hoy, no. 16, (September 29-October 5, 1972).

45. Trotsky, op. cit., p. 65.

THE INDUSTRIAL WORKING CLASS AND THE STRUGGLE FOR POWER IN CHILE
Patricia Santa Lucia

THE DEBATE OVER "PEOPLE'S POWER"

Throughout the three years of Popular Unity (UP) government it was the question of "popular power" (poder popular) that caused the most sustained and intense debate. The phrase is open to a number of interpretations; the mass struggle, however, obliged the Left to pose the problem at a very concrete level. In fact, it served as a focus for the debate between the two strategic conceptions that emerged and faced one another throughout the UP period. Undoubtedly the Industrial Cordones were the most important of the many forms assumed by popular power during that period. Any discussion of their role in Chile between 1970 and 1973, however, must wait on a more general analysis of the question of "popular power" itself and of the various ways in which it was interpreted.

The basic aim of the Popular Unity program was "to end the domination of imperialism, the monopolies and the landholding oligarchy, and set in motion the construction of socialism." This entailed a "struggle to conquer popular power," a struggle that would bring together the broadest range of popular forces. The Popular Unity Committees (CUPs) formed prior to the 1970 elections were to be a fundamental instrument in carrying out this task in the aftermath of Allende's electoral victory; their role was not limited to achieving the victory of the UP candidate in the presidential elections, but was to extend to making preparations for the exercise of "popular power." According to the program, "popular power" would contribute to the creation of a people's state that would emerge as the existing (state) institutions were modernized and democratized. The principal task

---

This chapter has been translated from Spanish by Mike Gonzalez.

of this new state, in its turn, would be to extend and purify that democracy.

The CUPs were established in each district and workplace during the electoral campaign of 1970, enabling both activists of the parties making up Popular Unity and any independents who identified themselves with the candidacy of Salvador Allende to collaborate in the campaign—mobilizing support, recruiting votes, collecting finances for the campaign, and so on.

These organizations never had any real life of their own; they virtually died on September 5, 1970. They had been limited to a simple* electoral function and could not be transformed into a different kind of organ capable of taking on new tasks and of exercising power. Further, the Chilean party political tradition also left its mark on them, so that independent supporters of UP had no weight in them at all; they had after all been established for and by the supporters of Popular Unity, and this effectively prevented their transformation into organizations representative of the masses as a whole. But the fundamental reason for their decline was that they lacked political leadership, coupled with the failure of the UP leadership to clarify what it was that they meant by popular power.

The CUPs were told that they should mobilize and educate themselves politically—yet they were never given a specific function nor a specific character. President Allende attributed to them the exercise of "popular power"—yet he never made clear what that meant, although it was to become gradually clear during the three years of the Allende regime that the concept of "popular power" did rest on a coherent underlying conception.

- Popular Power means that we shall destroy the basis of power of the minority that has always condemned our country to underdevelopment (Allende—November 5, 1970).
- To consolidate and extend popular power means to revitalize the popular parties on the basis of an effective unity (Allende—May 1, 1971).
- If we are to strengthen and consolidate popular power we must make the unions more powerful, provide them with a new consciousness that they are a fundamental pillar of government—not dominated by it, but consciously participating, assisting, supporting and criticizing its actions (Allende—May 1, 1971).

---

*"Simple" because decisions about the electoral front were taken by the constituent parties of UP at a national level, leaving the CUPs with very little scope for independent activity.

In various speeches, Allende stressed that workers' participation would be achieved through their political and trade union organizations. His definition of who the worker was covered "anyone who lives from the exercise of his labor." The workers were

> a social bloc which is constantly expanding as a result
> of capitalist development, and which is increasingly
> unified by its common condition as wage earners. For
> the same reason our government offers to protect small
> and medium industrialists. We seek the unity of all
> those sectors which to varying degrees, are exploited
> by the property-owning minority who occupy the
> centers of power (Allende–May 21, 1971).

The UP program defined the working class and the peasantry as the motor force of the revolution, placing them firmly at the center of a broad alliance that would include the small and medium bourgeoisie. It was this class alliance that would carry out the tasks put forward in the program and exercise "popular power." If anyone analyzes the speeches of Allende himself and of other leading members of Popular Unity, however, it becomes clear that only one fraction of the proletariat and peasantry as a whole was actually to be assigned tasks in the leadership and construction of the new society–namely, the organized workers. Since they were regarded as the expression or representatives of the working class as a whole, it was they who must exercise "popular power" on behalf of the masses.

- This is a government of parties, and of the workers organized in the CUT (Allende–June 16, 1971).
- A conscious, organized and disciplined people, together with the unequivocal loyalty of the Armed Forces and the Carabineros is the best defense of the Popular Government and the best guarantee of our national future (Allende–May 1, 1971).

Jacques Chonchol[1] and Jorge Insunza,[2] among others, asserted that the unorganized workers were not in a position to "support" the government, and Insunza went so far as to suggest that these sections of workers displayed deformations that could prejudice the active involvement of the masses in the struggle, "since, as they are new sectors with little experience of the great battles of the class, they reveal anarchist tendencies."[3]

The Labor Census of December 1971[4] shows that only 30.6 percent of the total salaried workforce over eighteen years were unionized and that the CUT, the highest organ of the Chilean working class, embraced a smaller percentage of the work force than this, as those voting in the national provincial election for the CUT in 1972 numbered only half a million, that is, scarcely 16 percent of the wage-earning work force. [5] Only 20 percent of the rural labor force were unionized by December 31, 1971 and nearly 50 percent of the industrial proletariat worked in plants employing less than 25 persons, and therefore had no union rights.* On the basis of these figures, it is not difficult to prove how large a proportion of the urban and rural proletariat were excluded from the exercise of "popular power." We shall see later that all the government's initiatives as far as the political incorporation of the masses was concerned were inspired to a greater or lesser degree by this conception.

The debate on the Industrial Cordones that took place later is closely connected with this question; we make no apologies, therefore, for devoting space to it before entering into the main theme of this discussion.

The conception of "popular power" enshrined in the UP program gave a special place within the vanguard to the workers in the Social Property Area†; they had a particularly important role to play, since this area would largely determine the character of the process of transition to socialism. The control of political power by the organized people whose expression was the Social Property Area in particular and the planned economy as a whole, provided the ultimate guarantee that UP's aims would be carried through. This was the popular power that would achieve and safeguard the realization of the tasks set out in the program.

The establishment of the Social Property Area and the mobilization of workers who were, or were to become part of it, was clearly of central importance in the UP program. It was this area of the economy that was to determine the transition from a capitalist to a socialist society "in the course of which all power would revert to the workers." [6]

> In the struggle against the old structure, the task of
> beginning to lay the bases for a new system (e.g. the
> development of a state-owned sector of the economy
> under a Popular Government) is of crucial importance.
> Equally important in the direct attack upon the previous

---

*The existing law on unionization in Chile required a minimum of 25 workers to form a union; industrial unions are not legally recognized, but only separate blue-and white-collar unions (obreros and empleados). In 1973, UP presented to Congress a draft law that would reform the labor laws in this and other respects.

†The UP program proposed the division of the economy into three areas: the private sector, the mixed sector, and the Social Property Area, comprising monopoly and other key industries that would be taken into state ownership.

> structure are, for example, voluntary labor, popular
> organization and a necessary increase in production
> and productivity; all of these provide a focus for
> political mobilization around the tasks to be realized
> in a particular conjuncture. [7]

The UP program stressed the importance of mobilizing the workers in
support of the transfer of industries to the Social Property Area. Yet,
since the objective was the transformation of society as a whole, it
is significant that this sector represented a very small proportion of
the Chilean working class as a whole.

> There are in Chile more than 35,000 firms. At this
> stage we intend to nationalize only 1 percent of the
> total (Allende-May 1, 1971).
>   Certain interests will be affected, but these
> will not include the vast majority of nonmonopolist
> industrialists. On the contrary, they will be offered
> extensive possibilities not only of permanence but
> also for development and growth. [8]

At first, 253 enterprises were regarded as of strategic importance;
within the first few months of UP government, however, the figure fell
first to 155 and later to 91. According to statistics provided by Luis
Vargas, [9] the number quoted before the Millas Plan was 90, of which
74 were industrial firms employing 55,884 people-in other words,
10 percent of the entire industrial labor force.

> The other 507,000 workers would continue in private
> or mixed-ownership enterprises; their mobilization
> would be limited by the continuing existence of the
> private relations of production. The struggle of the
> workers as a whole to move beyond the frontiers of
> the capitalist system, the struggle for socialism
> and for power, then, was not, as far as the 90 per-
> cent of the industrial proletariat that did not play a
> vanguard role in these struggles were concerned, to
> result in the destruction of the capitalist ownership
> of industry. [10]

Clearly, within the conception of the exercise of "popular
power" articulated in the UP program, the organized workers and
those within the Social Property Area had a fundamental role to play.
They were to be given concrete tasks and slogans of battle, and
provided with some organs of participation through which they could
make their opinions known. Generally speaking, these were the
most mature sectors of the working class, the soil out of which

Popular Unity—and the Communist party in particular—had grown, and over which they had almost total control. Although this sector represented only a small proportion of the total working class population, it was deemed preferable to sustain the sectarian divisions within the working class and straitjacket substantial sectors of the working class rather than take the risk of losing control of the movement.

Ninety percent of the working class remained within the private and mixed sectors of the economy. A part of that number were unionized and could express themselves through the CUT. As far as the process of transition as a whole was concerned, however, they were given no political direction, their capacity to mobilize was restricted, and they were thus never able to confront the bosses. The UP program proposed favorable treatment at this stage for private and mixed enterprises so that those workers within these sectors who were disciplined Popular Unity activists found themselves under an obligation to hold back their struggles in order to allow industrialists to "develop and grow." One of the consequences was that when workers in the private sector discovered sabotage or speculation they could do nothing, since any toma (takeover of a factory) or "strike" could be interpreted as "causing difficulties for the government" or "trying to leapfrog stages in the process."

> A proletarian political perspective must necessarily also include a permanent activity aimed at unifying the working class, struggling against bourgeois individualism within the working class whether at the organic, political or at the ideological levels. 11
>
> Equally, it is the task of the vanguard of the working class to organize an alliance of classes that will embrace all anticapitalist sectors. Here, too, we are discussing the unification of the people as a whole, while defining at the same time who are the enemies of the people, where and how they are to be found and what are their main objects of attack, an attack aimed at bringing down the system. 12

Thus it was the political task of the vanguard sectors to build a popular state that would emerge as a result of democratizing the existing state, while conquering at the same time those branches of the state that were as yet not under the control of the working class. The conditions under which this struggle was to take place were very favorable for the working class; the control of government meant that "part of power" had been won, thus creating a situation of "dual power." If the state was to be democratized, the forms of "popular power" for whose development the government was pressing would have to be given a mass character. These forms will be discussed later.

What precisely characterizes our present situation
is that the working class and its allies, brought
together in Popular Unity, have conquered a part
of power, expressed in their control of the executive
branch of government. Given the stage of development achieved by state capitalism in our country,
the executive branch is an important element of
power and probably the branch with the greatest
capacity for action. [13]

In Chile a situation has been created whose
special feature is that, from a class point of view,
dual power is expressed in the existence of a line
of demarcation within the existing State apparatus
itself, rather than in a confrontation between the
bourgeois state apparatus and an alternative state
expressing the interests of the working class and
its allies, as was the case, for example, of the
Soviets in the face of the provisional government. [14]

This conception was criticized by some sections of UP and by
the MIR, however, from the point of view of the Leninist conception
of dual power.

The fact that in Chile the popular forces have gained
control of government, of the executive branch of the
state, has given rise to incorrect formulations which
call into question the whole strategic orientation of
the revolutionary process. . . For example, the simplistic formulation that 'part of power' has been won.
The bourgeois state still exists in Chile; it is still
organized according to the liberal principle of the
separation of powers into executive, legislature and
judiciary. According to this principle, each of the
independent, institutional pillars that comprise the
state has an independent juridical status of power.

For similar reasons it is wrong to affirm that
in Chile there exists dual power within the state
apparatus. The formula 'dual power' corresponds to
a situation in which, as in Russia in 1917 when the
Soviets and the provisional government confronted
one another, there coexist two state powers which
cannot by definition exist within a single state apparatus. [15]

When, after the February revolution of 1917,
Lenin spoke of 'dual power', he was referring to the
parallel existence of two types of state: a bourgeois
state and a workers' state—the Soviets. Obviously,

the same is not true of Chile where, in any event, one
can only speak of two powers within a single state
apparatus. 16

Within this general discussion about the conception of "dual power,"
the government encouraged those organs of participation that corres-
ponded to its political plans, and there was still no prospect of any
alternative organizational proposal coming from the MIR or any other
section of the Left.

ORIGINS OF THE INDUSTRIAL CORDONES

The organs of participation developed by the government had no
more than a consultative function; they were created in order to democratize the Chilean state and to enable the economy to function
efficiently, but they were not to place any obstacles in the way of
the existing lines of hierarchy, whether in the institutions of the
state, in the management of the economy, or of the enterprises in
the private and mixed sectors.

On December 7, 1970, the government signed an agreement
with the CUT that set in motion "workers' participation in the transformation of the socio-economic structure of the country." In
February 1971, the CUT held an extraordinary congress that approved
a draft plan for workers' participation in the administration of enterprises in the Social Property and mixed areas of the economy.

This document was supposed to be discussed by the rank and
file of the workers' movement, but in practice it was only discussed
by the most developed sectors of the working class, those who held
union posts or who were members of the party leaderships (the
organized sectors). The plan was published in almost unmodified
form under the title "Basic Norms of Participation."

With the implementation of this organizational formula, workers'
participation in the economic management of the mixed and social
property areas was, in the UP's judgment, virtually assured. The
CUT also promoted, although without any great conviction, the
establishment of Committees to Supervise Production in the private
sector.

At the beginning of 1971 the government for its part created
the National Development Council (Consejo Nacional de Desarrollo),
whose function was to discuss national economic planning. This
council was composed of representatives of government, of the CUT
and of private enterprise. It was proposed that Regional Development
Committees should also be created with a similar composition—in
practice, however, these were never constituted. Indeed, the National
Council itself never really functioned.

What lay behind the idea of workers' participation in the Social Property Area was basically that workers should be consulted within the enterprise with a view to raising the level of efficiency and winning the "battle of production," though without altering the existing normal hierarchical structure of the enterprise. Only the highest internal body, the Administrative Council (Consejo de Administracion), comprising representatives of the state and of the workers, could make decisions; the organs that were created at various other levels within the enterprise were meant to facilitate consultation with the corresponding heads of section. All the representatives were directly elected by the respective assembly; it was taken as read, however, that all sectors of the enterprise would be represented, excluding neither technicians nor administrators from participation even though they were a minority.

All the new organs were subordinate to the trade union leadership, thus ensuring both that the "organized sectors" would retain the leadership of the movement and that, despite the fact that they now had access to decision making, power would not go to those young workers whose lack of experience might "lead them into anarchist deviations."

The Committees to Supervise Production were promoted by the CUT in the private property area in order to guard against sabotage and ensure the continuance of normal production. Their slogan, "win the battle for production," was one that both the CUT and the government were advocating in every sector of the economy. (It was under this slogan, too, that voluntary labor was called for). The committees went into action immediately; yet they were stillborn, for in practice neither the CUT nor the government possessed any means of acting upon the complaints received from workers. The government's lack of a coherent policy towards private enterprise, the contradiction implicit for the most radicalized parties of the UP in the policy of alliance with small and medium capital, and the struggles of the workers led these sectors into a trap. The lack of leadership of any kind meant that during their short life these bodies only served to frustrate even further those sections of workers who had helped to build them.

The Peasant Councils

Although not directly bearing upon the present discussion, it is important here to pause briefly to consider the characteristics of government-created bodies of a similar kind in other sectors.

In December 1970, the government signed a decree establishing a National Peasant Council (Consejo Nacional Campesino) that would enable peasant representatives to discuss government suggestions and proposals and thus participate directly in the formation of the government's agrarian policy. The council comprised two representatives from each national peasant organization, two from the national association of asentados,* two from the National Federation of Cooperatives and Small Producers, and the minister of Agriculture. Further, Peasant Councils would be established in each province, and later in each comuna.† These, too, had a consultative function, transmitting opinions and providing suggestions to the government agencies in charge of the agrarian reform. The radicalization of the peasant movement, however, gave them a new and more dynamic character, carrying them beyond the limits of their original function.

JAPs

Towards the end of 1971, the supply of goods was becoming an increasingly serious problem in Chile. The structural crisis of the Chilean economy made it incapable of responding to the considerable increase in the purchasing power of the mass of working people, to the informal blockade by the United States that stopped the import of essential machinery and spare parts, to the scarcity of cash caused by the fall in the price of copper on the world market or to the sabotage and speculation by the bourgeoisie that emphasized all these problems.

It was in order to overcome these problems, at least partially, that the minister of the Economy promoted the JAPs.

The object of the JAP (Committee for Prices and Supplies—Junta de Abastecimientos y Precios) was to rationalize distribution and control speculation by allowing consumers to participate directly. They included shopkeepers and traders, however, since according to the UP program they were supposed to form part of the class alliance supporting the UP. The JAPs were to be formed in each district and comuna and were to be composed of representatives of local mass organizations—mothers' groups, sports associations, neighborhood committees (Juntas de Vecinos, which had been formed in the poblaciones‡ during the Frei regime), plus the shopkeepers. Once the

---

*Asentados were the beneficiaries of the Christian Democrat Agrarian Reform Law later used as a basis for agrarian policy by UP. The law was designed to capitalize agriculture, and created a class of small farmers called asentados.

†An administrative division; a province would normally be divided into three or four comunas, though they may vary considerably in size.

‡Literally, a 'township', though shantytown is the way it has usually been translated here. Originally temporary living areas established by poor immigrants into the towns, they later became permanent in some cases. Basically, poor working-class areas.

committees had been formed, an executive would be elected who
would then be given official recognition by the corresponding government department (DIRINCO). "Honorary inspectors, who were supposed
to be the most respected citizens in the area, were elected from among
the members of the JAP; they then attended courses in DIRINCO leading
to an official diploma awarded by the Controleria."* With all this
paperwork behind them, the inspectors were then supposed to control
speculation, and ensure that official prices were adhered to and goods
were distributed equitably among the consumers in a particular district,
and so on. Although at certain moments and in certain areas they did
come to play a fundamental role, the JAPs very soon became a sort
of local branch of the state distribution agency; their job was to
collect those goods that were distributed by the state and deliver
them to those shopkeepers who had decided of their own volition to
participate in the JAPs, and to rationalize the distribution of goods
among all the inhabitants of districts or comunas affiliated to the
JAPs. But since in practice the JAPs had neither autonomy nor power,
there was no way of exercising control over those shopkeepers who
persisted in speculating or black marketeering. Like all the other
government-created organizations to which we have referred, the
JAPs had a vertical and subordinate relation to the state.

The JAPs grew and multiplied because with every day that passed
supplies became a more urgent problem; but they became increasingly
bureaucratic, and in the end prevented any autonomous initiative by
the masses on the question of distribution. New methods of supply
and distribution were sought. Towards the end of 1972 the government
began to promote workers' participation and consultation in the organs
of economic management. The National Development Council, which
had never worked in practice, was replaced by a ministers' Economic
Committee that included representatives of the CUT.

There were, however, intermediate levels of economic management between this committee and the Social Property Area where there
was workers' participation; in the final months before the coup the
government began to encourage workers' representation on the Sector
Committee Councils, organs of intermediate industrial planning linked
to CORFO;† but it was never realized.

---

*A state agency, originally set up to ensure that government or
congressional decisions did not conflict with the constitution. Under
Popular Unity government, it became a powerful weapon of the Right,
used in combination with the judiciary to place obstacles in the way
of antiruling class legislation.

†CORFO was originally set up by the state in 1939 in order to
channel or redirect public investment into industry and to establish
state control over an emerging industrial sector. Its original purpose—
the accumulation of industrial capital through the state—began to change

The development of the class struggle and the rising level of consciousness among the masses, however, led to a questioning of these bodies, which had after all been imposed from above. The criticism was based not only upon the fact that they had been founded in this way, but also because they failed to fulfil a mobilizing function.

Early Criticisms

In the Social Property Area, the rigid "Basic Norms" began to be widely questioned, and some groups of workers began to discuss the need to establish workers' control in the factories. It was in the Social Property Area itself that these proposals were first made, at the beginning of 1972. In the private sector, the Committees to Supervise Production died because their supervisory functions ceased to have any meaning, since the government lacked any meaningful sanctions that it could bring to bear against industrialists who were guilty of sabotage. In such cases, the workers pressed for the industry in question to be incorporated into the Social Property Area; and when they received no response from either the government or the CUT, they began to take their own initiatives.

It was at this point that the government began to recognize the necessity for a coherent policy towards the private sector. The workers, for their part, saw a need for workers' control and for new forms of organization that could go beyond the limits imposed by the Trade Union Law (Ley de Sindicalizacion) and by the rigid framework of an organization like the CUT whose experience was basically limited to the economic struggle against bourgeois capitalist governments. Workers in small enterprises began to understand the need for coordination on a geographical basis that would bring them the support of workers from other local industries in their struggle against a boss who engaged in sabotage and speculation and traded on the black market.

At the beginning of 1972 there took place a Congress of Textile Workers, whose struggles for the state takeover of their industry had taken almost all textile plants out of private hands. The object of the congress was to discuss and evaluate popular participation during the year; but it rejected the report of the government organ charged with the planning of the industry—the Comite Textil. The congress called into question the basic norms of participation, and demanded a greater power of decision making for the rank and file; it was agreed that union leaders and interventors should be brought under rank-and-

----

slowly after the Second World War, as in the fifties it came increasingly to subsidize private industry.

file control, that any who failed in their duty should be reported and
that the administrative committees should report back to the congress
on a regular basis, and so on. From this moment on, factory congresses
took place regularly, and the workers in the Social Property Area began
to go beyond the forms of participation proposed by the government.
At the same time, their discussions were not restricted to the contingent
problems faced by an individual factory but ranged across problems of
the economy and of the working class as a whole.

Bearing in mind the experience of the comuna peasant councils,
the MIR began in mid-1971 to agitate for the creation of comuna urban
councils. At that point in time the demand was far above the level of
consciousness of the masses; furthermore, it was posed in such a
general way that the urban masses were unable to grasp it. Yet the
MIR persisted in agitating around the slogan, and did find some echo
among those groups of slum dwellers and students where the MIR
already enjoyed some influence.

The Concepcion Popular Assembly

The first important mobilization on the basis of these proposals
was the Popular Assembly, which met in Concepcion on July 27, 1972.

This assembly of 2,000 workers and students heard a number
of analyses of how the Chilean process could be carried forward. The
result was the "Concepcion document," which made the following
basic demands: 1) the need to struggle for the achievement of workers'
control in both public and private sectors of the economy, 2) the
peasant councils to be given powers of decision, and 3) the unification of popular organizations into communal councils of workers,
which would discuss problems of supply, education, health, and so
on in rank and file assemblies. These proposals had a limited agita-
tional character, yet they put the question of popular power firmly on
the agenda of ideological discussion both among the constituent
parties of Popular Unity and among the most advanced sectors of the
working class. One paragraph of the Concepcion document, for
example, stated the following:

> . . . we are not dealing here with any supposed pro-
> grammatic rifts, but rather proposing an alliance which
> will discuss and put into practice a political line
> designed to ensure that the revolutionary process
> moves inexorably forward.

The Communist party, however, took no part in this assembly, on
the basis that "any action that tends to leapfrog stages in the revolutionary process goes against UP, the government and President Allende."
It was certainly the case that the proposals presented to the assembly

indicated a qualitative advance in the consciousness of the masses, going well beyond the forms of participation that had been set out on behalf of the working class by the government and in the Popular Unity program.

The debate on the question of power and the state became explicit at that point; as time passed the issue became one of increasingly general concern, and every day the different positions became clearer and more coherent—but they remained unresolved in practice.

Mario Benavente, a member of the central committee of the Communist party interviewed by the magazine Chile Hoy after the popular assembly, suggested that "for us communists this is a maneuver encouraged by the imperialists and the reactionaries, using elements of the ultra left and the MIR and its Revolutionary Workers Front in particular."[17] The Communist senator Volodia Teitelboim, for his part, felt that "it was a crazy idea thought up in the heat of the moment."[18]

Within Popular Unity itself, the debate made things much clearer for many workers; the slogan of "popular power" and the demands for Communal Councils of Workers (Consejos Comunales de Trabajadores) advocated by the MIR, which had up till then seemed very general and abstract to them, now became much more understandable. Workers began to discuss Communal Councils or Commands, Industrial Cordones or Workers' Coordinating Committees. Yet it was only during the October crisis that the masses came to understand their importance, when they responded to the bosses' strike by organizing themselves and infusing these organs with life.

The October Crisis

Using as a pretext a government proposal to establish a State Transport Enterprise, the association of truck owners brought about a national stoppage. They had the support of small traders, and later of the College of Engineers and of Physicians, as well as of private capitalists.

The transport strike by itself totally paralyzed all supplies; industries could not function without raw materials, while those that did have raw material had no means of distribution.

It was during this crisis that the Chilean working class created those organizations that provide one of the most valuable examples to emerge from the whole Chilean experience; by their efforts and organization alone the working class prevented the paralysis of the country. Now the Communal Commands of Workers emerged with real strength. Almost spontaneously, workers came together at local and regional levels, unified their organizations, and resolved the concrete problems caused by the strike.

Without political leadership from any group, whether within or outside the UP, the workers took over industries that the employers had tried to close and kept them working. They attempted to build mechanisms of direct distribution—economatos or people's super- markets—that would make retail traders unnecessary during this period. Some stores were reopened by shantytown dwellers and in some areas traders reopened their shops out of fear of the control and vigilance of the slum dwellers.

The Communal Commands were formed by the unions and by representatives from local factories, leaders of the JAPs, of neighbor- hood committees, student associations, and so on; leaders of left-wing parties, CUT leaders and in some areas mayors and local councillors also participated. The fundamental problem produced by the emergency was that for the most part the commands were elected from above and were not always completely representative of the rank and file.

Until then, the workers had channeled their struggles through the traditional organizations of the working class—the CUT and the unions—whose principal orientation was towards struggles of a social and economic character. It is not easy to understand the role of these organizations after September 4, 1970; in the Social Property Area in general the union leaders were subordinate to the executives of enterprises who were themselves members of the UP, either because they were members of the same party or as a matter of political disci- pline. The CUT for its part was clearly accountable on a national level to the Ministry of Labor. That is why it was not until October 1972 that the autonomous experience of the workers achieved concrete organizational form, when it was their spontaneous initiative that led them to organize and seek to forge the new organs demanded by the struggle.

The bosses' strike took the left-wing parties by surprise, and they were thus not able to respond and provide the masses with a correct political lead. In practice the two conceptions that had coexisted within the UP provided the basis for those responses that did emerge. The government and the more hesistant sectors of the UP strove from the beginning for a compromise with the striking sectors; they started discussions with the Christian Democrat party and with the armed forces, brought the masses under their control, and tried to hold them to a defensive position. The government took pains to create commands and commissions in order to maintain normal supplies and avoid any fall in production; generally speaking, these were technical measures that allowed the government to main- tain a normal situation at the economic level while they brought to a conclusion the "discussions" with those sectors who were demanding guarantees from the Popular Unity government. The government also created a "patriotic front of women" and a "patriotic front of traders, transport owners and businessmen" for propaganda ends—but they never gained any real strength.

The most advanced sectors of the Left, whether within or outside the UP, were unable to give a socialist lead in that conjuncture—indeed their political responses were weak, dispersed, and uncoordinated.

The CUT emerged in a slightly stronger position; it maintained a subtle independence from government throughout and called on the workers to build Coordinating Councils of the Unions to defend nationalized factories, and to create Committees of Transport, Supplies, and Health (COTAS) so that the crisis would not excessively affect the normal functioning of the social system. Although the measures taken by the CUT were correct, they had an exclusively defensive character.

Fascism launched its attack on a number of levels, strike action among them; in response, the masses went on to the offensive—but it was not only the masses who took an aggressive posture. Rank-and-file party activists also began to present and develop aggressive socialist tactics; in a diffuse way a left-wing leadership began to emerge within the masses themselves. The general slogans born out of the Concepcion Popular Assembly took on increasingly concrete forms. Yet they were never given support at the leadership level, at the level of government,or at the level of the party leaderships.

In October, the workers understood the need for Communal Commands, not only as organizations designed to solve the concrete problems posed by the strike, but also as embryonic organs of "local power" that, once constituted at the regional and national level, would constitute an "alternative power to the bourgeois state."

The growth and radicalization of the mass movement in October 1972 was one of the most significant qualitative advances made by the working class during the three years of Popular Unity, comparable only to the leap forward that occurred during the attempted coup of June 29, though this latter had a more limited duration.

The government's "solution" to the October strike was the establishment of the UP/Generals Cabinet. The large number of enterprises taken over by the workers were returned to their original owners, and the retail traders were given guarantees by the government that the mechanisms of direct distribution created by the workers would be suppressed; technicians who had gone on strike were re-employed without reprisal and did not even have the days they did not work deducted from their pay, while truck owners were given assurances that the Chilean transport industry would remain in private hands. This agreement was a cruel blow for the masses. Yet once again the Chilean working class movement offered proofs of its discipline and the respect in which it had always held government decisions and the party leaderships. While still on the offensive, just as the petty bourgeois associations were beginning to break down, they nevertheless accepted the "solution" without a single desperate act of protest. The result was a general demobilization; within a month almost all the organizations that they had created were dismantled, although the seeds of organization and the high level of mass consciousness as far as the need to create an alternative power was concerned remained.

During this period Communal Commands and Industrial Cordones were formed, though it was the commands that had grown and developed most notably. Although many industries were taken over by the workers, it was in the area of supply and distribution that the tactical confrontation actually took place. It was the organizations that had grown up in the poblaciones, together with the Communal Commands, that took on a decisive importance. This is not to deny the role played by the working class (whose job it was to ensure that production continued); it is important, however, to emphasize the role of the slum dwellers, for the working class itself took a relatively minor part in this period compared with its role in later crises. It serves, too, to underline the strong links that were established and maintained with other sectors of the population throughout this period.

The Communal Commands covered a given geographical area and brought together all the existing mass organizations: unions, JAPs, mothers' groups, tenants associations, student associations, and, according to the area, peasant unions or organizations. The Industrial Cordones, too, functioned as local coordinators, but were composed exclusively of factory representatives, and did not embrace either slum dwellers or peasants.

The more important Communal Commands, like Cerrillos-Maipu and Vicuna Mackenna, as well as other less important ones that had only a superstructural existence, had already been formed before October. That is why these two commands played such an outstanding role in October and why, later on, though demobilized, repressed, and suffering constant changes in their organic structure, they nevertheless continued to be of key importance. It was these cordones, for example, that mobilized their members to prevent the return of factories taken over during the bosses' strike.

Once the crisis of October had been resolved, the bulletin published by the Cerrillos-Maipu Command described the situation thus:

> The government has decreed the return of Tas Choapa, Chile Bus, Clarin, Asociacion Melipilla, Calgo Azul and Flecha Verde. Workers should respond to these decrees issued from above by creating Self-Defense Committees and Brigades for the Defense of Industry.

The same article continued:

> The bosses have got their courage up, they think they can do what they like. To begin with they want

to bring down the government and then walk all over
the workers. The main reason is that the government
and some sections of Popular Unity have been weak,
they have hesitated; instead of calling on the people
to smash reaction they preferred to turn to the armed
forces. But the armed forces won't solve the underlying problems; what is at issue is much more than
a return to normality and law and order.

After October, when the Communal Commands were a reality
and the demands of the Concepcion Popular Assembly had taken
concrete form, the debate within the Left began again.

Jorge Insunza suggests that the Communal Commands
should not be seen as parallel organs of power; the
task now is to find a way in which these Commands
can make their activities complementary to those of
government organizations. In this respect it is essential that the Comuna authorities participate in the
Commands. [19]

Hernan del Canto, interviewed by the same magazine, gave the
Socialist party position:

In order to avoid any suggestion that they are parallel
organs of power, our party feels that the Commands
should be presided over by the Intendente, Governor
or Subdelegado* in each case (SP Central Committee -
November Documents).

The secretary of the MIR, Miguel Enriquez, on the other hand, said
in a forum organized by the magazine Clarin,

Some people want to build the Communal Commands
not as embryonic organs of power, but as dependent
and subordinate organisms of the State apparatus; and
that is tantamount to suppressing them. The question
is not whether or not they should develop in line with
or in opposition to the Government; the political
question is this—how do we articulate the use of the
instrument of Government independently of those
organs of power which are progressively generated
within the mass movement, in such a way that both

---

*Local government official of the comuna.

factors contribute to the development of new instruments that will allow us to carry the process forward.

With the exception of the Communist party, whose central committee
made no statement, the UP parties supported the commands at this
stage—they were after all an undeniably concrete reality. As the
class struggle developed, however, the debate opened once again.
Orlando Millas, a member of the Communist party's political committee,
wrote several months later in El Siglo (the official CP newspaper), that
the Communal Commands were anarchist forms of social organization;
yet a large percentage of the Communist party rank and file took part
in them. The Socialist party still had no clear political perspective
at the leadership level—different leaders had different opinions—but
the party's rank and file either built or took an active part in the
commands. The MAPU held an ordinary Congress in November 1972,
at which the more radical sectors succeeded in gaining a majority
under the slogan "crear poder popular."* It was these sectors,
together with the MIR and sections of the Socialist party who gave
the greatest impetus to the slogan "popular power."
    Despite the open debate, and despite the fact that "popular
power" was now on the agenda, the UP/Generals Cabinet produced
confusion among the masses, who had not themselves developed any
alternative solution to that offered by the government; as a result
the organizations that were created in October began to fade away.
They emerged again in January 1973, under the impact of the electoral
campaign and of the mobilization of workers in the Social Property
Area in opposition to the Millas Plan;† this time, however, it was
the Industrial Cordones that gained strength. Even where Communal
Commands already existed they functioned in practice like cordones,
and it was the working class that led the mobilization; the return of

---

*The right-wing faction that had lost its hold in Congress was
incapable of facing up to the ideological debate; so it resorted to a
Stalinist maneuver, carrying out a coup and taking over local party
offices and the party infrastructure with the object of retaining the
name of the party. It failed, even though it had the support of Allende
and the Communist party; it was left without a working class base, and
a few government posts. It called itself MAPU OC (Workers' and Peasants MAPU) and joined the Popular Unity coalition under this name.
†The Millas Plan, proposed by Economics Minister Orlando Millas
in January 1973 proposed to cut the 90 enterprises comprising the
Social Property Area to 44, to pay compensation to the original owners
of the 44 enterprises, and to negotiate 'special cases' where enterprises in the hands of workers (whether as a result of state takeover
or of direct takeover by the workers) should be returned.

enterprises to private ownership was, after all, a problem that affected them directly. Yet these mobilizations did not enable the working class to draw other sectors of the population into their strength.

Once again the Cerrillos and Vicuna Mackenna Cordones took a leading role in rejecting the plan. The Cerrillos Maipu Cordon, for example, declared in a public statement:

> The Millas Plan is an agreement between the Govern-
> ment and the bourgeoisie from which only the bosses
> have anything to gain, and whatever they do gain will
> be fed into their unending efforts to defeat the working
> class once and for all; the first step is to bring down
> the government. In the end the government of Companero
> Salvador Allende is committing slow but certain suicide.

In the same statement, the cordon leadership went on to call for the coordination of all workers in defense of those enterprises that remained in workers' hands, for the establishment of workers' control over small and medium private enterprise and for real workers' control of the Social Property Area.

A statement from the Vicuna Mackenna Cordon was published in the cordones' newspaper Tarea Urgente (No. 1):

> To the workers: The workers of the Vicuna Mackenna
> Cordon call upon the working class to mobilize com-
> batively in defense of the Social Property Area and
> of the enterprises that were taken over during the
> October strike; these are now threatened by a proposed
> law that represents neither the feelings nor the opinions
> of the majority of workers, who are ready to carry to its
> ultimate consequences the struggle to defend their
> legitimate rights. For this reason the Vicuna Mackenna
> Cordon, in an Assembly held on Monday, January the
> 28th, passed the following resolutions: 1) Not to
> return any industry taken over during the bosses'
> strike of October: 2) unanimously to reject the so-
> called 'Millas Plan' because it does not represent
> the real ideas of the workers, but contributes to
> holding back the process that will carry us forward
> to a socialist revolution: 3) to demand that the authors
> of the proposed law explain to the workers the reasons
> why it was proposed and that they accept the histori-
> cal and political responsibility for it: 4) to demand
> that the parties of UP make clear public statements
> on their attitude to this projected law and bring an
> end to their silent complicity: 5) we propose that the
> working class should respond not only by refusing to

return any enterprise, but also by incorporating more
industries into the Social Property Area: 6) as workers
we give our most determined support to the statement
by the political committee of the Socialist party which
rejects the return of enterprises now included in the
Social Property Area as a result of the determined
struggle of the working class. We must advance without compromises. Not one enterprise must be returned:
many more must be taken over.

In the same paper, the Panamericana Norte Cordon issued the following
statement:

This is the government of the workers. Yet a decision
has been taken from above to consider returning 123
enterprises to their original owners; the decision was
taken without consulting the workers, and without
seeking their opinion. Those 123 enterprises were
wrested from the grip of the exploiters at the cost of
struggles, effort and sacrifice. Now those who control the law can count on favorable treatment from the
Congress and the tribunals. These are the people who
have lived on the breath, the sickness and the hunger
of workers and peasants, who have filled their own
pockets with the fruits of the sweat of workers. And
now they're going to be given another free gift—123
enterprises are going to be returned to them. Yet
these are the same people who have been trying to
kick out the workers' government since October, who
threw all their energy into an attempt to get rid of our
comrade president, who did everything in their power
to bring down the government of the workers, who
kiss the Yankee arse whenever they get the chance.
How much longer are the people up there going to go
on turning the screw the wrong way? It's beginning
to get on our nerves, and we're giving notice that
NOT ONE ENTERPRISE WILL BE RETURNED. On the
contrary, WE SHALL GO ON EXTENDING THE SOCIAL
PROPERTY AREA. And in case anyone has any doubts
WE SHALL REMAIN PERMANENTLY MOBILIZED IN
DEFENSE OF OUR RIGHT TO DECIDE AND TO GOVERN.

"The Coordinating Committee"

There followed declarations and proclamations in a similar tone from
all the other cordones. The result was an unprecedented mass mobilization that was clearly expressed in the 44 percent vote given to the

UP in the elections of March 4, 1973. The cordones were now a reality in Chile.

DEVELOPMENT OF THE INDUSTRIAL CORDONES

From that time on, the cordones were directly elected from the rank and file; unlike what had happened in October, assemblies were held in each factory and in each shop, each democratically electing its own representative to the respective cordon. The leadership of the cordon was then elected from among this number and working committees set up. At that time it was generally felt that the cordones had to assert themselves so that Communal Commands could then be formed. The elected delegates to the cordon did not have to be trade union leaders or officials.

MIR and Socialist party activists differed on the question of the Communal Commands. The MIR argued that the commands should be immediately established, while the Socialists felt that the cordones should first be strengthened. In practice the cordones were established and in some areas the commands achieved an even stronger position. This did not depend on the outcome of political debates, however, but on the character of the particular geographical area (whether it was a slum area, industrial, peasant, and so on) and on the level of class consciousness of the shantytown dwellers in relation to the workers.

During this period the working class took a qualitative leap ahead of other layers of the population; the shantytown dwellers, by contrast, progressed very little, for they were primarily concerned with the problems of supply and distribution of goods. They began to question the JAPs and to criticize their rigid structure; some sectors, in fact, did direct their struggle to building other kinds of organizations that could ensure the supply of goods—the Direct Supply Commands, for example (Comandos de Abastecimiento Directo). This was by no means universal to the shantytown movement, however; there was very little homogeneity in their activity. Most serious of all they did not, as they had in October, coordinate their activities during this period.

Despite the lack of political leadership from their parties (with the exception of the Communist party* and the MIR), the leaderships of the cordones were generally agreed on the objects and tasks of these organizations. They were not seen as alternatives to government—but they did make it clear that their basic struggle was against the bourgeois state. They declared their autonomy from the CUT, on

---

*The Communist party ordered its activists not to participate in the Industrial Cordones.

the basis that the cordones did not have economistic objectives, but aimed among other things to build the Communal Commands that would draw together all popular organizations in a given area. Power would then be exercised through the commands.

With small local variations, the cordones were constituted in the following way. In a given area an assembly of workers in each factory, including both manual and white-collar workers, would elect two or three delegates to the cordon. The factory delegates would then meet and elect an executive from among their number which usually included a general secretary, an organization secretary, executive members in charge of agitation and propaganda, disputes and conflicts, and security and defense (in some cordones there were also representatives with responsibility for culture and supplies).

The local or regional CUT officials were accepted into the cordon and could be elected by the assembly—but they had no automatic right to participate. Since the Communist party did not participate in the cordones, it was generally the Socialist party, MAPU, MIR, and CUT leaders who worked for and in the cordones, and they were usually elected by the assembly. Where the new leadership of the cordones was not yet directly elected from the rank and file, although it was agreed that they would be directly elected in the future, some CUT and trade union officials did remain on the executive on the basis that they had been involved in the establishment of the cordon.

Up to now the cordones had set out clear tasks for themselves: to build the Cordones and incorporate the maximum number of workers into them, strengthening them in order to move on to building the Communal Commands. On a more contingent level the tasks were to extend the Social Property Area, to ensure that factories taken over by the workers were retained, and to extend worker leadership and workers' control in the Social Property Area itself; to ensure control of distribution; to expropriate all landholdings over 40 hectares in size and give decision-making powers to the Communal Peasant Councils. To these general tasks were added the resolution of local conflicts and agitation around issues that might arise at any given moment as a result of developments on a national level.

Since the Socialist party was much stronger in workers' unions and regional CUTs than either the MAPU or the MIR, it had a significant majority in the leadership of the Industrial Cordones. The MIR's principal strength lay in the peasantry, the shantytown dwellers, and the students; for this reason it was clearly to their advantage to constitute the Communal Commands directly, since they drew together all the popular organizations. This was the basis of the debate between the Socialists and the MIR as to whether to work to strengthen the Cordones or the commands. The MIR's public position was that, by building the Communal Commands, the working class would not be separated from other layers of the masses. The Socialist party's reply—reply of the party's rank and file rather than of the central

committee, which did not clarify its position—was that the working
class was the vanguard class and thus needed to strengthen its
position before taking on the leadership of other sectors through the
Communal Commands. Their analysis of the October and post-October
experience, in which the Communal Commands had predominated, led
them to the conclusion that the working class had diluted and dis-
sipated its strength in discussion about supplies, problems of speculation, sanitary services in the shantytowns, and so on, rather than
devoting its attention to the central problems of the time.

The June Crisis

As the attempted coup of June 29, 1973 was set in motion,
confusion once again spread among the parties of the left; President
Allende's radio broadcast reflected his obvious surprise. The government failed to act in a unified way, and what it did do was based
principally on their faith in the attitudes of Generals Prats and Picker-
ing, and of the loyal sectors within the armed forces on whom they
felt they could rely. Although less apparent than in October, the
lack of political leadership was immediately clear.

The national CUT, hegemonized by the Communist party, gave
firm initial instructions: it recognized the industrial cordones, which
it had rejected until then on the basis that they were parallel unions.
The rank and file of the CP then moved rapidly into the cordones.

Once again the masses were on the offensive; tactical dis-
crepancies were overcome and the organization of the cordones reached
new levels. Although on June 29 it seemed obvious that the main thing
was the defense of the government and the celebration of the victory
that had been achieved, the slogans that filled the streets were not
the customary "Allende, Allende, the people will defend you" but
"A hard line, " "Fascists to the wall" and "Close the National Congress. "
The unity of the cordones and the commands, the embryonic organs of
"popular power, " was built around these slogans, despite the fact
that the CP rejected them as "ultraleftist. "

The cordones were now at a much more advanced stage of
organization than they had been in October; the workers now established
a system of offensive organization and every factory that could be taken
over was expropriated. The slogans that had been put forward by the
MIR and the left of the Socialist party stressed the need to destroy the
bourgeois state and establish the dictatorship of the proletariat. These
were now no longer abstract, general slogans; they had been given
flesh by the working class, as each cordon and command adopted them
as their aim and final objective.

The most important factor—and it cannot be emphasized enough—
was that the working class acted as a homogeneous whole. The CP

rank and file, who in obedience to party discipline had not joined the
cordones, nevertheless shared their aims and agreed with the program
they had adopted. The working class base of the Christian Democrat
party, which had become increasingly remote from the party in the
period since October, entered the struggle and took part in the defense
of factories and of the Popular Unity government.

Spontaneously, the workers organized paramilitary groups to
defend the factories; in every factory and workplace the creative
initiative of the masses took shape in homemade arms manufactured
by the workers to defend their factories. In this situation the vanguard role of the working class was proved beyond dispute, and the
industrial cordones stood above all other existing mass organizations.

The immediate tasks that the majority of the cordones set out
for themselves were: the creation of brigades to defend and protect
factories, permanent alert, and the mobilization of all the workers,
for a new fascist coup could come at any time. In Santiago, a Regional
Coordinating Committee of Cordones was set up that included the
Cerrillos, Panamericana Norte, Vicuna Mackenna, Santa Rosa-Gran
Avenida, Mapocho-Cordillera, and Conchali Cordones.

Cordones sprang up all over the country, and with the Communal
Commands they drew together the workers from almost all the factories
in their respective areas.

The central element of the program of action elaborated by the
coordinating committee was to ensure that factories taken over by
the workers from June 29 onwards were not returned—the number of
takeovers during this period had exceeded all expectations. The
other principal demands were workers' control in the factories,
control over distribution, the maintenance and extension of the
Social Property Area, and more power to the Communal Commands
and other rank-and-file organizations, which should be independent
of the CUT and present an alternative to the bourgeois state.

The bourgeoisie understood that the workers' principal weapon
was "popular power"; that is why one magistrate declared "If anyone
has a free hand, he should use it to tie the cordones to Allende."
And on July 6, the National leadership of the Christian Democrat
party declared:

> The de facto establishment of a so-called popular
> power, organized by official sectors and protected
> by state functionaries, and which is now taking over
> factories, distributing arms and setting up what is
> in effect an 'armed militia' which has arrogated to
> itself political, economic and military-defensive
> functions, constitutes the most serious threat to
> date against the constitutional regime and democra-
> tic collaboration.

The PDC leadership took this position when the interests of the monopolies and of imperialism were in jeopardy; yet these were the same
people who, in December 1972, had put on a democratic, populist
face and declared that "there is no effective transference of power
towards the organized workers taking place; the intermediate social
organizations—the family, the trade union, the cooperative, local
and regional government are in no sense under threat."[20]

Despite the demonstrations of strength by the working class and
the retreat of the bourgeoisie in the face of them, the government and
the vacillating sections of Popular Unity held back. The Communist
party began to question its own momentary participation in the Industrial Cordones and the national executive committee of the CUT made
a statement on July 19 asserting that it "understood these organizations to be the leadership of the rank and file which, as part of the
CUT, were thus part of the trade union movement of the working class
as a whole"; as far as the Communal Commands were concerned, these
they regarded as parallel to the CUT and thus "rejected them completely." The declaration ended by saying that it would be necessary to
return to their original owners all those factories that had been taken
over by the workers.

The order to return the factories was a peremptory decision taken
by the CUT and the government. The CUT wanted all factories returned
except those that appeared on the "list of 104," in other words the
monopolies and all those enterprises that had a key place in the
national economy, as well as factories where the problems with management had proved insoluble. This meant that enterprises taken over by
the workers on June 29, from which they had already been legally
evicted, had to be returned. It was this that caused the first rift in
the unity of the working class, a unity that had been forged during
and as a result of the June crisis. Apart from members of the Communist party and MAPU OC (Obrero Campesino), the workers refused
to return the factories.

On July 25, President Allende reminded the country in a speech
that his was a transitional, not a socialist government, and stressed
the need for a dialogue "in order to avoid civil war."

The tasks proposed in the cordones and the proposals that
stemmed from them were well synthesized in a declaration issued by
the Regional Coordinating Committee of the Cordones in Santiago;
although it was rejected by the MIR, it did represent the thinking of
the leaders of Santiago's 11 cordones.

> The Industrial Cordones of Santiago province have
> discussed and officially agreed to set up the Provincial
> Coordinating Committee of Industrial Cordones (CPCI),
> arising out of the initiatives of the working class in
> response to the fascist offensive of the bourgeoisie.
> In taking over factories, estates and other enter-

prises, and in strengthening their own organizations,
they prepared for the defense and continuing advance
of the popular government, and continued the struggle
to initiate the building of a socialist society.

In no case do they see themselves as parallel
to the CUT; on the contrary, they recognize the CUT
as the highest organization of the Chilean working
class at the national level. That is why the CPCI
has not been established as a provincial organization
parallel to the CUT, nor does it intend to assume the
leadership of the working class at the provincial level;
it has emerged as a result of the need to coordinate
the struggle in various individual cordones.

The cordones pose the problem of power and of
how to build the embryonic organs of popular power
(Workers' Communal Commands). This requires that
they have the autonomy necessary to carry out the
role of leading the various social sectors allied to
the proletariat in the struggle for socialism. We
should make clear that the instructions issued by
the CUT on (June) 29th were carried out by the Cordones, according to the particular characteristics of
each area.

The Industrial Cordones are broad class organizations, drawing together and organizing the workers,
whatever their political color. The political leadership will be given by the political parties of the working
class, who have a vanguard role to play in the struggle
itself, and within the working class.

In the present political conjuncture, the class
struggle has given the Industrial Cordones the character of complementary organizations to the popular
government, revitalizing the working class organizations; but under no circumstances must they be
allowed to become front organizations.

General Aims of the Cordones

1. To defend and extend the conquests of the
government and the class.

2. To represent the workers of the cordon in
a direct and democratic way.

3. To constitute themselves as organizations
to defend the present government, insofar as it represents the interests of workers.

4. To build organizations charged with deepening
and sharpening the political process and the class contradictions.

5. To struggle energetically for greater working class participation in decisions that affect their
inherent interests and to extend the power of the trade
unions and other class organizations.

6. To cooperate permanently in the organizations and training of the area defence organizations,
so that territorial and political control by the working
class can be guaranteed.

All the industries in each area, including small
factories and workshops, should send delegates to the
cordon to represent their comrades, with full speaking
and voting rights, thus ensuring the maintenance of
workers' democracy.

The Industrial Cordones should be based on the
broadest working class participation, giving free
expression to the creativity and revolutionary initiatives of the class. We must struggle against
sectarianism and against a bureaucracy that takes
decisions at a superstructural level and without
reference to the masses. In a word, workers' democracy should be established within the Industrial
Cordon.

The national executive of the CUT rejected the autonomy of the
cordones and refused to recognize the existence of the Coordinating
Committee. In the same declaration, the Coordinating Committee
responded as follows: "for some time now the CUT has advocated
reforming its organizational structure so that there could be a CUT
leadership in every Industrial Cordon. It sees the cordones, in
other words, as rank-and-file executives within the CUT and thus
as an integral part of the labor movement as a whole." The declaration added that "in Santiago the tendency has been not to organize
in the union and the CUT, and even to integrate into the cordones
people who are not members of any trade union . . . . At the same
time there has been a call for a higher Coordinating body of the
Cordones, which would replace the CUT, establishing a parallel
organization to it. "

On this last point the MIR and the Communist party, which
controlled the CUT National Executive, were in agreement. In
various workers' assemblies the MIR attacked the Coordinating
Committee, accusing it of being a parallel organization to the CUT.
The CPCI was mainly composed of Socialist party members, since
it comprised the presidents of the Santiago Cordones.

In response to government and CUT calls to return the factories
taken over by the workers, the Cerillos and Vicuna Mackenna Cordones
once again sprang into action. On Tuesday July 17 barricades were
set up in the Cordon Cerillos involving more than 5,000 workers as

well as students and the Maipu Peasant Council. Despite the opposition of their leadership rank-and-file members of the Communist party
were present at the barricade. That is why the CP, together with
MAPU OC,* called for the formation of a parallel cordon in Cerillos
despite their "energetic rejection of parallelism"; the call was ignored
by the rank and file. The same thing happened in Vicuna Mackenna,
at whose barricades one worker was murdered by the carabineros.

The debate between the CP and the rest of the left had become
much more intense; using its hegemony in the national executive of
the CUT, the CP used the CUT—an organization recognized by all
workers—to impose its position. It rejected the Communal Commands
out of hand, on the basis that they were parallel organizations; in
fact, neither their composition nor their program and objectives had
anything to do with the CUT, so they could hardly be acting parallel
to it.

Despite the argument between the MIR and the Socialist party
over the commands and the cordones, both agreed that the Communal
Commands did draw together all the vital organizations in each area.
This meant that the commands united the struggle of workers, shantytown dwellers, peasants, and students in any given geographical
area. The CUT, on the other hand, controlled only its affiliated
unions in the private and public sectors, and did not lead the struggles
of peasants, students or pobladores. Although it was recognized by
all sectors as the "highest organization of workers" it included only
30.6 percent of the working population, of whom 10.3 percent were
public sector or "white collar" workers (that is, 15.7 percent of these
were organized) and only 23.2 percent of the salaried workers in the
private sector (including the rural areas) were organized. [21]

The CUT's work was always aimed at leading the economic
struggles of the working class. The Communal Command, on the
other hand, was envisaged as the highest organization in each comuna.
"Popular power" would be exercised within the commands that, once
they were coordinated at a provincial and a national level, would give
birth to a "national popular assembly" capable of legislating and
administering justice and thus representing an "alternative power to
the bourgeois state." The popular assembly of the comuna would,
in its turn, emerge from the union of rank-and-file assemblies of
workers, peasants, pobladores, and students. Despite subtle differences between the MIR and the Socialist party over the composition
of the organization,† they agreed that its function was different from

————————

*Although the MAPU OC, had no mass base, it still retained
leading posts in the CUT that it had won before the party split.

†The Socialist party proposed that a regidor, the comuna governor,
or some local government authorities should participate in the council
of the commands, though without voting rights, and further, that the

that of the CUT, and that the Communal Commands would represent
an alternative power to the bourgeois state as a whole and not to the
Popular Unity government.

As far as the national executive of the CUT was concerned, it
saw the cordones as rank-and-file organs of the CUT under the leadership of the local, regional, and provincial CUT organizations. In
this light the first problem was the question of functions. The Industrial Cordones were not conceived as a trade union type of organization
designed to resolve economic conflicts, take matters to the factory
inspectorate and get them resolved, or deal with the problems of
unemployed or retired workers, and so on. * The Industrial Cordon was
conceived as an embryonic organ or power which brought the bourgeois
state into question and was the backbone of the Communal Command.
On the other hand, the cordon was not a coordinating committee of
trade unions, the cordon assembly was not composed of trade union
leaders but of delegates elected by the rank and file who were not
generally speaking trade union leaders. The trade union leadership
had enough to do with its internal tasks without taking on all the
further tasks that were being proposed for the cordones. This was
not hard and fast; there were many trade union leaders who were also
leaders of the cordones—but only when they were elected to that position by the assembly. Furthermore, there were many nonunionized
factories that had the right to send delegates to the cordon, as did
factories with less than 25 workers which, according to the Labor
Code then in practice, could not form unions.

The work of the cordones was determined on a geographical
basis: the large concentrated enterprises, some of a national character, usually had a single union; the union led all the workers in that
particular industrial complex, while plants that were a long way from
one another elected delegates to their respective cordon. The union
and the delegates dealt with different questions; the delegates to the
cordon coordinated defense and the guarding of factories at an area
level, for example, but did not deal with the economic problems of
the whole workforce in a single enterprise who would, in any case,
be spread over a number of factories.

These and many other arguments were raised in discussion with
the Communist party comrades; but they were firm in their ideas and
would not allow the movement to slip out of their control. Despite
having completely lost their control of the new organizations, they

---

Industrial Command should have a central role in the commands. The
MIR, however, gave more autonomy to the command, rejected official
participation, and proposed that all sectors (student, poblador,
peasant, and so on) should have equal weight within the command.

    *Work undertaken by the CUT at its various levels: comunal,
departmental (provincial), or local.

still maintained their hegemony over the unionized workers. As new
groups of workers became involved in the cordones, and as these
became more firmly established (even though they were still not in
any real sense organs of dual power) it became more and more difficult for them to control the movement. On the other hand, if the CP
did participate in them it might have jeopardized their dialogue with
the Christian Democratic party which had already declared its
opposition to the nascent organs of "popular power."

Allende sought a dialogue with the Christian Democratic party
and proposed the creation of a new cabinet; October repeated itself
as the cordones and the workers began to demobilize. The armed
forces began to search factories, using as their justification the
Arms Control Law that Congress had approved some time earlier; in
the course of these "arms searches" workers were beaten and killed.
The government did nothing and the dialogue continued.

Within the armed forces those soldiers who were opposed to
the coup began to protest; they were imprisoned and tortured. The
government did nothing about this either; the constitutionalist
generals retired from the armed forces, with Allende's approval, and
the three branches of the armed services were taken over by new
commanders, all of whom were known to be in favor of a military coup.

The bosses' organizations and the professional associations
embarked on a new October-style strike. A new cabinet, called the
Cabinet of National Security, was formed by civilians and the
commanders of the three services plus the director general of the
carabineros. This was the final stage in the frustration and demobilization of the rank and file. The bosses' strike continued, however,
despite the entry of the generals into the cabinet.

Armando Cruces, Socialist president of the Vicuna Mackenna
Cordon, put it this way:

> As far as the leaders of the cordones and the workers
> in general are concerned, this cabinet is seen as a
> betrayal of the working class; it shows that the govern-
> ment is still vacillating, that it has no faith in the
> working class. The military in the cabinet are a
> guarantee for the bosses, just as they were in Octo-
> ber; they're a guarantee for Vilarin,* not for the
> workers. We've had experience already; the military
> solved Vilarin's problem on the spot by providing
> him with new trucks and new tires. [22]

_____

*Leon Vilarin, leader of the transport owners' federation, was
a key figure in the bosses' strikes of October 1972 and July 1973.
After the coup he was sent abroad to restore the junta's public image;
he failed dismally.

The following is a declaration issued by the San Joaquin Cordon, an example of the many that came out of the cordones in this period. They were the last gasps of these organizations. When the fascist coup came on September 11, they were already practically dead.

> Cordon San Joaquin:
>   Faced with the social and political events now taking place in the country, the San Joaquin considers it to be its responsibility to make the following declaration:
>   1. Its most energetic rejection of the use of the Arms Control Law by the military; it has become the new ley maldita* directed against the workers. The discriminate application of this law has led to the death of one worker in an arms search carried out by combined Naval and Air Force personnel in the Austral woolen mill and another wounded by a bayonet; tools and machines were destroyed, forcing the factory to stop work while repairs were carried out. It should be pointed out that the Lanera Mill belongs to the Chilean people as a whole. We demand the immediate repeal of this law, and that exemplary punishment be meted out to the officers responsible for this murder, which has added one more victim to the list of working class dead.
>   2. The present lack of supplies, which affects workers and shantytown dwellers alike, is the result of the bosses' strike organized, as it was in October, with the support of armed fascist gangs. Their aim is to attempt to create the conditions favorable to a coup d'etat by the coup-minded military, which will lead to the bloody repression of the working class movement. This makes it necessary to coordinate the struggles of all workers, shantytown dwellers, students etc. in order to solve these urgent and serious problems. That is why the San Joaquin Cordon has formed commissions (for supplies, transport etc) into which the pobladores must become integrated, so that we can find a common solution to common problems.

------

*The ley maldita made the Communist party illegal and persecuted all active trade unionists and political activists of the Left. It was passed in 1947, during the Radical government of Gonzalez Videla; this same Radical party had formed part of a coalition with the Communist party some eight years earlier, before forcing the CP out and making it illegal.

> The unity in struggle of workers and <u>pobladores</u> will
> be the basis of a new organization that must be
> formed—the Communal Command—involving all sectors
> that are in alliance with the proletariat.
>   3. The present situation of the country is very
> serious; it is imperative that the workers in the cordones
> discuss and carry out the instructions they have received:
> to reinforce the guard on the factories and workers areas.
> It is imperative that all factories and working class areas
> are properly defended this weekend.

The leaders of the cordones and commands, who lived through this
dramatic experience, have now been killed or imprisoned by the
dictatorship. Today many of them are being tortured or at best are
underground or outside the country.

CONCLUSIONS

On September 4, 1970 Chile entered a profound prerevolutionary
crisis. The mass movement had developed to explosion point since
1967 as a result of the failure of Frei populism;* that movement underwent an important qualitative change and advance as a result of
Popular Unity's installation in government.

The victory of UP created the most favorable correlation of
forces that the working class and the Chilean people had ever
experienced. Despite the fact that the UP program proposed no more
than a gradual transformation of the bourgeois state, the broad possibilities opened up for workers' participation and the freedoms that no
Latin American country had ever known gave free rein to the organization and development of the creative initiatives of the popular movement. The beginning of the transformations envisaged in the program
in the cities and in the countryside, the confusion of the right wing
and its failure to reply to the blow it had received further stimulated
the mass movement.

The dynamics of the class struggle soon brought down the
preestablished schemes, even those of the government's program
itself, and the masses demonstrated a previously unimaginable potential, particularly during the period of crisis. They questioned and

------

*Eduardo Frei was the president of Chile from 1964 to 1970.
Leader of the Christian Democratic party, he was the prize example
of the Alliance for Progress' plan to install reformist governments in
some countries of Latin America under the slogan "revolution through
democracy." During his regime inflation remained uncontrolled, the
level of foreign debt and Chilean dependence on foreign capital
increased several times, and the agrarian reform policy on which the
Frei "development" program relied was only partially carried out.

began to go beyond bureaucratic directives at every level; the mass movement acquired its own autonomous dynamic.

The Chilean party political tradition, rooted in the discipline of the masses, prevented the movement from leading to a radical break with the hegemonic political leadership of Popular Unity, whose traditions in the Chilean workers' movement stretched back more than a century. Yet there were moments when that leadership found itself totally isolated, as proposals for an alternative leadership emerged from within the masses themselves.

On the other hand, despite the absence on the Left of any alternative leadership that could challenge the hegemony of reformism, * the popular movement spontaneously posed for itself socialist objectives.

There would have been no embryonic organs of popular power in Chile had there been no Popular Unity government; but if that government and the principal parties of UP had not held back that development, nor put obstacles in its way, events would have taken a very different turn.

Even so, the question of "popular power" is one of the most important aspects of the Chilean experience. The new vanguard will emerge from the surviving germs of that power.

The past is dead; there is a new future to build. The errors that were committed will be the chief source of the lessons that will enable us to take on the new tasks with a new and different vision.

APPENDIX

Some Industrial Cordones and Communal Commands
Existing in Chile in August 1973†

Santiago Province

Cordon Cerrillos. Established in mid-1972 as a result of the Perlak conflict. It was called the Cerrillos-Maipu Communal Command and drew in the peasants and pobladores of Maipu province. Once

---

*We are not setting aside here the important role played by the MIR in the radicalization of large sectors of pobladores, peasants, and students, but its lack of influence within the working class limited its potential for becoming a real alternative revolutionary leadership. The radicalized sectors of UP, although they did stand out at times, were never capable of providing an alternative socialist leadership either.

†These statistics are incomplete. Though the organization of the cordones was incipient and in some cases went no further than

established, it drew together workers in 169 factories, including among
others: Maestranza Calvo, Fensa, Fastuzzi, the Franklin Carriage
Works, Kamet Foundry, Mapesa, Lan, Avicola Farms, Adams Chewing
Gum, Ralco, Sindelen, Bata, Nylinsa, Insa, Inapis, Desco, American
Screw, Indura, Perlak, El Mono Aluminium, Policron, Copihue Pre-
serves, Metalpar, Enadi, Enap, Cintac, etc.

Cordon Vicuna Mackenna. Like the Cerrillos Cordon, it emerged in
mid-1972 as a Communal Command. At its height it mobilized 5,000
workers in 350 factories including: Chile Glass, Nitjana Liquor,
Eleemetal, Electromat, Siam Mellafe y Salas, Garcia y Geka Labora-
tories, Marquehue, Alyas Shoes, Radio Taxi 33, Indumet, Ready Lux,
Standard Electric, Luchetti, Vinex, Easton Chile and Ronitex, Alusa,
etc.

Communal Command Conchali-Area Norte. Emerged as a Command in
October 1972 and remained in existence after that despite certain
changes in its geographical area between then and August 1973. It
included the following factories: Dava, Libertad Foundry, Nobis,
Cerssita, Ferriloza, Pacifico Plastics, Via Sur, C.C.U. (Compania
de Cervecerias Unidas), Bunger, Magne, Edwards and Cerutti Construction, Imaur, Uniplac Belfi, Dalmiti Ltd., and Orion. It also
drew together the Communal Peasant Council of Conchali, the Comuna
Peasant Union Fidel, the JAPs, Mothers' Groups, workers in the San
Jose hospital, and students from the Medical Faculty.

Cordon Macul. The first attempt to establish this cordon was in
1969, as a result of certain trade union conflicts, even though the
conditions for its development did not yet exist. The idea was spread
among the workers by militant students, but it died soon afterwards.
It was definitively established in October 1972 as a Communal Command and then became a Cordon—but it covered few factories including
Biitig, Sudamericana Textiles, Bromack (textiles), Kattan, Kores,
Pollack (textiles), and Continental (textiles).

Cordon O'Higgins. Born in October 1972, it grew constantly from
then on. It operated in conjunction with the Communal Command
Estacion Central, and took in the following factories: ex-Yarur,

_____

its first meeting, they multiplied throughout the country. It has been
difficult to gather all the relevant material together, since most of
it was either destroyed or taken out of the country as soon as the
military junta directly accused the cordones of leading the organization of the so-called Plan Z, a plan for a left-wing coup. This plan
was miraculously "discovered" by the junta immediately after
September 11, and used to justify the coup.

Correa, Salinas y Fabres, Indugas, Seam Corfo, Burger, Gesco, Gemo, Distra, Precision Hispana, El Adarga, workers in the O'Higgins Park, Soquisa, Salomoni Building, and Roddenstock Optics.

Cordon Santa Rosa-Gran Avenida. Emerged as the San Miguel Communal Command in October 1972, but soon faded. It was established as a Cordon on the night of June 28th. It had a short life but managed to draw together some 80 factories and shortly before the coup of September the 11th called for the creation of a Communal Command. The factories involved included: Kademsa, Sumar, Polyester, Silberman, Hiato Bros., SGA, Lit, Los Aliados, Mibsa, Industrial School of San Miguel, Citroen, Ferromat, local hospitals, San Miguel Hilanderia, and Codigas.

Cordon San Joaquin. Born in June 1973 and fundamentally linked the Sumar factories. It never really built a mass base, but worked with the Santa Rosa Cordon.

Cordon Santiago-Centro. Formed after June 29th, bringing together all property and public offices in the center of Santiago, where only left-wing people worked. Its members were mainly office workers, so this cordon never really became a mass organization, since by this time the petty bourgeoisie had been totally polarized.

Cordon Panamericana Norte. Although it was one of the most important cordones, in a heavily populated working class area, we only have evidence of the involvement of Hirmas, one of the biggest textile factories in Chile, whose workers had fought hard to have it incorporated into the Social Property Area. It coordinated with the peasant organizations of Quilcura.

Cordon Mapocho Cordillera. This drew together the Disputada de Las Condes Mine, Cervecerias Unidas (breweries), TV Channel 9, and the Quimantu (state) publishing house among its most important elements. It was restructured several times and suffered from problems of demarcation with the Communal Command 5th Commune-Area Norte. Its development was limited and its geographical area included few workers. Its struggles were mainly concentrated on the defense of Channel 9.*

---

* Channel 9, the television station belonging to the University of Chile, was taken over by its personnel in mid-1972, and became the focus for a constant struggle for its control. The University of Chile administration was in the hands of the Right, and made every kind of attempt to either sabotage or take back the TV channel. It was finally handed back to the military shortly before the coup.

<u>Cordon Maturara-Mapocho</u>. Established in May 1973 and composed
principally of hospitals and service industries. Never developed
very far although it did occasionally achieve large-scale mobilizations. In effect, it covered an urban zone with no industry.

<u>Estacion Central Communal Command</u>. This command brought together
the following factories and organizations: Montero, Enafri, El Adarga,
Endesa, Trotter and Termometalurgica, and Mothers' Groups, JAPs,
and Tenants' Associations in the area.

<u>Other Communal Commands</u>. Many of the cordones that emerged in
October 1972 had effectively ceased to function, having been unable
to revitalize themselves in January 1973:

San Rafael-La Florida	Lo Espejo	La Granja
Nunoa Oriente	Barrancas	La Reina
7th Commune	Colina	Las Condes
2nd Commune	Las Viscachas	San Bernardo

Valparaiso Province

In the cities of Valparaiso, Vina del Mar, and Quilpue some
six highly combative Industrial Cordones were established, working
in conjunction with pobladores and in some cases with peasants.
We were not able to preserve the details of these organizations.

Cautin Province

Puerto Saavedra	Neuva Imperial
Lautaro	Loncoche
Cunco	

In Temuco City

Santa Rosa-Estacion	Avenida Alemania
Las Quilas	Padre Las Casas
Universidad de Chile	Pueblo Nuevo de Temuco

Linares Province

Yerbas Buenas
Parral
Retiro

Concepcion Province

Chiguayante
Penco

Tome
Talcahuano

The experience of "popular power" in Concepcion was one of the most advanced experiences of the period. Concepcion is a largely left-wing province, with a high level of radicalism and a considerable concentration of industry (coal mining, petrochemicals, Huachipato (CAP), and so on). There were incipient forms of workers' control emerging even before the Popular Assembly and these were strongly developed during and after the October crisis. In October Communal Commands were formed, and from January 1973 cordones were created that rapidly gained strength and became Communal Commands. Unfortunately, we lack more precise data.

Other Cordones and Comandos

Industrial Cordon Antofagasta—Antofagasta City
Cordon Alto Penuela ⎱
Cordon Serena-Centro ⎰ City of La Serena
Cordon Coquimbo-Centro ⎱
Cordon Puerto ⎰ City of Coquimbo
Constitucion Communal Command—City of Constitucion
Cordon Centro ⎱
Cordon Poblacional ⎰ City of Chillan
Cordon Centro—Osorno
Industrial Cordon of Llanquihue

NOTES

1. Jacques Chonchol, a leader of the Christian Left (IC) in "Elementos para una discusion sobre el camino chileno hacia el socialismo" in Cuadernos de la Realidad Nacional, no. 7, (March 1971).

2. Jorge Insunza, member of the Political Commission of the Communist party in the journal Principios, no. 138 (March/April 1971): 22.

3. See Julio Arredondo: "Los grandes ausentes: obreros no organizados" in Punto Final, no. 34, (1968).

4. Clotario Blest: "La Clase Trabajadora Chilena y la Estadistica Sindical," Punto Final, no. 151, (February 15, 1972).

5. See Emir Sader S.: "Movilizacion de masas y sindicalizacion en el Gobierno UP": CESO Working Document (Santiago: Universidad de Chile, 1972).

6. See Luis Vargas, "La formacion del Area Social: del Programa de la Unidad Popular a la lucha de clases," in the journal Marxismo y Revolucion, no. 1, (1973).

7. S. Ramos, Chile una economia de transicion? (Santiago: Prensa Latinoamericana, 1972).

8. Report by the Economic Minister Pedro Vuskovic to the Inter-American Committee for the Alliance for Progress, 1971.

9. Vargas, op. cit.

10. Ibid.

11. Ibid.

12. Ibid.

13. S. Ramos, "Acerca de demonios y tesis falaces, " in Chile Hoy, no. 6, (July 1972).

14. S. Ramos, Chile una economia, op. cit.

15. Pio Garcia, Socialist party activist, coeditor of the journal Chile Hoy, no. 31, (January 1973).

16. Marta Haernecker, Socialist party activist, director of Chile Hoy; "Los Comandos Comunales y el problema del poder, " in Chile Hoy, no. 26, (December 1972).

17. "La Asamblea Popular de Concepcion" in Chile Hoy, no. 8, (August 1972).

18. Ibid.

19. The Communist party, "Las bases organizan, " Chile Hoy, no. 26, (December 1972).

20. Report to the plenum of the Christian Democrat party, published in La Prensa (Santiago: December 3, 1972).

21. Figures as of December 31, 1971: "La Clase Trabajadora, " by Clotario Blest, op. cit.

22. "Los partidos deben informar a la base, " Chile Hoy, no. 62, (August 1973).

7

SHANTYTOWN DWELLERS
AND PEOPLE'S POWER
Monica Threlfall

The mass movement of Chileans in shantytowns and working class neighborhoods known as the pobladores' movement grew up around a series of demands relating to collective consumption and the struggle outside the workplace for better living conditions. In this sense it was a complement to the labor movement, taking up the secondary contradictions of the system, that is, not those relating to the relations of production but those emerging from the relations of consumption. Such secondary contradictions took a multitude of concrete forms: problems with housing, with urban infrastructure, with health, education, and transport, and in the case of Chile even problems that elsewhere would have been regarded as primarily a matter for the individual, such as food supplies and prices. The breakdown in Chile of the normal system by which goods went to individuals with the money to buy them, combined with structural impasses in the global supply system, led to these too becoming a collective issue.

What historical conditions made it possible for this type of movement to become a political movement of mass dimensions? First was the existence of a vast industrial reserve army of labor whose living conditions gave rise to a bitter struggle for survival. This reserve army of the unemployed is a consequence of Latin America's peculiar pattern of economic development and the dependent character of its process of industrialization. Its existence not only allowed capitalists to increase the rate of exploitation in the workplace, but also allowed them to ignore the need to provide an adequate environment for the reproduction of the labor force in the home.

For a more detailed analysis see Ernesto Pastrana and Monica Threlfall, Pan, Techo y Poder: El Movimiento de Pobladores en Chile 1970-1973 (Buenos Aires: Ediciones S. A. P., 1974).

Second was the weakness of the labor movement. In Chile,
the trade unions have grown up in extremely adverse and hostile
conditions, and they have been able to achieve only a limited power
of negotiation and a small margin of concessions from the bourgeoisie,
thus leaving the field open for other forms of struggle. This weakness
of the labor movement is itself a reflection of the oppressive character of the Chilean bourgeoisie and its dependence on imperialism.

Finally, inflation. Inflation is a problem that plagues many
dependent economies, but in certain situations it can become so
acute that wage claims cannot hope to keep up with the rhythm of
price increases. As a result, even the demands of the labor movement tend to shift towards the fight for better living conditions and
easier access to social services, as well as rises in pay. This
battle can be waged not only in the workplace, but also on the
"residential" front: the more so since the principal provider of services is not the industrialist or employers' class, but the state itself.
Hence the ability of some bourgeois administrations to organize such
a movement as a source of popular support, for example, as President
Velasco did through Sinamos in Peru and the Christian Democrat administration did in Venezuela.

In Chilean popular history before 1970 such struggles were by
no means unknown. The first tenants' league dates back to about
1925, while the first organized invasions of vacant urban land began
about 1946, led by the Communist and Socialist parties, the political
organizations of the labor movement itself. In the period preceding
Popular Unity, the Christian Democrats used such struggles on the
residential front as a way of articulating working class demands.
By setting up moderate organizations such as the Juntas de Vecinos
they provided an escape valve and a form of institutionalization for
popular claims for a better urban infrastructure, as well as a degree
of legitimacy: all of which served to lower the pressure of the masses
for social change. The promotion of such community organizations
also allowed the Christian Democrats to secure their own popular
base. Various housing programs for the low-paid were created (such
as the Plan de Ahorro Popular) as well as a scheme whereby urban
land was chopped up into tiny plots and handed over to homeless
families.

With the accession of the Allende government, the political
representatives of the working class achieved a historic victory.
Popular Unity was an instrument forged by the Chilean working class,
with which that class identified its class interests. Nevertheless,
this state of affairs alone was not enough to guarantee that the
masses were organized in any real or even any representative fashion,
or that its leading organization, the CUT (Central Unica de Trabajadores) actually included all the social layers of the exploited classes
within its ranks. Popular Unity represented the general interest of
the exploited classes as a whole. However, only 30 percent of the
salaried workers over eighteen belonged to the trade union movement,

this figure including the rural unions and a high proportion of white
collar workers—particularly civil servants and employees of state-
owned industries, since 90 percent of the public sector was unionized.
The Labor Code restricted unionization to plant unions, and these
could only be formed where there were 25 or more employees, while
50 percent of the industrial proletariat or more worked in firms employing fewer than 25. Furthermore, affiliation with the CUT was by no
means automatic: the decision whether to affiliate was left to the
discretion of individual unions, and depended on the whole on the
union's ability to pay membership dues. In general, the CUT's
membership was drawn from the larger unions, representing less than
25 percent of the working population. [1]

The rest of the working class, the self-employed and the under-
employed, could either have been incorporated into the trade union
movement de facto or by a reform of the Labor Code. Certainly it
would have helped to mobilize them to demand such a reform. But
none of these steps was taken. In early 1973, a bill for the reform
of the Labor Code was drawn up, but there was no public debate on
it and it never became law. Alternatively, if the position of these
social layers in the productive process made unionization unlikely
(as was the case with street vendors and unskilled service workers)
they could have been organized on a different basis. However, while
Popular Unity made no attempt to mount a public campaign to increase
the number of unions or to draw attention to the much-needed reform
of the Labor Code, its other attempts to create popular organizations
were along very similar lines to those once organized by the Christian
Democrats. Popular Unity's support for the homeless was a means
of generating a demand for housing geared to reactivation of the building trade, while the Juntas de Abastacimiento y Precios (JAPs) were
intended to provide the basis for an alliance with petty bourgeois
shopkeepers as well as a channel for "popular participation" in the
face of the growing problem presented by the black market.

The community movement of workers and shantytown dwellers
centered around three main organizational tasks: land invasion and
the subsequent setting up of campamentos; various methods of food
supply and distribution; and the formation of Comandos Comunales
(Communal Commands) to coordinate activities and demands on all
the different fronts within a particular geographical area, such as
a comuna or municipality. By centralizing these demands within the
framework of an organization that could take up the defense of working-
class interests as a whole, it was hoped to create local power centers.

THE SOCIAL BASIS OF THE SHANTYTOWN AND
WORKING-CLASS COMMUNITY MOVEMENT

Before going on to describe the work of the movement, let us
first attempt to clarify the ecological environment and social classes
among which it operated.

Traditionally the most visible expression of the movement has been the struggle for housing and urban infrastructure. In fact, the front in which it operates covers all those issues around which the oppressed classes can organize themselves at their place of residence, to satisfy needs for individual and collective consumption. So the movement is the organized expression of demands pertaining to the "residential" front.

The class roots of the pobladores and their universe or ecological environment present a more complex problem. Pobladores in Chile live in a variety of ecological situations, particularly in Santiago, including the following:

- the callampas or mushrooming shantytowns produced by slow cumulative invasions of empty sites, and the conventillos, deteriorating housing in the old urban center: 25 years ago these two accounted for the greater part of the proletariat's housing, but today their inhabitants are only an insignificant proportion;
- the poblaciones or planned estates of permanent, temporary, and often self-built housing;
- the campamentos, settlements formed on the basis of organized invasions of sites during the last few years;
- working class neighborhoods also popularly known as poblaciones, which have arisen as a result of unplanned urban growth, with temporary or permanent individually built houses on small plots acquired either through a cooperative or by individual purchase.

The inhabitants of all these areas participated in community organizations, but the poorest families suffering from the worst conditions were the most consistent in the struggle, and provided the main nucleus of the movement, and these are therefore the principal focus of attention here.

Even though theories of urban marginality and dual culture that define the poblaciones as economically and psychologically "marginal" were dropped in Chile some years ago, [2] the Left has still tended to treat pobladores as a social sector marginal to the productive process, and thus justify concentrating its efforts on workers in the large and dynamic industries. The Left argued that the poblador lacked experience of proletarian organization and therefore would have a low level of political consciousness, and furthermore that organizing around demands for consumption would lead to economist deviations, since pobladores, who had no experience of struggle against the bosses, would fail to visualize the bourgeoisie as a class.

Empirical studies and reinterpretation of data carried out during the Allende government has radically changed this picture. [3] The main conclusion that emerges is that the urban popular sectors are

remarkably heterogeneous. Though different criteria have been used
to provide a series of occupational categories allowing different class
factions to be distinguished, there are three basic variables:*
    1. type of insertion into the productive process. For those
pobladores working in industry, the size, sector and degree of modern-
ity of the firm they work for has to be taken into account, and for those
who work in services, the extent to which their work is unproductive.
Union membership tends to be a function of size of firm, although by
no means all large, dynamic, or monopolistic industry has the density
of union membership one would expect. [4]
    2. degree of occupational stability. This refers to continuity
of work, which can be gauged according to the level of unemployment in a particular sector. Work in construction, for example, is
relatively unstable.
    3. level of income as a determinant of consumer power.
    One could sum up the class characteristics of the social sectors
involved in the pobladores' movement along the following lines:

- Important contingents of the proletariat are involved, especially
  those in small- and medium-sized firms in nondynamic industries.
- The population of poblaciones and campamentos is composed
  of those class fractions receiving relatively low incomes,
  incomes that are lower than average for Greater Santiago.
- There is a higher percentage of construction workers in poblaciones and campamentos than in the rest of Santiago, and
  also a higher rate of unemployment.
- The percentage of union members is lightly higher than average
  for the whole city.
- In comparison with other areas, campamentos have a number of
  distinguishing characteristics. Incomes here are even lower
  than in other working-class districts, though there is a higher
  proportion of industrial workers than in the poblaciones or in
  Greater Santiago as a whole. The campamentos are mainly
  inhabited by recently constituted families with few young
  children or none at all, and there is a high proportion of migrants
  who have arrived in the city in the last 10 years.
- Finally, women make up an important part of the pobladores
  movement although they are hardly represented in the occupational categories since so few of them work.

    With respect to political consciousness, some studies suggest
that the level of consciousness in the pobladores' movement is no

———————

    *Level of skill among workers has not been used as a variable
due to inadequate data.

different from the "economist" consciousness prevalent in the trade
union movement, particularly in the modern industrial sector. [5]

So as Castells rightly suggests, it is not the peculiar class
composition of the pobladores' movement but the fact that it is organized around contradictions in the sphere of consumption that defines
the place of the movement within the class struggle, [6] as becomes
obvious in any discussion of the history of the pobladores' movement
between 1970 and 1973.

PHASES IN THE ORGANIZATION OF THE POBLADORES' MOVEMENT

The Campamentos

Occupations multiplied in the first nine months of 1970, during
the period before the presidential elections, reaching a peak during
the two months that elapsed between election day and Allende's
assumption of office in November, and continuing with declining
intensity during his first year in government. At the end of 1971 they
reached a new though less important peak, and fell sharply again in
1972. Police records give the following statistics for "occupations
of urban sites": 352 in 1970, 560 in 1971, and 148 before May 31,
1972. [7] By 1972, 15 to 18 percent of the Santiago population was
said to live in campamentos.

The immediate objective of an occupation was to achieve legal
right to a piece of ground that a family could live on without having
to pay rent, since buying a plot of land through the available schemes
was beyond the occupiers' means. Once the land had been occupied,
the government would be pressured into delivering a standard emergency prefabricated wooden hut (which Popular Unity did almost
immediately) and later into setting up plans for the construction of
permanent housing, the provision of electricity, water, transport,
and so on. The organization of an invasion began in most cases
with the formation of a Comite Sin Casa (Homeless Families' Committee), which recruited its members either through the network of
contacts of a branch of a political party, or from an overcrowded
neighborhood, through friends, or among workers in a particular
factory. The site to be occupied was carefully chosen in advance,
with particular attention to its owner. Land belonging to institutions
such as the Church was preferred to that belonging to individuals,
as likely to entail less police repression. Imperative needs such as
the need for protection from assault led to the formation of vigilance
brigades, sometimes of a paramilitary nature, which patroled the
site's boundaries and entrance. Afterwards, the participants began
to organize.

FIGURE 7.1

Social Characteristics of Inhabitants of Poblaciones and Campamentos

	SUBPROLETARIAT	PROLETARIAT		PROPERTIED PETTY BOURGEOISIE AND WHITE COLLAR EMPLOYEES
OCCUPATION	- SEMI-ESTABLISHED COMMERCE AND STREET VENDING - PERSONAL AND LOWLY QUALIFIED SERVICES - HABITUAL UNEMPLOYED - OCCASIONALLY EMPLOYED ("pololos," "changas")	BLUE-COLLAR WORKERS OF: SMALL — MEDIUM INDUSTRY, COMMERCE, AND SERVICES ARTESANS (includes modern medium industry) CONSTRUCTION	- LARGE MONO-POLY INDUSTRY BOTH MODERN AND TRADITIONAL - LARGE BASIC SERVICES (communications, energy, and transport)	- PRIVATE AND PUBLIC WHITE COLLAR EMPLOYEES - SMALL ESTABLISHED COMMERCE AND OTHER SMALL ENTREPRENEURS
STABILITY	VERY UNSTABLE	MEDIUM STABILITY	RELATIVELY STABLE	
UNIONIZATION	NOT UNIONIZED	HARDLY UNIONIZED (except by trade)	MEDIUM UNIONIZATION, BUT LOW NEGOTIATING CAPACITY	HIGHLY UNIONIZED ("Gremios" in case of commerce) - STRONG UNIONS
INCOME	LOW		RELATIVELY HIGH	
UNIVERSE — POBLACIONES	1972 - 6 poblaciones[a] 20%	60%	20%	
	1969 - 5 poblaciones[b] 18%	40%	26%	15%
	1969 - 4 poblaciones but 2 of them pre-1970 "compamentos"[c] 26.5%	36.5%	21.5%	15.5%
UNIVERSE — CAMPAMENTOS	1971 - 4 campamentos[d] 33%	55%	10%	2%

Source: The percentages come from: [a]Jose Bengoa study, CEA, Universidad Catolica, Santiago. Chile Hoy. No. 32, January 1973; [b]Vandershueren and Portes studies in Vandershueren, "Significado politico de las Juntas de Vecinos en poblaciones de Santiago," EURE, no. 2 (Santiago: June 1971); [c]Castells, "Movimiento de pobladores y lucha de clases," EURE, no. 7 (Santiago), and in Vandershueren op. cit.; [d]calculated on the basis of the data of the FLASO-CELADE study quoted in Duque and Pastrana, Revista Latinoamerica de Cienelas Sociales, no. 1, June-December 1971.

One of the main factors determining the character of the institutions set up in the new community was the political orientation of the leadership. Campamentos organized by the Christian Democrats were set up mainly after the 1970 presidential elections to cash in on Popular Unity's extensive building program: they tended to articulate demands without relating them to structural problems in the economy, thus furthering a vision of the state as a provider of goods and services. Such campamentos never developed a focus for rank and file participation, the leadership being responsible for "negotiating" what was needed independently of whether or not it had been democratically elected.

Campamentos organized by Popular Unity tended to view access to a roof and the infrastructure of urban life as a working-class right that ought to be satisfied as far as the government was able within the given circumstances. Thus the degree of pressure they saw fit to exert on the government to provide them with these rights tended to vary. Furthermore, many of the organizational practices that had grown up during the early stages of the organization would later be discontinued when the campamento's demands were met or when the promise of a solution was given. In general, after the initial period, Popular Unity's campamentos adjusted themselves to their environment, integrating into the surrounding poblaciones and fusing their representation and leadership with the local Junta de Vecinos if one existed, or creating one on the basis of the campamento's own original leadership if it did not. Wider questions such as the lack of medical, school, or shopping facilities in the area were sometimes made a focus for mass mobilization, but not in any systematic fashion, nor as a political issue—one more manifestation of the unequal access to services which the existing system imposed on the working class.

Finally, a third type of leadership can be distinguished in a smaller number of campamentos. This, corresponding to the political line of the Left of the Socialist party and the MIR, saw the movement as a political front of the class struggle. Within the poblacion it posed the need for organizational practices that would lead to a day-to-day questioning of economic and cultural contradictions, and that, by involving the masses in structures that encouraged participation and mobilization, would create a revolutionary political consciousness. [8] Thus representative organizations were created at a series of different levels, always democratically elected. In the most advanced cases, each block would elect a leader of the block, while the campamento as a whole would elect a Jefatura or Executive Committee by universal secret ballot: the block leaders and the Jefatura would then meet together to form the directorio, or intermediate level of leadership. Special activities were organized in a parallel fashion, through a series of fronts: cultural, health, education, work, and women's fronts that sought to involve the inhabitants in every facet

of social life by generating responsibility at the grass roots level.
In one campamento where a clinic was being organized, it was decided
that although the doctor had to be brought in from outside, the nurses
should be volunteers drawn from among the campamento's own comrades, because it was thought that such a system would be of more
value to the community in terms of the training and experience it
would provide than if qualified nurses were brought in, even if the
attention given was of lower quality.

In a study of the campamento Nueva La Habana, where mobilization was probably most successful, the following analysis of the
experience and its purpose was made by a poblador who was himself
a member of the executive committee:[9]

> Nuestra lucha es mas grande que la casa
> [Our struggle goes beyond the question of housing]
>
> Now then, there's no point for us to organize like
> this, let's say, just to get them to come and tell us:
> we're going to put you in such and such a place. Because
> before that happens the fundamental thing, the most
> important thing in all this, is that a political conscious-
> ness should be created in the minds of the comrades
> which enables them to visualize their fundamental enemies
> and their fundamental aims: basically, the taking of
> power along with the workers. That's why we've got
> to see that we've an obligation to make every one of
> the Comites Sin Casa—which will later turn into a campa-
> mento—make them into an instrument of power. Through
> its own organizations, that is, its own fronts for self-
> protection, culture, health, and building. And that it
> shouldn't be an official from the Ministry of Housing
> who decides that poblador so-and-so should be given
> such-and-such a house, but that the comrade should
> take part in the whole process of construction of his
> house. And that when he receives the key to the house,
> it should be the culmination of a whole process of par-
> ticipation and mobilization and not just the fact that in
> a paternalistic way they hand him the key and say: this
> is your house.
>
> And what's more, comrades need to be aware that
> the solution to the housing problem doesn't stop at
> having a roof and four walls, but that it includes making
> sure that we have all the equipment to be able to live
> in decent conditions, like human beings, with schools,
> clinics, supermarkets, all those things. And also to
> have them in the hands of the pobladores themselves,
> so that we avoid speculation with prices or robbery,
> or certain groups getting rich.

All this can only be got through a process, a
process we are living thanks to the way the campamento
functions, as a step towards getting a house.

But it's not just by solving the housing problem,
by building houses, that the pobladores' problem is
going to be solved. . . . the pobladores' problem is
one of living, one of surviving. Because there's no
point in having a good house if we are still being exploited and humiliated. There'd be no point in it if, for instance,
medicine continues to be controlled by the bourgeoisie;
just like education, justice and so on.

I'd see the housing problem as part of the global
problem. I mean, the only way for working people to
get their demands is by taking total power. And not
only by taking power, because even in socialist countries where they've made the revolution, the housing
problem hasn't come to an end. The housing problem
will end completely when we get beyond the stage of
socialism and arrive at communism.

Popular Organization of Supplies of Goods and Distribution

When meat began to go short because of increased consumption,
and the difference between official prices and actual prices began
to get out of hand because shopkeepers were speculating, the Popular
Unity government and the political parties in the coalition took the
initiative of promoting Juntas de Abastecimiento y Precios (Supply
and Price Committees) in every neighborhood. These were set up
on the same territorial basis as the already-established Juntas
de Vecinos—thus leading to a long drawn-out battle with the right
wing that we will not go into here. They were supposed to exercise
"control" over local shopkeepers and/or speculators and hoarders:
but as the committees had no legal rights to intervene or impose
sanctions, what in fact occurred in many cases was that the shopkeepers themselves took control of the JAPs and used them as an
easy way of obtaining supplies at official wholesale prices in order
to resell part of them at black market prices. However, even from
the beginning, the JAPs were a focus for organizing the discontent
of housewives and poor workers, and a means for them to begin to
mobilize around the defense of their access to basic foodstuffs.

Soon after the end of the bosses' strike, the problem of shortages
became much more acute. In campamentos, where there was no established commerce, and shopkeepers were mostly reselling what they
had bought in the central market at higher prices, the pobladores were
extremely mistrustful of this social group. This lack of faith, added

to their own peculiar disadvantages where shopping facilities were concerned (inaccessibility, bad transport, and so on) gave them a reason to launch into different forms of distribution. First a weekly or fortnightly canasta popular (people's food basket) was organized for each family according to its size, consisting of one unit of basic products such as sugar, margarine, tea, and oil. The canasta was organized by an elected "people's grocery" committee (Almacen del Pueblo), leaving the shopkeepers to sell nonbasic foodstuffs still in plentiful supply, about the only thing they could obtain on a small scale anyway. The people's grocery obtained supplies from state distributors or established contracts with private ones.

The idea of rationing distribution spread and was adopted in many working class neighborhoods, not as a means of bypassing existing commerce but as a way of establishing more effective control over this sector, which had become a very active source of opposition to the government. Rather than lose trade, shopkeepers would agree to cooperate with the JAP and register all families living in the area, selling them products on a rationed basis and taking only the margin of profit that was allowed by the official price ("rationing for the rich: supplies for the poor").

However, in the long run alliances with the small shopkeeper tended to break down as inflation soared and the profits shopkeepers could make from speculation became too much of a temptation: in any case the government controlled only 30 percent of distribution, and shopkeepers were under strong pressure from their ultraright-wing union. Eventually alternative forms of organization emerged on the initiative of the rank and file. Supply committees that the shopkeepers had abandoned or from which they had been expelled joined up to form area and provincial commands and organized distribution on a massive scale, supplying directly from the government distributor to the families without intermediaries. Run in conjunction with the National Distribution Secretariat, by mid-1973 the Santiago Comando Provincial de Abastacimiento or direct supply network was providing 180,000 families.[10]

This form of mobilization was very important. On the one hand, it involved directly or indirectly practically the whole of the working class population, entailing a vast amount of organization and antlike hard work and thus providing, on a massive scale, the beginnings of a political education for large sectors who were not involved in other forms of political activity, particularly women. The urgent need to involve women in political activity should not be underestimated, particularly given Popular Unity's dependence on elections, and the fact that its support from female voters lagged astonishingly far behind its support from male voters—in 1970, 26 percent of the female vote was cast for Allende as opposed to 46 percent of the male vote.

On the other hand, much of the mobilization was spontaneous. Popular mechanisms of distribution came under party controls only at the higher levels, and remained almost entirely independent of the trade union movement, as distribution was organized mainly on a residential basis. (Some supplies were secured through offices and factories of course, though not necessarily through the unions: but this was recognized as not being very egalitarian.) Much of what was achieved was gained against the initial policy of the government and at the cost of several bitter conflicts, producing occupations of government offices and distribution agencies and other mass protests. In such cases, the organizations of the masses were able to gain their demands through sheer weight of numbers most of the time.

Finally, the question of food supply and distribution was taken up not just in terms of the best way round a difficult situation, but as an issue in the class struggle, a demand that the government take adequate measures to maintain a minimum standard of living for the masses at the expense of the ruling class.

The Communal Commands

During the last year and a half of Popular Unity, the struggles of the pobladores' movement took a qualitative leap forward and the movement involved itself openly in the contest for political power as this was posed in Chile at the time. In this new phase in the history of the movement the key features were the following: a greater political capacity, expressed in the sharpening of conflicts between the movement and the bourgeoisie and the state; an irregular relationship with the organized trade union movement, in terms both of structures and of politics; and finally, the attempt to create local organs of "people's power" known as the comandos comunales (Communal Commands).

In practice, the Communal Commands led a rather fluctuating existence, according to the conceptions of their role and course of development favored by the political parties that promoted them and the conditions imposed by different political conjunctures.

The part played by the pobladores' movement in the formation of these new organizations was largely a consequence of the general linking up of local organizations of the movement over a larger area (for example, a municipality, or part of one) that had already been taking place for some time. On various occasions, the process of linking up had led to fairly widely coordinated protest action against local power centers, such as municipalities controlled by right-wing elements. In other words, a fairly well recognized vanguard already existed, based chiefly on the campamentos, and led by left-wing militants of the Socialist party and the MIR.

Simultaneously, new experiences of workers' participation had led some sections of the trade union movement towards a more radical political position, demanding that the government should take over more industries than it had originally planned, and that it should introduce workers' control. In the major industrial belt of Santiago, Cerrillos, this radicalization culminated in June 1972 in a series of joint actions by workers and pobladores, during which barricades were set up and the whole zone was taken over, and a Comando de Trabajadores—the first—was formed. The initiative spread to other areas.

When the bourgeois opposition organized a national "bosses' strike" in October 1972, conditions were ripe for the kindling of a massive and mostly spontaneous response from the trade union movement and the pobladores'. The attempt to halt production was a threat to the unions, the closing of shops and shortage of supplies, a threat to the pobladores. During this period about 20 comands or cordons or comites coordinadoras sprang up in the Santiago area alone, some based solely on the unions, some based solely on the pobladores, but most of them coordinating both groups under the leadership of the industrial proletariat. On the whole, the activities of these organizations were primarily defensive in character owing to the absence of support or political leadership from the government, the CUT, and the Communist party. For much the same reason, they were never effectively generalized. But they fought with success to overcome the obstacles created by the strike.

However, the wind was taken out of the sails of this movement by the end of the bosses' strike, accompanied by a government decree raising wages by the full amount of the cost of inflation. There was no real support from Popular Unity parties for the continued existence of the comands and cordons. As far as the parties belonging to the Popular Unity coalition were concerned, the government's agreement to invite representatives of the armed forces into the cabinet in order to solve the strike implied a sharp cutback in any attempts to promote autonomous activity on the part of the masses. Furthermore, although the bosses' strike had generated a massive mobilization, only vanguard sectors were prepared to take up the question of "people's power, " dual power, or the creation of soviets, which for the masses as a whole was a novel experience.

Thus coordination between the trade union movement and the pobladores came to a sudden end: activities continued on a lesser scale, but each front became absorbed in its own tasks. Some comands and cordons disintegrated and some others were formed, particularly in the provinces, but few grew to the point that they had any real capacity to mobilize on a mass scale or to exercise any power.

During the period just before the Tancazo (the attempt to trigger a coup by a Santiago tank regiment, on June 29, 1973) the pobladores' movement took a more political turn. Its militant sectors were involved in demonstrations outside factories in conjunction with the

more radical sections of the trade union movement, calling for increased
government takeovers and people's control of the factories that produced foodstuffs and of the distribution agencies. For a short period
after the tank regiment's mutiny there was heightened activity, and
a series of new comands were formed in response to popular realization of the government's fragility. Then came a second strike by the
truck owners, who had provided the backbone of the first bosses'
strike, and with it a new wave of shop closures and public transport
stoppages. The pobladores' movement was forced to devote all its
energies to immediate tasks such as food supply and transportation.

The vanguard of the movement had reached an understanding
that it was vital to bring together all the different fronts of struggle
and all the different classes and factions of classes involved, if
there was to be any hope of organizing a resistance to the onslaught
of the bourgeoisie; just as it had also reached an understanding of
the political necessity for organs of workers' power to be set up that
were capable of challenging the power of the state and generating a
situation of dual power. But the nature of the Chilean political situation meant that there was considerable controversy over the different
roles of government and masses, as well as over the role of the
embryonic organs of workers' power vis-a-vis the state. The two
most important political representatives of the mass movement, the
Communist and Socialist parties, were after all also the dominant
political forces in government, and the Ministry of Labor was under
the control of a unified trade union movement represented by the CUT.
Because a reformist political leadership dominated the labor movement, organizations of the masses were treated as something that
ought to be subordinated to the government or that at best should
serve to complement it. Thus they never became an alternative to
the bourgeois state apparatus in which the government was entangled,
and dual power can only be an alternative to the bourgeois state.
Only the vanguard had begun to question this subordinate role allocated to the movement by mid-1973. But the deterioration of the political
situation as a whole happened at too fast a pace for their views to
make much difference. Significantly, the military coup of September
1973 occurred at a moment when the masses were uncertain and
confused about the role of the government and the course of action
they should follow.

The Significance of the Pobladores' Movement

There are two different angles from which the significance of
this movement of shantytowns and working class neighborhoods can
be evaluated: by focusing on the size of the movement and its
"quality," or by focusing on the role the movement played within the
class struggle taken as a whole.

Early analyses of the pobladores' movement that were made while Popular Unity was still in government underlined the numerical size and spread of the movement as this was manifested both in the seizure of sites and setting-up of campamentos and in the cumulative increase in neighborhood organizations from the time of the Frei administrations. They also laid fundamental emphasis on those aspects of the struggle that, it was thought, led to a generalized questioning of the system and to the creation of embryonic organizations of "people's power."

As we have seen, the traditional role of the movement had been one of exerting pressure on the state to meet immediate needs of consumption. Originally, in other words, the movement played the role of client to a paternalistic state, stopping short of any demands for fundamental change in the system in the hope that less fundamental demands might be satisfied. However, between 1970 and 1973 the movement was able to pose demands that went far beyond the traditional limits to its actions, at the same time as it expanded to involve broad social layers in its activities. New methods of organization and forms of struggle were invented as the movement took responsibility for food supply and distribution and joined the Communal Commands.

The Size of the Movement

Official statistics and sociological surveys give an astonishingly high estimate of the number of organizations involved in the movement and the number of people affiliated to it. One survey, for instance, suggests that in 1972 there were "800,000 families affiliated to organizations inspired and motivated by the housing problem, or active in its periphery,"[11] that is, four million people or about 40 percent of the Chilean population. Figures for 1969 given by the Consejeria Nacional de Promocion Popular indicate that at that time there were already 3,500 Juntas de Vecinos in existence with nearly 350,000 members, and over 6,000 Centros de Madres with 240,000 members: furthermore, the Consejeria tells us that between 1964 and 1969 it organized over 39,000 training courses with more than 1,350,000 participants.[12]

Exaggerated or not, these global figures fail to tell us anything about the rhythm of formation of different types of organizations or their ability to involve growing numbers of people. Still more important, they have nothing to say about the degree of effective participation. Such phenomena are a function, not only of national political conjunctures, but also of the internal dynamics of the movement and its individual organizations. For instance, there was an upsurge in the movement between 1970 and 1971 in the form of increased occupations of urban sites. Then a period of consolidation followed, marked by ups and downs, until the campamentos reappeared as a force on the national political scene in late 1972 and early 1973, well in the lead with respect to the organization of new methods for direct distribution of food.

Periods of upsurge in the mass movement can be identified by increases in the formation of new organizations, the rapid involvement of new members, and a rise in the number, size, and militancy of the movement's demonstrations. Such periods alternate with periods of drift when the movement is in the doldrums and with periods of consolidation characterized by a slow accummulation of experience, political training, and maturity on the part of the movement's leaders. The movement's participation in the building of the Communal Commands, for instance, owed much to the prior existence of community organizations and their experience of earlier struggles.

The Quality of the Movement

Quantitative analysis shows clearly that the movement managed to mobilize vast sectors of the population: however, 100 people willing to join a Junta de Vecinos have a very different political significance from 100 people willing to join in an occupation, organize a People's Supply Committee, or form a Communal Command, forms of action that belong to a more advanced stage of the class struggle. Consequently, we shall look at the following features in order to assess the movement's achievements: the enemies it identified; the long-term class interests that it envisaged; the tactics and strategy it developed to further these; the political content of the demands it posed and of the forms of organization that it adopted as a way of reaching immediate and long-term aims.

In what ways did the movement surpass its traditional sphere of action? Let us study some of its experiences, and the repercussions these had on the class struggle as a whole.

"Socially-transforming" Practices in the Campamentos

One study in particular has made an attempt to look at experiences of social change within the campamentos, and analyze the structural and conjunctural factors that effect the emergence of new social practices for good or ill. Its authors conclude that on the whole campamentos "do not constitute a focal point of cultural change, properly speaking, but can represent a source of social change in some dimensions and in some cases." They go on:

the more the problem is related to basic structural
contradictions (i. e. the bourgeoisie's power over the

state apparatus and the means of production) the less
will be the capacity of a popular government to satisfy
people's demands; the stronger the leadership of revolutionaries within a campamento, the higher the level
of social creativity expressed in the way in which day-
to-day problems are solved. [13]

The most highly developed attempts to create alternative social
practices and institutions occurred in those campamentos that developed
their own structures of power and framework of social relations within
the community. Whereas the Juntas de Vecinos organized by the Frei
government in a legalistic fashion stopped short at providing a formal
cohesion within the sprawling "marginal" areas, a cohesion that
rarely came close to breaking down class barriers or fomenting class
consciousness, practices of a completely different nature were instituted in certain campamentos. Here an internal power structure was
consolidated and the basis of social relations among the inhabitants
was changed, the new structure being legitimated by the awareness
of residents that it constituted a continual challenge to the status
quo. In the most advanced examples, the inhabitants gave active
but not unquestioning support to a leadership that undertook a wider
range of community responsibilities, and that in turn was given
greater rights to intervene in the life of the community. In some
cases, a high degree of legitimation for the new authority structures
led to the elected leadership going as far as the formation of a disci-
plinary body; in one or two cases this was actually endowed with
the attributes of a "people's tribunal of justice" (a grass roots
response to a government bill that envisaged the creation of "neighborhood tribunals," but never saw the light of day because of right-wing
opposition).
    In the midst of other experiences of social change, the work
of the different "fronts" provided a day-to-day source of political
education "bringing out the real meaning of immediate demands,
placing them clearly in the field of capitalist relations of production,
thus raising the political and ideological consciousness of the
majority of the inhabitants." [14] Though experiences of confrontation
with the state were more general before Popular Unity won the presidential elections of 1970, the struggle for demands that the state
could not satisfy continued afterwards on a massive scale, provoking
a new attitude and awareness of the nature of the state even while
the direct challenge to the existing order waned.

Links With the Process of Production and the Labor Front

As suggested earlier, the traditional separation between the
class struggle in the factory and the class struggle on the residential
front was an obstacle to the rise of a political movement that could

bring together different factions of the oppressed classes and was
capable of rising above the "economist deviations" that characterized
both fronts in isolation.

Between 1970 and 1973, the gap between the two fronts was
bridged in some individual campamentos, as well as in the concepts
and methods of struggle embodied in the Communal Command. In
several campamentos committees of the unemployed were formed on
the basis of demand that the committee as a whole should be found
work. Often the members of these committees were construction
workers made redundant during the 1970 slump in construction (though
some of them were industrial workers who had lost their jobs because
of factory occupations). Pobladores in the most militant campamentos
demanded that the unemployed be taken on as paid employees to build
the campamento new houses, in direct contrast to the Christian Democrat policy of "self-help," which encouraged individuals or at best
cooperatives to build their own houses; residents of the poblacion
were then represented in the workers' council in charge of the construction site. Alternatively, pobladores demanded that the unemployed
be given work in state construction companies under workers' control.
Another way in which the gap between the residential front and the
labor front was bridged was through the active support that some
campamentos gave to industrial conflicts in their area, turning out
massively to take part in workers' demonstrations and pledging the
solidarity of their organization.

These on the whole were limited experiences, however. The
Communal Commands provided a framework for coordinated action
with the labor front on a much larger scale; however they too functioned for only a limited period, and with sharp fluctuations. Although
the comands were originally conceived as an alliance between different
factions of the oppressed classes and the different fronts of the class
struggle, once the October 1972 strike was over they tended in many
cases to narrow their focus to the organization of a preponderantly
industrial or preponderantly residential base, and to orient their
activities accordingly. Where subproletariat and proletariat (industrial
and nonindustrial) did work together in a united front of different
organizations, the unionized sectors played the leading role, as
would be expected from their longer tradition of struggle and their
political position as the revolutionary class.

During the October crisis, the comands constituted a significant step forward in the relationship between the two fronts, although
collaboration was largely confined to the level of leaders and there
were only a few coordinated activities at the level of the rank and
file. After the crisis was over, the mass movement went through a
period of slackened activity until the Tancazo: as a result, there
was a partial disintegration in united action between the two fronts,
industrial action being organized through the industrial cordons and
community action through the comands, while different mass organi-

zations at local and provincial level grew up to confront the problems posed by the acute shortage of supplies. There were, however, some notable exceptions to this fragmentation, such as the coordinated takeover of the small town of Constitucion. Furthermore, distribution of supplies directly from the factories and farms to the shantytowns through the people's organizations continued.

Identification of the Principal Enemy

Though contact and organizational ties with the labor movement contributed towards raising the consciousness of the more highly mobilized sectors of the pobladores' movement, specific political conjunctures and the general rhythm of the class struggle were more important in the political steps forward taken by the movement as a whole. The economic crisis, particularly the bosses' strike, accentuated class polarization and threw light on the real nature of the capitalist system whose mechanisms for exploitation are usually veiled by bourgeois ideology. The crisis revealed to workers in general that production depended on them, and in particular it revealed the link between consumption, production, and distribution, and the dependence of one or the other.

In earlier periods of the class struggle in Chile, demands for individual and collective consumption had rarely transcended the act of pressuring the state to go some way toward satisfying the elementary needs of the masses. The art of combining welfare state demagogery with outright repression was one at which populist governments were adept, and it served successfully as a means of containing the movement, preventing demands that might have strained the system's ability to control the situation from even being posed. If the pobladores blamed anyone for the lack of an adequate response it was always the government of the moment, not the system as a whole.

During its first year, the Popular Unity government showed an unprecedented ability to respond to the movement's demands on a massive scale; but because of the dependent nature of Chile's economy, it was impossible for the government to maintain this rhythm in the redistribution of income or in the expansion of the building industry without taking full control of the economy. Furthermore, the initial effort had hardly begun to meet the real needs of the masses, while still greater demands were being put forward.

One can assess the political development of the movement in the new range of these demands. Pressure was still directed towards the state, but now the demands were not merely for the state to deliver the goods (literally), but also that it should take over the privately owned systems of production and distribution, and put them at the service of the oppressed classes: demands, for example, that the state should take over construction firms and monopolistic distributors, and that it should accelerate the rate of agrarian reform.

Thus, the brittleness of the economic system meant that even economistic demands quickly became political, and the class nature of
the process of production was recognized by shantytown dwellers
and working class housewives alike. During Popular Unity, the
movement began to recognize that its enemies were the same as those
of the labor movement, and linked its demands with those of the
industrial proletariat and the peasantry, directing them at the bourgeoisie: an important step towards the formation of a common class front
against the bourgeoisie.

Identification of the Class Nature of the State Apparatus

If one of the often-cited weaknesses of the pobladores' movement was its tendency to visualize its enemy as an impersonal
government body, instead of the bourgeois class—a tendency rooted
in the very nature of its demands—this, during the later stages of
Popular Unity, also became one of its strengths.
    When the Popular Unity government was in its early phases, the
movement gave way to a tendency to regard the state apparatus as
legitimate, in spite of its past experiences of the state's negative
features. Land occupations had had to face severe police repression
under the outgoing Frei administration, and the consciousness of
those who participated in them was marked by the experiences of
this period, and of the need to organize a defense against police
attacks: these experiences had crystallized in the most advanced
forms of people's power found among the campamentos. And yet,
when Popular Unity took office, we find

> . . . all the potential of the movement to generate forms
> of power starting from their direct clashes with the
> state power, were put into question by the new situation
> . . . The change was felt by the pobladores. In fact,
> perception of the change that had occurred went even
> farther than reality itself. The statement became common
> that the courts, carabineros, and police, previously
> unjust, were now just. [15]

However, the movement was not in a position to blame the
boss when problems were not solved, since its demands continued
to be directed at the government, even if the government was "ours";
thus its followers were able to see the nature of power more clearly.
The difference between the government and the state apparatus began
to emerge, as protests were voiced against bureaucracy and red tape,
and actions were taken against municipalities, ministries, and other
state bodies. As Popular Unity's very limited powers over the state
and the state's class character became more obvious, the most
militant sectors posed the need to change the nature of the state as

well as to take power from the bourgeoisie. The banner of "people's
power" was relevant beyond the sphere of the factories: it was taken
up as a central slogan by the shantytowns and other organized communities. To the extent to which the Chilean masses as a whole did
come closer to a consciousness of the bourgeois nature of the state—
in circumstances where Popular Unity was drawing a curtain over
precisely this question—the struggles of the shantytown movement
made a contribution that the labor movement would possibly not have
made on its own.

CONCLUSION

The urban land seizures of 1970-71 signaled the appearance
of the poorest sections of the working class on the national political
scene: the "sin casas" (homeless families). This first massive
phase of struggle over living conditions was an integral part of the
upsurge of political activity among the masses as a whole during
this period, a product of the deepening crisis within the ruling classes.
The movement's importance both before and after the 1970 presidential
elections lay in the coincidence of a natural expression of certain
social contradictions with the tactical approval of all the important
political forces: at this moment in time the Christian Democrats as
well as the parties of Popular Unity and the MIR were encouraging
this type of mass demand, though obviously with different aims.
The social significance of the movement was heightened by its
appearance within a limited area in a very short space of time.
However, it is interesting to note that the struggle on the
residential front was not, numerically at least, the dominant form
of mass struggle in the postelectoral period. Its protagonists were
drawn from the lowest income strata of the proletariat, recently
unionized and traditionally with very limited powers of negotiations:
but these were precisely the sectors who now found an outlet for
their demands in industrial action, and not only through the struggle
for housing. Thus the same period saw a numerically significant
wave of strikes, concentrated particularly among the same faction
of the working class, those employed in small- and medium-sized
firms. What did distinguish the pobladores' movement during this
period was its ability to involve sectors of the population who had
previously never engaged in political activity: certain layers of the
nonindustrial, unorganized urban poor, housewives, and unemployed
workers. At the time, the pobladores' movement was politically the
most important form of the class struggle.
One can distinguish a second phase of the movement that begins
slowly in the second half of 1971 and becomes obvious by mid-1972,
in which the movement developed, broadened its horizons, and began

to take up a greater range of secondary contradictions of the system
in its demands. With the creation of new community organizations
such as the JAPs and the Consejos de Salud (Health Councils) the
movement began to look like a model of popular participation as this
was being promoted by Popular Unity. It provided the Left with a
source of active popular support, and its organizations were strong
and broadly based enough to allow for mobilization on a national scale.
In fact, its capacity to give a mass response in situations of conflict
developed to the point that it sometimes went beyond the defensive
type of action engaged in by the masses as a whole, its most militant
sectors demonstrating that they were in a position to carry out local
offensives against the bourgeoisie.

The October bosses' strike was a political experience that
provoked a qualitative leap forward in the types of tasks undertaken
by the shantytown and community movement: these became more
political and began to entail a higher degree of autonomous organization and independent action on the part of the participants. The
third phase of the movement followed; the campamentos led other
sections of the masses both in organizing the rationing of food supplies
and in the effort to set up communal commands. While on the one hand,
the economic crisis was forcing the movement to dedicate itself to the
distribution of basic foods, on the other hand, the increasing level of
social and political tension imposed a new set of conditions on its
struggle. The fight to be able to eat became implicitly a problem of
political tactics and the movement's political consciousness developed
at the same pace as its understanding of the functioning of the system
of domination that threatened it. If rationing was to continue it was
vital for the government to extend its control over production and
distribution, striking a blow against the bourgeoisie by expropriating
more firms, and of this the movement was aware. By the time the
movement's vanguard had reached the stage of forming comands as
embryos of "people's power," and thus at least potentially of calling
into question the power of the state, the movement had gone far beyond
the model imposed upon it by Popular Unity and was on the way to
constituting centers of dual power—but it was unable to progress beyond this stage.

The community movement had already developed in Chile as a
result of the populist policies of the Frei administration before the
Popular Unity period; and one of the peculiar features of the Chilean
experience is that it already constituted a movement with definite
characteristics when Allende was elected president. However, the
Chilean Left traditionally tended to identify the working class with
unionized workers, at least where politics was concerned, relegating
other strata or factions of the proletariat and subproletariat to the
status of tactical allies of the working class in its political struggle,
nothing more. At the beginning, Popular Unity's relationship with
the pobladores' movement was a function of its economic policies,

aimed at providing a building program and increasing the masses'
level of consumer power. At a later stage, Popular Unity deliberately
stimulated the creation of community organizations as a way of increasing popular welfare: but in spite of this shift, Popular Unity
clearly did not take advantage of the movement's full political potential, or even of the advances achieved by the movement itself.

The classes and factions of classes mobilized in the community
movement were therefore only superficially involved in Popular Unity's
political project. In the Popular Unity view, they remained passive
agents on the receiving end of economic benefits, or at most, a source
of popular support for government measures. Thus, the tendency for
Allende's government to rely fundamentally on the proletariat in large,
dynamic industries continued. The organization of the Area de Proprie-
dad Social (Social Property Area), the nationalized sector of the
economy, was designed to mobilize only a small sector of the proletariat. [16] Another example of Popular Unity's unwillingness to take
up the defense of broader class interests is the lack of a concerted
attack on the discriminatory and inhibiting union laws mentioned
earlier. Finally, those organizations that sprang up at rank-and-file
level as an attempt to bridge existing divisions within the proletariat,
such as the cordons and the Communal Commands, remained bereft
of government support in their attempts to carry out this task.

Recently, there has been a demystification of the social composition of the pobladores' movement and its experiences during the
years of Popular Unity, confirming that the classes and class factions
involved in the movement were strategic allies of organized labor.
These social layers were able to identify their chief enemies as the
bourgeoisie and imperialism, and took an active part in the struggle
against their own domination; they also made attempts to coordinate
their defense of their own interests with the interests of the labor
movement. The fact that the working class remained politically
divided greatly hindered the consolidation of the mass movement as
a whole under a single leadership, and this in turn hampered the
coordination of struggles on the various different fronts. Though the
pobladores' movement had its own limitations—because of its class
heterogeneity and the nature of its fundamental demands, the movement was inevitably subject to ups and downs—the weakness of
efforts at coordination was not, on the whole, the fault of the pobladores. In a series of different political conjunctures, the pobladores'
movement demonstrated a constant search for ways and means of
coordination. It was imperative that the political leadership of the
mass movement as a whole should allow the pobladores' movement
to play an active role in the political struggle, precisely because
it could draw together the different class factions of the proletariat
and take up the defense of the interests of all the exploited classes.

The Chilean experience has shown that any revolutionary political strategy for Latin America must take into account the potential of
a community movement.

NOTES

1. See Emir Sader, Mobilizacion de masas y sindicalizacion en el Gobierno UP, mimeographed, (Santiago: Universidad de Chile, Documento de Trabajo, CESO, 1973).

2. See in particular, Hacia un diagnostico de la marginalidad urbana. Caracteristicas socioeconomicas de las poblaciones marginales de Gran Santiago, mimeographed, (Santiago: Consejeria Nacional de Promocion Popular, 1970).

3. In particular, see the research sponsored by CIDU of the Universidad Catolica and FLACSO-ELAS, UNESCO, Santiago.

4. For the best study of unionization see Emir Sader, op. cit.

5. F. Vanderschuren, "Significado politico de las Juntas de Vecinos en poblaciones de Santiago," EURE, no. 2 (Santiago, June 1971): 82.

6. M. Castells, "Movimiento de pobladores y lucha de clases," EURE, no. 7, (Santiago): 20-21.

7. Quoted in Joan Garces, El estado y los problemas tacticos en el gobierno de Allende (Santiago: Siglo XXI, 1973), p. 151.

8. Cf. also, James Petras, "Political and Social Change in Chile," and "Chile: Nationalization, Socioeconomic Change and Popular Participation," in Petras, ed., Latin America: From Dependence to Revolution (New York: John Wiley, 1973), pp. 30-32 and 58-60, for comments on the political consciousness of the pobladores.

9. Organizacion y lucha poblacional en el proceso de cambios en la experiencia del campamento de Nueva La Habana, H. Saa, R. Urbina, A. Victoria, Directorio y pobladores de Nueva Habana, DEPUR (Santiago: Universidad de Chile, 1972).

10. Quoted by an official of the secretariat.

11. See L. Alvarado, R. Cheetham, and G. Rojas, "Mobilizacion social en torno al problema de la vivienda," EURE, no. 7 (Santiago). Castells, op. cit., quotes the same figure from Alvarado et al., but gives it as 800,000 Chileans affiliated to territorially based organizations, "that is, more than the total number of unionized urban and rural workers in the productive sphere."

12. Cited by Giusti, Organizacion y participacion popular en Chile, el mito del hombre marginal (Buenos Aires: FLACSO ediciones, 1973), p. 139-40.

13. "Reivindicacion urbana y lucha politica: los campamentos de pobladores en Santiago de Chile," CIDU Study Group, in EURE, no. 6 (Santiago).

14. Castells, op. cit.

15. S. Quevado and E. Sader, "Algunas consideraciones en relacion a las nuevas formas de poder popular en poblaciones," EURE, no. 7 (Santiago): 76-77.

16. For an analysis of the labor force in the Social Property Area see Luis Vargas, "La formacion del Area Social: del programa

de la UP a la lucha de clases, " in <u>Marxismo y Revolucion</u>, no. 1
(Santiago, 1973).

REVERSING THE REVOLUTION:
THE CHILEAN OPPOSITION
TO ALLENDE
Ian Roxborough

This chapter addresses itself to two interrelated questions:
First, why it was so difficult for the opposition to overthrow Allende,
why it took them three years to get around to doing what many powerful Chileans (and foreigners) thought should have been done in 1970;
and second, how these difficulties led to a specific manner of organizing the coup, something that might well have important consequences
for understanding the nature of the present regime in Chile.

The first question is important for understanding the constraints
and choices open to the actors in the Chilean political system between
1970 and 1973. There is sometimes a tendency when looking at the
coup of September 11, 1973 to analyze the sequence of events leading
up to the coup and implicitly conclude that the coup was more or less
inevitable. Most observers do, at least, go one step beyond this
and ask what might have been done to avoid the coup. This suggests
that the coup was not completely inevitable, but did depend to a
certain degree on the policy decisions made by various actors.

But if this is the case, then one must ask not merely what might
have been done to avoid a coup on September 11, 1973, but also what
was done to avoid a coup in the period up to that date, or at least,
what political forces made a coup unlikely before September 11.
Once the question is formulated in this manner, then it becomes
obvious that there did exist several conjunctures during the three-
year period with which we are concerned in which some form of military intervention was possible and indeed, had been planned or even

Earlier versions of this chapter were presented as a paper at
seminars of the Centre for Latin American Studies at Cambridge
University and at the Institute of Latin American Studies at Glasgow
University. I am grateful for the participants for their comments.
The fact that I have not always heeded their advice is my fault alone.

attempted. (Aside from the assassination of General Schneider, Colonel Labbe was forced to retire in December 1971 for plotting a putsch, General Canales was forced to retire in September 1972 for the same reason, and there was a brief uprising led by Colonel Souper in June 1973. These are the attempted military interventions that are well documented. There were certainly a great many more rumors that a coup was in the offing.)

By choosing to focus on the problems inherent in the military coup as a successful enterprise, one is led to a stress, not on the inevitability of the 1973 coup, but rather on its contingent nature. That is, the successful outcome of the September coup was contingent on a whole series of decisions taken by a multiplicity of actors in the Chilean political system over the three-year period and even before 1970.

This is not to say that the outcome of the political process was dependent only on the decisions of these actors, nor to claim that these decisions were themselves not products of a given historical situation. Clearly, we are not dealing here with totally free agents acting in a historical vacuum. What is stressed, however, is the role of choice and consciousness in history.* Concretely what is at issue here is whether a decision by the Allende government to compromise with the Christian Democrats in 1972, or a decision by the Socialist party to leave the Popular Unity coalition and form (together with the MIR and MAPU) a mass revolutionary party committed to insurrectional strategy, could have prevented the September coup either through some kind of compromise or through a preemptive revolution. To take the second alternative, there are good reasons to suppose that had the leadership of the Socialist party followed a policy of developing the revolutionary process even at the cost of breaking with the Allende government, then to have hoped for a successful socialist revolution in Chile before September 1973 would not have been unrealistic. Those of a determinist persuasion would

---

*There is not space in this chapter for a lengthy discussion of the philosophical issues involved. Briefly, it may be said that I find the position taken by Lucian Goldmann more cogent than that taken by Althusser. In terms of the history of Popular Unity in Chile, there is a school of thought that claims that the coup of 1973 is best understood as a response to a long-term structural crisis in the Chilean state. It is argued that the Chilean political system had been in a state of crisis or decomposition for some years, certainly since the Frei presidency, and possibly even antedating 1964. There had been a decline in the legitimacy of the state, accompanied by an upsurge of political participation and the emergence of a new, antidemocratic right. In contrast to this position, the analysis in

no doubt argue that the constraints on the ability of the leadership
of the Socialist party to choose this path were such that a choice of
revolutionary tactics by the leadership of the Socialist party was
most improbable, and therefore this line of historical development
was foreclosed. These constraints might include the petty bourgeois
origins and following of the Socialist party, and its long involvement
in parliamentary politics. Clearly, the argument must move to a more
specific and empirical level in order to assess the plausibility of
these claims.

Similarly with the hypothesis that agreement with the Christian
Democrats in 1972 might have prevented the coup. It is possible to
argue that the leadership of the PDC could not afford to ignore the
feelings of a body of "hard-liners" within the party (grouped around
ex-President Frei) who were already at that date pushing for a military
intervention. Again, such a claim must be assessed at a specific
and empirical level.

Two alternative paths of development that might have avoided
the September coup have been briefly presented. In gross terms,
these were two of the most plausible alternative historical outcomes.
Since this chapter is concerned with the decisions made by the
opposition, a study of the possibilities for a revolutionary strategy
cannot be fully discussed here. The rest of this chapter focuses on
the alternatives open to the opposition and the effect of the choices
made between these alternatives on the Chilean political process.

It is here that the second question—the specific manner of
organizing the coup—becomes central. The argument that will be
presented here runs as follows: because the opposition to Allende
was badly divided in 1970 a military intervention was not realistic
for some time; during this period the National party and the extreme
Right sought to polarize Chilean politics and thereby forced the PDC
to develop and organize a militant mass base in order to respond to
the challenge from its right flank; the net result was the growth of
a mass movement of the middle class that gave the military coup
(when it was finally organized in September) a number of fascist
overtones. This argument will be spelled out in more detail in the
following pages and some evidence will be produced to support this
interpretation. It should, however, be stressed that much of this
line of reasoning is in the nature of a series of hypotheses, to be
substantiated or invalidated at a future date by more detailed research.

----

this chapter is more conjunctural. That is, the position taken is that
if Allende had not been elected in 1970 there would not necessarily
have been a crisis or decomposition of the Chilean political system.
What occurred in 1973 was not some abstract crisis in the political
system but a concrete threat of a socialist revolution.

THE INITIAL SITUATION

The coalition led by Salvador Allende that won the presidential elections of September 1970 was considerably to the left of most social-democratic reformist governments of a European variety. Besides the reformist sector, the UP coalition contained within it both avowedly revolutionary elements, and sections which were committed to far-reaching structural changes in Chilean society on such a scale that any serious attempt to implement the program was likely to be highly destabilizing. The UP represented a potentially dangerous challenge to the Chilean ruling class.

This potential threat was intensified by the very factor that had enabled the Popular Unity coalition to win the elections; namely, the deep-seated division of the Chilean Right and its inability to agree on a common program and candidate.

Such agreement had been reached in 1964, in the face of a clear threat that the Left would win the presidential elections in that year. In 1964 the Right had joined together in an uneasy coalition around the reform-mongering candidate Eduardo Frei. The rich and powerful classes of Chilean society temporarily joined in a common cause with the dispossessed and alienated "marginal" elements around the slogan of a "revolution in liberty." This vacuous theoretical formulation did not last long in trying to paper over the contradictions inherent in such a populist alliance, and by the late sixties most of the members of this unholy alliance had become disenchanted with "their" government and had moved either to the Left or to the Right. Chile's one chance at the needed self-reform by the ruling class (carried out by a Centrist party) had failed, and the polarization spiral that was to lead via September 1970 to September 1973 had begun.

However, the Chilean ruling class had one crucial advantage: its hegemonic position. The history of the development of Chilean capitalism has been such that a highly integrated and cohesive ruling class has developed over a relatively long period. This class, although it embodies factions with somewhat diverging interests, does have a high degree of internal unity, based to a considerable extent on extensive economic and kinship linkages between the core families of the ruling class.[1] In addition to this structural (economic and kinship) unity, the ruling class had managed to legitimate and institutionalize its position as ruling class in the political and juridical sphere. Chile's long and more or less continuous bourgeois-democratic tradition had permitted the growth and development of a deeply-rooted ideology of legalism and respect for the constitution that permeated important sectors of the working classes and the various middle strata. Indeed, some of the parties forming the UP coalition—such as the Radical party and the API—were profoundly committed to these ideological positions. Thus, the very "maturity"

of the Chilean working class and its early incorporation into a basically clientelistic system of politics, [2] in conjunction with the extent
to which middle class elements had been incorporated into the state
apparatus, would facilitate the maintenance of ruling class power.
This is what is meant by saying that the ruling class continued to
hold a hegemonic position in Chilean society.

Unlike many other prerevolutionary situations, the bourgeois
state apparatus was intact in 1970. There had not been a civil war
or revolution, nor a crisis in the ruling class resulting from a major
war or civil disaster. The bourgeois social order, the bourgeois
political parties, the armed forces and police, and the capitalist
economy were all intact.

The question of state power confronted Allende in a highly
complex and formidable way. If it was true, as his supporters claimed,
that his inauguration would mean that the representatives of the working class had captured a part of state power, it was by no means the
case that they had the totality of state power, and much less the
case that they were in a position to constitute themselves as a
socially dominant class.

For these reasons, many analysts, both on the Left and on the
Right, believed that the most probable course of events would be the
hemming-in of the Allende government by bourgeois institutionality,
and its transformation into yet another social-democratic, but essentially bourgeois, administration. [3]

Such a course of events was not the only one possible. Despite
its hegemonic position, the Chilean ruling class was badly split
politically, reflecting its inability to successfully solve the crisis
besetting Chilean society, a crisis whose roots lay in the dependent
nature of Chile's economy and its position within the world economy.
With the failure of the reforming attempt of the Frei government, the
Right had little to offer by way of solutions except either more of the
same (this was the Tomic position) or a return to the discredited and
ineffectual orthodox stabilization policies pursued by the conservative Alessandri administration (1958-64). This political bankruptcy
was reflected in differing solutions to the ruling class' latest head-
ache: Allende's electoral victory.

THE INITIAL OPTIONS

During the two-month period between Allende's election and
his subsequent ratification by the Congress as president of Chile,
three basic options were mooted among the members of the opposition. These form the first expression of a three-way choice of
strategic line that continues in changing formulations throughout
the three years of the Allende government. It should be emphasized
from the start that these basic options or strategic choices need not

coincide with the positions of the opposition parties. The options available at any given time have a logically independent status, and it is a matter for empirical investigation which parties and factions adopt various options at different times. Of course, these options will tend to correspond closely to the position of identifiable parties and factions, but when we discuss options or strategic choices in this chapter it should be understood that there is no assumed identity with party or factional positions.

These three basic options in 1970 were, starting from the Right, the golpista formula, the Alessandri formula, and the statute of guarantees deal.

As is well known, there was an attempt by a small group of people around Roberto Viaux who conspired to kidnap the commander in chief of the army, General Schneider, known for his support for the constitutional ratification of Allende's election, and stage a military coup. The kidnapping attempt backfired when General Schneider resisted, and he was killed. The military coup never materialized. Although it is difficult to estimate the degree of military support there might have been for a coup at this time, it would be unwise to dismiss the attempted kidnapping as being merely the work of a small and isolated group of men. Viaux was a figure with a considerable following in the army, as had been demonstrated by the widespread support he had received during the affair of the Tacnazo in 1969. [4]

The second option, the Alessandri formula, was rather more subtle, though whether it was less bloodthirsty may be open to question. A quote from ITT's men in Chile, Hendrix and Berrellez, gives the substance of the Alessandri formula:

> The big push has begun in Chile to assure a congressional victory for Jorge Alessandri on October 24, as part of what has been dubbed the "Alessandri Formula" to prevent Chile from becoming a Communist state.
>
> By this plan, following Alessandri's election by Congress, he would resign as he has announced. The Senate president (a Christian Democrat) would assume presidential power and a new election would be called for 60 days ahead.
>
> Such an election would most likely match President Eduardo Frei, then eligible to run again, against Allende. In such a contest, Frei is considered to be an easy winner.
>
> Late Tuesday night (September 15) Ambassador Edward Korry finally received a message from State Department giving him the green light to move in the name of President Nixon. The message gave him maximum authority to do all possible—short of a Dominican Republic-type action—to keep Allende from taking power.

At this stage the key [emphasis in original]
to whether we have a solution or disaster is Frei—
and how much pressure the US and the anti-Communist
movement in Chile can bring to bear upon him in the
next couple of weeks. . .

Looming ominously over the successful application of the "Alessandri Formula" is the threat of an
explosion of violence and civil war if Allende loses
the congressional vote. Allende, the UP and the
Castroite Revolutionary Movement of the Left (MIR)
have made it clear they intend to fight for total victory.
Thus, some degree of bloodshed seems inevitable. [5]

As it transpired, the Alessandri formula—a last ditch attempt to
repeat the coalition of 1964—did not get the necessary support from
the PDC who, at that time under the control of the moderate faction,
preferred to bargain with Allende and have him sign a statute of
guarantees dealing with freedom of the press, noninterference in
the armed forces, and so on. A transgression of this agreement by
Popular Unity would provide a reason for demanding Allende's
removal from office.

This third option, a hedging in of the Allende government with
a view to facilitating its transformation into a reforming bourgeois
administration, was favored by those sectors within the PDC who
clearly perceived the continuing nature of the crisis of Chile's
economy and sought once again to apply structuralist reforms aimed
at creating the preconditions for a more healthy capitalist development. In this sense, it was possible to view the Allende government
as being Chile's last chance for a reforming, redistributionist and
developmentalist program. UP was to be given a chance to prove
that it did not intend to subvert the bourgeois social order and
capitalist economy, and the statute of guarantees was designed to
keep it on this straight and narrow path. For woe betide those
reforming governments that stray too far from the primrose fields of
bourgeois virtue in search of some other promised land. The statute
of guarantees ensured that the Damoclean sword (whose concrete
embodiment was the armed forces) was to remain suspended over
the heads of the erstwhile revolutionaries. Care had to be taken
or heads would roll: such was the message.

These then were the three basic choices: a military coup, a
united front of the opposition around the figure of Frei, and the hope
that Chilean society was mature enough to have a tame social-
democratic government (coupled to a suspicion that this was not the
case and an insistence that this government be carefully constrained
and placed under a vigilant surveillance). In 1970 it was this last
option that won out.

With the opposition divided and the extreme Right discredited, the UP clearly had the initiative. During the first year it appeared to many observers and to many in the UP itself that the peaceful road to socialism would be a painless road to socialism characterized by economic growth and stable, orderly change, by increasing popular support among ever wider sections of the population, and by relative political tranquility. That at least was the dominant tone of the avalanche of academic eulogies that greeted this supposed new way of building socialism without engaging in class struggle. If Keynes had talked of the euthanasia of the rentiers, then surely what was about to happen in Chile was the euthanasia of the entire bourgeoisie. They were expected to sit quietly by, with arms folded, as their economic and social power was slowly eroded. With the benefit of hindsight (though if one looks carefully one can find dissenting voices who refused to be swept up in the stampede) one can only wonder at the political naivete and myopia displayed by many leftist academics. But that is a problem for the sociology of knowledge and need not detain us here. The point that needs to be made is that within a year or eighteen months, the UP had been forced on the defensive and by, say, mid-1972, the Chilean Road to Socialism was clearly an anachronism, incapable of being carried through. What happened?

THE MIDDLE CLASS

An adequate account would necessitate a discussion of the initial strategy of the UP and the constraints on the successful carrying out of that strategy. (This is dealt with elsewhere in this book and will not be repeated here.)

In those aspects that are of most concern here, the UP program sought to generate economic growth by utilizing idle capacity and by carrying through a rapid and massive agrarian reform. It would nationalize the copper mines and the major industrial monopolies and banks, thereby creating the basis for a rational control over the economy. Together with these measures, the UP would redistribute income in favor of the less well-off sections of the community and institute a series of reforms designed to increase social welfare and popular participation. The underlying political rationale for this program was the hope that these measures would consolidate the UP's support in the working class and win over large sectors of what were loosely described as the "middle sectors' (capas medias)—the substantial, amorphous middle class and petty bourgeois groups without whose support the UP's voting strength could not be increased. It was an electoral strategy aimed at buying off the middle sectors, based on the assumption that the contradictions between the middle sectors and the ruling class (defined by the UP as consisting of

monopolists and landowning oligarchs tied to foreign capital) would
be too great for the ruling class to enlist the support of these middle
sectors.

It might perhaps have worked. It would be unreasonable to
state categorically that the Chilean road to socialism was foredoomed
to failure. It has been argued above that many of the measures proposed by the UP could easily have fallen within the acceptable limits
of a 'structuralist' reform of Chilean capitalism, and the UP might
have evolved in the direction of a domesticated and 'loyal' social-
democratic administration. That the Chilean road to socialism in
such a case would have led somewhere else is, of course, another
matter.

However, it didn't work (and was not likely to have) because
the strategy was based on a number of assumptions about Chilean
society that are rather questionable.

The first and most obvious point is that the strategy was silent
on some of the central questions concerning state power. It was not
clear how the UP would proceed from its conquest of a part of state
power (the executive) to control of the totality of state power. This
would require not merely gaining a majority in the Congress and
somehow reforming the judiciary, but also controlling the government
bureaucracy and the armed forces. Moreover, there would arise the
need to thoroughly transform the state apparatus. For a socialist
society to emerge, the old bourgeois state would have to be destroyed
and new forms of power created by the working class. Chilean
Marxists were well aware of the classic writings of Marx, Engels,
and Lenin on the subject; but this found no reflection in the UP's
political program. It was only the action of the working class in
creating its own forms of organization in the heat of the class struggle
that put the issue of state power on the agenda.

But even in terms of its own theoretical premises, there were
great flaws in the UP's early strategy.

As the internal contradictions of the UP economic model began
to become obvious in early 1972, it became clear that the UP would
no longer be able to continue to deliver the goods without cutting
into the real income of some groups in order to favor other groups.
The Allende government had to face the problem of administering a
capitalist economy while trying to create the economic bases for
socialism. [6] Clearly the capitalist class would react in some way.
In Chile this took the form of capital flight, disinvestment, speculation, black marketeering, and so on. Given the climate of uncertainty
and the government price controls, it became increasingly less realistic to expect profit-minded capitalists to continue to produce for the
official market—or even to produce at all, unless it were for speculative motive.

In more concrete terms, the failure of the economic model was
related to a seeming inability to anticipate the bottlenecks that would

arise when existing capacity was being used fully, if there occurred, as there did, a fall in the price of copper. This meant a foreign exchange bottleneck that, given the UP's commitment to a policy of infrequent devaluations, would tend to produce either inflationary pressures, or shortages, or both.

All this would have occurred even if there had been no direct sabotage on the part of the bourgeoisie. The evidence seems to suggest that there was, in fact, a considerable amount of such direct sabotage, though it is impossible to get any precise estimates of the extent of sabotage.

Again, these economic problems would have occurred in the absence of U. S. hostility. As was to be expected, business interests in the United States did not take kindly to the UP's program of nationalizations and retaliated in a number of ways. There is a great deal written on the subject of U. S. involvement in Chile;[7] in this chapter the only point that needs to be made is that the actions of U. S. government agencies and U. S. companies (whether concerted or otherwise) undoubtedly added to the economic difficulties of the UP government.

The net result of the increasing economic problems was to undercut the UP's attempt to buy off the middle sectors. But even if the UP hadn't faced the difficult economic conjuncture that it did, it might be wondered whether in fact this is an adequate way for a revolutionary movement to relate to the petty bourgeoisie. There were alternative strategies. For example, Trotsky (who certainly had his followers in Chile) claimed that since the petty bourgeoisie was, by nature of its peculiar position in the class structure—balanced between the proletariat and the bourgeoisie—it would tend to oscillate politically and give its allegiance to whichever side appeared to be about to win in the decisive class confrontation. According to Trotsky, the way to win over the petty bourgeoisie was not to temporize and try and buy them off, but rather to take decisive steps towards winning the class struggle and thereby attract the timid petty bourgeoisie as hangers-on.

Whatever the merits or demerits of Trotsky's theory, the weight of Marxist theory tends to support the view that the petty bourgeoisie is highly prone to bonapartist mobilizations and, even though in many underdeveloped countries such bonapartist and populist regimes tend to be left-wing,[8] there is no guarantee that the petty bourgeoisie will not be mobilized by the Right.

Perhaps the most important premise of the UP's political strategy was the continued division of the opposition. By mid-1972 there was an increasing convergence of the two principal parties of the Right, the National party (PN) and the Christian Democratic party (PDC), and this fundamentally altered the entire political situation.

Although there were many differences between the PDC and the PN, they were both deeply committed to the defense of bourgeois

institutionality.   It was this growing challenge to the bourgeois
social order that drew them together into a loose and antagonistic,
but nevertheless effective, alliance.

Throughout the first year the position of the PDC was that it
too was a legitimate reforming party; in this way it entered more or
less directly into competition with the UP, hoping thereby to win
over the middle sectors. 9 The PDC's position was that the revolution
in Chile could be made in two ways: either in a violent and ultimately
totalitarian one represented by the UP insofar as it was a coalition
dominated by the Marxist parties, or a democratic road represented
by a PDC recombined with certain more 'responsible' elements of
the UP. In marked contrast, the National party repeatedly called
for the formation of a united front of the bourgeoisie capable of
toppling the government. As it turned out, these seemingly antithe-
tical positions combined in a curious way to produce an effective
opposition. While the militant stance adopted by the National party
forced the PDC to turn increasingly to more direct forms of opposition
to the UP government and thereby prepared the ground for an eventual
violent confrontation and polarization, the fact that the PDC remained
'flexible' and committed to bargaining with the UP meant both a ham-
stringing of the government (through the extraction of concessions)
and at the same time strengthened the position of the reformist elements
within the UP coalition since they could continue to hold out the
rather illusory hope of some kind of deal with the opposition to avert
a showdown.

Initially the prospect of a deal had not been entirely unrealistic,
but as events unfolded and the militancy of the working class increased,
the parties of the bourgeoisie closed ranks. By the end of the first
year the possibility of compromise between the government and the
opposition had become quite unlikely.

The UP had clearly underestimated the extent to which the
bourgeoisie, still controlling the bulk of the state apparatus, and
of the mass media, with much of its economic power intact, and
organizationally intact as a class, could both at the organizational
and at the ideological level forge an identity of interests—or at least
the semblance of one—between it and the middle sectors. This identification, and the convergence of the PDC and PN, were facilitated
by an upsurge in the class struggle which took the form of a wave
of working-class militancy in May-June 1972.

CLASS CONFLICT

It may be helpful at this stage to provide a brief periodization
of the UP period in terms of the class conflict taking place. Clearly
this periodization could be the subject of considerable debate. In
order to minimize these problems, the periodization has been left at

a rather crude level, and is meant principally to give the reader some
general notion of the tempo of political conflict during the Allende
regime.

The three years may be roughly divided into six periods:

1. November 1970-December 1971: initial success and euphoria
2. December 1971-May 1972: emergence of problems and search
   for new strategies
3. June 1972-November 1972: intense crisis and attack from
   the opposition
4. November 1972-March 1973: stalemate and armed truce
   with activity directed toward the congressional elections,
   presided over by the civil-military cabinet
5. March 1973-May 1973: following the favorable election
   results the UP takes the offensive
6. May 1973-September 1973: intense crisis and attack from
   the opposition.

Unfortunately space does not permit an extensive discussion
of this six-period scheme here. [10]
The discussion so far has taken us through the first two periods
(roughly up to May 1972). During the first part of 1972 it became
apparent that there were growing economic problems and that the
UP's strategy had reached something of an impasse. Faced with
this situation, and with continuing harassment from the part of the
state still firmly in the hands of the bourgeoisie, the working class
and peasantry began increasingly to take a series of initiatives.
These actions by the working class were frequently led by parties
of the UP, but not by the UP or the Allende government as such.
In fact they are a response to the lack of leadership offered by the
UP at this time. The UP did not turn to the Left at this point; rather,
the working class turned sharply to the Left as a direct result of the
inability of the UP to offer a concrete program to meet the situation.
As a result of their direct activity, this period (May-June 1972),
marking the transition from the early, comparatively tranquil phase
of the UP government to the later crisis-ridden phase, sees a qualitative jump in the level of organization and consciousness of the
working class.

These events included the impeachment by the Congress of
Allende's minister of the interior, Jose Toha, and a number of mass
demonstrations in his support; a demonstration led by the Socialist
party calling for the abolition of the Congress; the widespread discussions around the Hamilton-Fuentealba project for constitutional
reform defining the form of the state sector of the economy; a number
of violent demonstrations in the southern industrial city of Concepcion
(some months later, in August, that same city was the site for the
organization of a people's assembly, an initiative that produced

considerable internal conflict within the UP); the organization of the
first cordon industrial in the important Cerrillos-Maipu industrial
district of Santiago;[11] and the peasant movement in support of 44
peasants imprisoned in Melipilla for the occupation of the farm
"Millahuin";[12] and a number of other incidents.

These events signaled a change in the nature of working class
action under the Allende government. Previously the working class
had played a rather passive role, relying on the government to carry
the struggle forward; by mid-1972 the working class was beginning
to develop a higher level of combativity and a certain degree of
autonomy vis-a-vis the government. This did not go unnoticed by
the opposition.

If it had not been anticipated previously, it was by now clear
to the bourgeoisie that their position was being threatened and that
the social and political processes set in motion by the UP were in
danger of getting out of control. By letting its own base get out of
control, the UP had definitely gone off the rails and some form of
drastic corrective action was now needed. It was no longer possible
to rely solely on the statute of guarantees and the strength of bourgeois
institutions and ideology to constrain the government; a more direct
method was needed. (Interestingly, it was about this time that the
specter of an impending civil war was first raised by sectors of the
opposition.)

Faced with these changed circumstances, the first option
available to the bourgeoisie—the strategy embodied in the statute
of guarantees deal—was in need of considerable revision. What was
sought now was a more direct limitation on the freedom of action of
the government. While the possibility of PDC participation in the
government was not discounted, the central thrust of this opposition
strategy was contained in the Hamilton-Fuentealba reform, and in
the discussion that took place between the UP and the PDC on this
issue.

Some time after the Allende government had assumed office,
two leaders of the Christian Democratic party in Congress, Senators
Renan Fuentealba and Juan Hamilton, introduced a bill in the form
of a constitutional amendment. The purpose of the bill was to define
by a specific law the constitution of the nationalized sector of the
economy. That is, a list of industries to be nationalized was drawn
up, and only those industries that had the express approval of the
Congress could be nationalized. The fundamental aim of this bill
was to limit the government's powers to expropriate industries. In
a sense, this was the constitutional form in which a central issue
in the economic struggle was to be fought out.

After many months of drafting and discussion in Congress the
Hamilton-Fuentealba amendment was approved and sent to the president in early 1972. Allende, acting within his constitutional rights,
vetoed some of the provisions of the bill and sent it back to Congress
for reconsideration.

Congress now had to consider whether to accept or reject the presidential veto on certain clauses of the bill. At this point a constitutional conflict arose, as a result of a disagreement over whether Congress needed a two-thirds or a simple majority to override the presidential veto. For while the opposition parties held a majority in Congress, they did not have enough seats to constitute a two-thirds majority.

Both sides also disagreed as to which constitutional authority had the power to decide the outcome of the conflict.

Because such a conflict of powers brought with it the danger of a military intervention to resolve the conflict, the UP and the PDC entered into negotiations. Both sides stood to gain from a postponement of the confrontation. After lengthy discussions negotiations bogged down over the exact composition of the list of industries to be nationalized, and the left wing of the Socialist party and the hardliners in the PDC (grouped around Frei) took initiatives to call off the discussion. An immediate confrontation was avoided by allowing the Hamilton-Fuentealba project to proceed slowly through Congress a second time, but no substantive agreement between the UP and the PDC was reached, and the attempt to implement the first strategic option of the opposition had failed.

THE RUSSIAN MARSHALS

With the breakdown of these negotiations, there was a shift to the second basic strategy of the opposition. In mid-1972, the Alessandri option was no longer possible, and had to be reformulated. Rather than attempt to constrain the government to act within what the bourgeoisie could regard as acceptable limits, that is, limits that did not challenge the capitalist order as such, it was now assumed by the dominant forces within the opposition that sooner or later the UP government would bring about a situation in which a totalitarian dictatorship would be imposed. The aim, therefore, of the opposition was to defend bourgeois institutionality by preparing for an eventual confrontation which would force Allende to leave the presidency.

Within this general strategy, it is possible to discern a number of different interpretations. It was left open, for example, whether Allende would be made to leave peacefully by a plebiscite or impeachment, or whether he would have to be removed by a military coup. And there was disagreement between those who wished an immediate confrontation and those who thought that the time was not yet ripe.

The most articulate exponent of the latter tactic was the PDC theoretician, Claudio Orrego. He described his position as the strategy of the Russian marshals. In an analysis replete with military metaphor, Claudio Orrego polemicized with the National party, taking

them to task for precipitating a confrontation when the armies of
democracy (read opposition) were in a disadvantageous position.
In his own words:

> One tries not to present battle at the moment in which
> the enemy suddenly breaks through the frontier and
> has at his disposal a maximum level of fire-power,
> morale and organization. To give battle in these con-
> ditions is to risk the very survival of one's own army,
> weakened by surprise and thereby risk being totally
> defenseless at a later date. For this reason, you
> retreat to Moscow. Meanwhile the enemy is harassed
> to sap his strength, to disorganize him, to slow down
> his advance, and to demoralize him. And one retreats
> to Moscow burning the lands and abandoning towns
> until winter approaches and the first snows begin to
> fall. That is the hour for the first great battle and for
> the final offensive. [13]

For Orrego, a truly class-conscious theoretician of the bourgeoisie, Moscow is the Chilean constitution and the institutional framework
of bourgeois rule. The nature of the contest is clearly seen for what
it was: a contest between capitalism and socialism. Allende had to
be removed not because inflation was unmanageable or because the
economy was in chaos (though these were present as central complaints of the opposition) but because the nature of Chilean society
and the right of the dominant class to continue to rule were being
called into question, if not by the government itself, then by the
supporters of the government acting with the tacit approval of important sections of the Popular Unity coalition.

According to Orrego, the first battle was opened in the bosses'
strike of October 1972; the final victory, however, would come in
the elections of March 1973, when the government would be disastrous-
ly defeated at the polls. (Orrego wrote his book in November 1972.)

One of the implications of the strategy of the Russian marshals
was that a certain time would be necessary to mobilize the forces
that would eventually defend Moscow. This then, was the immediate
task of the opposition—to mobilize a powerful mass base. In a
sense, it meant merely a continuation of the ideological campaign
that had been pursued since Allende's election. But it also meant
adding an organizational dimension to the campaign.

The opposition developed a number of organizational forms:
neighborhood self-defense committees (PROTECO), mass marches,
Juntas de Vecinos, and so on. But the most important organizational
form was the gremio.

Briefly, it is possible to distinguish three quite distinct types
of gremial organizations: (1) the small but powerful associations

of large landowners, industrialists, construction contractors, and large retailers (a group that has been described as the oligarchic gremios), (2) the associations of the small entrepreneurs and petty bourgeoisie, and (3) the professional colleges (of doctors, lawyers, engineers, and so on. [14]

The important thing about the gremios was that they facilitated the development of a sense of identity between the small businessmen and professionals on the one hand and the large industrialists and wealthy landowners on the other. A factor that contributed greatly to the success of this interest aggregation function was the predominance of corporatist notions in the ideologies of the opposition political parties and press. Both the PDC and Patria y Libertad had important corporatist strands in their ideological makeup, and not even the National party was willing to openly espouse capitalism as such but chose rather to operate with concepts such as "participation" and "profit sharing" as well as with the more familiar notions of nationalism, authority, and tradition. [15]

In addition, the PDC had a certain following among sectors of the working class and peasantry. This provided the basis for a demagogic campaign to unite these disparate class segments into a syndicalist movement with clear corporatist overtones. Behind this corporate-syndicalist front the opposition was able to claim that it represented a nonpolitical movement of all sectors of society aimed at overthrowing the totalitarian menace of the UP. This syndicalist movement provided a mass base for the employers' strikes of 1972 and 1973, and an excellent ideological cover to obfuscate the defense of the class interests of the bourgeoisie.

THE HARD LINE

It has been argued above that by June 1972, the opposition had shifted from a primary emphasis on the strategy of social-democratic entrapment to an emphasis on a hard line aimed at the eventual overthrow of the government. This was the second basic option. The third, that of a military coup, had not yet become predominant.

Perhaps it will be useful at this stage to review briefly the development of these options.

	A (National party)	B (Frei)	C (Tomic)
1970	immediate coup	Alessandri formula	Social democratic entrapment— statute of guarantees
1972	impeachment and coup	Russian marshals	Entry into cabinet— Hamilton-Fuentealba compromise

The three basic options have been tentatively identified with political parties and factions within parties. This has been done only to provide the reader with some idea of the sorts of political forces supporting the various lines. The caution mentioned above must be repeated: the identification of these options with specific groups in the opposition is not entirely legitimate and underplays the fluidity of the situation. For what was central in the development of the opposition strategy was the way in which these strategies were combined, and the way in which different strategies at different times came to dominate the action of the opposition taken as a whole, forcing the exponents of other strategies into a subordinate position.

In mechanical terms, we may ask, do we get a combination of options A + B or of options B + C? (The crucial role of the Freista group should be apparent.) We may also ask, in each combination, which strategy dominates? That is, if A and B are in alliance, does A's strategy dominate over B's, or vice versa? Similarly with the Frei-Tomic alliance within the PDC, who controls the party, the Freistas or the Tomicistas?

But such questions are posed at a purely formal level. The more interesting question is, how do these shifts in the internal correlation of forces in the opposition come about?

Some of the more obviously relevant considerations include: the degree of crisis in the political system; the extent of polarization in the population; the availability of compromise solutions; the situation in the armed forces and the feasibility of a military intervention; the degree to which the working class or the UP government appears to threaten bourgeois interests; and the degree to which the opposition has developed a mass base that can be used to generate a precoup atmosphere. This last element, the development of a mass movement of the petty bourgeoisie and bourgeoisie, is perhaps the most interesting theoretically, and we shall return to it below.

Before doing so, however, it is necessary to elaborate the analytical framework somewhat. Up to this point, the opposition has been analyzed mainly in terms of political responses, in terms of the selection of a specific strategic option. It is necessary to go beyond this and look at the opposition not merely in terms of political factions but also in terms of institutional spheres.

So far, the analysis has confined itself to one institutional sphere: political parties. It is likely, however, that the three basic options that have been identified have differing degrees of acceptance and support in a variety of institutional spheres, besides political parties. The gremios and the armed forces are institutional spheres in which the basic options are debated and selected. Similarly, one might include U. S. policy makers as a fourth institutional sphere for such political decision making.

If it is assumed that each of the three basic options has some base in each of the institutional spheres, then it is possible to talk about the relative strength and dominance of the basic strategies in

each sphere, and about the relative strength and dominance of institutional support for each strategic option. For example, the coup
option might be very strong in the PN and in the gremios, but weak
in the PDC and the army.

Viewed in these terms, the process of coalition building within
the opposition can be seen to be quite complex and will involve the
building up of subcoalitions within sections of the opposition. A
hypothetical example of two subcoalitions within the opposition is
presented in the accompanying diagram (Figure 8.1). In this illustration, the dominant strategy within the opposition as a whole is
strategy A, and this strategy is supported by many who would prefer
strategy B. There is a subcoalition of the more liberal elements
within the opposition that is unwilling to go along with strategy A,
but does not have control over the opposition as a whole and must
therefore reluctantly follow the dominant subcoalition in its pursuit
of strategy A, while trying to bring about a change in opposition
policy. This subordinate subcoalition contains some groups who
would prefer strategy B, but if given a choice between strategies A
and C would prefer strategy C.

FIGURE 8.1

Subcoalitions Within the Opposition

Options

Institutional Sphere	A	B	C
PDC	nonexistent	strong	dominant
PN	dominant	strong	nonexistent
Army	dominant	strong	weak
Gremios	strong	dominant	weak
USA	dominant	strong	weak

dominant sub-   subordinate
coalition   subcoalition

Perhaps this set of analytical boxes looks overly elaborate;
there is certainly no intention of employing it in detail here. What
the scheme is intended to do is sensitize the analyst to the complex
ways in which coalitions may be constructed. It suggests the possibility of direct contacts between the supporters of a given line in
different institutional spheres. This contact need not be mediated
by the political parties. Thus, for example, one might hypothesize

direct contacts between the armed forces and the gremios, without
the direct mediation of political parties. The traditional nonparty
apoliticism of the army and the claim of the gremial movement to
transcend party politics would tend to favor such contacts. The
result would be a strengthening of the corporatist elements in the
dominant group within the opposition.

In suggesting this, there is no intention of denying or playing
down the links that both the PDC and the PN did have with the armed
forces and with the gremios. Nor is there any attempt to minimize
the importance of the political parties. The point here is merely that
it is quite possible that there were direct links between members of
the armed forces and leaders of the gremios in the periods of crisis.
This is important for the discussion of fascism below.

With the sabotage of the UP-PDC conversations by Frei and
the Altamirano group in the Socialist party, the opposition moved
decisively into the second major strategy, that of an eventual overthrow of the government, the strategy of the Russian marshals.

It is probable that the strategy of the Russian marshals, with
an orientation towards the legal, rather than the military, overthrow
of Allende was predominant in the opposition during the period from
the breaking off of the UP-PDC conversations until the March elections. During this period it appears that the PDC was firmly controlled
by the Freista faction and that there was a struggle between the PN
and the PDC for leadership of the opposition.

At any rate, the spate of impeachments increased, and the
opposition developed forms of mass mobilization: the march of the
empty pots, strikes of shopkeepers and students. At the same time
legal and parliamentary obstruction increased and agitation in the
armed forces was stepped up. September 1972 witnessed a tense
atmosphere in which a coup was imminent, but was discovered and
defused by the government. (This resulted in the revelations about
the "September Plan" and the retirement of General Canales.)

Despite the government's action, the opposition regained
momentum and the October bosses' strike began. As the strike got
under way, the leadership of the opposition passed increasingly
towards the PN.[16] But as the strike dragged on, it became apparent
that not enough preparatory mass mobilization had been done, and
that the movement would be unable to topple the government or
provoke a military coup. It was necessary, then, to open negotiations and seek a compromise with the government.

At this stage the PDC resumed leadership of the movement,
and the moderate wing within the PDC also increased in strength,
though it seems not to have had the strength to displace the Freista
dominance within the party. The softening of the PDC caused alarm
in the National party and the PN tried to put pressure on the PDC
to return to a harder line. It did this by trying to persuade the PDC
to join with the PN in impeachment proceedings against Allende in

the Congress. Since the opposition did not control the necessary
two-thirds majority in the Congress such proceedings could only
be interpreted as a call to the armed forces to intervene.

This maneuver did not succeed, and the October strike was
finally resolved with the entrance of the military into the new cabinet,
the so-called cabinet of social peace.

The period between November 1972 and the congressional elections of March 1973 saw a kind of armed truce between both camps.
During this period, the opposition parties took up the position that
the UP was using the military in order to cover up an incompetent
government with totalitarian aspirations, and that the armed forces
were in danger of being manipulated for sectarian political ends.
The demand was raised that the military participate not only at the
level of cabinet ministers but also at the intermediate command posts
in the governmental apparatus. The opposition claimed that the
functionaries of the UP were deliberately sabotaging the instructions
of their military superiors. It would seem that the fundamental aim
of the opposition was, on the one hand, to politicize the armed
forces and, on the other hand, to drive a wedge between these and
the UP. Information on the armed forces is, of course, difficult to
come by, but it would seem reasonable to suppose that this campaign
of the opposition parties was not without a certain degree of success.
One indicator of this would be the way in which the military played
a key role as a veto group in the discussions over the proposed educational reform embodied in the project for the Escuela Nacional Unificada.
At a later date, the demonstrations against General Prats would seem
to indicate the same.

However, in the period leading up to the elections, the main
thrust of opposition activity was concentrated not in the armed forces
but in the organization of an electoral campaign.

There were two interpretations of the significance of the March
elections. One interpretation (which seems to have been that of the
PN) was that the PDC and PN would between them get enough votes
to have a two-thirds majority in Congress and would therefore be
able to impeach Allende. The other interpretation, identified with
the position of the PDC and in particular of the Frei group, held that
the March election would have the character of a plebiscite. If the
UP got less than 50 percent of the vote, then it could be claimed that
it no longer had a mandate to govern. This view, while more realistic
in its appraisal of the probable results of the election, was on very
shaky constitutional ground, as the Tomic faction within the PDC
pointed out. However, by March 1973 the Tomic faction within the
PDC seems to have lost most of its influence and may be discounted
as an effective force.

The result of the March election was that the UP gained 44 percent of the vote, considerably more than had been anticipated by most
analysts.[17] This meant that the opposition was not building up mass

support as rapidly as it had thought, and seemed to bring with it the prospect of three more disastrous years of UP government. The gloom of this prospect was deepened when the UP moved onto the offensive, forming a purely civilian cabinet and expropriating a number of industries.

In this situation, as the armies of the opposition fell back on the gates of Moscow, the strategy of the Russian marshals became indistinguishable from the strategy of an immediate coup. The hour of action was at hand. The choice between revolution and counter-revolution was clearly posed; it could be only a matter of months before the decisive confrontation arrived. The opposition began to mobilize on all fronts and within six months the Chilean road to socialism had been drowned in a sea of blood.

To summarize briefly, it has been argued that the Tomic strategy of social-democratic entrapment became unviable after May-June 1972. Given this, the inability to carry out the initial strategy of the Chilean road to socialism (because of increasing economic difficulties and the failure to win over the middle sectors) led to initial economic dislocation that both increased working class militancy and created an impression of the weakness of the UP government. These events in turn led to increasing levels of opposition activity and set off a polarization spiral. The center positions became increasingly less viable. But until one side or the other could win definitively, the center could continue to reassert itself. However, this periodic reassertion of the moderates could not stop the polarization cycle from proceeding since a stable center solution was never worked out. Sooner or later one side had to win. Even though the dynamics may have been somewhat different, the positions within both Left and Right hardened and moved increasingly towards intransigent extremes.

FASCISM?

When the September coup came, the bourgeois social order was rescued from the imminent peril of social revolution. But although the capitalist economy was saved, the opposition political parties, the parties of the bourgeoisie, did not benefit from the coup in any immediate sense. This, and the prolonged nature of the military intervention, poses a theoretical problem.

One obvious possibility—that the military would rid the country of the Marxist menace and then turn over rule to the bourgeois politicians—did not occur. A straightforward capitalist restoration did not happen. It is possible to account for this in part by noting the magnitude of the task of repressing the Left in Chile. But this is only part of the explanation.

The military is clearly acting on behalf of the bourgeoisie and at the instigation of the mass petty bourgeois movement, and in this sense is a bonapartist regime, basing itself on two social classes and mediating the contradictions between them. There is nothing very unusual in this; in times of crisis the bourgeoisie abandons its political parties and entrusts power directly to the armed servants of the bourgeois state. Moreover, it usually does so reluctantly and with reservations and misgivings about the relative autonomy of the armed forces, an autonomy that enables them to rule in the interests of the bourgeoisie as a whole yet simultaneously enables them to act against the specific interests of sections or fractions of the bourgeoisie.

There are two features of the autonomy of the armed forces in Chile that deserve comment. The first concerns the extent to which the armed forces came to occupy a position of dual power before the September coup. This was a kind of dual power of the Right, and was more than the armed forces' usual veto power. The veto power of the armed forces as a Damoclean sword had existed throughout the three years and was reinforced by the Allende government's inability or unwillingness to either purge and reform the armed forces or to build up an effective counterweight in the form of a revolutionary militia. The dual power of the military began to emerge in the period of crisis beginning in May 1973. Using the newly approved Law for the Control of Arms, which gave the military far-reaching powers to search people in the street, in their homes, and at their places of work, the armed forces began to systematically harass the working class movement, gather information on the Left, and assess the military preparedness of the revolutionary forces.[18] They were able to do so because the effective power of the Allende regime had virtually disappeared; control over the situation was rapidly slipping out of its grasp. Unlike the situation during the October 1972 strike, when the UP could count on the army to support the government, any recourse to the army in 1973 was a two-edged sword. The army was just as likely to act against the government as for it. True, the army put down the attempted Souper coup of June 29th. But the reasons for this action were not respect for the constitutional role of the armed forces, but a lack of preparation for an effective military intervention. There still remained organizational work within the armed forces: the removal of certain 'unreliable' officers from key positions, and the detection of constitutionalist and pro-UP sections within the armed forces. Colonel Souper's farcical attempt to launch a coup was a desperate gamble of a man whose involvement in a conspiracy had been discovered and who was about to be arrested.

The second feature that increases the autonomy of the military in present-day Chile is the development of the gremialista movement. At the moment the utilization of this movement to organize a corporate state appears to be more a potentiality than an actuality, since the military seems undecided on this question.

The curious thing is that, given the peculiar way events unfolded, the extremist position finally adopted by the opposition was not that of the immediate coup (advocated principally by elements associated with the PN) but rather the strategy of the Russian marshals put forward by the Freista wing of the PDC. It seems plausible to hypothesize that had the strategy of immediate coup been adopted in 1970, there might simply have been a capitalist restoration. However, because the strategy that was followed during the important period from early 1972 until early 1973 was that of the Russian marshals under the leadership of the Freistas, a mass middle class movement was mobilized. What happened, it may be suggested, was that this mass base shifted slowly and steadily—and imperceptibly—to the Right all the time. The PN, waiting in the wings, was able to take over the leadership of this movement after March 1973. Was it the case that this mass movement played a role somewhat analogous to a fascist movement, bringing about a military intervention that would create a new corporate state?

This is not easy to answer. The fascist movement in Chile, Patria y Libertad, remained relatively small during the three-year period, and neither the PN nor the PDC could easily be characterized as fascist or profascist parties. They did, indeed, have important corporatist elements in their ideologies, and in many ways some of their ideological pronouncements closely approximated the overtly fascist statements of Patria y Libertad. Nevertheless, Dick Parker's early assessment of the situation is probably the most accurate description of what actually occurred:

> . . . it can almost certainly be expected that the tradi-
> tional forces of the Right will be opposed to the upsurge
> of a powerful independent fascist movement. The only
> way of stopping it, however, is to take over the poten-
> tial social base of the fascist movement, adopting methods
> of mobilization as effective as those of the fascists.
> We will point out that this is precisely the policy pur-
> sued by the National party after the municipal elections
> of April 1971. [19]

The only point that needs to be added is that by 1972 the PDC was also actively engaged in precisely the same policy. This seems to be the historical importance of the development of the gremialista movement in Chile. As this movement moved steadily to the Right and became increasingly less dependent on the official parties of the bourgeoisie (a process paralleled on the Left by the rise of the cordones industriales—Industrial Cordons) it developed into the social base for an authentic fascist counterrevolution. Whether this potentiality is actualized in the construction of a corporate state in Chile depends on a variety of factors, which would require another chapter to discuss.

Thus it seems that, whatever label is attached to the present regime in Chile—fascist, bonapartist or merely authoritarian—we are left with the seemingly paradoxical notion that it was Frei and his supporters, Frei the exponent of the revolution in liberty, who turned out to be the most dangerous menace to both revolution and liberty.

NOTES

1. The evidence presented by Maurice Zeitlin and his associates on this score seems conclusive. See Richard Ratcliffe, "Kinship, Wealth and Power: Capitalists and Landowners in the Chilean Upper Class" (Ph. D. diss., University of Wisconsin, 1973); and Linda Ann Ewen, "Ownership and Control of Large Corporations in an Underdeveloped Capitalist Country" (Ph. D. diss., University of Wisconsin, 1970).

2. Norbert Lechner, La Democracia en Chile (Buenos Aires: Ediciones Signos, 1970); Faletto, Ruiz, and Zemelman, Genesis historica del Proceso Politico Chileno (Santiago: Quimantu, 1971).

3. Zemelman and Leon, "El Comportamiento de la burguesia chilena en el primer ano de Gobierno de la Unidad Popular," Revista de Sociologia, no. 1 (Santiago, August 1972); and Zemelman and Leon, "Political Opposition to the Government of Allende" in Medhurst, ed., Allende's Chile (London: Hart-Davis, MacGibbon, 1972).

4. Florencia Varas, Conversaciones con Viaux (Santiago, 1972); and Eduardo Labarca, Chile al Rojo (Santiago: Universidad Technica del Estado, 1971).

5. Hendrix and Berrellez to Gerrity, September 17, 1970.

6. Kyle Steenland, "Two Years of Popular Unity in Chile: a Balance Sheet," New Left Review, no. 78 (March-April 1973).

7. North American Congress on Latin America (NACLA), New Chile (New York: NACLA, 1972); Dale Johnson ed., The Chilean Road to Socialism (New York, 1973).

8. Nigel Harris, "The Third World," International Socialism, no. 42 (February-March 1970).

9. Zemelman and Leon, op. cit.

10. A more detailed discussion of the politics of the UP period is to be found in O'Brien, Roxborough, and Roddick, Chile: The State and Revolution (London: MacMillan [forthcoming]).

11. A brief analysis of the cordones is to be found in Philip J. O'Brien, "Soviets in Embryo: Chile 1973," Critique, no. 2 (1973).

12. Accounts of the Millahuin events are to be found in Roxborough, "Political Mobilization of Farm Workers in the Chilean Agrarian Reform" (Ph. D. diss., University of Wisconsin, in progress); Roxborough, "Agrarian Policy in the Popular Unity Government," Occasional Paper no. 14, (Glasgow: University of Glasgow, Institute

of Latin American Studies, 1974); Jose Bengoa, "Movilizacion Campesina, " Sociedad y Desarrollo, no. 3 (July-September 1972).

13. Claudio Orrego, El Paro Nacional (Santiago: Editorial del
Pacifico, 1972), p. 47.

14. Los Gremios Patronales (Santiago: Editorial Quimantu, 1973);
Thomas Bossert and Nora Hamilton, "Chile's Gremios, " CALA Newsletter
3, no. 3 (1973).

15. James Petras, Politics and Social Forces in Chile (Berkeley:
University of California Press, 1969); Dick Parker, La Nueva Cara
del Fascismo (Santiago: Prensa Latinoamericana, 1972).

16. Jorge Larrain, "Orientaciones y actividades de la Confederacion Democratica de Partidos durante la crisis de Octubre, " Cuadernos
de la Realidad Nacional, no. 16 (April 1973).

17. White Book of the Change of Government in Chile, (Santiago,
1973).

18. O'Brien, Roxborough, and Roddick, op. cit.

19. Parker, op. cit., pp. 150-51.

9

**WAS THE UNITED STATES
RESPONSIBLE FOR
THE CHILEAN COUP?**
Philip J. O'Brien

The revelations of William Colby, head of the CIA, to the House of Representatives Armed Service Intelligence Committee in April 1974 concerning the interference of the CIA in Allende's Chile must have come as no surprise to anyone who had closely followed the events in Chile from the electoral victory of Salvador Allende on September 4, 1970 to the military coup of September 11, 1973. Indeed it should not surprise anyone who has studied the role of the United States in Latin America and underdeveloped countries in general. In the aftermath of Watergate and Vietnam it was also perhaps not surprising that parts of Colby's secret testimony were leaked to the press, in this case by U. S. Congressman M. Harrington. [1] Thanks to this and other evidence it is thus possible to piece together some aspects of U. S. involvement in the Chilean military coup of September 11, 1973.

The facts of U. S. involvement (although useful to know) are of less importance than an assessment of the role that involvement had in Allende's downfall. In many ways this assessment is crucial to the worldwide debate about the possibilities of a peaceful transition to socialism in light of the Chilean coup. For if the crucial factor in the coup was U. S. interference, then presumably other attempts at a peaceful road to socialism may succeed provided the United States does not interfere. But if U. S. interference was of relatively minor importance, although admittedly of assistance, then one of the clear lessons of Chile is that a transition to socialism is likely to lead at some stage to armed confrontation.

Reactions to the role of the United States have varied. For President Gerald Ford and Secretary of State Henry Kissinger what the United States did in Chile was as Ford put it in a press conference, "in the best interests of the people of Chile, and certainly in our best interests." This comment was in keeping with one made by Kissinger in June 1970: "I don't see why we need to stand by and watch a country

go communist due to the irresponsibility of its own people." Both
Ford and Kissinger have attempted to minimize, and even to deliberately conceal the part the United States played against Popular Unity.
But even so, many people would still agree with Kissinger's judgment
that "it was the policies of the Allende government, its insistence
on forcing the pace beyond what the traffic would bear much more
than our policies that contributed to their economic chaos."[2]

Opposed to this position, James Petras and Morris Morley
have argued that the United States' "sustained policy of direct and
indirect intervention culminated in a general societal crisis, a coup
and a military government."[3] And Armando Uribe argues that without
the joint action of the United States and traitorous members of the
armed forces there would have been no coup.[4] The belief that the
United States is responsible for the Chilean coup is one widely held
particularly by those unwilling to criticize Popular Unity's basic
strategy and tactics.

The position taken in this essay is that there would have been
an armed confrontation in Chile even if the United States had remained
strictly neutral. The United States did not, of course, remain neutral
and there is little doubt that it actively aided and abetted the downfall
of Popular Unity. But this surely was to be expected. When, particularly in Latin America, has the United States not tried to bring down
a government opposed to its interests? But there is a distinction
between aiding and abetting, and being primarily responsible for a
coup. Given the development of the class struggle in Chile, at
some time the Chilean bourgeoisie and their allies, particularly the
military officers, were bound to launch an armed offensive. No ruling
class in history has given up its privileges peacefully, and there
was no reason to expect that the Chilean ruling class would be any
different. It is true that in a dependent country like Chile, it would
be misleading to confine external pressures and internal social structures to two watertight, separate compartments, but it would be
equally misleading to assume that without the external pressure, the
internal social struggles would have followed a different course.
Thus it is not enough to document and condemn U. S. involvement
in the Chilean process as many (particularly the U. S. New Left)
do; it is also important to assess the impact of that involvement.

THE U. S. STAKE IN CHILE

The Economic State

Throughout most of the nineteenth century Chile's trade and
capital flows were predominantly with Europe. In this period Chilean
foreign policy makers were generally consistent in their distrust of

the United States, regarding the Monroe Doctrine and its subsequent interpretations by the United States not as a form of protection for Latin America from outside aggression but as a declaration for a separate American system in the interests of the United States. During the War of the Pacific, Chile believed that the United States had sided with Peru and Bolivia. A contemporary Chilean journalist wrote: "as is usually the case, the United States is impelled by economic considerations, in this case, to give American capital a better chance of challenging British pre-eminence."[5]

Thus until the 1880s diplomatic relationships between the United States and Chile were cool. From the 1880s onwards the situation changed. Until then, the United States had been unable to challenge European economic predominance in Latin America. But by 1890 the United States was in a position to expand outwards. U. S. investments in Latin America increased very rapidly from $304 million in 1897 to $1,641 million in 1914. Chile's share of these investments rose from $1 million in 1897 to $171 million in 1914. U. S. investment in Chile thereafter continued to expand: to $423 million in 1929 to $484 million in 1936 to $540 million in 1950 to $736 million in 1958.[6] By 1958 over 80 percent of foreign investments in Chile were owned by the United States. The bulk of these investments were in mining as the following data from the U. S. Department of Commerce show (in millions of dollars):

Mining and Smelting	483
Manufacturing	40
Trade	13
Other	200
Total	736

In terms of mining investments, almost entirely copper, Chile was very important to the United States, although in terms of manufacturing Chile had only 2.3 percent of total direct American manufacturing investments in Latin America in 1958.

After the Second World War, the U. S. view of Latin America quickly became dominated by cold war considerations. This perspective entailed a picture of the Communists, not only as exploiters of world revolution, but also as being to a large extent its creators. Thus the increasing social instability of Latin America was either interpreted as being instigated by Communist agitators, or as liable to lead to the growth of communism. From the point of view of U. S. security it was considered important either to prevent this instability or to control it so that it did not develop into a threat to U. S. interests.

A good example of the extension of this cold war perspective into Latin America was Chile's Law for the Defense of Democracy, which outlawed and persecuted the Communist party from 1947 to 1958.

One of the reasons for the original introduction of this law was U. S. pressure. Business Week's "Chile letter" of November 8, 1947 commented that to obtain loans from the World Bank and the United States the Chilean president had to remove all Communists from the Chilean government.

Surprisingly, given the growth of Marxist parties in Chile, for many years after the Second World War the United States did not regard Chile as one of the important potentially "unstable" countries of Latin America. This optimism can be partly explained by the U. S. success in getting the Communist party of Chile outlawed, and partly by the reassuring reports of the American ambassador in Chile from 1939 to 1953, Claude Bowers, who "heaped uncritical praise upon all the superficial aspects of Chilean life, and judged the country by its lustrous veneer."[7] Thus, for Bowers the Chilean urban poor were "the most picturesque segment of the Chilean masses," and Salvador Allende was "an uncompromising foe of communism."[8] This blind optimism continued almost until the elections of 1958, when the narrow defeat of the Socialist-Communist coalition led by Allende made the United States aware that its dominance in Chile was potentially fragile. This new awareness, followed by Castro's conquest of power in Cuba, led to a massive increase in all aspects of U. S. assistance to the new Chilean government.

The new massive involvement of the United States in Chilean internal affairs was not without its stresses and strains with the Chilean ruling class which maintained some nineteenth century trappings of anti-Americanism, though only at the superficial level of disdain over the supposed lack of U. S. cultural and spiritual values. These stresses and strains became particularly apparent during the Alliance for Progress reforming period when the United States pressed for some land, tax, and educational reforms. Nevertheless, at the practical level the Chilean ruling class knew that the role of the United States was crucial in helping them to maintain their position. U. S. military and financial assistance, and continuous anti-Marxist propaganda, helped them to maintain their political and economic hegemony in a situation in which this was under continual threat.

From 1946 to 1958 Chile received a total of $253.6 million from the United States, of which $154.8 million were Export-Import Bank Loans. Thereafter, loans poured into Chile at such a rate that by 1970 Chile had the second highest per capita debt in the world, the highest being Israel. In 1959 the United States listed its key aid objectives as follows: to help avoid any swing to the Left, to foster the growth of democratic patterns, and to encourage freedom and development of private enterprise of capital mainly through private foreign investment.[9] From 1961, in keeping with the public relations rhetoric of President Kennedy, the declared U. S. objectives became those of the Charter of Punta del Este, which established the Alliance for Progress. But in practice the first objective of 1959, to prevent a swing to the Left, dominated U. S. involvement in Chile. A U. S. government report put it, "as a political leader in Latin America, Chile's importance to the U. S. A. is obvious. If she remains on our side of the ideological fence, she is a sober and steadying influence in hemispheric affairs. If she were committed to communism or extremism, the results would be spectacular and disastrous."[10]

At the start of President Alessandri's term of office in 1958, the United States regarded his administration as being filled with competent business and management people, the failure of whom "almost automatically ensures a marked swing to the left."[11] But by the end of 1962 the U. S. officials had decided that the Alessandri government was unwilling and unable to tackle Chile's serious social problems and that an alternative to the traditional Chilean ruling elite had to be found. They found this alternative in Eduardo Frei of the rapidly growing Christian Democrat party. Loans continued to pour into Chile with the main objective of maintaining "Chile's current levels of economic activity and investment and to support the balance of payments so that financial deterioration and unemployment would not occur in an election year."[12] Aid was rushed to "short-term social impact projects to improve social conditions in the densely populated urban low income areas and thereby to produce short-term political and social results"[13] favorable to U. S. objectives in Chile.

At the same time, according to a U. S. journalist, about $20 million was channeled into the Frei election campaign.[14] U. S. companies in Chile also assisted this campaign. The result was a substantial victory for Frei and the Christian Democrats, although the size of his victory—55.7 percent of the vote against Allende's 38.6 percent—makes it dubious that all the U. S. activity was necessary to secure Frei's victory.

U. S. involvement in Chile under President Frei continued to grow. U. S. investors who had traditionally shown little interest in Chilean manufacturing industry, began to invest more heavily in Chile after 1967, as data on foreign investment in manufacturing in Chile show:

(U. S. dollars, millions)

	1965	1966	1967	1968	1969	1970	Total
Total	9.24	5.07	9.27	30.02	42.29	45.65	141.54

Between 1965 and 1970, investment in manufacturing was almost the equal of that in mining, the traditional field for U. S. investment in Chile. By 1970 U. S. interests were increasingly becoming the dominant force in the largest and most dynamic Chilean industries: of the top 100 firms in Chile, 61 had foreign participation.

TABLE 9.1

Distribution of Foreign Investment, 1965–70

Sectors	1965	1966	1967	1968	1969	1970	Total
Agriculture	0.11	–	–	–	–	–	0.11
Mining	2.25	–	0.57	73.23	10.83	56.54	143.42
Industry	9.24	5.07	9.27	30.02	42.29	45.05	141.54
Services and others	0.35	0.01	0.02	0.57	2.47	–	3.42
Total	11.95	5.08	9.86	103.82	55.59	102.19	288.49

<u>Source</u>: Corporacion de Fomento de Produccion: Inversiones Extranjeras en Chile, May, 1971.

Nevertheless, although there was a trend towards increasing U. S. participation and control in manufacturing and also insurance, banking, communications, wholesaling, and retailing, the dominant U. S. economic stake in Chile remained copper. With the exception of coal, the United States had investments in all the main Chilean minerals: copper, iron, nitrates, iodine, and salt. Copper was by far the most important of these, comprising 75.8 percent of the total value of Chile's commodity exports in 1970. The two major U. S. copper companies in Chile, Anaconda and Kennecott, regarded their investments in Chile as being of major importance. The reason for this can be readily appreciated from a Chilean government advertisement in the New York Times (see Table 9.2).

TABLE 9.2

Anaconda and Kennecott Profitability
and Investments, 1969
(in dollars)

	Anaconda	Kennecott
Investments		
worldwide	1,116,170,000	1,108,155,000
in Chile	199,030,000	145,877,000
percent in Chile	16.64	13.16
Profits		
worldwide	99,313,000	165,395,000
in Chile	78,692,000	35,338,000
percent in Chile	79.24	21.37
Rate of return		
percent worldwide	8.5	15.0
percent in Chile	39.5	24.1

Source: Chilean government advertisement in the New York Times, January 25, 1971.

Under President Frei, the Chilean government had acquired a majority share in the largest Chilean copper mines. The acquisition was carried out with the full cooperation of the U. S. companies and many important decisions remained in the hands of the U. S. copper companies. Compensation for the shares was high, and a new tax agreement allowed the companies to triple their profits (between 1965 and 1971 Anaconda made $426 million profit in Chile, and Kennecott $178 million). The copper expansion program under

Frei was not financed out of the U. S. companies' own funds, but was financed by contracting debts of $632.4 million that the Chilean government guaranteed—a useful hedge against nationalization. In 1970 copper was still the key to Chile's dependency on the United States.

Throughout most of its history the Chilean balance of trade has been positive: current export revenues being greater than imports of goods. Nevertheless for most of the period since the Second World War, Chile has been plagued by a constant balance-of-payments deficit. The main cause of this deficit has been the large amounts of profits remitted to the metropolitan countries, particularly the United States. These profit remittances have generally exceeded the entry of new private foreign capital: Chile has been a net exporter of capital. In the short-run, foreign aid helped to cover this balance-of-payments deficit.

Thus, U. S. loans to Chile had for some time exceeded the inflow of U. S. foreign investment. Between 1960 and 1970 Chilean public foreign debt rose from $698 million to $3,127 million with more than half of this debt owed to the United States. In addition to this external public debt there was an external private debt of $659,000. The strategy of development through contracting foreign debt had incidentally the effect of increasing the consumption levels and the expectations of Chileans. But contracting foreign debt was only a short-run solution as interest and amortization payments on this debt rapidly placed an additional burden on Chile's foreign exchange earnings. In 1965 with an official debt service charge of over 40 percent of the value of Chilean exports, President Frei had to negotiate and reschedule debt repayments. The constant need to obtain new credits and aid and to renegotiate the debt placed Chile in a weak bargaining position over both internal and external policies with its main creditors, the United States and the international financial community. Thus when it came to power in 1970, Popular Unity faced a situation in which profit remittances from private direct foreign investment and the debt service charges comprised about 30 percent of the total value of Chilean exports. This gave the United States, with its power to ensure that the flow of aid and credits to Chile could cease, a powerful tool for disrupting the Chilean economy.

In addition, the structure of Chilean imports gave the United States other powerful leverage to disrupt the Chilean economy if it so desired. Unlike the refusal to buy Cuban sugar, a U. S. refusal to buy Chilean copper would have had little effect as the United States took only 23 percent of Chilean exports in 1970. However Chile was in a weak position on the import side, 39 percent of which was supplied by the United States. More importantly, 70 percent of all capital goods came from the United States, and thus the bulk of crucial spare parts and machinery came from U. S. sources.

The Political Stake

U. S. dominance in Chile was not just confined to economic relations. Within a short space of time after replacing European economic predominance in Chile, Chilean cultural and military relationships became increasingly tied to the United States. In place of the German and English advisers who had modernized the Chilean army and navy at the end of the nineteenth century came American advisers and American equipment. News services, sources of technical expertise and cultural and educational exchanges, became dependent on the United States. After the Second World War these sorts of U. S. activities increased dramatically.

These activities served a variety of purposes ranging from straight charity organizations to fronts for the covert actions of the CIA. [15] But overall they all formed part of the U. S. informal empire in Chile, a fairly conscious attempt to maintain the United States as the dominant influence in the Chilean development process. In nearly all key sectors—the military, communications, trade unions, education, community organization, and government departments—there was a U. S. organization giving advice, training, and money. Thus in addition to the various U. S. government agencies there were in 1970 about eighty private U. S. institutions in Chile ranging from the Ford Foundation program for higher education to the Seventh Day Adventist Welfare Service. [16]

Apart from the political parties, two Chilean organizations were considered particularly important by the United States: the Chilean armed forces and the trade union movement. For the size of its population, ten million, Chile has one of the largest armed forces in Latin America—about 75, 000 men or 7. 5 men in uniform for every thousand of its population. From the enactment of the U. S. Mutual Security Act in 1951, Chile has been the highest per capita recipient of U. S. military aid in Latin America and in absolute terms of military grants and surplus stocks ranks second only to Brazil. U. S. military aid particularly since the 1960s has been designed not only to strengthen the recipient armed forces but also to tie these armed forces to the United States. [17] If the need arose the United States clearly would prefer not to have to intervene directly itself but to leave it to its client armed forces. Although the Chilean military receives relatively little antiguerrilla training, most of the Chilean officers have been trained in the United States or Panama if they have gone abroad at all. U. S. military assistance to Chile clearly reflected the conclusion of a U. S. congressional study of U. S. military assistance to Latin America: that the assistance is "political and economic in nature rather than strictly military, " and that "the military assistance programs are primarily an instrument of American foreign policy and only secondarily of defense policy. "[18]

The United States very early on singled out the trade union movement in Chile as a problem area. In 1961 a report to Washington stated: "due to the stepped up activities of the Communist forces in the labor movement it will require considerable effort to assist democratic trade unions to combat the totalitarian threats and permit the development of free trade unions undominated by outside forces."[19] The outside forces did not of course include the United States. The problem facing the United States was Chileans workers' susceptibility to "revolutionary doctrines and class consciousness."[20] To combat these the United States undertook a number of training programs and projects. Trade union leaders were sent to the United States and Puerto Rico for training, and the American Institute for Free Labor Development established an office in Chile to conduct seminars and training programs. The American Institute for Free Labor Development (the AIFLD) is described by former CIA agent Philip Agee as a "CIA-controlled labor center financed through AID programs in adult education and social projects used as a front for covering trade-union organizing activity."[21] The AIFLD was also partly financed by U. S. companies, and included on its board J. Peter Grace of Grace Company and Charles Brinckerhoff of the Anaconda Company—all this presumably to illustrate "the unique pluralism and consensus in American society: Labor-Government-Business," as an AIFLD brochure put it. Over $2 million was spent on this program and more than 4,000 labor leaders trained. How successful the program was from the point of view of U. S. objectives is difficult to judge. The AIFLD claimed that the leadership of many trade unions and trade union departments of some of the political parties were in the hands of former participants in U. S. programs. But the attempt by the United States to establish a rival trade union body to the Socialist-and Communist-dominated Confederacion Unica de Trabajadores failed.

In 1964 another CIA front, the International Development Foundation (IDF), began working among the newly formed peasant trade unions. Over $1 million was spent in an effort to set up a rival peasant confederation to the left-wing one and also, somewhat unusually, given the close cooperation of the United States and the Christian Democrats, to the organizations being established by one of the Chilean Agrarian Reform agencies, Indap. The reason for the latter was that the head of Indap, Jacques Chonchol, was regarded as too socialistic. In this they were right: Chonchol later became minister of Agriculture under President Allende. Again it is difficult to judge the success of the IDF, but undoubtedly it recruited peasant leaders to work for the United States.

Thus, by the time of the elections of 1970 the United States had a substantial stake in the Chilean economy and was deeply enmeshed in all aspects of Chilean society. After so much money and effort it was unlikely to sit back and allow the new Popular Unity government to fulfill its electoral program and entrench itself in power.

THE DETERMINATION OF U. S. POLICY
TOWARD CHILE

Having made a consistent attempt over the years to keep the Chilean Marxists from power, the United States was not likely to stop its activities because a Marxist-dominated coalition had won the presidential election. As a memo written by an employee of the American International Telephone and Telegraph Co. (ITT) in Chile commented, "Why should the United States try to be so pious and sanctimonious in September and October when over the past few years it has been pouring the taxpayers' money into Chile, admittedly to defeat Marxism? Why can't the fight be continued now that the battle is in the homestretch and the enemy is more clearly identifiable?"[22] The ITT's impatience was unjustified; the fight was to be continued.

Two other factors made it likely that the United States would not sit by and allow Popular Unity to consolidate its power. At the end of the 1960s a new anti-Americanism emerged in Latin America headed by Chile, Peru, and Bolivia. Only Brazil seemed uninfluenced by the left-wing nationalism sweeping Latin America. Chile with its mass-based Marxist parties was the key nation in this new nationalism. Bolivia under Torres was in a weak and unstable position; and in Peru the economic nationalism of the military, for example, the nationalization of the American International Petroleum Company, was not intended to lead to a socialist transformation of society but to a redefinition of dependency. Only Chile posed a clear threat to U. S. interests, a threat that if carried out successfully could influence the pattern of development in other Latin American countries. As Kissinger put it: ". . . .we should harbor no illusions: the taking of power by Allende in Chile poses serious problems for us and our allies in Latin America." Also the importance of Chile extended beyond Latin America. To quote Kissinger again: "Further, Chile's political evolution is extremely serious for U. S. national security interests because of its effects on France and Italy."[23]

The policy of detente with both the USSR and China pursued by Nixon and Kissinger did not imply a move towards isolation on the part of the United States. It did not even imply a lessening of the fight against communism within U. S. spheres of influence. Chile, because of its ideological influence within both Latin America and Europe, threatened the balance of power as conceived by Kissinger. Thus Chile, although of little military strategic importance, was to be faced with the new U. S. policy of interference, a policy whereby the reactionary internal forces of a country are supported by the United States in their efforts to defeat the Left.

But although the general contours of U. S. policy towards Chile were set by the time of Salvador Allende's victory in September of 1970, the specifics needed to be worked out. The U. S. ambassador

in Chile, Edward Korry, had been confidently predicting a victory for
Jorge Alessandri, the right-wing candidate in the Chilean presidential
elections. So confident had he and others been that they had not set
up a coordinated machinery with Washington for dealing with an
Allende victory. In the presidential elections of September 1970
Allende had gained 36 percent of the vote, more than either of his
rivals, Alessandri and Tomic. Under the Chilean constitution, he
still had to be confirmed by Congress as president seven weeks
after his electoral victory. The seven-week interregnum was to be
a period of intrigue and panic as frantic efforts were made to prevent
Allende's confirmation. It was during this period that most of the
International Telephone and Telegraph Company memos revealed by
Jack Anderson were written.

The ITT memos make it difficult to decide who precisely was
initiating U. S. policy towards Chile in this period, particularly as
someone like John McCone, an ITT director and a former director of
the CIA, seemed to be working for both ITT and the CIA. The ITT
memos together with the hearings of the Senate Foreign Relations
Subcommittee on U. S. corporations abroad (March-April 1973) give
a fairly clear picture of the role of ITT in these weeks.[24] Unfortunately we do not have a similar account for the CIA and the State department
so the following account is one as seen by ITT.

Prior to the Chilean elections of 1970 ITT officials contacted
the CIA to say they were worried about the Chilean elections and
to offer a substantial sum to stop Allende. When the United States
failed to prevent Allende's victory, ITT met again with the CIA and
made a second offer. In addition an ITT official tried to inform
Kissinger that ITT was "prepared to assist financially in sums up
to seven figures."[25]

Shortly after the election, according to an ITT memo, the State
Department gave Ambassador Korry "maximum authority to do all
possible–short of a Dominican Republic-type action–to keep Allende
from taking power."[26] Also, shortly after the election the U. S.
government's interdepartmental "Committee of Forty," chaired by
Kissinger, met to discuss policies towards Chile and to approve
whatever covert CIA operation might be necessary. We do not know
what was decided at that meeting. But on September 29 the head
of the Clandestine Services Western Hemisphere Division of the
CIA, William Broe, met an ITT vice-president, Edward Gerrity, to
discuss a plan for encouraging economic chaos in Chile. As Broe
explained: "There was a thesis that additional deterioration in the
economic situation could influence a number of Christian Democratic
Congressmen who were planning to vote for Allende."[27]

During this time there was indeed an economic panic in Chile.
And in the midst of the panic the chief of staff of the Chilean armed
forces, Rene Schneider, was shot during a kidnap attempt on him by
an extreme right-wing group. However, the assassination and

Allende's acceptance of a statute of guarantees ensured that Congress officially approved Allende as president. A more coordinated long-range strategy for defeating Allende was needed.

In November of 1970 Anaconda suggested that an ad hoc committee of U. S. companies opposed to Popular Unity meet regularly to discuss strategy against the Chilean government. In January the first ad hoc committee meeting of the major U. S. companies in Chile, ITT, Anaconda, Kennecott, and so on, met in the office of the head of ITT in Washington, William Merriam. This committee was to meet again in February and March. The agreed objective was "to make it clear that a Chilean takeover [of their investments] would not be tolerated without serious repercussions following."[28]

In his 1970 report to Congress on foreign policy, President Nixon stressed the need to have a body coordinating and centralizing U. S. foreign policy. In keeping with this Nixon had made the National Security Council, headed by Henry Kissinger, his main foreign policy-making body on national security affairs. Chile was considered a problem of national security and it was the National Security Council that decided the tactics and strategy of U. S. policy towards Chile. The ad hoc committee of U. S. companies established contact with the National Security Council to coordinate efforts. In February 1971, through one of Kissinger's advisers, Arnold Nachmanoff, the ad hoc committee was informed that the National Security Council considered that "the best way to get at Chile is through her economy."[29]

By February of 1971, then, the general strategy of attack against Allende was agreed: weaken the Chilean economy. And as Merriam told the February meeting of the ad hoc committee, the CIA and Kissinger's office were handling Chile: the State Department was peripheral. (Kissinger was not yet Secretary of State.)[30] But although there seems to have been some tough talking, and although the ITT in particular seems to have rushed all over in an effort to get rid of Allende, the overall conclusion on this period of U. S. policy was that it had little impact on events in Chile. There was little support within the armed forces or the civilian population for any drastic move to topple the Popular Unity government.

THE APPLICATION OF U. S. POLICY IN CHILE: THE INFORMAL BLOCKADE

In his testimony to Congress the CIA director, William Colby, is reported to have said that Chile was a "prototype or laboratory experiment to test the techniques of heavy financial investment in an effort to discredit and bring down a government."[31] Although Colby has denied using the phrase, this policy has become known as "destabilization." It was a policy that involved all relevant branches of the U. S. government together with interested companies in a coordinated effort of clandestine interference and diplomatic and economic pressures. Between 1969 and 1973, according to Colby, the CIA spent $8 million in clandestine activities to defeat the Chilean Left.

Throughout his first year in office President Allende consistently maintained that Chile "wants to maintain cordial and cooperative relations with all nations in the world and most particularly with the United States."[32] He carefully refrained from making any demagogic speeches attacking the United States. Chilean policy towards the United States was to be firm, polite, and nonaggressive, while at the same time making it clear the U. S. hegemony over Chile had now ended. One aspect of ending this hegemony was the nationalization of U. S. companies in Chile. The United States had clearly begun its efforts to undermine Popular Unity before the Chilean government nationalized the U. S. copper companies without compensation. But after the nationalization there seems to have been a firm resolution on the part of U. S. policy makers to make destabilization effective. One can see this partially from the ITT memos. ITT had quietly been trying to betray its deal with the U. S. copper companies by making its own private deal with Allende. But when Allende nationalized the U. S. copper companies, and by legally deducting "excess" profits earned by the companies in Chile from compensation (profits in excess of 12 percent over the previous fifteen years were deducted), paid virtually no compensation, and when he appointed an interventor to manage ITT in Chile (an indirect form of nationalization), ITT openly advocated deposing Allende. Merriam sent an eighteen-point plan to Peter Peterson, President Nixon's assistant for international economic affairs, advocating that "everything should be done quietly but effectively to see that Allende does not get through the crucial next six months."[33] The eighteen-point plan bore a striking resemblance to what actually happened: all loans to be stopped; discontent fomented within the Chilean military; subsidize the Chilean right-wing newspaper, El Mercurio; disrupt Allende's diplomatic plans; set up a special task force to put pressure on Chile, and so on.

The U. S. government however had already probably decided to go ahead with its own destabilization plans. The ITT proposal was perhaps no more than an encouragement. Destabilization had two main focuses: an informal blockade to disrupt the Chilean economy, and assistance and encouragement to Chilean internal opposition to Popular Unity in order to create a mass basis for a military intervention.

In his address to the General Assembly of the United Nations on December 4, 1972, President Allende accused the United States of conducting an "informal" blockade against Chile:

From the very day of our electoral triumph on 4 September, 1970, we have felt the effects of a large-scale

external pressure against us which tried to prevent
the inauguration of a government freely elected by the
people, and has attempted to bring it down ever since,
an action that has tried to cut us off from the world,
to strangle our economy and paralyse trade in our principal export, copper, and to deprive us of access to
sources of international financing. . . . This aggression is not overt and has not been openly declared to
the world; on the contrary, it is an oblique, underhand,
indirect form of aggression, although this does not
make it any less damaging to Chile. [34]

According to Allende this indirect form of aggression involved
pressure by the United States on the World Bank and the Inter-American
Development Bank (IDB), to sever all loans to Chile; the ending of all
U. S. government loans; the withdrawal of credit facilities by both
the public and private sector in the United States; the suspension of
disbursements of loans granted to previous Chilean governments;
forcing Chile to pay in advance for imports from the United States
to keep in continuation projects already started; and attempts to
hamper Chile's normal financial transactions with Western Europe.

The United States maintained its "informal blockade" until the
coup of September 11, 1973. The rationale for this blockade was
described in general by President Nixon on January 19, 1972, as
follows:

Thus, when a country expropriates a significant U. S.
interest without making reasonable provision for such
compensation to U. S. citizens, we will presume that
the U. S. will not extend new bilateral economic benefits to the expropriating country unless and until it is
determined that the country is taking reasonable steps
to provide adequate compensation or that there are
major factors affecting U. S. interests which require
continuance of all or part of these benefits. In the
face of the expropriatory circumstances just described,
we will presume that the United States government will
withhold its support from loans under consideration in
multilateral banks. "[35]

Even before Chile nationalized the U. S. copper companies
and by deducting excess profits in effect paid no compensation, the
United States had taken a number of concrete steps to cripple the
Chilean economy, to "not extend new bilateral economic benefits"
and to "withhold its support from loans under consideration in multilateral banks." In early 1971 the Export-Import Bank refused a
Chilean request for $21 million to purchase three Boeing passenger

jets. And in August 1971 this was followed by an announcement from
the Export-Import Bank that Chile could expect no loans or guarantees.
Since 1945 Chile had received about $600 million in credits from the
Export-Import Bank, and had made use of the Bank's insurance and
guarantee programs. The latter is crucial if a poor foreign government wishes to obtain credits from private banks, and obtain suppliers'
credits for its imports. The decision of the Export-Import Bank had
an immediate effect: in 1972 Chile was able to obtain only $35 million
in short-term credits from private U. S. banks compared to an average
of $220 million in previous years. In addition nearly all suppliers'
credits were suspended. Also, the U. S. government aid agency,
AID, immediately cut off all U. S. aid to Chile from the moment of
Allende's victory, and even went so far as to refuse to disburse loans
signed with the previous Chilean government.

The United States also successfully exerted pressure within
multilateral banks. Since 1959 the Inter-American Development Bank
had granted Chile $310 million in loans. All requests from the Allende
government to the IDB for loans were refused—with the exception of a
$7 million loan to the Catholic University of Santiago, and a $4.6
million to the Austral University, in the south of Chile: both opposition-
controlled universities. The World Bank, which had loaned Chile
$235 million since 1944, refused all requests for loans from Chile
during the Popular Unity period. The head of the World Bank, the
former president of the Ford Motor Company and a former U. S.
secretary of State for Defense, Robert McNamara, even went so far
as to state publicly that "the primary condition for bank lending—
a soundly managed economy with a clear potential for utilizing
additional funds—has not been met. The Chilean economy is in
severe difficulty."[36] This remark of Robert McNamara's affected
the credit standing of Chile with, for example, its Western European
creditors, as the president of the World Bank must have known it
would.

Along with the informal blockade by the U. S. government, U. S.
multinational companies with investments in Chile launched their own
attack. Unfortunately the ITT memos end in October so we have no
evidence whether ITT tried to implement any part of the eighteen-
point plan to bring down Allende. The U. S. copper companies,
Anaconda and Kennecott, however, reacted fairly openly to the
nationalization of their assets without compensation in Chile. Both
companies declared that they would fight by every means possible
against their failure to obtain adequate compensation.

In pursuit of its compensation claims, Kennecott tried to
disrupt sales of Chilean copper to Western European countries, who
buy about 66 percent of Chile's total copper exports. Kennecott
sent a letter to all importers of Chilean copper informing them that
the company regarded copper from the El Teniente mine as still belonging to them and that they would "take all such action as may be

considered necessary in order to protect our rights."[37] The action undertaken was an attempt to block legally payments for copper to the Chilean Copper Corporation. In France the legal action had some success and Chile temporarily had to put up in escudos a sum of money equal to that which might have to be paid to Kennecott in the case that Chile was found by a French court to owe money to Kennecott. In other countries Kennecott's legal injunctions were less successful. But overall Kennecott's actions created uncertainty among buyers of Chilean copper and made it difficult for Chile to sell its main resource.

There was therefore a consciously planned informal blockade of the Chilean economy. But what real effect did this have on the Chilean economy? Some commentators have argued that the effects of the informal blockade in Chile are an indication of the success of the new "low profile" policy of Kissinger (after Vietnam the United States will have to achieve its aims through means other than U. S. military intervention). For, after all, did not the United States put into practice the ITT proposal of creating economic chaos in Chile so that Popular Unity would be overthrown? And did not the majority of the Chilean middle classes mobilize against Allende when the economy ran into problems?

The U. S. blockade did damage the Chilean economy. Chile, which imported about 40 percent of its imports from the United States in 1970, found itself importing only about 15 percent in 1972. Chile therefore had to find alternative sources of supplies. But for many spare parts, replacements, and machinery there are no exact alternatives available. Some industries therefore had to cut back on existing production and halt new construction, some of which was already in process. For example, the Chilean Steel Company (CAP), which obtained a $25 million loan from the U. S. Export-Import Bank in 1969 for expansion, had to halt that expansion because the Export-Import Bank refused to disburse the remaining $13 million of the loan when Allende became president. In the vital transport sector, where the bulk of Chilean transport vehicles comes from the United States, a Chilean source estimated that in 1972 about 30 percent of the private buses, 21 percent of the taxi buses, and 33 percent of the public buses were out of use because of lack of parts or tires.[38] The shortage of parts and tires was one of the excuses for the truck owners' strikes.

But a careful examination of the Chilean economy reveals that, although damaging to the Chilean economy, the effects of the U. S. blockade were somewhat mitigated by the success the UP had in finding alternative sources of supplies, aid, and credit.

The amounts of loans to Chile, in fact, increased during the Popular Unity period. Between 1970 and 1973 the medium and long-term debt increased by 16.7 percent, and the short-term debt increased by a staggering sixfold (the figures for 1973 include debt contracted after the coup of September 11).

TABLE 9.3

Evolution of the External Debt, 1970-73
(millions of U. S. dollars)

Group of countries or institutions	1970	1971	1972	1973	percentage variation 1970-73
1. Multilateral agencies	349.0	381.4	435.6	483.4	38.5
2. Paris Club	2020.0	2060.0	2094.3	2159.3	6.9
3. Socialist bloc	14.0	6.6	17.6	40.0	185.7
4. Other European countries and Latin American countries	9.0	18.9	65.2	149.8	1564.4
5. Capital contributions in the form of credits	111.0	111.0	111.0	111.0	0.0
6. Total external medium and long-range debt	2526.0	2577.9	2743.7	2943.6	16.7
Annual growth in percent	–	2.1	6.4	7.4	
7. Short-term credits	78.0	90.5	353.0	478.0	512.8
Annual growth in percent	–	16.0	290.0	35.4	

Source: Memoria, Central Bank of Chile, Santiago, 1974.

The overall picture therefore is that the UP successfully obtained aid and credit to replace that withdrawn by the United States. The bulk of this credit was however short-term, involving harsher financial terms than in the past. Credit came from a wide variety of sources: approximately $90 million from the Socialist bloc; $148 million from the International Monetary Fund in 1971 in compensation for the fall in copper prices, and from Chile's normal drawing rights; $32 million from Brazil in 1972; and $100 million from Argentina in 1973. The bulk of the short-term lines of credit seem to have come mainly from France and Argentina.

Popular Unity was also not unsuccessful in postponing the payment of the Chilean foreign debt. In November of 1971 the Chilean government declared a moratorium on its foreign debt repayments while it tried to negotiate a rescheduling of its remaining 1971 debts and the debts due in 1972. The United States canvassed the other debt holders, mainly European, to try to make renegotiation conditional on two factors: that adequate compensation should be paid for expropriated companies, and that Chile should accept an IMF standby agreement (in return for a standby loan from the IMF a government often has to agree in a "letter of intent" to a series of monetary, fiscal, foreign and public sector policies negotiated with the IMF). The United States failed to win agreement on its two conditions. At the Paris Club meetings in April 1972, Chile managed to reschedule about 70 percent of the debt service payments falling due between November and December 1972. It was much less than Chile had hoped for and terms of the renegotiation were harsher than Chile had tried to obtain. But the U. S. ploy to completely isolate Chile had failed. All the members of the Paris Club bilaterally negotiated the rescheduling of the debt owed them except the United States. It was only after the coup of September 1973, in December of 1973, that the United States agreed to reschedule its outstanding $130.5 million debt with Chile.

The economic situation of Chile in 1973 was such that Popular Unity in effect declared a moratorium on debt repayments in 1973. At the 1972 Paris Club meeting it had been agreed to hold another meeting in 1973 to discuss the possibilities of further extending the period of payments of the debt. Throughout 1973 this meeting was postponed, which meant in effect that the $328 million of debt due to be paid in 1973 was not paid. In 1974, the military junta went to the Paris Club, and seemed to have little difficulty in renegotiating the external debt service payments due. In 1975, as an indication of their repudiation of the junta's bloody policies in Chile, many European countries refused to attend the Paris Club meeting to reschedule Chile's debts. This decision created serious problems for the economic policies of the Chilean military.

The informal blockade was undoubtedly a contributory factor in the Chilean economic crisis. Nevertheless, as indicated above, it was no more than a contributory factor: the main cause of the crisis has to be sought elsewhere. In any case, something like the informal blockade must have been expected by Popular Unity and presumably taken into account when designing policy. Perhaps not all the U. S. policies were anticipated, particularly the cutting off of suppliers' credits and the drying up of private credits. But a government bent on antiimperialist policies can only expect a response from the imperialist country. There is nothing in the history of U. S. relations with Latin America to suggest that it would continue to supply aid and credits to a Latin American government that expropriates U. S. property and attacks U. S. policies. To blame the United States for not assisting economically the Popular Unity government is illogical.

THE UNITED STATES AND THE MAKING OF THE
CHILEAN COUP

Two factors need to be kept in mind when considering direct U. S. involvement in the Chilean coup. The first is that there is just not enough information on the internal politics of the Chilean military and other groups, and on the precise extent and nature of U. S. involvement with these groups to be able to analyze in depth the U. S. role. What reliable information there is, however, tends to disprove the U. S. State Department briefing, the day after the Chilean coup, which stated that "it is unequivocally clear that the United States government and all elements of the United States government were not—repeat not—involved." The evidence available also tends to disprove President Ford's claim that the $5 million spent by the CIA in Chile, 1971-73, was "to help and assist the preservation of opposition papers and electronic media and to preserve opposition parties." (It is worth noting that throughout the three years of Allende, opposition parties and papers were allowed to operate; since the coup not one opposition party or paper has been allowed to operate.) The United States was involved in the Chilean coup.

The second factor is that, given the evidence on U. S. direct involvement, how does one interpret that evidence? In an interview on the CIA, former CIA officer Philip Agee made the following observation:

"But it doesn't matter how much a man is being paid, it's what he actually does that is important. In many cases very high government officials will be exceedingly effective without receiving a salary from the C. I. A. They understand that the interests of the class they belong to are identical with the interests of the C. I. A., the U. S. government and U. S. companies."[39]

This is an important point to bear in mind when examining direct U. S. involvement in the Chilean coup. When one looks at the continuous series of mass mobilizations of the Right in December 1971, March 1972, October 1972, May-June 1973, and August 1973 (just to tally up the peaks of frenzy reached by the opposition campaign) it would be surely giving too much credit to the CIA's political and organizational ability to claim that it or any U. S. agency was responsible for these movements—although it is probably true they helped finance them.

One lesson that both the United States and the extreme Right seemed to draw from the failure to prevent Allende's victory in the presidential elections and the failure to prevent his becoming president was that the conditions for the defeat of Popular Unity had to be carefully prepared. The key group in these preparations was the armed forces. The Chilean armed forces did have a constitutional tradition, and some, particularly the head of the armed forces, General Prats, were clearly opposed to a military coup against a democratically elected government of Chile. But in spite of this tradition it was also clear that there was a good deal of anticommunism among the officers, and that as a group the officers adhered closely to their class of origin. There was also a tradition of military conspiracies in Chile that in the past was almost exclusively the property of retired officers. Thus it would not be new to discuss the possibilities of a military conspiracy among the officer corps. What would be new, and what was required was to make a conspiracy the united action of the whole armed forces.

One way to stir up discontent is to worsen the economic situation. The ITT memos described the purpose behind this as follows: "A more realistic hope among those who want to block Allende is that a swiftly-deteriorating economy will touch off a wave of violence leading to a military coup."[40] This the United States tried to do through the informal blockade. Another way, complementary to the first, is to actively mobilize a mass campaign against Popular Unity. El Mercurio, the major bourgeois paper of Chile and one reported to have received a substantial part of the funds used by the CIA in Chile, described how this should be organized:

"However the opposition organizes itself, its methods of action must have an immediate root in the bases of society: it cannot confine itself to the general propaganda and traditional use of assemblies by the old political parties. Neighborhood councils, mothers' unions, cooperatives, trade unions, and other professional bodies require the permanent involvement of those representing the best political thinking of the citizens, not the reduced contacts characteristic of an electoral campaign. The explicit or implicit unity of the opposition should give rise to concrete actions at work, in the suburb, in the supermarket which will be capable of counteracting the dictatorship which the Marxists are prepared to put into practice at the base. It is not enough for the democratic forces to try to reach the public through the mass media. They must link themselves with the masses. Such a program implies great sacrifice, often a substantial change of peoples' habits and style of life . . . ."[41]

The "masses" that were organized in this way were drawn from those disparate groupings that make up the middle sectors—professionals, small factory owners, shopkeepers, truck owners, middle-class housewives, bureaucrats etc. Faced with an economic crisis and fanned by the skillful propaganda of the Right, this group formed themselves into a mass opposition to Popular Unity. Reading Philip Agee's account of CIA activity in Ecuador and Uruguay, it is hard to believe that the CIA did not have a hand in this campaign. After all, they spent their money on more than subsidizing El Mercurio. Unfortunately the information on this aspect of U. S. involvement is patchy.

In December 1971, five thousand women, mainly from the wealthy part of Santiago, marched through Santiago banging cooking pots and saucepan lids in protest against so-called food shortages. This was the first mass demonstration by the opposition since Allende had taken power, and it bore a striking resemblance to the mass march of women in Sao Paulo shortly before the military coup in Brazil. This march marked the beginning of a unified right-wing campaign of openly mobilizing the opposition against Popular Unity. The climax to this campaign came in October of 1972 when the Union of Truck Owners launched an indefinite strike against the government ostensibly over the government's proposal to establish a state transport system in part of the south of Chile. The strike quickly revealed its purely political nature when it was joined by the capitalists and some of their allies among professionals and shopkeepers. It is widely held that the United States helped these strikes with finance and advice. An article in the Sunday Times claimed that "108 Chileans from the gremios and unions were trained at A. I. F. L. D's school at Front Royal, Virginia. These were the cadres for the truck-owners, and other Right-wing strikes."[42]

After the congressional elections of March 1973, the Chilean right-wing stepped up their campaign against Allende. Strikes, demonstrations, riots, and assassinations built up into the climax of an attempted coup on June 29. Although the mutiny of the second tank regiment failed, it was clear that the armed forces were not an apolitical "constitutional" body. In the last weeks of July, the truck owners launched another strike, and again they were soon joined by other transport owners, professionals, and shopkeepers. This was the final civilian buildup to the military intervention on September 11. Again it is clear that the U. S. government, especially the CIA, was involved in this buildup—although not all the details are known. In an interview with the New York Times, R. S. Cline, the former head of the Intelligence Office of the State Department, claimed that one of the activities of the CIA was financial support for the truck owners and shopkeepers' strikes. The New York Times also quoted an unnamed official as saying that the truck owners could well have received CIA money: "If we give it to A and then A gives it to B and C and D, in a sense it is true that D got it, but the question is: Did we give it to A, knowing that D would get it?"[43] In an article for the New York Times (for which he was expelled from Chile) Jonathan Kendell claimed that some members of SOFOFA, the most important organization of Chilean industrialists, told him that they had received some $200,000 from a number of companies: Protexa in Monterrey, Mexico, from the Grupo Mendoza in Caracas, Venezuela, and a Peruvian company. These dollars were said to have been changed in the Chilean black market at about 500 percent more than the official exchange rate and distributed weekly to the striking truck owners and shopkeepers.[44] In the New York Times, Seymour Hersh reported that a series of documents prepared for meetings of the Committee of Forty between 1970 and 1973, revealed that the CIA had recommended giving $200,000 to the Chilean National party, a party that had links with the terrorist group Patria y Libertad, and that was openly calling for a military intervention against Allende.[45] It is still not known whether the money was given to the National party, but William Colby is reported to have told the congressional subcommittee that in August 1973 he had authorized the spending of $1 million in Chile and that $50,000 had been spent by the time of the coup.

Indirect corroboration of outside financing of the right-wing strikes can be found from the movement of the dollar in the black market. Throughout the three years of Allende's government the black market rate for the dollar rose substantially, except during the bosses' strike of October 1972 and August 1973 when the rate actually fell, indicating a large influx of dollars onto the black market. This and other evidence even led one of the Christian Democrat senators, Renan Fuentealba, to express his concern about foreign intervention on television on August 22, 1973, when he said that he believed that foreign agencies were financing and helping to organize the insurrectionist campaign of the Right.[46]

Yet the crucial group remained the armed forces. However much the Chilean Right, with U. S. assistance, organized strikes and demonstrations it could not hope to defeat Popular Unity and its working class supporters without the intervention of the armed forces. There were of course very close ties between Chilean officers and U. S. officers, and over the years the Chilean armed forces had become increasingly dependent on the United States. This policy of building close military ties with the Chilean military yielded rich dividends for U. S. interests not only in Chile but also in the whole of Latin America.

The informal blockade involved among other things the cutting off of U. S. aid to Chile. There was however one exception to this: military aid. During the three years of Allende, U. S. military aid to Chile actually increased: in fiscal years ending 1970, it was $800,000; by mid-1971 it had increased to $5.7 million, and in

1971-72 it was $12.3 million.[47] The U. S. military maintained their
close contacts with their Chilean counterparts. And in spite of
protests from his left wing, Allende allowed the Unitas maneuvers,
joint U. S.-Chilean naval maneuvers off the coast of Chile, to
continue.

We do not know how the coup was prepared. But, according
to the former head of the Chilean armed forces, General Prats,
"the real coordination and planning for the coup took place in Valparaiso."[48] The Sunday Times article reported that the U. S. marine
attache, Lieutenant Colonel Patrick Ryan, liaised with Admiral Turibio
Merino, second-in-command of the Chilean navy and senior naval
officer at Valparaiso, over preparations for the coup. Merino is
generally recognized as one of the key figures in the coup and is a
member of the Chilean junta. The Sunday Times suggested three
reasons why U. S. naval intelligence was the main liaison with the
Chilean conspirators. The first is that in the late 1960s special
secret communications networks with Latin American navies were
established. This meant that Chilean and U. S. navies could communi-
cate directly in total secrecy. The second reason is the traditionally
close ties between the U. S. and Chilean navies. The third reason
is the existence of the joint U. S. and Chilean naval maneuvers,
Unitas. These maneuvers were scheduled to begin on the day of the
coup, September 11, 1973. Four U. S. navy vessels were involved:
two guided missile destroyers, the USS Richmond K. Turner and USS
Tattnall, the destroyer Vesole, and the USS Clamagore. On September 11 the State Department reported that "on receipt of information
about the situation in Chile they were redirected and ordered not to
go into Chilean territorial water or ports."[49] In the interview given
with the journalist Marlise Simons, General Prats is reported to have
said that on September 10, the day before the coup, Admiral Merino
requested the United States to keep their four Unitas ships out of
Chilean waters, but at the same time to remain on the alert offshore.[50]
Throughout the period of the coup the four U. S. warships remained
off the coast of Chile. Presumably if the armed forces had divided
and civil war ensued they could have been used. As it was, the
coup that began with the navy in Valparaiso on September 10 met
relatively little armed resistance. U. S. direct intervention was not
needed.

But what does all this add up to? A not inconsiderable sum
(especially if, as seems reasonable to suppose, most of the CIA
dollars were exchanged on the black market) was spent assisting the
Chilean right-wing campaign. We may also be sure that the United
States gave ample advice and technical assistance to that campaign.
But the emergence of the right-wing campaign was essentially a
response to the dynamics of the internal class struggle in Chile and
not the result of some Machiavellian conspiracy by the CIA or whom-
ever. The importance of the role of the United States should of course

not be underestimated, but at the level of direct support this assistance was of secondary importance in the making of the coup.

CONCLUSIONS

In his evidence to the Senate Foreign Relations Committee on January 22, 1975, former director of the CIA Richard Helms admitted that he had misled Congress in his earlier evidence claiming that the CIA was not involved in politics against Popular Unity. Helms went on to claim that "I know that the Nixon administration wanted it overthrown, but there was no way to do it that anybody knew of, and any probes that were made in Chile to ascertain whether there was army force that was likely to bring this about produced no evidence that there was any such force."

This may have been true in 1971, but by October of 1972 there had emerged both a civilian and military group determined to defeat Popular Unity. The emergence and organization of such a group was helped both directly and indirectly by the United States. But the emergence and organization of this group was primarily a response to the development of the internal class struggle in Chile and not a response to the machinations of North American groups. The United States assisted the making of the Chilean coup, but was not the prime promoter of that coup.

NOTES

1. New York Times and Washington Post of September 8, 1974.

2. Henry Kissinger before the Senate Committee on Foreign Relations. See U. S. Congress, Senate, Committee on Foreign Relations, Nomination of Henry A. Kissinger, part 2 (Executive Hearings) (Washington, D.C.: U. S. Government Printing Office, 1973), p. 304.

3. J. F. Petras and M. H. Morley, How Allende Fell: A Study in U. S.-Chilean Relations (Nottingham, Eng.: Spokesman Books, 1974), p. 9.

4. Armando Uribe, Le Livre Noir de l'Intervention Americaine au Chile (Paris: Seuils "Combats," 1974), p. 9.

5. Quoted in F. B. Pike, Chile and the United States 1880-1962 (Notre Dame, Ind.: University of Notre Dame Press, 1963).

6. External Financing in Latin America, Economic Commission of Latin America, (1965), p. 15.

7. F. B. Pike, op. cit., p. 272.

8. C. G. Bowers, Chile through Embassy Windows 1939-1953 (New York: Simon and Schuster, 1958), pp. 10, 340.

9. International Cooperation Administration, Chile: Country Economic Program – 1959, U. S. Department of State, 1960.

10. Agency for International Development, Field Proposed Program for Fiscal Year 1962/1963. Chile, U. S. Department of State, 1963.

11. I. C. A. , op. cit.

12. U. S. Congress, Senate, Committee on Government Operations, Subcommittee on Foreign Aid Expenditures, United States Foreign Aid in Action: A Case Study (Washington, D. C.: U. S. Government Printing Office, 1966).

13. A. I. D. , Country Assistance Program, – Chile – 1963. U. S. Department of State, 1964.

14. Lauren Stern, "U. S. Helped Beat Allende in 1964, " Washington Post, April 6, 1973.

15. Philip Agee, Inside the Company: CIA Diary (Harmondsworth, Eng.: Penguin Books, 1975).

16. For an analysis of U. S. attempts to influence policy making in Chile see Philip O'Brien, "La Alianza para el Progreso y los prestamos por programa a Chile, " Estudios Internacionales 2, no. 4 (Santiago, January-March 1969).

17. See U. S. Congress, Senate, Committee on Foreign Relations, Subcommittee on Western Hemisphere Affairs, United States Military Policies and Programs in Latin America (Washington, D. C.: U. S. Government Printing Office, 1969).

18. U. S. Congress, House, Committee on Foreign Affairs, Subcommittee on National Security Policy and Scientific Developments, Report of the Special Study Mission to Latin America (Washington, D. C.: U. S. Government Printing Office, 1970), p. 31.

19. A. I. D. , Field Proposed Program for Chile, Section on Labor. U. S. Department of State, 1961.

20. I. C. A. , Chile-Economic Country Data and Forecast. Section on Unstable Trade Movement. U. S. Department of State 1958.

21. Philip Agee, op. cit. , p. 600.

22. The I. T. T. Memos. Subversion in Chile: a case study of U. S. corporate intrigue in the Third World (Nottingham, Eng.: Spokesman Books, 1972).

23. J. F. Petras and M. H. Morley, op. cit.

24. For an analysis based on both see A. Sampson, The Sovereign State (London: Hodder and Stoughton, 1973).

25. The I. T. T. Memos . . ., op. cit.

26. Ibid.

27. U. S. Congress, Senate, Committee on Foreign Relations, Subcommittee on Multinational Corporations, Multinational Corporations and United States' Foreign Policy (Washington, D. C.: U. S. Government Printing Office, 1974).

28. Ibid.

29. Ibid.

30.   Ibid.

31.   Quoted in "Destabilisation" by G. Hodgson and W. Shawcross (London: the Sunday Times, October 27, 1974).

32.   Salvador Allende, Chile's Road to Socialism (Harmondsworth, Eng.: Penguin Books, 1973), p. 106.

33.   Quoted in A. Sampson, The Sovereign State (London: Hodder and Stoughton, 1973), p. 255.

34.   Salvador Allende, Spokesman Pamphlet no. 31 (Nottingham, Eng.: Spokesman Books, 1973).

35.   Quoted in North American Congress on Latin America, New Chile, Berkeley, 1972.

36.   Ibid.

37.   Quoted in J. Petras and M. Morley, How Allende Fell (Nottingham, Eng.: Spokesman Books, 1974), p. 87.

38.   Chile Hoy, August 11-17, 1972.

39.   Interview with Philip Agee, Red Weekly, January 1, 1975.

40.   The I. T. T. Memos . . ., op. cit.

41.   El Mercurio, March 10, 1973.

42.   The Sunday Times (London), October 27, 1974.

43.   Ibid.

44.   New York Times, October 15, 1974.

45.   New York Times, October 21, 1974.

46.   Quoted in A. Zimbalist and B. Stallings, "Showdown in Chile," Monthly Review, October 1973.

47.   The Sunday Times (London), October 27, 1974.

48.   Ibid.

49.   Ibid.

50.   Ibid.

10

THE CHILEAN ARMED
FORCES AND THE
MAKING OF THE COUP
Alain Joxe

The problem we must come to grips with in this chapter is the
following: how can a civilian army, based on conscription, dedicated
to the constitution, and not suffering from any current economic neglect,
turn itself into an instrument that is capable of intervening violently
against mobilized popular forces to prevent a legal transition to
socialism from taking the first timid steps towards becoming a real
transition to socialism?

It is a problem one can approach from two very different angles,
and we shall try not to ignore either of them. Structurally and historically, it can be argued the Chilean armed forces were in a sense
already prepared for intervention when Allende took power. Historically they have always intervened at political conjunctures that were
critical for capitalism and imperialism, as they did in 1891 to bring
an end to President Balmaceda's brief attempt at economic nationalism,
and almost continuously during the prolonged period of crisis from
1920-33.[1] Sometimes the armed forces have split in the face of
contradictory tensions; but in general the winning side has always
been the one backing the interests of the imperialist nations to which,
willy-nilly, a modern army in an underdeveloped country is tied.

On the other hand, almost any other military establishment
in Latin America would have acted to prevent the Allende government
from taking power. The three-year delay in the reaction of the armed
forces in Chile to a Marxist assuming the presidency has to be
explained. So too does the actual process by which the army was
prepared for the coup. Let us take it for granted that the Chilean

Translated from French by Jacqueline F. Roddick and K. M.
Field. Edited by Jacqueline F. Roddick. Partial versions of this
chapter appeared in "L'Armee Chilienne," Les Temps Modernes,
May 1973, and "Comment une armee devient putschiste, cas de
l'armee chilienne," Critique Socialiste, March 1974.

army's takeover in September 1973 was not a sudden breach of discipline, but was something prepared for little by little while Popular Unity still nominally controlled the government. The successive stages in the military takeover of power must then be analyzed in terms of the rising class struggle that was taking place in Chile during the Popular Unity period, the rhythm of polarization of the country between bourgeoisie and proletariat, and the progressive development of political consciousness on both sides. In this process, the key "trigger" for the action of the right wing within the armed forces was the mobilization of the Chilean working class: and the key question we must try to answer is, how did the right wing succeed in consolidating the armed forces as a whole behind its position?

CIVIL AND MILITARY POWER IN
UNDERDEVELOPED COUNTRIES

Nowhere are the armed forces "simply" a tool in the hands of the ruling class, as for instance control over the issue of currency is a tool that allows the ruling class to determine the level of real income from salaries. The armed forces necessarily have a greater autonomy than other sectors of the state apparatus, because their role is not merely one of transmitting economic or judicial orders, but one of guaranteeing the preservation of the existing relations of production and at the same time of maintaining discipline in the final instance within the ranks of the ruling class itself.

Thus in general, it is safe to see the armed forces as a "state within a state," a social formation with its own distinct methods of organization that are important and must be understood if one wants to analyze the way it is integrated into a larger, national and international world. One of the defining characteristics of the armed forces as an institution is the political function of the officer corps. The army is a "state" where paradoxically it is not possible for the rulers to resort to violence on a global scale in order to maintain their control, because those they rule also have arms. Thus it is only through intense political activity that the officers can ensure the obedience of the lower ranks; the importance of their political role is revealed in the norms that govern their promotion, where prestige and an aptitude for command are required, rather than the simple qualifications of seniority or the other professional qualifications that serve in a mandarin organization. The foundation of military power and the source of the officers' own authority lie in the obedience of their subordinates. This is one of the key reasons for the autonomy of military power from civilian authority relations; for by force of necessity, the sole responsibility for the troops' esprit de corps lies with the officers themselves, it being their task to maintain discipline even though their fire power is inferior to that of the rank and file.

In a traditional army, particularly in an army where military service is compulsory and many of the lower ranks are conscripts, the power of the officer corps over its subordinates is only maintained by a constant flow of real and imaginary services, very much as among the lords of feudal society. The colonel can appear as "father of the regiment," because he controls and distributes the regiment's means of subsistence—but since armies do not produce their own means of subsistence through productive economic activity or even for the most part their own arms, he can only play this role thanks to the civil power. It is the civil state that supplies the means of subsistence necessary to maintain troop morale, and thus the officer corps' authority ultimately derives from the civil state. This is the reason why the military "state within a state" is totally dependent on the civil power and on civilian society; and it explains why the civil state as immediate source of all necessities is a natural object of reverence for military men just as it is for other bureaucrats, though in a rather more archaic fashion. The military attitude towards civilians, however, is rather different: the civil state, that holiest of warehouses, may be the military man's god, but he is more likely to see the civilian as a serf.

Such archaic social relations are characteristic of traditional armed forces. However, as the social formation to which the military power belongs moves from its own feudal heritage and feudal-style social relations, under the impact of capitalist development, the military enclave's relations with civil society run the risk of becoming increasingly artificial. Backwardness is dangerous. In order to maintain its own power and authority over the military enclave, the bourgeoisie in power must necessarily transform the officer corps into a model force of businessmen and technicians, another capitalist elite. This happens in all developed countries, though in a variety of ways; through the development of a more and more sophisticated armaments industry or the creation of military-industrial complexes. The final step in the modernization process consists in eliminating the need for officers to dominate their contingent of conscripts politically through the distribution of uniforms and food, rewards and punishments, in a fashion that is completely out of key with the norms of civil society. In various ways, armies in the developed countries have moved towards the end of obligatory military service and the creation of a professional army with considerable technical skills, where the troops are paid a good wage.*

In underdeveloped, dependent countries that do not manufacture arms, this evolution is either impossible or very slow, or—from the capitalist point of view the most satisfactory solution—the initial source of armaments and technical skills is provided by imperialist

---

*For example, the German army.

formations in the developed countries. But modernization of the armed forces under such conditions is a delicate game. In fact, the local ruling class and its representative, the chief of state, risk seeing their authority questioned whether or not they have made provision for modernization. The risks involved are a reflection of the local bourgeoisie's own dependence on the imperialist bourgeoisie.

If the civil power pushes modernization too far, the military may come to constitute the most modern force in the society, that is, the force most dependent on capitalist relations of production for its local power; and in military eyes, the local state may lose authority in comparison with the state or states that supply them with arms. Alternatively, the officer corps may begin to question the very existence of the local political system, in the name of a capitalist class that does not exist locally—Nasserism in Egypt, Peronism in Argentina, and so on.

On the other hand, if the civil power fails to push modernization far enough, it risks losing authority over an enclave that is archaic by comparison with the expanding capitalist relations of production in the country as a whole. The armed forces may then survive by falling back on values that are not shared by the ruling class; or it may feel that it has been denied a status that it could obtain elsewhere and which when the time comes it has the means to obtain by force.

Between "too far" and "not enough," one may assume that it is impossible to reach a final balance, the more so since the dosage prescribed is never arrived at as a result of a simple strategic calculation on the part of the local ruling class, but also depends on the level of consciousness and organization of the oppressed classes, and on the global economic interests of imperialism. Thus, in a peripheral capitalist formation there is almost always a certain weakness in the ruling class' control over the military power, a weakness that is not merely a result of the peculiar circumstances of a particular political conjuncture, but arises from structural contradictions rooted in the imperialist system as a whole.

In the case of Chile the structural weakness in ruling class control over the armed forces when Allende became president was its thirty-year-long failure to maintain the original impetus of modernization begun during the 1880s with the help of Germany. From the Second World War onwards, bourgeois governments consistently ignored the army's need for better wages and more sophisticated equipment to maintain its status as a leading Latin American military power. As a result, in 1969 the Christian Democrat administration faced an overt mutiny from one regiment over economic issues, which undoubtedly had widespread support within the military as a whole: the so-called "Tacnazo."

Much of Popular Unity's strategy towards the armed forces was based on a belief that the new government could use existing military resentment against the traditional political elite, in order

to secure their loyalty to the transition to socialism: thus its attempts
to provide better wages and better equipment, and also to upgrade the
army's status as a source of technical and managerial expertise by
involving it in broader issues of Chile's development. This theory
ignored a great deal of historical evidence on the Chilean armed
forces' close ties with imperialism, as well as the impossibility of
insulating the military from a class struggle that had polarized the
country as a whole.

IMPERIALISM, THE CHILEAN ARMED FORCES, AND THE LOCAL BOURGEOISIE 1880-1933

Military interventions are rare in Chilean history; but when they
have occurred, it has always been at a critical point in the history
of world capitalism. In 1891, the first military intervention, capitalism
was inaugurating its imperialist phase. When the military took power
for a period of six years during the 1920s, U. S. imperialism was
beginning to assume a dominant role within the world system and
one of the functions of military dictatorship was to reorient Chile's
economy towards the emerging U. S. power. The crisis of central
capitalist formations during the Great Depression, which gave birth
to a national bourgeoisie in the peripheral countries as administrators
of a process of industrialization through import-substitution, * also
gave rise to a succession of military coups. These were points in
time at which the Chilean state changed character, and the existing
power bloc was modified; and at such points the armed forces have
always split or taken sides on the question of reorganization of the
state as a whole.

Prussianization and the Crisis of 1891

The origins of the Chilean army and its peculiar traditions lie
in an unusual attempt at "prussianization" during the first phase of
modernization that followed the War of the Pacific (1879-81). The
War of the Pacific was fought against Peru and Bolivia to gain control
over the nitrate-rich northern desert, nitrates from then onwards

------

*An industrialization process whereby goods previously imported
are excluded by high tariffs and other policies in an attempt to stimulate their internal production. This strategy tended to take as given
existing demand patterns, that is, existing patterns of income distribution. In Latin America it often led to a proliferation of high cost,
inefficient consumer goods assembly plants.

supplying the bulk of the country's foreign exchange as copper was later to do. As a result of the war, the strength of the army suddenly shot up from a normal 3, 000 during the nineteenth century to 41, 000, * and the war gave Chile the momentary appearance of being an autonomous imperialist power. However, the reality of the world balance of forces quickly reasserted itself, though in a somewhat paradoxical fashion. It was British imperialism that recaptured the nitrate mines, having briefly lost them to a Peruvian attempt at nationalization through the mechanism of the Chilean armed forces and the policies of the Chilean government. [2]

An unsuccessful nationalist attempt to reverse the British takeover was made by President Balmaceda in 1890, in defiance of the local agrarian oligarchy and importing bourgeoisie, who were quite willing to risk Chile's nascent industries in order to make concessions to imperialist commercial interests. Balmaceda planned to nationalize the mines and invest this extraordinary resource in industry, thus directly challenging British interests—and to do so, in part at least, by building up an anti-British base within the army. It was Balmaceda's hope that he could balance the influence of an oligarchic parliament tied to British interests and a navy with strong British connections by building up presidential power based on the populace, the national bourgeoisie, and a strong, modern army. The Prussian doctrine of the soldier-citizen as well as the Junkers' traditional loyalty to the monarchy were supposed to serve these ends. At the time, following a victory over France, Germany seemed to be emerging as a rival to British imperialism: the supreme military power on land matching the supreme military power at sea.

The crisis of 1891 showed that such calculations were based on an illusion. In the civil war that followed a confrontation between Balmaceda and the Congress, the German mission that Balmaceda himself had hired to retrain the army took the side of the constitutionalist Congress, along with the British and the navy. Its head, Captain Koerner, personally trained the constitutionalist militia and supplied it with modern arms from Germany that originally had been destined for the army. The army suffered a military defeat: Balmaceda committed suicide, and Captain Koerner was made chief of staff by the new regime. Prussianization of the army continued, although without the old impetus.

After the event, it is easy to see that German and British imperialism shared some common interests even if they were rivals, and that it was no part of this interest to allow the industrial faction of the

_____

*During the nineteenth century, following the war against the Federation of Peru and Bolivia, the army normally numbered about 3, 000 men; however, the armed core of the state was in fact counterbalanced by a rural militia and a bourgeois urban guard that in the 1830s reached 25, 000 men, though thereafter it progressively declined.

Chilean bourgeoisie to gain hegemony over the commercial faction,
or to permit the emergence of a new imperialist nation on the Pacific
coast. Germany's policy of selling armaments to Chile and offering
technical help with modernization brought certain commercial advan-
tages, but its primary purpose was to create a state that would look
favorably on foreign investment. Looking at the birth of the modern
Chilean army, one can see that modernization was the point at which
an essential link in the imperialist chain was forged, a link that
then had to be remolded periodically to meet the needs of different
phases of imperialist development.

Thus in Chile, even if towards the turn of the century the
military with their pointed caps and monocles provided a perfect
mirror image of the Prussian army, modernization had a very different
significance from what it would have had in a central capitalist
country. The military apparatus was not being brought to perfection
in order to prepare the way for a systematic policy of territorial
expansion. On the contrary, after the army was modernized the
Chilean bourgeoisie fought no further wars, made no attempt to export
their capital, and not only failed to build up a heavy industry but
from the manufacturing point of view actually regressed. In Chile
the formation of a modern army was equivalent to the colonial conquests that imperialism was carrying out elsewhere, with the difference
that here the conquest was carried out by imperialist agents within
the country.

Nonetheless, Prussianization left certain permanent marks on
the consciousness and organization of the Chilean armed forces.
The prestige of the Prussianized Chilean army allowed it briefly to
play the role of intermediary in modernizing other Latin American
armies, and it was Chile as subcontractor that took charge of the
Prussianization of armed forces in Colombia, Ecuador, and El Salvador
at the beginning of the century. This favored position, together with
the memory of having been at the head of the best-policed state in
the continent during the nineteenth century, fostered a self-complacen-
cy that took the place of a more aggressive nationalism, and that
tradition has been preserved. Conscription was another lasting benefit. It was introduced in 1900 as the crowning glory of Captain
Koerner's work, and in Chile as in Europe it served as a delicate
instrument for the repression of the trade union movement, particularly
in the mines. But as existing social forces at the time posed no real
political threat, a truly efficient compulsory service program was
never introduced.

Modernization of the army also introduced a new political
dimension into the officer corps. Over the first decades of the
twentieth century, one can see new political and social concerns
emerging within their ranks, indirectly expressed in the form of
professional grievances and of misgivings about the multiplication
of the army's repressive duties. Thus the appearance of secret military

societies and of plotting among junior officers in 1907, 1912, and 1919. [3] These new preoccupations reflected developing contradictions within the bourgeoisie, caused on the one hand by the state's new importance in redistributing nitrate revenues and the consequent rise of a petty bourgeoisie tied to the state apparatus, and on the other hand by the rebirth of a certain national industrial bourgeoisie during the First World War.

The Role of the Military in Consolidating Presidential Rule 1924- 31

Changes that demanded a readjustment were simultaneously occurring in a whole series of other fields. Global economic trends were combining to undermine the economic and political power of the agrarian/commercial oligarchy that controlled the state apparatus: the price of agricultural raw materials had begun a long-term decline, and the economic importance of Chilean nitrates to the world market was also being eclipsed by the invention of an industrial process for synthesizing ammonia and the consequent appearance of artificial fertilizers. By resorting to inflation the oligarchy was able to pre- serve its agrarian interests, [4] but only at the cost of alienating the salaried petty bourgeoisie, including the military. Thus the ruling classes began to lose political support internally and the foundations were laid for a tactical alliance between the petty bourgeoisie and the proletariat.

Between 1924 and 1932, U. S. -owned copper began replacing British-owned nitrates as the most important source of Chile's foreign exchange:* only the most obvious sign of the contemporary, worldwide decline of British imperialism and the growing hegemony of U. S. imperialism. This shift in international centers of economic power also served to weaken the position of the contemporary Chilean ruling class. Each imperialist nation had its own peculiar method of inte- grating with the social formations it dominated. The British tended to invest in the primary sector of the economies they controlled, looking for a source of raw materials that were lacking in the British Isles with which to supply their home industries: thus British imperial- ism was a willing ally of the agrarian and commercial oligarchies whose only interest in imports was confined to luxury goods. By contrast, the United States was already well-endowed with essential raw materials, and although it was undoubtedly interested in investing in mining, it was also interested in exporting its own mass-produced

---

*U. S. companies first obtained control of the Chuquicamata copper mine in 1910 and Potrerillos in 1916.

industrial products. Thus the United States was looking for a middle-
class clientele capable of providing a bigger market. After the Great
Depression, this tendency for the United States to favor a shift in
the social structure of the dominated countries was reinforced by the
U. S. desire to export intermediate goods, machine parts, and tools
as a way of reviving its own home industry, thus servicing the market
created by the renascence of the local industrial bourgeoisies that
had also been fostered by the Great Depression—local bourgeoisies
who were also, perforce, oriented towards the needs of a middle
class.

In the case of Chile, such changes in the favored classes of
the imperialist economy and the concomittant weakening of the old
ruling class were aggravated by a headlong process of urbanization:
towards 1927, urban population began to outstrip the rural. This
fact of itself was sufficient to change the working conditions in the
traditional electoral kitchen. An electoral majority could no longer
be guaranteed by bribery during the campaign. A new class of political
orators with a popular turn of phrase was necessary.

All these factors combined to force a change in the ruling group
within the power bloc and a remodeling of the state apparatus. The
military were an active agent in this process of social change, just
as much as the more radical strata of the petty bourgeoisie. Two
successive coups in 1924 and 1925 secured the passage of a great
deal of reform legislation that had been blocked by the old Congress,
including income tax legislation, and a Labor Code legalizing trade
unions under close government supervision. [5] A certain populist
ambiguity in the appeal of the leading military man of the period,
Colonel Carlos Ibanez, allowed him to win 98 percent of the vote
for president in an election in 1927. As president and dictator from
1927 to 1931 Ibanez strengthened the presidency immensely, providing
it with its own source of military support in the form of the carabineros,
a unified national police force quartered in barracks, replacing the
hitherto independent local forces.

Two years after Ibanez was installed as president the Great
Depression arrived: in Chile as elsewhere, it led to an internal
social and political crisis, which accelerated the development of an
antiimperialist consciousness among broad layers of the urban population and even within the armed forces themselves. Successive coups
between 1931 and 1932 saw progressive elements within the military
emerge to national prominence, particularly in the naval mutiny of
1931 and the Socialist republic of 1932. In both cases, they were
defeated. But their very existence and the vivid impression of having
once been near to a military takeover of power left a lasting impression on the Socialist party formed in 1933, very largely around one
of the key figures in the short-lived Socialist republic, Colonel
Marmaduke Grove.

The Emergence of Military "Soviets" and a "Socialist Republic"

When the Great Depression arrived, the Ibanez government was actively pursuing a policy of development based on state intervention and the repression of popular protest. Its rigorous measures could only be justified if they were associated with prosperity. Economic paralysis combined with inflation and a catastrophic foreign debt led to the reemergence of an alliance between certain new social layers who saw the foundations of their relative prosperity crumbling and the old oligarchy. Faced with the opposition of such social forces, and a student rebellion, Ibanez gave up his attempts to retain power by force and resigned.

His successor took a series of exceptional measures to safeguard the country's finances, among them a general reduction of civil service and military salaries by 50 percent. This decision led to a rebellion among naval crews and officers: soviets were briefly organized in Coquimbo harbor, in more or less conscious imitation of the 1917 Russian model, but the mutiny remained isolated, and after a series of declarations that became increasingly revolutionary in character, it was put down by the combined power of army and air force. [6]

In spite of its defeat the naval mutiny of 1931 did serve to break the traditional political role of the navy as a source of support for the oligarchy. In 1932, thus encouraged, a new and much more left-wing military movement emerged from the scattered plotting of civilian and military socialists, populists, and left-wing Ibanistas against the right-wing president duly returned by popular vote in 1931. In June 1932, a Socialist republic was installed on the wings of the air force, which made a series of low altitude flights over Santiago. It was headed by General Puga, but its minister of War was a future founder of the Socialist party, Marmaduke Grove. The new republic lasted only 13 days, but among its decrees was emergency legislation allowing the state to intervene in industries whose owners had interrupted production. [7] This decree, never repealed, was used by President Allende to extend the Social Property Area of nationalized industries between 1971 and 1973. [8]

The Socialist republic had also proposed to nationalize the copper and coal mines, but before it could do so, a countercoup was engineered from within the armed forces by a former Ibanista and past ambassador to Washington, who gave the U. S. State Department a guarantee that U. S. interests would not be jeopardized. This new regime instituted a savage repression of strikes and popular mobilizations, before falling victim to a coup engineered by supporters of the traditional oligarchy; and this in turn was forced to hand over power to the Supreme Court pending new presidential elections by the "legalist" rebellion of the garrisons of the key provincial cities of Antofagasta and Concepcion. This legalist pronuncamiento of 1931 was to be the last intervention of any political importance by the Chilean army until the Tacnazo of 1969.

From this welter of events it is worth rescuing a few facts of historical significance. One is that the armed forces were profoundly split by the economic crisis created by the Great Depression, with antiimperialist, proimperialist and prooligarchic elements all playing a role. A second fact, perhaps more important in understanding Popular Unity's policy towards the armed forces, is this: the origins of the Chilean Socialist party lie in an adventurist, putschist clique of civilians and military officers, left wing certainly, antiimperialist very clearly, but with a history of connections with Ibanismo, for all the latter's corporativist overtones and its importance in the creation of a strong presidency. These roots have never been entirely abandoned. Even during Allende's government, the ruling coalition included a few old Socialist partisans of Ibanez who supported the founder of the modern presidential regime during his second presidency, from 1952 to 1957, as, briefly, did a wing of the Socialist party itself. *

None of this invalidates the Socialist party's claim to be a Marxist party of the proletariat, nor the reasons for such a party's emergence in the 1930s, long after the foundation of the Communist party. The contemporary need was genuine enough: the Socialist party was founded to provide the means for a united front between the proletariat and the petty bourgeoisie, and thus outflank the sectarian and "pure" proletarian politics of the Communists during the Great Depression, imposed upon them by the Third International. But much of Popular Unity's sympathy with the military surely has its roots in this historical peculiarity. The Socialist party has always had a military wing—paradoxically, this was to be the one party that made a serious attempt to fight the armed forces during the 1973 coup—but it also retained an intimate connection with the army as an institution as late as 1970, and President Allende himself could claim certain personal ties with the generation of officers then in posts of command.

For the next thirty-three years, the Chilean military accepted a succession of populist and reactionary bourgeois governments without any significant political reaction. Perhaps they had been burned by the divisions within the armed forces from 1931-32: in any

---

*The left-wing Partido Socialista Popular joined Ibanez's cabinet for the first few months of the administration until its anti-working class bias became obvious. See Fernando Casanueva y Manuel Fernandez Canque, El Partido Socialista y la Lucha de Clases (Santiago: Editorial Quimantu, 1973).

case, the bourgeoisie had no need of a military coup to maintain its hegemony, as the industrial bourgeoisie consolidated its power over the oligarchy within the new power bloc on the basis of a compromise that denied the rural areas any serious effort at agrarian reform. When the Allende government came to power in 1970, the most notable characteristic of the Chilean armed forces was their record of political passivity. But in a sense this long period of political inaction was not uneventful. What has to be analyzed is the declining importance of the military within the state apparatus during the years of stable bourgeois rule—a decline that was far from fully compensated by the considerable aid they received from the United States for the nominal purpose of common defense.

THE DECLINING IMPORTANCE OF THE MILITARY
IN CHILE

Between the Popular Front of 1938 and the Christian Democrat administration of 1964-70, Chile's defense budget decreased in comparative importance by almost any yardstick one cares to use, * as the new ruling classes turned more and more towards a reliance on their own political skills in manipulating popular opinion, backed at critical conjunctures such as presidential elections by imperialist sources of military aid. The declining importance of military expenditure is most striking if one looks at it as a percentage of government expenditure as a whole. Between 1941 and 1947, defense expenditure accounted for more than 25 percent of the national budget. Under President Gonzalez Videla—notorious for outlawing the Communist party in 1948 in response to American pressure, though at the time the Communist party was part of his own cabinet—it dropped to 18

———

*Calculated in constant dollars, the defense budget fell from $90 million in 1946 to $57 million in 1948, when in response to American pressure President Gonzalez Videla took a sharp rightward turn and outlawed the Communist party, at the time part of his cabinet. During his first year as president, Ibanez raised the armed forces' budget to $130 million, and thereafter it stabilized during his administration at about $120 million, after a fall in 1954 due to the Chilean financial crisis that followed the collapse of the copper market at the end of the Korean War. When Jorge Alessandri assumed the presidency in 1958, the defense budget fell to about $100 million, and by the end of his mandate it was even lower. There was a recovery under President Frei, and by 1967 and 1968 the military budget had reached $127 million: following the Tacnazo rebellion in 1969, it climbed to $157 million.

percent in 1948. During President Ibanez' second term (1952-58), in spite of Ibanez's own military origins, it reached a maximum of 22 percent, and from 1957 onwards began a precipitous decline that was only halted by the Tacnazo rebellion in 1969: and this in spite of the use of the army in 1957 to repress an explosive rebellion of the squatter settlements around Santiago, at a cost in lives that has never been calculated.* Chile had always devoted a higher percentage of its national budget to defense than the average for Latin America as a whole. But, partly due to the expansion of the state's civilian activities, this percentage suddenly fell well below the Latin American average: 9 percent in 1965, compared with a 15 percent average for Latin America as a whole.

The same pattern emerges if one looks at military expenditure as a percentage of Gross National Product (GNP): it declined from a maximum of 3. 3 percent under Ibanez—a percentage that has never been surpassed in Latin America, and is now only equaled in Peru— to 2. 2 percent when Jorge Alessandri assumed the presidency and 1. 7 percent when he left it in 1964. As the number on the military payroll not only remained constant during this period but even increased from 40, 000 to 46, 000 men, plus another 27, 000 carabineros, it follows that the army must have sacrificed its officers' real salaries and new equipment to cope with the reduction in its budget that was paradoxically being imposed by the Chilean Right. The fact that it was the traditional Right that forced the military to tighten their belts certainly did not help strengthen their political ties with the armed forces. Even the Christian Democrats who came to power in 1964 only gave in to military demands when their administration's hand was forced by a threatened coup d'etat. Thus in 1970 there were initially a number of reasons why Popular Unity should hope to be able to secure the loyalty of the military.

This declining importance of the armed forces within the national context has to be kept in mind when evaluating the relative importance of U. S. military aid. In 1952 Chile signed the U. S. Mutual Assistance Pact with a metaphorical gritting of the teeth, and refused outright to send a battalion to Korea. But considering its size it did extremely well out of the Grant Aid Program, receiving benefits that by most standards were second only to those received by Brazil. From 1953 to 1965, the Chilean military received more than $66 million

----

*On March 27, 1957, there were demonstrations against cost of living increases. These demonstrations, led by the students union, FECH, in Santiago, Valparaiso, and Concepcion were broken up by the police. In subsequent protests a student Alicia Ramirez, was killed. The students then called a general strike, and attacked public buildings and some commercial shops. A state of emergency was declared in Santiago. See Jorge Barria, La Historia del CUT (Santiago: Editorial PLA, 1972).

in financial aid and between 1960 and 1966, $22 million in equipment. *
Between 1960 and 1965, a total of 2,064 Chilean officers were sent
abroad on U. S. training programs, though until the Christian Democrat administration of 1964-70 very few were sent to the schools for
guerrilla warfare set up by the United States in the Canal Zone.

One useful measure of a country's comparative dependence on
U. S. military aid is the proportion of aid in its total military budget.
Between 1953 and 1965, U. S. aid in all its forms accounted for
about 9.7 percent of Chile's military budget, halfway between countries such as Peru, Ecuador, and Bolivia where such aid accounted
for nearly 20 percent of the military budget, and the more developed
countries such as Mexico and Argentina, where U. S. aid was minimal, under 3 percent of the military budget as a whole. One might
conclude that the importance of U. S. military aid in Latin America
varied strictly with the country's underdevelopment. However,
where Chile was concerned, U. S. aid played an important role in
compensating for the miserliness of the local ruling class, particularly in strategically important political conjunctures such as election
years, and this pattern is reflected in the sharp fluctuations in aid
that are concealed in an overall average: between 1960 and 1971, for
instance, the proportion of U. S. aid in the defense budget fluctuated
between 4 percent and 30 percent. During Ibanez' second term as
president (1952-58), U. S. aid never exceeded $5 million a year
from 1952 to 1957: but in 1958, an election year, it suddenly shot
up to $12 million, only to fall to less than $5 million again by 1960.
As Ibanez' successor, President Jorge Alessandri, began to pursue
a policy of reducing government expenditure on defense, U. S. aid
began to increase in compensation, and by the next presidential
election year, 1964, it reached $25 million. These elections may
have seemed particularly important to the United States, given the
possibility of a triangular contest between Allende as the Socialist-
Communist candidate, Frei as candidate for the Christian Democrats,
and a third right-wing candidate—an election Allende might well have
won. Frei's final victory was only firmly secured through the tacit
support of the Chilean Right.

This decline in the importance of the military is closely connected with the development of new tendencies within capitalism
after the end of the Korean "boom." The possibilities of the import-
substitution model of development were now virtually exhausted,
and the shadowy class of national capitalists characteristic of this

---

*In terms of financial aid, the Chilean military took second
place in Latin America after Brazil, and were well ahead of Peru.
The same order of preference can be seen in gifts of military supplies.
In terms of the numbers of officers sent to train in the United States,
Chile came third after Brazil and Peru.

model had begun to disappear.   Manufacturing industry was quickly
being taken over by foreign capital.

In Chile, the disappearance of the national bourgeoisie led to
a neglect of the military machine, as the classes in power felt able
to rely on their political abilities to maintain the existing system
without too many confrontations, and were able to look for support
from the imperialists, on whom they were more and more dependent,
at particularly critical conjunctions such as elections or a rise in
popular protest.   Thus, measured by the standards of the ruling class
the armed forces were rapidly becoming an archaic institution—
precisely the opposite of what was happening in Peru, where modernization had turned the armed forces into the most progressive force in
the country.   This imbalance between the military power and civil
society was only made worse by the contradictory global policy during
this period of the imperialists themselves.

During this era, there were two different and contradictory
imperialist models for Latin American development.   One was the
Kennedy model (the Alliance for Progress), based on an alliance with
the remnants of the national bourgeoisie and the state apparatus,
which saw a solution to the problem of economic stagnation in enlarging the popular market for manufactured goods.   The Kennedy model
has now been abandoned everywhere.   The other, more successful
model, was that favored by the multinational companies and pioneered
by Brazil.   Industry was to be oriented towards an upper middle-class
market that might be limited in any individual country, but would in
any case be very dynamic and could be extended, thanks to the
various policies for regional integration (the Andean Pact, the ALAC,
the Latin American free trade market, and the Central American Common
Market).   Development was to be financed by a superexploitation of
the labor force, and this in turn was to be made possible by military
repression.

In Chile, favorable conditions existed only for the Kennedy
model, for the popular movement was strong, influencing even the
Christian Democrat style of populism and imposing a need for a
clear program of distribution.   The Christian Democrats swept home
in the presidential elections of 1964 because their policies of dependent modernization seemed to be linked to promises of redistribution,
though any form of modernization of the armed forces was excluded
in this perspective as costly and useless.   But President Frei arrived
too late: in point of fact, the Alliance for Progress had already been
buried.   The development of a monopolistic bourgeoisie completely
dependent on the foreign multinationals was accelerating the decline
of the old national bourgeoisie that now barely survived in the nonmonopoly sectors of industry.   The old power bloc, based on a
compromise between this national bourgeoisie and the landed oligarchy,
was breaking up.   Even the moderate attack on the rural latifundistas
implied in the Christian Democrats' agrarian reform program called

into question the feudal component of the power bloc as it had stood since the Popular Front.

Thus, the two principal components of the old power bloc were gravely altered. Meanwhile, the armed forces continued to rely on conscripts of popular origin, in line with the norms of an earlier era. There was no real attempt to provide the military with sophisticated modern equipment of the kind that following the collapse of the Kennedy model was being purchased by armed forces throughout Latin America: the occasional order of some subsonic British jets (Hawker Hunters) was a compromise typical of this confused conjuncture. Under President Frei's administration antiguerrilla training did become standard practice—in spite of the fact that the serious risk of a guerrilla movement in Chile was minimal—and officers were sent to the Canal Zone for training in preference to the mainland of the United States, as they had been before. Special antiguerrilla units, the "black berets," were formed: but these did not really have sufficient time to diffuse new norms through the armed forces as an institution.

Thus the armed forces remained a typical survival from an earlier stage of dependent capitalism, taking no part in the Kennedy project except as one sector of the populist clientele among many others. Professional bitterness over the material progress of those Latin American armies that had taken part in coups began to accumulate. Under President Frei, the morale of the professional officer corps sank lower and lower while at the same time their tranquility was shaken by profound changes in Chilean society, changes in which the ruling classes clearly wanted them to take no part. During this period any consciousness of national responsibilities among the officer corps gave way to a morose retreat into legendary "professional" values and manufactured rumors about the "danger of war" with Argentina.

In October 1969, the coincidence of professional demands for modern equipment and trade union demands for a higher real income gave rise to the Tacnazo, the first military intervention for 37 years. In much the same way as the year before, students had occupied the university and left-wing Catholics had occupied the cathedral, the tank regiment "Tacna" occupied its own barracks. General Viaux, dismissed just days before for putting forward intemperate proposals that reflected the armed forces' malaise, was chosen as leader, and the regiment set forward demands for a raise in salaries and money to purchase arms. Loyal troops spent an inordinate time in "surrounding" the rebellious unit and avoided all contact, while officers, pupils of the War Academy, and all kinds of politicians visited the barracks where the officers willingly allowed themselves to be interviewed by the press. The air force, ordered to fly over the regiment as a measure of intimidation, suddenly developed an attack of "flu." Left-wing parties and the CUT called for a mobilization in defense of democratic institutions, and the dustmen's union dispatched its dump-trucks to protect the presidential palace.

The mutiny disintegrated as soon as the government gave
guarantees that the demands should be satisfied as far as salaries
were concerned, and the government announced for its part that Valdes,
the minister of Foreign Affairs, had gone to London to negotiate "the
arms purchase of the century. " Those activists of the extreme Right
who had attempted to turn the mutineers towards political action
found themselves isolated. Order returned, at the cost of certain
sanctions against the ringleaders. However, though materially the
winner, the army emerged from this trial extremely troubled. The
rupture of military discipline had left its mark, and during the last
year of the Frei administration the army's commanders were above
all interested in wiping that mark out.

THE ROLE OF THE ARMED FORCES DURING
POPULAR UNITY

It was this structural weakness in the relationship between the
ruling class and the armed forces that allowed Popular Unity to inaugurate its legal transition to socialism, and explains why the experiment
was not nipped in the bud by a violent reaction from the hegemonic
sectors of the bourgeoisie. At the time the sectors with the best
claim to be hegemonic, representing the monopolies tied to international
companies, did not have the necessary command of the armed forces.
The attempt by the Right to kidnap General Schneider, the commander
in chief of the armed forces, and thus provoke an intervention on the
eve of a vote in Congress over the validity of Allende's election,
backfired seriously when Schneider was accidentally killed. His
assassination shocked the armed forces and led them to reaffirm in
this moment of crisis that the constitution was the only valid norm. [9]
Nevertheless, this temporary restraint of the military could
never really serve as a guarantee of the peaceful road. Nor should
one confuse Popular Unity's search for a means of neutralizing the
armed forces over the next three years, with a belief in their neutrality. Reformists within the government might refuse all talk of a
confrontation with the military, while revolutionaries claimed to be
preparing for a confrontation that was inevitable. But in a strategic
sense, both of them shared a common purpose: both were looking
for ways to draw the armed forces or part of them at least into the
Left's own camp. (This was, for example, the policy of the MIR.)
It is best to understand Popular Unity's policies towards the
armed forces as a reflection of the kind of historic alliance of classes
projected by the government when it was elected, an alliance between
the working class and certain sections of the nonmonopolist bourgeoisie. As it happened, by 1970 the nonmonopolist bourgeoisie had only
secondary contradictions with imperialism, and indirectly, tied as it
was to Chile's own monopoly sector, could have been considered as

a dependent bourgeoisie in its own right. But Popular Unity set itself the historic task of transforming this nonmonopolist sector back into a national bourgeoisie, relying on state initiatives and the economic support of socialist countries and even certain sections of European capital. Until this task had been accomplished, no new power bloc favorable to the Left could be consolidated, and the alliance remained a tactical one that would one day disappear. Nonetheless, the struggle to preserve this alliance was one of the dominant themes for certain sectors at least of the Popular Unity coalition.

During the three years of Allende's government, the debate between reformists and revolutionaries was to run through the heart of the Chilean Left. It cannot be reduced to a debate between the parties of Popular Unity and the MIR: the contradiction between policies encouraging class struggle and policies protecting the government's all-important economic strategy ran through all left-wing political parties, and was in fact no more than the manifestation on the political plane of a much more fundamental contradiction between the interests of the working class in a period of profound social upheaval and the interests of the bourgeoisie. The Popular Unity coalition did include petty bourgeois parties such as the API and the Radicals, but these, because of their lack of autonomous power and their inability to represent real social forces, were never of key importance. Paradoxically, it was the Chilean Communist party that took on the responsibility for representing bourgeois interests within the coalition, perhaps as a conscious tactic, but certainly as the objective result of its concrete actions. Such was the significance of the Communists' systematic search for an agreement with the Christian Democrats over the nationalized Social Property Area—the search necessarily entailing ever-increasing concessions to the interests of the private sector. Such, too, was the significance of its policy of encouraging military participation in the ongoing political process, and of placing military men at the head of important strategic tasks such as distribution. Objectively, as the tempo of class struggle grew more frantic, an alliance with the military often served the government as a substitute for the elusive alliance with the Christian Democrats and other traditional political representatives of the non-monopolist bourgeoisie.

The first year of Popular Unity was characterized by an economic euphoria and except in the rural areas by a low level of class struggle. After Popular Unity's success in the March 1971 municipal elections, appeals launched by the left wing of the Socialist party for a rapid transition towards socialism and an offensive strategy on the military question were ignored by the government because of the inevitability of a confrontation. Popular Unity's strategy towards the armed forces was one of integrating the military into the process of social change as a source of technical assistance, particularly in those industries that had been nationalized or were in the process of being nationalized.

Economically, the government took care to preserve the gains the
armed forces had made after the Tacnazo in wages and other benefits,
and it set out a plan of acquisition of new equipment on a significant
scale. The army and the police had never been so well looked after
since the administration of President Ibanez.

In the period between his election by the people, and his
confirmation as president by Congress, President Allende gave
Congress a statute of guarantees, promising to preserve the armed
forces from structural reform, and he kept his word. Such measures
as amending the constitution to allow ordinary soldiers and NCOs
the right to vote, or establishing a single scale of promotions (thus
breaking the caste barriers between them and the officer corps) were
never considered. Thus, the officers' mode of domination was not
called into question, and the government took no steps that might
have let loose a class struggle in the heart of the armed forces. The
president avoided overturning the hierarchy of command that he had
inherited from President Frei by any means that entailed a modification
of the rules of promotion or normal usage. Generals more or less
favorable to the government's program were slowly promoted to posts
of command, at the "normal" rhythm established by the Commission
on Promotions and Qualifications, where the executive had the right
to a certain quota of "discretionary retirements." This period of
prudent management allowed the government to secure a situation
by early 1972 in which the commanders of all three branches of the
armed forces and of the police were favorably inclined to Popular
Unity, or rather to the class alliance that was intended to restore the
nonmonopolist bourgeoisie to a position of economic importance.
Whatever the political views of the junior officers trained by the
United States (who in certain cases were much more closely linked
to the monopolist, proimperialist bourgeoisie than their older comrades)
it was control over the hierarchy of command that counted.

In fact, just as the government preserved the privileges of the
small and medium bourgeoisie and waited for them to invest their
profits from the boom in its plans for national development, so, too,
it protected the privileges of the officer corps, in many ways a
corresponding social layer, and hoped fervently that they would
invest their satisfaction with a new, improved economic and social
status in political support for the executive. In both cases the
government's expectations were based on a miscalculation, though
the small and medium bourgeoisie were to disappoint it sooner.
In the case of its chosen "national capitalists," Popular Unity overlooked the fact that this sector's defining characteristic was its
search after the greatest profit to be had at any particular moment
in time. A slightly higher profit margin in speculative deals and
black market transactions was enough to turn its interest away from
investment in industry, thus bringing it into conflict with the government and its national plan. The bourgeoisie saw this conflict as a
battle over fundamental principles.

In the case of the armed forces, the government "forgot" that for many years back army officers had received their training in the United States, in an ideology of control over the class struggle by violence if necessary. The armed forces' abstention from politics could only hold up in the absence of a mass movement that called into question the nature of the state. But economic disorder unleashed by the bourgeoisie's economic politics, compounded by its growing hostility to the government's attempts to restrain it and also by the failure of the government's own economic plan, was to spur on the creation of just such a mass movement.

The year 1972 saw a rise in mass mobilizations and a series of successive crises that, each in their own fashion, revealed a growing polarization between the camp of the bourgeoisie and the camp of the proletariat. [10] The common interests of the two classes represented by the hypothetical role of the nonmonopoly bourgeoisie as a new class of national capitalists grew fewer and fewer. From the government's point of view, agreement was never reached with the Christian Democrats over the definition of the Social Property Area, and began to grow more and more unlikely in spite of the government's attempted concessions. One notices that it was these successive negotiations and their failures that provided the framework for a progressive introduction of the armed forces into positions of political power; just as if the lack of a political agreement with the sectors representing the interests of the nonmonopolist bourgeoisie, the Christian Democrats, and the PIR or right-wing faction of the Radical party could be replaced by a political agreement with the other social category that equally represented the interests of this faction of the bourgeoisie, the army. The possibility of finding a compensation in one for the unwillingness of the other existed because the armed forces' own political consciousness was out of phase at this point with the political consciousness of the Christian Democrats. The armed forces were preoccupied by the need to maintain order. The Christian Democrats were firmly committed to the need to defend capitalist relations of production against government intervention.

In January 1972, the armed forces accepted the transfer of Jose Toha from the Ministry of the Interior to the Ministry of Defense. Toha had been voted out of office by a congressional motion of censure, and military willingness to accept him in this new post was a measure of their support for the executive against Congress. [11]

In April 1972, the first military cabinet minister appeared. He replaced a member of the PIR, a faction of the Radical party that had broken away from the party over the government's failure to suppress farmworkers' takeovers of rural property towards the end of 1971. The PIR had originally joined Popular Unity and the government, only to leave it again in the hopes that from the outside, it would be able to exert greater pressure on the planned negotiations with the Christian Democrats over the Social Property Area. Thus politically, this first military appointment to a position of power was a way of warning the traditional political parties representing the nonmonopolist bourgeoisie that they had no monopoly over the right to represent this social layer. The government felt that providing its economic policies had some real success behind the backs of these negotiators in congressional corridors, the army could play the role of representative just as well. The left wing of the Christian Democrats in particular, would have to take a political position on the negotiations or run the risk of losing its political power.

The first military cabinet minister left the cabinet in the following reshuffle, which should have been a signal for the reopening of negotiations in June or July. The same reshuffle eliminated the popular Vuskovic as minister of the economy, and installed Orlando Millas, a Communist, in his place. But negotiations were stranded in spite of these efforts. Meanwhile, the working class, shocked by tactical concessions made at this point in time that went as far as the repression of certain actions of the masses, began to organize itself in the urban industrial areas on the periphery of Santiago and formed the first cordon, the Cordon Cerrillos-Maipu (see Chapter 7).

This form of organization became generalized when the opposition organized a strike of truck owners, professionals, and industrialists in October, the "bosses' strike." In October the great majority of workers succeeded in reorganizing themselves on the basis of common class interests whether or not the government had seen fit to include them in the Social Property Area and even regardless of whether their normal political allegiance was to the Christian Democrats: a major achievement. More important still, the different forms of organization that were consolidated at this time, with the limited aim of securing some kind of continuity in production and distribution in the face of the sabotage of the bourgeoisie and the petty bourgeoisie, clearly prefigured the institutions of a republic of soviets and the supercession of the bourgeois state. The JAPs (Juntas de Abastecimiento y Precios), Industrial Cordons, and Communal Commands would in the future be very difficult for the government to control.

The Christian Democrats and the traditional Right lost considerable political ground over this adventure, and even as the March elections were to prove, some working class votes. Thus the "solution" of the strike through the entry of the heads of the three branches of the armed forces into the cabinet at the beginning of November was to some extent a way of allowing the opposition to save face: a compromise solution to a trial of strength in the economic arena, from which the opposition would have emerged beaten. From the point of view of the Left, such a compromise may well have been necessary as a way of gaining time and avoiding a premature confrontation in the military arena, for which the working class and its allies were not prepared. On the other hand, as the left wing of Popular Unity was very well aware, the three military cabinet ministers were a working-class concession to the interests of the medium-sized bourgeoisie, a concession that the working class itself would have to struggle to overcome.

From the point of view of the armed forces this was a key moment. Discussion within the ranks of the officer corps had already gone far beyond the issue of military wages and new equipment. In September, rumors of a military coup timed to coincide with the truck owners' strike were rife in Santiago, and the government forced the resignation of General Alfredo Canales, supposedly the leader of the right wing within the armed forces. Canales subsequently gave an interview to Chile Hoy in which he revealed indirectly that a discussion had already taken place on the best method of taking power: "mutiny by the barracks," he said to the interviewer, "seems to me a very crude system."[12]

What seems to have restrained the armed forces from a coup at this point was a hope that without the working class noticing or feeling any pain the Allende regime might yet be saved by its internal transformation into a Peruvian-style regime. The real power of the armed forces within Popular Unity could thus be used to secure a kind of peaceful transition to a gentle fascism: or rather, to a mono-poly capitalist state in which only the most limited and carefully structured form of workers' participation, consistent with a corpora-tivist outlook, would be allowed. The fact that the military had been given the key posts of Ministry of the Interior and vice-presidency of the republic seemed to prepare the way for a possible further slide towards a government of "national security" like that advocated by military ideologues; and all but unnoticed by the Left at the time, the government had already made a major concession to the armed forces along these lines by allowing the passage of the Arms Control Law that gave the military the sole right to police illegal arms. The same cabinet incorporated the president and secretary-general of the CUT, confirming the armed forces' hope that it represented a step towards corporativism: one could now speak, in fact, not of an alliance between Popular Unity and the military but of an alliance among the trade unions, the government, and the armed forces—and, given that fascist sectors were represented within the ranks of the military and the Christian Democrats were represented with the CUT, the armed forces could delude themselves that this was unity on a very broad basis indeed.

This military dream was fated to be short-lived. Hopes of a low level of class struggle were perhaps realistic in Peru, where industry was relatively weak and capitalist relations of production were limited, but not in Chile, which had a large and traditionally well-organized industrial working class. In any case, whatever nominal justification the November "cabinet of national unity" might have gained from a tallying-up of its participant forces, it failed completely to reflect the overwhelming evolution of political conscious-ness among the masses during the October strike, and thus was doomed to remain a superstructural solution without any real hopes of imposing itself on the level of government policy. Over the next months the working class, newly organized through the cordons, confronted the state's attempts at consolidation head-on on a number of different fronts: most importantly over the issues of the nonreturn of occupied factories and maintaining popular control over distribution.

Certainly, however, the ministries taken over by the armed forces in November were of great strategic importance for the control of the new "people's power": Ministry of the Interior, Ministry of Transport, Ministry of Mines. At the time, the importance of the new military ministers within the cabinet was seen as a gain for the policies of Popular Unity's reformist wing, although—from the point of view of the Left—this concession to the interests of the bourgeoisie was supposedly compensated for by the presence of prestigious trade union leaders in the cabinet. Everybody, even the MIR, might be in agreement over a minimal rationalization of the existing circuits of distribution that had sprung up anarchically during the October crisis: in particular, the duplication of distribution by the JAPs with distribution by cooperatives based on individual firms for their own members' benefit, which created an inevitable source of supply for the black market, obviously had to be suppressed. However, the measures taken by the cabinet to control the new popular forms of organization and bring them back within the framework of Popular Unity's original strategy confirmed that the new government represented the reformists within Popular Unity rather than the working class.

On January 21, military control moved nearer when the socialist who held the post of Secretary of State for Distribution and Commerce was forced to resign, and an air force general was appointed in his place. Four high ranking officers (three of them still on active service) were appointed at the same time as his assistants. The police were put in charge of reducing the JAPs to some kind of order, and behaved with a certain authoritarianism.

This blow on the distribution front was followed by an even more serious blow at the gains of the working class in industry during the October owners' strike. On January 23, a bill defining the Social Property Area was put before Congress by the Minister of the Economy, Orlando Millas, a Communist. It provided that forty-two firms should pass into the Social Property Area without delay, by government decree. The cases of another 123 firms, the majority of them occupied by workers during October and either administered by the state or managed by workers' committees, were to be put before a Commission of Special Cases chaired by the Minister of Labor, and might even be returned to their former owners by the commission, on the grounds that "they were not of a strategic character for national industry." The bill also envisaged a compromise formula allowing for joint administration of firms by the state, the workers, and the previous owner.

Millas' bill was clearly aimed at opening the road to new negotiations with the Christian Democrats, if possible before the elections, its proposals for comanagement of enterprises by workers and owners being seen as something that the Christian Democrats were committed to ideologically in any case, and so would have difficulty turning down, at least on paper. Its fundamental aim was thus, once again, to rally the nonmonopolist bourgeoisie to the government's support, and solve the grave problem of lack of investment that was paralyzing the private sector of industry, and that could be partly explained by the uncertainty among the middle classes over just how large the nationalized sector would turn out to be.

However, the day after the bill appeared, workers of the cordon Maipu occupied their district and threw up symbolic barricades. The Socialist party reaffirmed that it was against any steps backwards opposed by the workers, and the Undersecretary of State at the Ministry of the Economy, a socialist, resigned. The division within the heart of Popular Unity over the bill was only ended in February when the bill was simply withdrawn.

The reformist wing of Popular Unity, and the Communist party in particular, found itself placed in an increasingly delicate position after the mobilization and radicalization of the working class in October 1972. The communists had been acting in the long term interests of the proletariat, defining those interests as if the proletariat was already in a hegemonic position not only within Popular Unity but within the social formation as a whole. Thus they felt they could seal a strategic pact that preserved the interests of a bourgeois class allied to the proletariat. Unfortunately, in spite of the considerable profits that it made during the boom in Popular Unity's first year, the middle bourgeoisie was not willing to consider itself a subordinate ally of the proletariat. The proletariat was not in a hegemonic position, and the Communist party's policies left the field wide open to the revolutionary wing of Popular Unity to monopolize a representation of the real interests of the proletariat as these developed out of the existing political struggle: to the left wing of the Socialist party, and even those organizations that had their origins in the left wing of Christian Democracy, radicalized petty bourgeois parties such as the MAPU and the Christian Left.

If this growing representativeness of the non-Communist organizations within Popular Unity had only been a question of the dissidents taking a harder political line, a line much closer to that of the MIR, the Communist party could have ignored it as a discussion among intellectuals. History has shown that the means to make at least the MAPU keep quiet did exist, in the form of an internal "procedural" coup that at the time of the March elections brought back to power within the party a minority faction that supported the government unconditionally.[13] It was the mutiny of the cordons against the Millas plan that posed the gravest problem. The Communist party saw workers themselves questioning its authority within the heart of the working class. Workers in the cordons were organized on the basis of trade unions affiliated to the CUT, but in fact they escaped from any kind of centralized control, the CUT never having been a centralized organization. In early 1972, responsible Communist trade union leaders began to question the party's line within the party: and doubts were sown that undoubtedly contributed to the decision to drop the military from the cabinet after Popular Unity's success in the March elections, although Secretary-General Luis Corvalan had let it be understood in a public interview in December that a military presence in government could become a permanent, and original feature of the Chilean transition.

Meanwhile, the struggle between the working class and the government over the question of a strategic compromise with the middle-bourgeoisie shifted towards the field of distribution, where following General Bachelet's appointment in January the military were now in control. General Bachelet began by trying to reduce popular control of distribution and the popular organizations themselves to a role of adjunct or assistant to the government as represented by its administrators: and this in a fashion that ran directly counter to the plan for distribution submitted in early January by a MAPU minister, Fernando Flores, and approved in theory by the Communist party before the military took over the administration.

On March 12, a week after the élections, the general reaffirmed in a circular that the biggest enterprises of the nationalized sector should not encourage the generalization of "people's groceries," shops owned and controlled by the JAPs, or any growth in the system of distribution, a carefully rationed quantity of goods directly to working class estates, in the form of the so-called "people's basket" (see Chapter 8). Wherever private retail commerce existed, it should be given priority. The government-owned sector in any case controlled only 30 percent of total supplies, so its resources were limited, and the "people's groceries" and "people's baskets" were generally seen as one of the pillars of "people's power," particularly given the increasingly rightward drift of the retail trade. This was an attempt to put an end to one experience of direct mass control over the economy, in this case distribution, which by attacking the monopoly of private commerce confronted the interests of the bourgeoisie head on. At the same time, paradoxically, workers in the private sector's wholesale firms were mobilizing behind the demand that their own firms should be nationalized: in October 1972, the principal firms had been taken over and managed by workers' councils, only to be turned back to the private sector when the military entered the cabinet in November.

Bachelet's attack on popular control over distribution continued, in spite of the installation of a new, purely civilian cabinet; on

March 31 he demanded and obtained the removal of all incumbent administrators in the nationalized sector of distribution, and their replacement, in the majority of cases, by military officers. In spite of the fact that the military were, from Popular Unity's point of view, no longer productive politically (reflected in the Communist party's growing willingness to talk about "the struggle against reformism"), Allende seemed to want at all costs to maintain them in their posts.

The March elections reflected the rise in mass struggles, as well as the growing political consciousness of the working class. The elections also showed that Popular Unity had lost the support of the middle classes, at least in Santiago. From the time of the government's victory, or near-victory, it became clear to the masses themselves, to the bourgeoisie, and also to the overtly fascist sector of the armed forces that a confrontation was inevitable.

Thus between March and April the politics of the armed forces underwent a sea change, at least for the outside observer. In fact, what was happening was that the fascist sector had reached an awareness that in the contemporary situation of political confrontation the issue could only be decided on the basis of the military balance of forces, that is, by a decisive military battle between the two sides. From this point onwards, fascist officers began a military operation. In doing so they were representing more and more consciously the interests of the bourgeoisie, rather more so than bourgeois politicians, who as politicians continued to think in terms of political negotiations backed by threats. This time it was the politicians who were out of phase.

However, it must be understood that the armed forces did not turn united towards a coup because they were moved to do so by the Holy Spirit. What led the officers to their conclusion that the time had come for a decisive military confrontation was the rise of mass struggles and the growing "disorder" that was anathema to military ideology. Within the armed forces, unity on this point was secured by the internal military activity of those who favored the coup, and their correct use of the threat of death against their opponents in order to increase their internal power.

On June 29, a tank regiment whose leading officer was in danger of being charged by the government with sedition suddenly moved against the presidential palace. This mutiny was put down by the commander in chief of the armed forces personally. It was in fact a pure piece of adventurism, completely unprepared: the fascist Right has its own voluntarist elements just as much as the revolutionary Left. What followed was a moment of indecision that the Chilean Left failed to seize. The army had laid bare its own divisions about the course of action which should be followed, procoup and anticoup. The working class on the other hand was united in action at the level of the cordons, no longer simply the kinds of organizations that had appeared in October 1972, set up to maintain production but

oriented towards geographic and military control of the situation.
After a moment of hesitation and real disarray the faithful supporters
of the bourgeoisie within the armed forces took charge of operations
once more, and the impetus of the military towards a coup continued.
On July 8, ex-President Frei made a speech denouncing the formation
of armed working class militias. This was a signal for the armed
forces to throw themselves into enforcement of the Arms Control Law
passed in late October 1972, and not vetoed by the president through
some unforgivable and not very credible oversight.

During the month of July, under cover of searches for illegal
arms, the right wing within the armed forces organized the first
violent operations against workers in factories and against the parties
of Popular Unity. These confrontations helped to restore the unity of
the armed forces, damaged by the Tancazo or tank mutiny of June 29.

In July, too, the government for its part renewed efforts to
negotiate with the Christian Democrats. Once again this move was
accompanied by the formation of a joint civilian-military cabinet.
The new cabinet was installed on August 9, and took as its title the
"national security cabinet," echoing the hopes the military Right had
once placed in the cabinet of October 1972. However, this time the
armed forces were not willing to put their faith in politics. While the
cabinet was being installed, a new military operation was launched
against rank-and-file support for the government in the naval bases
of Valparaiso and Talcahuano. On August 4, sailors and NCOs who
had demonstrated their opposition to the plans for a coup were imprisoned, tortured, and charged with sedition. The cabinet formed
on August 9 was powerless to come to their defense, even when news
of their ill-treatment at the hands of the navy filtered through to the
public.

On August 24, Commander in Chief General Prats resigned,
following demonstrations outside his house by the wives of other
generals. His resignation was a sign that the Left had met a strategic
defeat within the armed forces. But this defeat had been achieved
not so much by a political campaign as by a military struggle for
control over the military apparatus.

The right wing took control over the armed forces because it
knew how to wage a battle in stages: first, class struggle within
the army; then, class struggle between the army and the working
class. Popular Unity had never been willing to pass beyond its
institutional game of chess with the individual commanders of different units, for fear of questioning the monolithic unity of the armed
forces. But the officers who supported the coup had no such inhibi-
tions; they unleashed a class struggle within the heart of the armed
forces, beginning with the navy, where class tensions were traditionally most violent. The dissuasive effect of terror, used against the
sailors, had its repercussions on other ranks. After this example the
Right restored troop morale by throwing the rank and file into more and

more frequent commando operations against factories during August
and after August 15 against the Mapuche peasant regions as well.
This confrontation with an enemy external to the institution created
a new fascist esprit de corps among the ranks, and erased the
divisions that in certain units at least had been opened up by the
Tacnazo and the repression of progressive NCOs.

These are the two classic operations of reassertion of control
over a military formation in wartime. They were undertaken with
greater energy because, thanks to the Arms Control Law, they were
legal. Popular Unity could not counterattack on this terrain without
involving itself in illegal actions. But what was at issue was no
longer the legality or illegality of the government. The coup of
September 11 was the final move in a military operation correctly
led by the right wing within the armed forces. To the end, it may
have seemed a new maneuver of right-wing politicians, using the
armed forces as a tool—not only to the responsible men within Popular
Unity, but even to leading right-wing politicians such as Frei. The
masses however had no illusions about the meaning of this military
drive.

Briefly, as we have seen, the armed forces were not acting as
tools of the traditional political right, but as conscious agents of
the immediate interests of the bourgeoisie. After March, when
Popular Unity showed that it was able to make gains in an electoral
contest in spite of the opposition's efforts, these interests entailed
the continuation of politics by other means: i.e., war. Allende
himself could not envisage this passage from politics to war as a
fait accompli: he took it as a mere threat, which is why he believed
to the very last that he would be able to divide the armed forces and
the congressional Right by some political coup, such as his offer
of a national referendum on the government, the Social Property Area,
and the constitution on the very day of the real coup.

As for the rest of Popular Unity's political personnel, they were
dominated by the hope that the confrontation could be put off for days
or weeks, for a better moment. Perhaps only the Communists and
the MIR clearly understood that events now were going to be determined by the military situation, and that the situation was desperate,
because the armed forces would not divide. In the last days of
Popular Unity, the two parties drew divergent conclusions. The
Communist party was in favor of negotiating at all costs to gain time.
The MIR was in favor of breaking off negotiations, so that when the
confrontation came, it would at least be in conditions of political
clarity. But both were aware that the first phase of the confrontation
would involve a defensive withdrawal. From a military point of view,
there was no alternative. This may explain, for example, why
neither party attempted to distribute arms to the people. In the
existing situation the people were bound to suffer a crushing defeat,
and the arms would only have been lost.

Thus the terrible paradox of Popular Unity's last days: a people mobilized and demanding arms, while their political and military leaders had gone into hiding. Only the Socialists, who had proclaimed their willingness to fight a few days before September 11 through Secretary-General Altamirano (a trifle unrealistically), fought and lost a few sporadic battles, notably in Sumar Factory. These, and Allende himself, were the only ones to die with their arms in their hands. The old president of the peaceful road voluntarily demonstrated with his death that another stage in the process had been reached, the stage of armed struggle; and he was the first combatant.

NOTES

1. For a more detailed analysis of the historical development of the Chilean armed forces see A. Joxe, Las Fuerzas Armadas en el Sistema Politico Chileno (Santiago: Editorial Universitaria, 1970).

2. See H. Ramirez Necochea, Historia del Imperialismo en Chile (Santiago: Editorial Austral, 1970).

3. See F. Nunn, "Military Rule in Chile: the Revolutions of September 5, 1924 and January 23, 1925," HAHR 47, no. 1 (February 1957).

4. For an analysis of this viewpoint, see F. Fetter, Monetary Inflation in Chile (Princeton, N.J.: Princeton University Press, 1931).

5. See J. O. Morris, Elites, Intellectuals and the Consensus: A Study of the Social Question and Industrial Relations System (Ithaca, N.Y.: Cornell University, 1966).

6. See P. Mans, La Rebellion de la Escuadra (Valparaiso: Ediciones Nueva Universidad, 1973).

7. See J. C. Jobet y A. Chelen, Pensamiento Teorico y Politico del Partido Socialista de Chile (Santiago: Quimantu, 1972).

8. See Eduardo Novoa, "Via legales para avanzar hacia el socialismo," Revista de Derecho Economico (Santiago, February 1971).

9. See E. Labarca, Chile al Rojo (Santiago: Editorial Austral, 1971).

10. For a detailed analysis of this and other points, see Philip O'Brien, I. Roxborough, J. Roddick, Chile: The State and Revolution (London: Macmillan [forthcoming]).

11. See Joan E. Garces, Revolucion, Congreso y Constitucion: el caso Toha (Santiago: Quimantu, 1972).

12. Interview of General Canales, Chile Hoy, September 1971.

13. See Philip O'Brien et al., Chile: The State and Revolution, op. cit.

11

THE MILITARY IN POWER AND THE LESSONS OF CHILE
Philip J. O'Brien

THE COUP

The coup, when it came, was swift and effective. As Alain Joxe has shown, the military officers had prepared their ground carefully and thoroughly. Months before the coup, under the pretext of the Law for Arms Control the armed forces had forcibly entered factories, left-wing party headquarters, and <u>poblaciones</u> to search for any arms the working class might have had. These searches served a number of purposes: they helped prepare the rank and file of the armed forces for an attack on the working class and the left-wing parties; they tested the likely resistance of the working class and the extent to which workers were armed, and they allowed the armed forces to control large parts of the country, for example, whole towns in the south of Chile, prior to launching their armed offensive proper.

The coup proper began on September 10, 1973, when a series of purges took place within the armed forces themselves. Then on the morning of September 11, the navy seized control of Valparaiso. On receiving this news Allende rushed to the presidential palace, the Moneda, where he learned that the whole of the armed forces was in revolt and that the three heads of the armed forces, and one of the lower ranking generals of the police, General Cesar Mendoza Duran, had issued an ultimatum which demanded that President Allende immediately resign. Allende, a loyal respecter of the bourgeois Chilean Constitution to the last, refused. At 9:30 a.m. the president broadcast his last message to the nation, just before the last remaining government radio station was forced off the air. In his broadcast Allende pledged that faced with the military revolt, "there is only one thing I can say to the workers: I shall not surrender." Some time after midday, with the presidential palace bombed and in flames around him, President Allende died. Whether he committed suicide as the military junta immediately claimed, or whether he was shot is irrelevant: in either case he died fighting rather than surrender.

Within hours of launching their coup, the military were in effective control of the whole of Chile. Sporadic fighting, however, continued for about another week, particularly in Santiago. This armed resistance was mainly led by militants of President Allende's own party, the Socialist party. When it became obvious that the armed forces were not going to split, the Communist party, MAPU, and the MIR advised their militants to organize a strategic retreat. But some of the left wing of the Socialist party, perhaps hoping that armed resistance would provoke a split in the armed forces, fought heroic battles in isolated factories,[1] government offices, and poblaciones. However, against the united force of the military, resistance was doomed to failure. After a week Chile was firmly under the heel of the military.

In that first week after the coup it might have been possible to think that the brutality of the military was a result of the fear psychosis whipped up within the military prior to and immediately after the coup, and also of the armed resistance. The myth of Plan Z assiduously propagated by the military junta—that the Chilean Left with the assistance of an army of Cubans and North Koreans were planning to exterminate thousands of people, including military officers—must have been believed by many of the young, and inexperienced conscripts. The man who believes he is going to be shot at, shoots first and asks questions later. But as time passed it became obvious that the brutality of the repression was consciously implemented as part of a plan to terrorize the working class into submission.

The ferocity of the repression came as a shock to all of the Chilean Left, and indeed to many who originally supported the coup. How many died in Chile after the coup will probably never be known. Many people accept as close to the truth the figure given unintentionally by Duran, Chile's representative to United Nations Committee 3, when he declared on October 16, 1974, that the official figure of people killed since the military coup was 30,000.[2] It was undoubtedly one of the bloodiest coups in the recent history of Latin America.

In the beginning the most savagely treated were the many Latin American refugees living in Chile. The air force dropped a leaflet all over Santiago with the following message: "No compassion will be shown to foreign extremists who have come here to kill Chileans. Citizen, be on the alert to discover who they are, and report them to the nearest military authority."

Chileans received little better treatment. Thousands were arrested and herded into football stadiums. The world outcry at the treatment meted out to prisoners in the football stadiums (in the National Stadium of Santiago, one of Chile's leading folksingers, Victor Jara, was beaten to death) forced the Chilean junta to set up a number of concentration camps in remote parts of Chile, and well-concealed torture centers in the towns. In a country which had thought itself immune to such barbaric practices, torture became systematized and prevalent. [3] For the military leaders the country was in a state of internal war; anything to obtain information was justified.

Some of the brutality was random in its choice of victims. This was particularly true for shantytown dwellers. Men, women, and children were picked up, beaten, tortured, or shot often without regard to whether they were left-wing political militants or not. In this way a reign of terror was created in the poblaciones, a terror designed to atomize their inhabitants into complete passivity. But as time passed, although indiscriminate brutality still continues, the repression as a whole has become more systematic. The International Commission of Jurists' Report on Chile estimated that about 60,000 people had been arrested and detained for at least twenty-four hours between the coup and the end of March 1974. And at the end of March they estimated that there were about 9,000 to 10,000 still in prison. As the report points out many of those arrested are detained illegally even under the junta's own decrees, that is to say, without a prior written warrant. A substantial number of those arrested have been tortured.

The style of repression in Chile today is reminiscent of fascist regimes. Nearly all the arrests are conducted by the DINA (the National Department of Investigations). This Chilean Gestapo was established in January 1974, and is responsible to no one except General Pinochet himself. Its members wear civilian clothes, use cars without registration numbers, and can arrest anyone without a warrant or document of any sort. As DINA is responsible to no ministry, people can just disappear without any official record being made of their arrest. Another method of arrest is the "sieving" system used by the Nazis in the Second World War. Whole areas of a town are sealed off, and every inhabitant in that area checked. Anyone under suspicion in the check is carted off to a detention center for further interrogation.

But although the scale and style of repression is similar to that of fascist regimes, there are a number of important differences between the European fascist regimes and the Chilean military dictatorship. One of these is the failure to consolidate a political movement based upon the petty bourgeoisie. Another is a failure to create a corporate state structure.

The Nature of the New Regime

The armed forces have declared that they intend to stay in power for a long time. On March 11, 1974, the military government issued a Declaration of Principles in which it stated: "The Armed and

Order Forces do not set fixed periods of time for their administration
of Government because the task of building the country morally,
institutionally and materially requires a profound and prolonged
period of action. Inevitably, it becomes imperative to change the
mentality of the Chileans. But, further than that the present Government does not pretend . . . that it represents a reorganizing truce in
order to return power to the same politicians who had so much responsibility—because of their actions or omissions—in the virtual destruction
of the country."

The reference to politicians, and not just Marxist politicians,
was not without significance. It was a clear warning to the Christian
Democratic and National parties that the junta did not intend to hand
power over to them. The Christian Democratic Party in particular had
expected otherwise. A few weeks after the coup the Christian Democrats had issued a declaration which blamed Popular Unity for making
a coup necessary, and which stated the Christian Democrats' belief
that the armed forces "will keep faith with their promise to establish
a transitional, apolitical government for the purpose of reestablishing
the institutional, economic and social normality of the country and
that as soon as circumstances permit, they will return the power to
the people . . ." The Christian Democrats interpreted "the people"
as themselves. But it was not to be: the military did not see themselves as transitional.

A few weeks prior to the coup, the MIR in an article published
in Chile Hoy argued that two different types of coups were being
plotted within the armed forces: the golpe blanco—the "white coup"—
and the golpe negro—the "black coup."[4] The first, argued MIR, was
associated with Christian democracy, and referred to a military coup
which would destroy the government, suppress the left-wing political
parties, and then quickly return to some form of guided bourgeois
democracy. The second, associated with the National party and
Fatherland and Freedom, was thought to lead to an eradication of all
working-class organizations and the replacement of existing institutions and organizations with fascist or corporatist ones.

The coup itself was a golpe negro: the repression was harsh
and systematic. But MIR had overlooked the extent to which the
Chilean armed forces, having made a coup, were determined to keep
all power solely within the hands of the military apparatus. The
military had no intention of sharing power as a corporatist state
would have required.

Within weeks of the coup the hard-won rights of the century-
old labor movement to establish its own political parties, the right
to elect its own trade union leaders, the right to strike, hold meetings,
and negotiate on behalf of its members, had all disappeared. All
left-wing political parties were declared illegal, their buildings and
equipment confiscated, their presses destroyed, and their political
militants persecuted. The CUT was declared an illegal organization,

its property confiscated and its leaders branded as criminals. Trade
unions became in effect completely state controlled: there were to be
no meetings, no right to strike, no elections of officials, and wages
were to be strictly controlled by the state.

But the changes were to go further than just a repression of
the working class and the left-wing organizations. All democratic
institutions and all political organizations were seen as dangerous.
Thus the existing constitution was suspended, Congress dissolved,
and the activities of the Christian Democratic and National parties
temporarily suspended. In effect no political activities were allowed.

The suppression of open discussion and debate was extended
to all spheres of life. The left-wingers were denied access to any
form of media. Strict censorship was established over all forms of
communication. As time passed, fewer and fewer, even censored,
forms of semiindependent media survived. By the end of February
1974 the Christian Democrats' semiofficial daily newspaper, La Prensa,
had closed. The official reason given was financial difficulties; but
it is worth noting that by February, the Christian Democratic party
had slowly edged its way towards publicly and privately opposing
some of the policies of the military. The only national newspapers
to survive were El Mercurio and the less important La Tercera.
El Mercurio, which had attacked Popular Unity almost daily for threatening the freedom of the press in Chile, has never once objected to the
total suppression of free communications in Chile.

No institution was exempt from reorganization. The universities
were extensively purged: rectors, regardless of their politics, were
replaced by military officers, whole faculties and departments were
closed down, and all students were forced to reregister, a process
which led to thousands being dismissed; for example, in the University of Concepcion about 6,600 students were expelled. The education
system was completely reorganized—curriculum, administration staff,
and students. The purpose of education as seen by the military was
to instill nationalism, discipline, and harmony of opinions. As a
result, thousands of teachers have either been dismissed from their
post or have resigned. The same emphasis on nationalism pervades
Chilean culture. Books, films, theater, music, mass media, artists
of all kinds are censored. The junta's assessor for cultural affairs,
Enrique Menendez, has summarized the purpose of cultural activities
as being "to form the student with a feeling for his nation, emphasizing
the teaching of the concepts of the fatherland, flag, and heroes."

The underlying theme of a narrow nationalism, and the book
burning in the early weeks of the coup, are reminiscent of fascism.
Indeed, in September 1973 Chile looked ripe for the installation of
a corporatist or fascist regime. There had arisen in opposition to
Allende a mass movement of petty bourgeoisie, professionals, and
some white-collar employees organized in pseudo-trade unions,
gremios. The larger capitalists too had their gremios. If the military

had wished to replace the professional politicians once and for all,
the gremios could have been used to form a corporatist congress,
thus giving this existing mass movement some organizational and
constitutional form. The junta clearly toyed with this idea (and at
times still does), and even set up a commission of right-wing jurists
to draw up a new constitution. But military distrust of civilians
was too great, and the military preferred to rely solely on their own
organization.

Gradually the fairly widespread social base which supported
the military coup began to evaporate. Its disappearance was partly
the consequence of the junta's economic policies, which favored
foreign and local monopoly capital at the expense of all other sectors;
but it also reflected the failure of the military to incorporate any
civilian group in the decision-making process. Various groups,
although not going as far as to oppose the military actively, began
to withdraw their support from the junta. The National Confederation
of Retailers, one of the most vociferous groups opposing Allende,
found itself complaining to the military authorities about the tough
measures—fines, closing down of shops, imprisonment—taken against
some of its members for infringing the junta's decrees.

Slowly, virtually all those groups who had once actively supported
military intervention withdrew any comparable support from the junta.
Fear of the Left as much as fear of reprisals from the military prevented
them from moving into active opposition. But, apart from the monopoly
bourgeoisie in a remarkably short space of time the military were left
without any social base. It thus became increasingly essential for
the stability of the military regime in Chile that the Chilean economy
enter a period of growth, if only to lessen tensions with important
political sectors such as the petty bourgeoisie and small capitalists—
as well as with the working class.

The Restoration of Capitalism

Few military regimes have appointed military men to take charge
of economic ministries. The design of economic policies is usually
left in the hands of civilians, and the choice of the civilian minister
of economics is therefore a good indication of which faction of the
bourgeoisie the government favors. The appointment of Fernando
Leniz, director of El Mercurio, a member of 130 boards of Chilean
and foreign firms in 1970, clearly marked the ascendency of Chilean
monopoly capital closely linked with foreign interests. Leniz,
together with a group of economists from the Catholic University of
Santiago, most of whom had been trained at the University of Chicago,
devised a series of short-, medium-, and long-term models for the
Chilean economy which broke with the pattern of Chilean development
since the turn of the century.

Over these decades the Chilean state had acquired a pivotal role in the Chilean economy not only as the main means of distribution of the revenues from copper, but also as one of the main sources of productive activity. The state intervened to establish a process of import substitution industrialization by creating a heavily protected domestic manufacturing industry catering for an internal market. And later it had begun a process of agrarian reform to widen that market. Fluctuating copper revenues, deficit financing by the state to meet its commitments, and the contradictions of an underdeveloped dependent economy had led to a combination of inflation and stagnation. It had been Popular Unity's intention to end inflation and stagnation by altering the class nature of Chilean development—ending dependency on the United States, replacing the oligopolistic, capitalist structure of the Chilean economy and the pivotal role of the state in the accumulation of private capital with a socialist organization of production and state accumulation of capital. But Popular Unity never intended to change radically the overall direction of the Chilean economy, an economy which was essentially built around the state catering to an internal market.

The military, however, suddenly and drastically altered the whole path of development. "There is no worse businessman than the state," declared Admiral Toribio Merino, and so all state activities, except repression and control of wages, were to be pruned to the minimum. In its place the economy was to be regulated by the "social economy of the market" (a phrase coined, it seems, by Arnold Harberger of the University of Chicago)—prices were to be freed, labor was to be dismissed wherever and whenever necessary, tariffs were to be reduced, exchange rates to be "realistic," a capital market was to be established, foreign investment to have preferential treatment and few controls, and the economy to pivot around an export led development path. The Chilean economy was to be run according to the simplistic model of certain economic textbooks, a model which has a certain logical elegance in textbook form, but which has never been practiced in the real world since the nineteenth century.

The "realistic" economic policies announced by the junta involved an acceptance of capitalist economic ideology. [5] This entailed reversing the process of state ownership of sectors of the economy in favor of private ownership. At the time of the coup the bulk of the Chilean economy was under control of the state—about 95 percent of banking and finance, 90 percent of mining, 40 percent of manufacturing industry, and about 60 percent of distribution. The firms involved had been acquired in one of three ways: by the state purchasing a majority share, by the state intervening to administer the property although the property remained legally private, or by the workers seizing control. About 500 industries taken over

by the last method were immediately returned to their former owners.
For the others CORFO was asked to propose methods of returning them
to the private sector.

By September of 1974 according to the vice-president of CORFO,
General Palacios, all firms taken over after June 1973 had been
returned, and of the 304 firms which made up the social property area,
188 had been returned to their former owners, 21 were in the process
of devolution, 17 had been sold by CORFO to the private sector, 31
were in the process of being sold, and 111 were earmarked for sale;
the status of 33 firms was unclear as their former owners had not
indicated to CORFO whether they wanted them back or not, and 14
firms were to remain under CORFO's control. The extent of this
privatization of the Chilean economy, including as it did state sub-
sidiaries created by the state, went beyond anything advocated by
the Christian Democrats.

However there were two areas where the junta was slow to
return property: banking and agriculture. One year after the coup
the majority of Chilean banks remained in state hands, partly because
the government's antiinflation policies were thought to require a
tight control over the financial sector. But gradually the banks too
were returned to private ownership. In the agrarian sector it became
clear that the military were unwilling to return to the unproductive
latifundio system. All land illegally expropriated was handed over
to its former owners, and an end was declared to further expropriations.
By the end of May 1974 some 1.4 million hectares had been returned
to their former owners. But some 8.4 million hectares still remained
in the reformed sector, and the junta declared that it was willing
to accept the expropriation of land which had not been used produc-
tively. The intention, according to the vice-president of CORA,
was to parcel out "family economic units" to campesinos of "good
social and economic conduct." In this way it was hoped to modernize
agriculture along capitalist lines in an attempt to increase production.

Complementary to the privatization of the Chilean economy was
the normalization of relations with the capitalist world, particularly
the United States. The American copper companies received a total
of $363.3 million in compensation for the mines nationalized by
Allende, [6] $87.1 million in down payments, and the rest in install-
ments. The American copper companies were not unhappy with the
deal. Other companies received back their firms or were handsomely
compensated, for example, ITT. The community of multinational
companies was satisfied and Chile could now be integrated again
into the international capitalist system.

The model being proposed by the junta's economists required
such integration, for Chile was to specialize in those branches of
production where she had international comparative advantage. To
ensure that the economy functioned along these lines a competitive

market economy had to be introduced. To this end the multiple
exchange rate system of Popular Unity was replaced by a single,
unified rate which was subject to periodic, and at first very large,
devaluations to keep Chilean prices in line with international ones.
In addition the whole complex system of protection, that is, tariffs
for Chilean industry, was drastically reduced, and Chilean industry
subjected to international competition.

Accompanying the above measures the military permitted
internal prices to rise to find their natural market level. This,
together with the increased cost of imported products, added a new
twist to the inflationary spiral. In 1973 and 1974 Chile experienced
the worst inflationary process ever experienced by any country in
peacetime. Using the official Chilean statistics one can see how
the inflationary process spiraled out of control (see Table 11.1).

In the first months of their rule the military did not seem
preoccupied with the problem of inflation. But as prices continued
to spiral upwards two years after the coup, and as it became increasingly difficult to blame the "distortions" of Popular Unity for the problem,
inflation became the major economic preoccupation of the junta.

The system of reajustes, readjustment of wages and salaries
in line with increases in the consumer price index, had allowed the
Chilean wage and salary earner in the past to keep up to some extent
with the rate of inflation. The bargaining over the reajuste had been
one of the major tasks of the Chilean trade unions. But under military
rule, with the unions suppressed and with labor almost the only
price outside the market, the Chilean worker found himself powerless
in the face of the rapidly escalating inflation.

Using the official statistics released by the military, one
can see the movement of wages and salaries (see Table 11.2).

There have, of course, been exceptions to this downward
trend in real wages and salaries—most notably the real wages and
salaries of the armed forces have increased. However, even supporters
of the coup have complained about the wage and salary policies of the
military. For example, in March 1974 the Confederacion de Empleados
Particulares (CEPCH—the Confederation of White Collar Workers in
the Private Sector) presented figures to the government showing that
one of their typical members with a family of four had to spend
virtually all of his salary on food.

Food in fact became a serious problem, particularly for the
growing number of unemployed. One of the major objectives of
Popular Unity had been to maintain a policy of full employment.
And in spite of the economic difficulties full employment was maintained throughout the Popular Unity period. When they seized power,
the military, who regarded many industries as overmanned, simply
dismissed thousands of workers, particularly if they had a history
of trade union or political militancy. One year after the coup,

TABLE 11.1

Percentage Variations of Price Indexes

Year	Consumer Price Index		Wholesale Price Index	
	Yearly Average Variation	December to December	Yearly Average Variation	December to December
1970	32.5	34.9	36.1	33.7
1971	20.1	22.1	17.9	21.4
1972	77.8	163.4	70.0	143.3
1973	352.8	508.1	511.4	1147.1
1974	504.7	375.9	1,028.9	570.6

Note: Data represent the annual average index variation during one year in relation to the same average index of the preceding year, and the variation in twelve months, measured from December to December.

Source: Instituto Nacional de Estadistica.

TABLE 11.2

Wages and Salaries: Real Index Variations Base
(January 1973 = 100)

Month	Wages and Salaries, Real Index	Percentage Variation with Regard to January 1973
1973		
January	100	—
April	91.4	-8.6
June	82.7	-17.3
October	39.4	-60.6
1974		
January	86.6	-13.4
April	69.8	-30.2
June	83.4	-16.6
October	76.6	-23.4
1975		
January	81.4	-18.6

Source: Instituto Nacional de Estudistica.

dismissals of members of three important unions had reached more than 30 percent, according to the CUT in exile:

	Total Work Force	Dismissals	Percentage
National Federation of Mineworkers	65,000	20,000	30.8
National Federation of Metalworkers	35,000	12,000	34.6
National Federation of Textile Workers	35,000	15,000	42.9

Not surprisingly, unemployment increased rapidly. According to the official figures unemployment among the active labor force in the greater Santiago area was 10.4 percent in October of 1974 and 9.5 percent in November and December of 1974. It has been argued that this figure underestimates the extent of the problem. This is particularly so if one adds to the official figure of unemployed a figure for the subemployed. The Jesuit magazine Mensaje estimated this to be about 10 percent in September 1974. The combination of unemployment and the fall in real wages led to a fairly widespread problem of malnutrition among the poorest sectors of the population. [7]

In the first months after the coup, when prices were drastically increased and wages reduced, there was a severe crisis of under-consumption—that is, although goods began to appear in shops and elsewhere, the general purchasing power of the Chilean population was such that they could not afford to buy goods. The armed forces were forced to overcome this crisis by allowing wages and salaries to increase somewhat.

But gradually, in terms of output, certain sectors of the economy began to pick up. The government planning agency ODEPLAN, estimated that the gross geographical product grew by about 5.5 percent in 1974, the main areas of growth being agriculture, mining, and construction. The one area which remained stagnant was industrial production. But 1974 was in many ways an exceptional year: the price of copper reached an all-time high, rising from $0.46 per lb. in 1972 to $0.71 per lb. in 1973 and to $0.95 per lb. in 1974. With this windfall gain exports rose from $658 million in 1972 to $1,088 million in 1973 and to $1,650 million in 1974. With this boost to the economy it is in many ways surprising that there was not more growth, particularly in the industrial sector.

But from July of 1974 onwards the price of copper began to slide downwards, reached an average of $0.58 per lb. by December of 1974, and remained low throughout 1975. The low price of copper threw the export-led growth model of the armed forces into disarray. Not only did the problems of unemployment, unequal income distribution, and inflation continue but the economy also faced a balance-of-payments crisis and a decline in economic growth.

As inflation continued to spiral upwards in 1975 two international "experts," Milton Friedman and Arnold Harberger of the University of Chicago, visited Chile. In a well-published statement both talked about the need of a "shock treatment" to combat inflation, a treatment which in their view required a drastic reduction in public expenditure in order to cut back the money supply. Shortly after their visit the entire Chilean cabinet resigned. General Pinochet then appointed two superministers to tackle the economic problems: Raul Saez, minister of economic coordination and development; and Jorge Cavas, minister of finance. Fernando Leniz was replaced by the Chicago-trained economist Sergio de Castro at the Ministry of Economics.

On April 24, Cavas announced a Program of Economic Recuperation—it followed the general lines indicated by Friedman and Harberger in their advocacy of "shock treatment." The object of the program was to reduce the rate of inflation drastically by the end of 1975. Government expenditure was to be cut by between 15 percent and 25 percent at whatever social cost, taxes were to be increased, and wages and salaries controlled. Cavas emphasized that the program involved increased hardships, and although he did not mention it specifically it seemed clear that unemployment would rise over the coming period and the standard of living of the majority of Chileans fall.

But it remains doubtful whether the program of economic recuperation and the overall model of development can succeed. And as long
as the economy remains in crisis it is doubtful whether the armed
forces can legitimize and stabilize their position. The military can,
of course, continue to use massive repression, but eventually "one
can do many things with a bayonet except sit on it."

The Chilean armed forces clearly hope to be able to imitate
their Brazilian counterparts and create a Chilean economic miracle.
But the situation of Chile is very different from that of Brazil in 1964.
By 1967 Brazil was in a position to take advantage of the growth in
the world economy; in 1975 Chile is faced with a world recession.
The effective Brazilian market of about 25 million people with a per
capita income close to that of Sweden was able to sustain the Brazilian
industrialization drive not only into consumer but also into intermediate
and capital goods; the effective market in Chile, less than one-tenth
that of Brazil cannot possibly do the same. The Brazilian state played
a key role in controlling and intervening directly in the Brazilian
economic miracle; the Chilean state seems to believe that the free
play of market forces with a minimum of state activity can somehow
bring about the desired results. And last but not least, Brazil was
able to attract large inflows of foreign capital. Chile hopes to do
the same, but so far, foreign capital, both public and private, has
not entered Chile in the amounts required.

The failure to attract sufficient amounts of foreign investment
has been a blow to the whole economic strategy of the Chilean junta.
If the price of copper remains low, and Chile fails to attract large
sums of foreign capital, then the Chilean economy and political
system is likely to remain unstable; and the more unstable it remains,
the more unlikely it is to attract large amounts of foreign capital.
The international reaction to the Chilean coup and subsequent events
has played a not insignificant part in maintaining the possibility of
change within Chile.

THE INTERNATIONAL ISOLATION OF THE CHILEAN
JUNTA AND THE RESISTANCE MOVEMENT IN CHILE

On November 7, 1974, the United Nations Human Rights
Commission condemned by 90 votes to 8 with 26 abstentions the
Chilean junta for its gross violations of human rights. This vote
brought home clearly to the Chilean armed forces its growing isolation
within world politics and economics. Shortly after the vote, the
Chilean newspaper El Mercurio commented that the U. N. vote
"enables us to evaluate the magnitude of the growing campaign
against Chile, because traditional friends have turned their backs
on us. Even Spain abstained."

The U.N. vote was not some isolated incident, but the outcome of a growing movement of international solidarity with the plight of the Chilean working class and their allies. Probably not since the Spanish Civil War has the world seen such a widespread campaign. It was clearly more than an "international Marxist conspiracy" as the junta originally tried to claim; and the effects of the campaign had deep repercussions within Chile.

When thousands of refugees fled from Chile the plight of ordinary people in Chile was vividly brought home to all those countries which accepted refugees. By December of 1974 it was estimated that there were 12,000 Chilean refugees in Western Europe, 5,000 in Eastern Europe, 500 in Australia, 200 in North America, and 250,000 in Latin America. [8] The bulk of the refugees in Latin America were in the countries bordering Chile, Argentina, and Peru. They often crossed the borders unofficially and particularly in Argentina suffered harassment.

The refugees helped to bring home to ordinary men and women what was happening in Chile. And they gave an added weight to the demonstrations, denunciations, and widespread repudiation of the Chilean junta. Slowly the international campaign began to affect the viability of the Chilean regime, particularly when feelings of repudiation were translated into concrete actions. Groups of workers in Great Britain, for example, boycotted armaments destined for Chile, notably the overhaul of Rolls Royce engines for the Hawker Hunter aeroplanes. And the International Federation of Transport Workers organized a two-day boycott of all Chilean goods. The constant pressure of many groups and countries around the issue of human rights forced the armed forces to release some political prisoners and to tone down somewhat the brutality of their methods.

When the price of copper fell, the Chilean junta became increasingly vulnerable to international pressures. In 1974 the Chilean minister of finance estimated the deficit on the balance of payments to be of the order of $198 million. A World Bank report gloomily forecast that "due to the continuously rising interest payments in the external public debt, the current account balance, most probably, will continue to be negative all through the rest of the present decade." Estimates of the deficit in the balance of payments ranged from $658 million to $1,028 million, and the gross foreign capital requirements ranged from $936 million to $1,328 million if Chile failed to renegotiate her debts due in 1975. It thus became critically important for the junta to achieve two objectives: renegotiate the debt, and attract in a substantial amount foreign public and private capital. [9]

The junta did not probably envisage any major problems in pursuit of these two objectives. But they were wrong. In 1974 Chile had successfully renegotiated its debt, and its main creditors (the Club of Paris) had agreed to allow Chile a further seven years to

repay at $7\frac{1}{2}$ percent interest—better terms than those offered Allende.
But by 1975 the international campaign against renegotiating the debt
had grown. The British Labour Party Conference called for no renegotiation until "full civil and political rights are restored in Chile."
The pressure on the British government was such that the government
agreed not to renegotiate because of "Chile's policy on human rights."
In other countries a similar campaign was undertaken, and on March 22,
1975, the French government announced the postponement of the Paris
Club meeting because 7 of the 11 creditor countries had refused to
attend.

In 1974 Chile had received in loans a total of $1,207 million
of which $363.6 million came from international organizations,
$449.7 million from governments, and $394 million from private
banks. It was a substantial amount, and the speed with which the
Inter-American Development Bank and the World Bank rushed in loans
(they had refused to make any loan to the Popular Unity government),
and the large loans from the United States indicated that initially
the United States was willing to help the Chilean military. By 1975
there was a growing opposition within the United States to large-scale
financial assistance for Chile. And in March 1975 Sweden, Norway,
and Denmark protested in an International Monetary Fund meeting at
the terms of a fund report on Chile. Great Britain and other nations
expressed "scepticism." At that meeting Chile received a $100 million
"standby" credit; but future credits would probably be harder to obtain.
Also, and somewhat surprisingly, the World Bank refused a $20 million
loan to Chile for agricultural development on the grounds that as Chile
cannot reschedule its debts, it is no longer credit-worthy. The decision of the World Bank was undoubtedly influenced by Great Britain
and other nations indicating that they would abstain in the vote on
the loan. Thus, although in 1974, Chile had received large financial
loans, it was doubtful whether it could get as much in 1975 and thereafter.

Foreign private capital was intended to play a key role in the
social market economy. It was hoped that it would substantially
assist the Chilean economic miracle as it had the Brazilian. To
this end the Chilean armed forces tried to make Chile as attractive
as possible to foreign investors: wages and salaries were low; trade
unions and social pressures were powerless; and access to internal
credit and easy repatriation of profits granted. The junta feared
that Article 24 of the Andean Pact, of which Chile is a member, might
discourage foreign investment given the restrictions this article
placed on foreign investment. To overcome this they passed Decree
900, the Statute for Foreign Investment, which in effect, annulled
most of the clauses of Article 24 which attempted to control foreign
investment. But in spite of giving a free hand to foreign investors,
foreign investors remained wary about investing in Chile. For them
Chile remained a high-risk, unstable country. Although many investors

expressed interest in investing in Chile, only $4 million of new
foreign private capital was actually invested in Chile in 1974. [10]
It was unlikely that this would increase substantially in the near
future.

But by itself international pressure, and over time that pressure
will begin to lessen, cannot topple the present military regime in
Chile. That depends on internal resistance.

Any resistance in Chile is extremely difficult: the brutality
of the new regime was designed to make it so. Although the coup
did not destroy party organizations, it did considerable damage.
The largest party of the Left, the Socialist party, was the worst hit:
many of its local and regional units ceased to function for a time
after the coup. Most of the known working class leaders were either
arrested (for example, the secretary-general of the Communist party,
Luis Corvalan) or had to flee the country (for example, the secretary-
general of the Socialist party, Carlos Altamirano). MIR was the
only party which ordered its leaders and militants to stay in Chile.
And that proved to be a costly mistake. Its secretary-general,
Miguel Enriquez, died in a gun battle on October 5, 1974, and most
of its central committee were either arrested or killed by the armed
forces.

All the parties on the Left faced a slow and painful task of
regrouping and reorganizing themselves. The coup of September 11,
1973, was a massive defeat for both the parties of the Left and the
Chilean working class: it would take years to recover from such a
defeat. Slowly the working class did begin to recover: workers
went on strike for brief periods, underground newspapers and pamphlets
began to circulate, and slogans began to appear on walls again. All
left-wing organizations (including the MIR) held a meeting in Santiago
shortly after the coup, and agreed to coordinate resistance against
the junta. A broad anti-Fascist front was formed, and, as in the
days of Popular Unity, each party was allowed to put forward its
own policy. In December of 1973 all parties of Popular Unity and
the MIR issued a declaration from Rome setting out the basis of the
anti-Fascist front:

> The Chilean people are reorganising their ranks. They
> are regrouping for the struggle in the midst of a diffi-
> cult clandestine environment. A far-reaching and united
> movement is being set up for mobilising the majority
> of our compatriots. The anti-Fascist resistance is
> headed and shaped by the Chilean people inside the
> country. They must decide on its character, form,
> scope and the factors making it up. They will surely
> set it up as strong as possible, with absolute deter-
> mination to win, with a spirit of unity that seeks to
> increase the vast well-spring of anti-Fascist feeling
> that is developing throughout the country.

The formulation was left deliberately vague. Within the anti-
Fascist front there were difficulties, particularly between the MIR
and the Communist party, over sectors of the Christian Democratic
party, and in the long run the role of the Christian Democratic
party as a whole. MIR was generally opposed to having representatives of the bourgeoisie, and in particular, a party such as Christian
Democracy committed to the maintenance of bourgeois democracy,
formally within the front; the Communist party wanted to be more
flexible on this point. But whatever the disputes all were committed
to the overthrow of the military junta. The problem remained as to
how one overthrows a military regime.

The reality of the situation was such that by itself the Chilean
Left could not hope to topple the junta. Divisions within the armed
forces were a sine qua non for any changes, and for this the Christian
Democrats were probably crucial. Thus, whether the Left liked it
or not, the vocal opposition to the junta's policies began to center
around the church and the Christian Democratic party. The church
began to voice more and more openly their disquiet at the lack of
fundamental human rights and the economic situation of the poor.
The left wing of the Christian Democratic party voiced their opposition
against the military: some of them left Chile (for example, the former
vice-president of Chile, Bernardo Leighton, went to Rome where he
established with other Christian Democrats a Documentation and
Research Center which published a review, Chile-America, attacking
the military), others were expelled, for example, Renan Fuentealba.
Gradually, and extremely cautiously, the official Christian Democratic
party expressed disquiet over some of the policies of the armed forces.
The official seal of opposition was finally given when ex-President
Frei broke his long silence by giving an interview to the Chilean
magazine Ercilla in which he criticized the economic policies of the
junta. But the unknown still remains the armed forces: there are as
yet few indications of major divisions within the military.

THE LESSONS OF CHILE

One should always be suspicious of people who draw cut and
dried lessons, according to their own political formula, from the
experiences of other countries and other times. As emphasized
throughout this book, Chile is a unique society with its own peculiar
social economic and political structures, and with its own historical
development. Nonetheless, there is a basic similarity of historical
situation between Chile's experience in 1970-73 and the possible
future experiences of "parliamentary roads to socialism" in Europe
and elsewhere. After all, Chile was a democratic country, with a
social structure and culture not all that unlike Western European countries such as Italy and France, or even Great Britain. West Europeans

have not been the only ones to notice the similarities. In the case of
Great Britain, as noted an American news commentator as Eric Severeid
was quick to draw the parallel with the country's contemporary political difficulties:

> As a rough analogy, Wilson's Government is at the stage
> of Allende's Chilean government when a minority tried
> to force a profound transformation of society on the
> majority. . .11

With Portugal suffering from political upheaval, and communist
support in Italy growing, other rough analogies are not difficult to
find.

Thus the response of many, particularly in Europe, to events
in Chile was not only indignation at the brutality of the military
coup and the destruction of all democratic and human rights but also
the realization that it could happen here. It is this which explains
why the reaction in Western Europe has been stronger in the case of
Chile than it was to military dictatorship in Greece. Interpretations
of the Chilean experience have not just been academic exercises:
Chile is too close for comfort to the world we live in ourselves.

The Chilean road to socialism, so-called, was important as
a model to West Europeans even before the coup, since its underlying
strategy was already almost identical with that envisaged by West
European Communist parties and even the left wing of some Social
Democratic ones: election to government (the parliamentary road)
followed by a series of measures within the framework of capitalism
designed to curb the power of the monopolies, and correct some of
contemporary capitalism's worst weaknesses and abuses, plus
advanced social policies aimed at securing the firm support of the
majority of the population for greater state control over the economy
in preparation for the transition to socialism ahead. For this reason,
a procession of progressive politicians made its way from Europe to
Chile while Allende was still in power.

What conclusions do they draw now, those who went and those
who merely took an interest in Chile from afar? The Italian Communist
party seems to have been driven farther to the right, confirmed in its
search for a historic compromise with the Christian Democrats by a
belief that at least for a period, left-wing social reformism is the
only viable choice. The British and French Communist parties have
generally taken the line that, whatever the fate of the Chilean road
to socialism, the British road and the French road will not suffer from
the same weaknesses. In Great Britain, the strength of the national
trade union movement is often pointed to, as a force capable of
preventing any attempt at a coup: though what British trade unions
would do if faced with all the sophisticated methods of population
control currently developed by the British army in Northern Ireland,

is a question which has not so far been answered satisfactorily.
There is a greater awareness in France and Italy, of the need to
democratize the armed forces, assisted in France by the fact that
military conscripts have begun to strike in protest against their own
conditions of service.   In Great Britain, in spite of the close proximity
of Northern Ireland, where the army has been accused of torture before
the Human Rights Commission and certainly has maintained concentration camps, the question is still virtually taboo.   But on the whole,
European Communist parties seem to have drifted towards the right.
Only in Portugal, where the Communist party feels that the armed
forces are on its side, has there been any tendency to take a tougher
line: even so, the communists have supported a vigorous crackdown
on the ultra-Left and the government has shown great sensitivity to
the possibilities of intervention by the CIA.

Looking at Western Europe (with the exception of Spain and
Portugal) it is hard to imagine a transition to socialism beginning
outside the parliamentary framework.   The key lessons to be drawn
from the Chilean experience relate to what must be done after the
elections.

If there is one dominant theme running through this collection,
it is that there were always two different strategies within Popular
Unity on this question: that of the reformists and that of the revolutionaries.   At each critical conjuncture of the Chilean process genuine
alternatives were posed for the Left.   In a document in March 1973,
the Cordillera Regional Committee of the Socialist party summed up
what these different choices, these different roads were in concrete
practice:

> Two tendencies cohabit in our party at all levels.
> There is a revolutionary tendency, whose historical
> roots go back to the "workers' front"; this tendency
> defends the position that simultaneous accomplishment
> of the democratic bourgeois revolution, and the transi-
> tion to socialism, is the cornerstone of the Chilean
> process.   Its slogan is, "ADVANCE WITHOUT COM-
> PROMISE".   The reformist tendency can trace its
> origins to the idea of the National Liberation Front,
> the cornerstone of the Communist Party's politics.
> According to the reformists, any attempt to achieve
> socialism immediately would isolate the proletariat,
> weaken it, alienate it from the middle sectors of
> society, and in the end lead it to defeat.   Although
> the reformist tendency sees in theory a decisive value
> in the alliance between Communists and Socialists,
> in practice it subordinates the views of the Socialist
> Party to those of the Communist.

Thus there are two clearly defined choices of action:

(a) While the revolutionary tendency looks for support from the urban and rural poor, the reformists push the party towards alliances with the parties of the Centre—hence the entry of the PIR (The Left Radical Party) into the Cabinet in 1972, the agreement with the Christian Democrats in June, the entry of the armed forces into the Cabinet in November.

(b) While the revolutionary tendency expects the on-going process to lead inevitably to an armed confrontation provoked by the bourgeoisie, and therefore considers that it is necessary to prepare oneself and the masses for such a confrontation, the reformist tendency considers that a confrontation can be avoided by renouncing socialist goals. It also considers that the people would be able to count on the majority of the armed forces, if the reactionaries went beyond the legal Constitution. Therefore, it rejects any need to prepare for an armed confrontation.

(c) The revolutionary tendency considers that the present economic problems are the result of a struggle against imperialism and the sharpening of the class struggle, and that scarcity of goods, the black market and speculation must be fought by establishing a war economy (which would entail rationing certain articles of mass consumption) and by organizing at the base popular organizations to take control over supplies for workers. On the other hand, the reformists believe that existing problems can be solved through greater efficiency in production, reorganising the public finances, and regaining the confidence of the national bourgeoisie in order to give the capitalist dynamic new life.

(d) The revolutionary tendency argues that it is necessary to extend the socialized sector of industry, this being a question of life or death, as it implies the passing of real power into the hands of the workers. The reformists argue that to extend nationalization of industries beyond the original list of 90 monopolies can only provoke a crisis in the whole Chilean process, by alienating medium-sized producers . . .

Looking back over the history of Popular Unity, one can see that it was the reformists within the coalition, especially the Communist party and the right wing of the Socialist party, who determined

most of the government's decisions. The majority of the contributors
to this book would have preferred those who advocated "advance
without compromise"; if only on the grounds that there is no point
in trying to compromise with an adversary who is convinced that he
must eliminate you in order to survive.

A priori judgments are dangerous, in any political situation:
a good politician, even a good revolutionary, must have a feeling
for the correlation of forces and judge his tactics accordingly. Yet
what happened in Chile suggests that the most important issue is not
how to avoid a confrontation, but how to win it—particularly in countries dominated by imperialism, where the army has almost certainly
been trained to set the interests of the self-styled free world above
all others, and the local Right can count on outside help in its efforts
to overthrow any unsympathetic government. Any attempt within this
framework to confront the interests of imperialism as a first step
towards fundamental social changes, is likely to be met in turn by
an unholy alliance of international capital, local capital, the CIA,
and the national armed forces—the alliance Chile faced in September
1973.

Whether Western Europe is in the same position remains to be
seen.

NOTES

1. For an account of one such battle see the summary of the
interview with David Iturra on the battle of ex-Sumar in P. O'Brien,
I. Roxborough, and J. Roddick, Chile: The State and Revolution (London: Macmillan, 1975).

2. United Nations reference, no. A/C35R 2067.

3. Cf. Hernan Valdes, Tejas Verdes, diario de un campo de
concentracion en Chile (Barcelona: Ed. Ariel, 1974); see also
Amnesty International report, Torture in Chile, London, 1974.

4. Chile Hoy, September 7-13, 1973.

5. Cf. Bartolome Hernandez, "La Economia Politica de una
Politica Economica: el modelo Economico de la Junta Militar Chilena, "
Boletin Antifascista, 1974, Havana.

6. Cf. C. Fortin, "Compensating the Multinationals: Chile
and the United States Copper Companies, " mimeographed (University
of Sussex: Institute of Development Studies, January 1975).

7. Cf. M. Chossudovsky, "The Neo-Liberal Model and the
Mechanisms of Economic Repression: The Chilean Case, " mimeographed
(Ottawa: University of Carleton, November 1974).

8. Cf. Chile Fights, no. 10, (London, December 1974).

9. For a more detailed analysis of the external sector economic
policies, see Pablo Lira, "La Politica Economica de la Junta Militar

Chilena," mimeographed (University of Glasgow, Institute of Latin American Studies, March 1975).

    10.   El Mercurio, January 10, 1975.

    11.   Quoted in The Guardian, May 8, 1975.

Aguirre, C., "El abastecimiento y las tareas del poder." Chile Hoy no. 65, September 1973. See also Chile Hoy no. 32, January 1973 and 40, March 1973.

Alvarado, L.; Cheetham, R.; and Rojas, G. "Movilizacion social en torno al problema de la vivienda." Revista Latinoamericana de Estudios Urbano Regionales. EURE, no. 7, Santiago: Centro Interdisciplinario de Estudios de Desarrollo Urbano, CIDU, University Catolica de Chile, April 1973.

Bengoa, J., "Pampa Irigoin: lucha de clases y conciencia de clases." Santiago: Universidad de Chile, CESO, mimeo, 1972.

———. "Racionamiento para los ricos, abastecimiento para los pobres." Chile Hoy no. 32 and "Las JAP rompen el empate." Chile Hoy no. 33, February 1973.

Carmona, A., "Comites Coordinadores: Ruta del poder obrero." Punto Final no. 111, November 1972.

Castells, M., "Movimiento de Pobladores y Lucha de Clases." EURE no. 7 (Santiago), April 1973.

Cheetham, R., Rojas, G. and J., Rodriguez, A. "Comandos Urbanos: alternativas de poder socialista." Revista Latinoamericana de Planificacion, no. 30 (Buenos Aires) June 1974.

CIDU study group (M. Castells et al.) "Reivindicacion urbana y lucha politica: los campamentos de pobladores in Santiago." EURE no. 6, 1972.

Consejeria Nacional de Desarrollo Social, "Las Jap," 1972.

DIRINCO (Ministry of Economics), "Las Juntas de Abastecimiento y control de Precios." February 25, 1972.

Duque, J., and Pastrana, E. "Elementos teoricos para la interpretacion de los procesos organizativo-politicos poblacionales." Santiago: ELAS-FLACSO, mimeo, 1972.

———. "Las estrategias de supervivencia economica de las unidades familiares del sector popular urbano." Santiago: ELAS-FLACSO, mimeo, 1973.

_____. "La movilizacion reivindicativa urbana de los sectores populares en Chile: 1964-72." Revista Latinoamericana de Ciencias Sociales 4, Santiago: FLACSO, June-December 1971.

Duque, J. "La movilizacion reivindicativa urbana en la provincia de Concepcion." Santiago: ELAS-FLACSO, mimeo, 1972.

Fiori, J. "Campamento Nueva Habana: estudio de una experiencia de autoadministracion de justicia." EURE no. 7, 1973.

Germana, C. "El estado y las masas marginales en Chile." ELAS Bulletin 4, no. 6, 1970.

Giusti, J. "Organizacion y participacion popular en Chile, el mito del hombre marginal," Buenos Aires: FLACSO ediciones, 1973.

Nazal, J. "Las JAP: respuesta del pueblo a la especulacion." Principios, May-June 1972.

Quevedo, S., Sader, E. "Algunas consideraciones en relacion a las nuevas formas de poder popular en poblaciones." EURE no. 7.

Rama, G., and Schlaen, N. "El estrato popular urbano." Santiago: CEPAL/ECLA, U.N., Social Development Division, mimeo, 1973.

Sader, E. "Movilizacion de masas y sindicalizacion en el Gobierno U.P." Universidad de Chile, CESO, Facultad de Economia Politica, mimeo, 1973.

Sader, E., Cordero, M. C., Threlfall, M. "Cordon Cerrillos-Maipu: Balance y Perspectivas de un embrion de poder popular." Santiago: University Catolica de Chile, CIDU, 1973.

Santa Cruz, E. "Comandos Comunales: organos de poder del pueblo." Punto Final, no. 189, July 1973.

Vaccaro, V. "Los Comandos Comunales: Iniciativa de las masas." Chile Hoy no. 26, December 1972.

Vandershueren, F. "Significado Politico de las Juntas de Vecinos en poblacionas de Santiago." EURE no. 2, June 1971.

PHILIP J. O'BRIEN is lecturer in economics at the Institute of Latin American Studies, the University of Glasgow. He studied at the University of St. Andrews and at the Institute of Development Studies, University of Sussex. He was in Chile on a Ford Foundation Fellowship 1966-1968; and visited Chile in 1971. Author of articles on Chile and Latin America, is coauthor of Chile: The State and Revolution (London: Macmillan, forthcoming).

JACQUELINE F. RODDICK studied at Queen's University, Ontario, London School of Economics and the University of Sussex, where she is currently finishing a Ph. D. thesis on "The Political Behaviour of Chilean Teachers." She was in Chile during the Popular Unity period; and is coauthor of Chile: The State and Revolution (London: Macmillan, forthcoming).

PABLO LIRA is a pseudonym for a Chilean economist from the University of Concepcion. During the Allende period he worked in the copper industry. He is presently doing a study on foreign capital in the Chilean industrialization process at the University of Glasgow.

ALEC NOVE is Bonar Professor of Economics and Director of the Institute of Soviet Studies, the University of Glasgow. Author of various articles and books on Economic Theory, Eastern Europe, the Soviet Union and Latin America, including An Economic History of the U. S. S. R. Was in Chile in 1972 as Visiting Professor at the Centro de Estudios de Planificacion Nacional (CEPLAN) of the Catholic University.

CRISTOBAL KAY studied at the Universities of Chile, Oxford and Sussex where he received a Ph. D. He was a fellow of the Centro de Estudios Socio-Economicos (CESO) of the University of Chile 1971-73. After the coup he was Visiting Fellow to the Institute of Latin American Studies, University of Glasgow, and is currently a lecturer in economics in the Department of International Economic Studies at the same university. Author of various articles on historical, social, and economic aspects of agrarian systems in Latin America and Europe and on agrarian reform in Chile.

PATRICIA SANTA LUCIA is a pseudonym for a Chilean economist formerly in charge of workers' participation in the energy sector at CORFO, and member of the research team at the Centro de Estudios Socio-Economicos (CESO) of the University of Chile. Editor of A Un

Ano del Golpe Militar en Chile, with contributions by Pedro Vuskovic and Andre Gunder Frank et al. published by the Coordinating Centre of CESO in Buenos Aires.

MONICA THRELFALL studied at the University of Oxford and Leeds. She worked in Santiago in 1972 at the Catholic University on popular participation in urban municipal development and in 1973 at the Centro de Investigaciones de Desarrollo Urbano, CIDU. She coauthored a study of the emergence of the first industrial cordon in Santiago, and is joint author with Ernesto Pastrana of Pan, Techo y Poder: El Movimiento de Pobladores en Chile 1970-1973, (Buenos Aires: Ediciones Siap, 1974). A member of the Coordinating Centre of CESO, she is at present working on the Latin American labor movement.

IAN ROXBOROUGH is lecturer in the political sociology of Latin America at the London School of Economics. He studied at the Universities of York and Wisconsin (United States) and spent two years doing research in Chile during the Allende administration. He was on the staff of the Institute of Latin American Studies at the University of Glasgow 1973-75. Coauthor of Chile: The State and Revolution (London: Macmillan, forthcoming).

ALAIN JOXE is a political scientist at the Centre d'Etude de Politique Etrangere, Paris, France. Author of various articles and books on Chile and Latin America, including Las Fuerzas Armadas en el Sistema Politico Chileno.

MIKE GONZALEZ is lecturer in Hispanic Studies at the University of Glasgow. He studied at the Universities of Leeds and Essex, and worked in Mexico for two years. He has translated La Philosophia de la Praxis by A. Sanchez Vazquez into English.

THE ECONOMIC DEVELOPMENT OF REVOLUTIONARY
CUBA: Strategy and Performance
Archibald R. M. Ritter

ECONOMIC NATIONALISM IN LATIN AMERICA
Shoshana B. Tancer

EXPROPRIATION OF U.S. INVESTMENTS IN CUBA,
MEXICO, AND CHILE
Eric N. Baklanoff

EXPROPRIATION OF U.S. PROPERTY IN SOUTH
AMERICA: Nationalization of Oil and Copper
Companies in Peru, Bolivia, and Chile
George M. Ingram

NATURAL RESOURCES AND NATIONAL WELFARE:
The Case of Copper
edited by Ann Seidman

THE PORTUGESE REVOLUTION AND THE ARMED
FORCES MOVEMENT
Rona M. Fields